that underpin great bakes—flour, sugar, eggs, fat—before delving into the techniques that bring recipes to life: texture, color, how things rise, and a technical overview of all things baking. The 100 tested, thoroughly tested recipes are organized by difficulty and time commitment, ranging from easy 30-minute cakes to spectacular showstoppers you can devote a weekend to.

SIFT

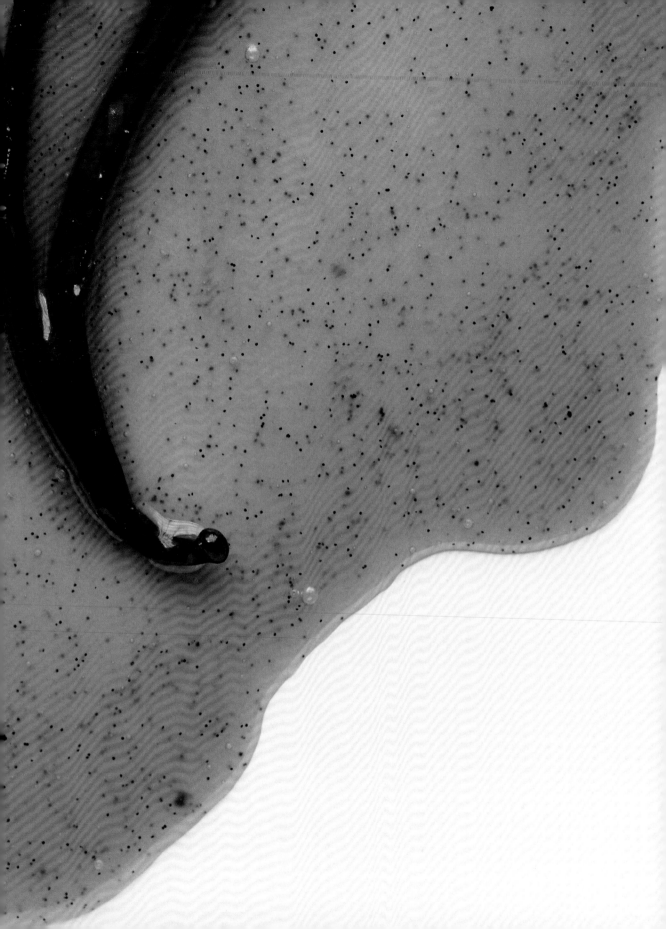

SIFT

The Elements of Great Baking

Nicola Lamb

Photography by Sam A. Harris

Clarkson Potter / Publishers

New York

To Carole and her brownies

I

Welcome   6
Equipment list   8

II

All about flour   10
All about sugar   24
All about eggs   36
All about fat   50
How things rise   66
Color   82
Texture   90
Technical overview   102
How to build a bake   114

III

Recipes I: Base recipes   116
Recipes II: An afternoon   138
Recipes III: A day   230
Recipes IV: A weekend   278
Recipes V: Extras   330

IV

Matrix of joy   344
Index   346
Acknowledgments   352

WELCOME

•

Welcome to the world of baking, a wonderful place where ingredients transform right before your eyes. It's a place where lumps of butter and dough become impossibly fragile flaky croissants, where the wobble of a custard tart appears to defy physics and egg whites are whipped into a frenzy of creamy clouds. When you learn to bake, it sometimes feels like you're becoming a magician. And although it IS magical, it isn't magic.

And I want to tell you why.

Learning to ask why is one of the most important lessons I have ever learned while baking. Once you start asking this question and pulling at the threads, you'll discover that baking is an interconnected puzzle, a sprawling family tree of ingredients and reactions. In this book, I hope to provide you with a map so you can explore this kaleidoscopic world with confidence.

I know how frustrating it can be to attempt a recipe off the bat only to be disappointed with the results and not understand why. The reality is, effortless-looking bakes coming out of professional kitchens are often down to one thing, and trust me (because I am speaking from experience), it's not just natural talent. It comes from years of information gathering and repetition.

Holding a piping bag, judging when the dough is proofed, and defining what "golden brown" really means are no simple feats. In fact, when you are baking at home, it's near impossible to replicate the rote memory that comes with rolling 10,000 croissants a week or frosting hundreds of cakes. I mean, who has the time (or budget) to take on such a task? It's obviously not practical. But as a result, it can be harder to feel comfortable and natural in the kitchen when the stakes (The! Dinner! Party! Is! In! Two! Hours! And! My! Ganache! Has! Split!) feel so high.

Part of this is because we set the bar much higher for baked goods. Unlike savory cooking, which seems to be endlessly fixable, once a cake is in the oven, there's no real way to go back. And what we consider baking "failures"—the burns, the explosions, curdled eggs, the weird textures, the odd colors— always seem more unforgivable and egregious than cooking "failures," which tend to be considered edible.

Although this high expectation means that a curdled custard may be destined for the trash, while menacingly dry roasted chicken will likely make the cut, it's for a good reason. At the end of it all, baked goods and desserts have a role in our life that extends far beyond sustenance. Baked goods have an incomparable ability to bring us joy.

In this book, I want to help pave a direct path to that joy. I want to teach you the fundamental principles and techniques that underpin and connect our recipes. Learning to understand the why of baking through the lens of science has helped me feel more confident and independent in the kitchen: imagine a detective's investigation board with string connecting all the different elements of pastry, showing how choux buns are connected to bagels, how brioche relates to ganache, and what jam and ice cream have in common. I'm no scientist, but I have learned to play by the rules set by each ingredient, which ones play nicely together and which should be kept apart!

I want to share with you the defining factors of successful baking with technique-driven recipes that will show you these skills in action and help to sharpen that baking Spidey sense I know you have. When a recipe asks you to whisk the eggs for 10 minutes or tells you to bake at a sky-high temperature, I want you to know why it's worth it, and when it's not. I want this book to make you pick up another baking book with confidence or return to a recipe that previously confounded you. More than anything, I want you to be able to look at any recipe and think, no, *know*: "I can make this!"

From the pearls of wisdom handed to me in the early days of my career to all of the knowledge generously shared in the pages of in-depth research by chefs, writers, and scientists, to my own hard-earned lessons along the way, it is my greatest honor to help lay a foundation for you on your baking journey.

This book is divided into two sections. The first is a practical reference guide to the key building blocks of baking. From how to make egg foams to the melting points of fat, my goal is to arm you with the details that underpin successful baking. Yes, there will be graphs.

The second section will lead you through a series of recipes broken down into what I hope is a valuable metric: time. Split into An Afternoon, A Day, and A Weekend (I will never lie to you about how long something takes, that's a promise!), the recipes will be a practical way for you to see everything described in the reference section in action. From speedy cookies to awe-worthy croissants, each recipe has a timeline, so you'll be able to transform your kitchen into a patisserie to suit your schedule.

But the first lesson I want to teach you is this: there will be burned crusts, pastry stuck to pans, unset jellies, and everything in between, but try not to let these knock your confidence. Failures are a crucial part of the learning journey. And any journey that ends with cake is one worth taking.

Shall we begin?

RECIPE NOTES

I'll be here to guide you the whole way through the book, but here are a few pointers and rules that the book abides by:

- The recipe section begins with a series of base recipes. From doughs to pastry, these are big-hitter recipes that you can build upon.

- The timeline on each recipe represents the approximate time it would take to do each step.

- Many elements of the recipes can be made in advance, so please check each recipe for more details on that.

  - Recipes that are one afternoon take up to 4 hours (not including resting time) and have relatively simple steps.

  - Recipes that take one day are above 4 hours and/or have multiple steps. Sometimes the day is split over two half days.

  - Recipes that take a weekend must be split over multiple days and they have much more involved steps and techniques.

- You can check the main techniques used in the recipe to refer back to the reference section if you want to go deeper into the theory behind what makes them work.

- All egg weights are the weight out of the shell.

- I opt to use Dr. Oetker Platinum gelatin sheets (4½ x 3 inches) for my recipes but you can use powdered gelatin. See page 100 for more information.

- Unless stated, all butter is unsalted butter.

- I use instant dry yeast that does not need to be activated before using. Please always proof your yeast according to the manufacturer's instructions on the back of your packet.

- Rising times are assuming optimal rising conditions: 75–81°F. Doughs may take longer to rise in your own home environment.

- Bread flour is flour with a protein content between 12–14%.

- For the best results, always seek out the best quality ingredients you can afford, be it eggs, dairy, chocolate, or fruit and veg, trying to keep it as seasonal as you can!

EQUIPMENT LIST

ESSENTIAL

8-inch/20cm cake pan
This is a great size for single and layer cakes.

8-inch/20cm square pan
Another useful size for baking buns.

8-inch/20cm tart pan
A loose-bottomed 8-inch/20cm tart pan will get you where you need to go. An 8-inch/20cm tart ring is also very useful.

Baking sheets
My standard heavy baking sheet is 16 x 10½ inches/40 x 27cm. I have about five and they all stack up beautifully.

Bowls
Assorted sizes for measuring, weighing, scaling, and mixing.

Chef's knife (8 inches/20cm)
Perfect for all-purpose cutting tasks. But remember: if it can't cut through a tomato, it's not sharp enough.

Circular cutters (assorted sizes, fluted and unfluted)
These get lost (often) and the worst thing ever is when they get put away dirty (a crime), but any self-respecting cookie lover must have these on hand.

Digital scales
No questions, this is 100% needed for good baking. Get a pair of scales that has a sensitivity of 1g so you feel confident when using it. Accuracy is key.

Digital thermometer
I've destroyed many digital thermometers over the years thanks to their proximity to hot oil, sugar, or ovens. So, choose an economical one!

Dough scraper
My absolute favorite piece of equipment. SO USEFUL. I like small, rounded ones for scraping and slicey, right-angled ones for dividing doughs and cleaning.

Fine-mesh sieve
I have a few sieves at home, but you need one for sifting and a smaller/finer one for decorating. Avoid plastic ones that could melt from straining hot liquids!

Hand mixer
If you don't have a stand mixer, a hand mixer does a decent job of whipping, creaming, and aerating. But it won't perform heavy-duty tasks.

Measuring spoons
Although I don't reach for these often, I find it's still important to have a set. While I don't mind asking you to weigh 3g of a spice, most recipes will include the volume measurement, so it's worth having a set on hand.

Medium saucepan
For all your poaching and caramel-making needs!

Mini tart rings/pans
I always keep a range of tart rings and pans, but the most useful are 3¼-inch/8cm rings and the loose-bottomed fluted 4-inch/10cm pans.

Offset spatula
Offset spatulas (mini and large) are ideally designed for decorating and finishing, but are also very handy for lifting and for serving guests.

Oven thermometer
All of our ovens are built differently and may not run to an accurate temperature. An oven thermometer will provide insight into the hot (or cold) spots and help get your bakes coming out as expected.

Pastry brush
A natural flat-bristled brush is worth investing in (I like 1¼-inch, 1½-inch, and 2-inch), Make sure you clean them properly and then allow them to dry, flat.

Peeler
I'm partial to the speed peeler with a good grip handle—if your peeler isn't sharp, just replace it. Working with a blunt peeler is a unique torture.

Rolling pin
A reliable rolling pin is so helpful—tapered ones are useful for control pressure but not essential. Also great for crushing spices.

Scissors
Truly the cornerstone to any good set of kitchen tools. Never let a good pair out of your sight!

Serrated knife
Perfect for slicing through cakes without damaging or squashing the layers.

Spatula
Any kind of really good, firm, basically unbreakable silicone spatula that can be used for everything. A few different sizes are helpful.

Tongs (heatproof)
My favorite: I use these to remove hot pastry rings from tarts and move stuff around in the oven so I don't get burned. Also useful for deep-frying.

Whisks
A good metal whisk with lots of overlapping steel wires to increase the aeration factor. A silicone whisk is essential if you have non-stick pans.

HELPFUL

6-inch/15cm cake pans
My favorite size to build layer cakes. Because of the smaller diameter, the cake looks more impressive once you build it up and still feeds a crowd.

Acetate
Food-grade acetate is useful for lining pans when building mousse cakes for super clean finishes.

Blenders
A countertop blender is useful for liquefying purées and can even make nut paste pretty well. Immersion blenders are brilliant, especially for emulsifying ganache, and for saving split custard in an emergency.

Cooling rack
Having at least one cooling rack on hand is worthwhile. I have a few types—my favorite has fold-out legs for easy storage.

Electronic timer
Your phone timer will only get you so far. Keep a few electronic timers nearby—you won't regret it!

Food processor
Perfect for blitzing up nuts, making dough, or whipping up cake mix. I don't use mine every day, but I often feel very grateful for its existence.

Mortar and pestle
Great for grinding or crushing whole spices.

Piping bags
Disposable or reusable piping bags are very useful. I tend to go for big blue professional ones (18 inch).

Piping tips
Having a variety of piping tips is useful, especially a range of star tips. Oh, and a long bismarck tip for filling everything!

Ruler or measuring tape
Essential for making neat and tidy pastries. I know it's tempting to borrow a tape measure from the DIY drawer, but it's better to have your own.

Silicone mat
These non-stick mats are great and reusable—really good when you are making sticky things like brittles.

Stand mixer
Essential for long mixing of doughs and making fluffy foams.

FEELING EXTRA?

Assorted molds/pans
A simple pastry can be elevated by a great mold or pan. I personally love a cube to trick people into thinking I'm fancy!

Blow torch
A proper industrial-looking blow torch is a bit of an investment but is so worth it. Use it to warm up your stand mixer bowl to help emulsify, or torch meringue or crème brûlée perfectly.

Canelé molds
Specialty molds to make the perfect Bordelaise pastry. I've had good results in copper and steel!

Cast-iron/oven-safe frying pan
A must for stovetop to oven-baked desserts like tarte tatin.

Deep-frying thermometer
A thermometer you can affix to the edge of a saucepan safely will make deep-frying easier. A digital thermometer will also tell you the temperature, but having a gauge fixed in place is helpful.

Fine grater
I think a Microplane grater is one of the greatest gifts you can give to anyone, including yourself. Although a standard box grater is OK, fine graters make such quick work of zesting citrus fruits, grating Parmesan cheese, garlic cloves, and more. You can get different shapes, but I like the long slim one as it's quite effective for spherical fruits!

Gram scale
For getting those super accurate rising agents, yeast, and salt measurements, a gram scale cannot be beat!

Mandolin
I love my mandolin—I use it all the time! It makes the best salads, the most perfectly cut fruit for the top of tarts, and beautiful thin slices for pickles. It might seem a bit expensive at first, but I think you'd end up using it more than you reckon.

Melon baller
A tool that can remove chunks of fruit in a perfect spherical ball shape—useful for coring apples and pears.

Spice grinder
One step up from the mortar and pestle—useful if you're working with a lot of whole spices.

1

ALL ABOUT FLOUR

Conjure up an image of a stereotypical baker and I bet you see someone surrounded by a floating cloud of white dust. Flour is just a veritable trademark of the profession.

From toasty whole-wheat to earthy ryes, bright white cake to hardy bread flours, the flour we use is an excellent jumping-off point, laying a foundation for great bakes to come. Getting to know flour is essential because it's often the parameter by which we understand recipes. It regularly gets the top billing for our bakes, and its influence extends far beyond flavor. Flour determines the structure and character of our bakes because it contains two of the most significant structure providers in baking: gluten and starch.

These two titans are key to the crackle of a baguette, the chew of a cinnamon bun, and the crunch of a well-baked pie crust. To get the best out of flour, we need to learn how to coax out these characteristics, when to push it and when to let it be.

In this chapter, we'll look at the way we use flour to build structure, the techniques that underpin it and understand when it's best to push it and when we should just leave it alone. We'll also learn to speak flour, from demystifying protein content to decoding baker's percentages. Let's get into it.

THE STORY OF FLOUR

Flour refers to any grain that has been ground into a fine powder. From rye to rice, buckwheat to chickpea, tapioca to corn, the range of flours is huge. But there is one dominating force in the flour world: wheat.

Wheat is one of the world's most widely grown and consumed grains. Evidence of domesticated wheat goes all the way back to 9000 BC in the Middle East, and its importance and relevance are yet to wane. Millions of acres around the world are dedicated to this crop. But not all wheat is created equal. the two main types are hard and soft.

The terroir (a word that refers to the unique environmental factors of an area, including soil, topography, and climate) significantly impacts the wheat grown in certain regions. Wheat grown in harsher climates with more dramatic winters and summers—like Canada and Eastern Europe—tends toward hard wheat with high protein content, while wheat that thrives naturally in the UK tends to be softer with a lower protein content.

Softer wheat works well for cakes, cookies, and biscuits, but when it comes to bread, we tend to reach for imported flour with a high proportion of gluten. These imported flours produce lofty loaves that align with our idea of what bread should look like. In recent years, these standards have shifted as more bakers seek local grains and challenge our idea of what responsibly sourced, good-for-you bread looks (and tastes!) like.

A kernel of wheat has three parts: the endosperm, the bran, and the germ. During the milling process, wheat kernels are cracked and finely ground. It's then sifted in stages, the flour becoming more refined each time. Eventually, the bran and germ are entirely filtered out, resulting in white flour.

This white wheat flour is almost entirely comprised of the endosperm. The endosperm is the part of wheat rich in protein (which leads to gluten) and starch, but it is not nutritionally rich. Most of the goodness and flavor—the fiber, minerals, and vitamins—come from the bran and germ. Flour that contains endosperm, bran, and germ is known as whole-wheat flour. It is coarser and more flavorful than white flour, and more absorbent, meaning recipes made with whole-wheat flour are adjusted to contain more water.

What are heritage grains?

You may have noticed bakeries adding heritage grains to their breads, buns, and cakes.

These are grains that were grown in the local area before the introduction of mass selective plant breeding in the early 20th century. These heritage grains tend to be forgotten varieties of wheat, barley, oat, or rye and have now begun to be reintroduced. Einkorn is a popular heritage grain in the UK—it is one of the earliest cultivated plants, with evidence it was domesticated some 10,000 years ago!

A PEEK INSIDE THE KERNEL

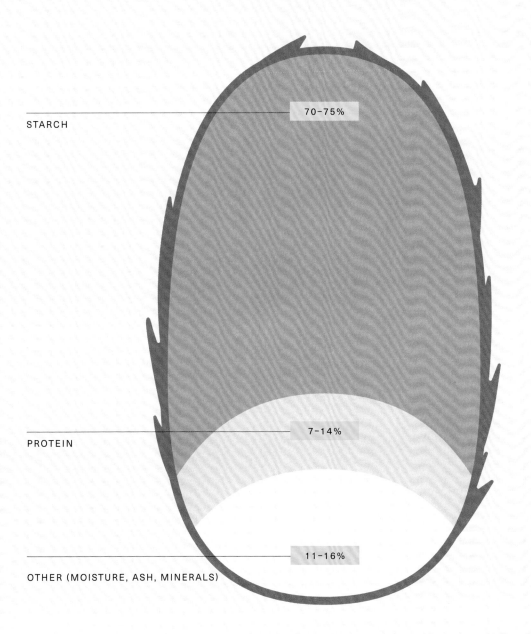

STARCH — 70–75%

PROTEIN — 7–14%

OTHER (MOISTURE, ASH, MINERALS) — 11–16%

STARCH	70–75%
PROTEIN	7–14%
OTHER (MOISTURE, ASH, MINERALS)	11–16%

LET'S TALK GLUTEN

One of the key ways to categorize flour in baking is in relation to its strength. We can find out the strength of flour by looking at its protein content. This is important because, when we add water, these proteins emerge from their dehydrated hibernation to create gluten. The amount of protein in wheat flour tells us how much gluten it can develop or how strong a dough will be. The easiest way to check the gluten content is to check the nutritional table on the back of a bag of flour—the protein value will reveal everything.

The amount of gluten in the flour should be thought of as the capacity or potential for gluten because gluten is not implicit—gluten needs to be built! There are a few ways to do this, which we'll cover in this chapter.

Once gluten is developed, it will stubbornly spring back into shape. This impressive, flexible network can capture gases, like CO_2 and steam, and will help your bakes hold shape when baked. Without gluten acting as a net, bread could not rise effectively—the gases produced by yeast fermentation would just escape! (See How Things Rise on page 76.)

Understanding protein content

Protein Content Range (%)

6–8%	8–9.5%	9–12%	12–14%	15%
Low	Low/medium	Medium/high	High	Very high

WHEN FLOUR MEETS WATER

Take a bag of buckwheat flour and check out the nutritional table on the back—it might have a very high protein content. But you can't make a lofty loaf with just buckwheat flour. Why?! Well, it's not the right mixture of proteins. So, what IS the right mix?

The proteins glutenin (the strength protein) and gliadin (the stretch protein) in wheat flour bind together to form gluten in the presence of water. Without water, gluten cannot form. As soon as wheat flour is hydrated, the glutenin and gliadin unfold (aka denature) and form gluten.

A series of sticky bonds develop between adjacent gluten proteins, creating a spring-like network that forms the backbone of many of our baked goods. From a fragile, oily bubble puffing excitedly out of focaccia to a satisfyingly stretchy and supple milk bread, we have gluten to thank.

The windowpane test

A failsafe way to judge how well your gluten has developed is by pinching off a small piece of dough and stretching it. This is known as the windowpane test.

How we mix our ingredients has a major impact on how gluten develops. Folding, the gentlest technique we reserve for batters like genoise sponge, results in the least amount of gluten formation. Whereas whisking or stirring will encourage more gluten to form, increasing the interaction between proteins. Vigorous or continuous kneading or mixing will result in the most gluten formation.

See right →

The deal with alcohol

Ever seen a recipe that suggests a splash of vodka in your pie dough or batter? Well, there's a method to this madness. Because gluten only forms in the presence of water, by using a high percentage alcohol like vodka, which is only 60% water, you are reducing the proportion of liquid contributing to the gluten development.

Even though vodka will make your dough look wet, ethanol does not hydrate the proteins! This results in a dough that is as easy to roll out as one made with 100% water but with implicitly less gluten, resulting in a more tender final product.

Stages of gluten development

Low — The dough will not stretch without breaking

Medium — Dough stretches but tears easily

High — The dough stretches easily to a very thin pane

Overmixed — Dough is sticky and cannot be stretched

MECHANICAL INTERVENTION

We can speed up the formation of gluten by mechanically agitating and mixing the dough, also known as kneading. During the kneading process, the proteins are stretched and realigned, allowing for more opportunities for bonds and links to be made—it's like chaotic speed dating. The kneading action also incorporates air, which strengthens the bonds. Eventually, the bonds are put under so much stress that they break and the dough relaxes.

This has the effect of the dough becoming more and more elastic as we continually stretch the gluten and force the bonds to break and reform. Gluten also forms in the direction it is kneaded. Bakers often turn the dough as they knead it to ensure that the gluten is developed evenly. This is also why we rotate the dough between each turn when we laminate croissants and puff pastry. (See How Things Rise on page 69.)

This is why recipes will often be precise about the mixing method. It's also why a cake method may ask you to mix the flour until it is just combined, while a bread recipe may have you knead the dough for upward of 15 minutes. The former is to ensure excess gluten isn't formed, while the latter is to maximize gluten formation.

When it comes to timings, recipes will guide you on how long to mix the dough to develop gluten, but you must learn to trust your senses. In any case, with yeasted doughs, you must not allow your dough to rise (also known as the bulk development stage) until the gluten is developed. (To find out why, see How Things Rise on page 79.)

Kneading techniques

Classic
Best for low-medium hydration doughs, e.g., flatbreads, bagels

Using a work surface for resistance, repeatedly push the dough away from you with the heels of your hands, then fold it back over itself. Repeat.

Slap and fold
Best for medium-high hydration doughs, e.g., milk bread, brioche

Place the dough on a clean work surface. Slide your hands under the dough and lift in the middle to release from the work surface. Bring the dough up (it'll hang a bit) and slap the bottom half on the counter. Stretch it up slightly (it should have stuck) and quickly fold the dough in half over itself. Rotate it 90 degrees, then repeat.

Stretch and fold
Best for high-hydration doughs, e.g., focaccia

This is usually reserved for wet doughs that cannot hold their own shape. It is a very gentle method. Stretch each corner of the dough into the center, lift the dough up, stretch gently, and place it back down into the container.

Rubaud
Best for high-hydration doughs, e.g., ciabatta

This is usually reserved for wet doughs that cannot hold their own shape. Using a dough scraper or your hand as a flat paddle, repeatedly lift, stretch, and turn the dough, to act as a mechanical mixer.

AUTOLYSE—SWEET NOTHING

You know that phrase "work smarter, not harder"? Well, let me introduce you to **autolyse**. Autolyse is a period after mixing flour and water when you do . . . nothing. We step away from the mixing bowl and allow the flour to fully hydrate and form gluten without us lifting a finger. This could be anywhere from 20 minutes to 1 hour. The word *autolyse* is French for "self-digestion" or "self-breaking down." It's derived from the Greek *auto*, meaning "self," and *lysis*, meaning "to break down."

During this time, the structure (by way of gluten) begins to form without any intervention. The key here is time. With enough time, flour and water will develop significant gluten—kneading simply speeds this up. It's also a much gentler way of distributing water through a dough, rather than fully working it in during the mix.

Processes similar to autolyse happen when we rest other baked goods. For example, when we rest pie dough in the fridge, water distributes itself evenly throughout the dough and gluten forms, making it much easier to work with and roll out.

STRENGTH VS. STRETCH

When making dough, there are two properties to consider: elasticity and extensibility. Although they may seem similar on the surface, they are actually opposites. Compare paper-thin filo pastry to a puffy batch of buns. Though both are made of wheat flour, we are seeking different characteristics in each.

Elasticity means your dough will go back to its shape/can hold a shape. In contrast, extensibility refers to how much the dough can stretch without consideration of it returning to form. In fact, a very extensible dough, even if it can stretch over your entire table, is actually considered weak.

You can think of these simply as strength vs. stretch. Doughs that excel in strength may have a chewy final texture (think pizza dough or bread), while doughs that excel in stretch will be tender and fine (think filo pastry).

THE IMPORTANCE OF RELAXATION

There's a lot we can learn from dough and one of those things is the importance of relaxation. When dough relaxes, it becomes extensible, aka more stretchy. All the strength (and elasticity) created during the kneading process adjusts to its new capacity. Imagine gluten as a magical rubber band, which, over time, learns to accommodate its new range without sacrificing elasticity.

If the dough isn't allowed time to relax, especially if it is high in gluten, it will be hard to shape and could become malformed while baking. For intensively stretched doughs, like croissants or puff pastry, at least 45 minutes is recommended for the dough to relax.

This is also relevant during the mix. If you are mixing a high-hydration dough that needs intensive kneading, taking rest periods, 2–3 minutes every 5–10 minutes, will give your dough a chance to relax, resulting in improved flexibility. Dough is not unlike a muscle after a workout. Like muscles, gluten networks become tight and tense after the kneading, so allowing the dough to relax means the proteins can untangle and loosen, making the dough easier to work with.

The deal with no-knead doughs

No-knead bread is a category of hands-off doughs that slowly develop strength over time. It is the perfect example of a trade-off in baking: effort (not having to knead) vs. time (24–36 hours). Pioneered by Jim Lahey, in its simplest form you simply mix flour, water, and yeast together and allow the dough to develop for 24–36 hours without touching it.

It's essentially one huge autolyse with added yeast. This is usually reserved for sourdough bread. (See How Things Rise on page 77.)

So, what exactly is happening here? Well, the enzymes present in the flour begin to break down the proteins, which make the dough really stretchy and developed. As the yeast processes the sugars, the CO_2 expands, which has the effect of very gently kneading and stretching the dough.

FLOUR POWER

Most doughs need a yin/yang mix of strength and stretch. Although our gut reaction when preparing a dough that requires a lot of volume or stretching may be to use bread flour, this isn't always necessary.

Recipes that require your dough to rise and hold its shape will usually benefit from a higher protein flour, while recipes that only need to stretch can be made with all-purpose flour. You see, all-purpose flour isn't so great at creating the sort of coiled-spring gluten network capable of trapping masses of CO_2 that we need for bread. That's where bread flour excels.

Though specific recipes will vary, here's an overview of which flour characteristic dominates in various pastries.

Effects of flour

Baked goods made with all-purpose flour will have a softer, cakier, or fluffier texture, while baked goods made with bread flour will be crisper or chewier and have better definition after baking.

SWAPPING IN FLOURS

Almost all recipes calling for bread flour can be made with all-purpose flour by reducing the hydration by around 10%. Lower protein flour absorbs less water than higher protein flour. However, this swap will come at a cost. The resulting bake will be cakier and less springy in texture, spongy rather than springy. It will likely have a lower profile since there isn't enough gluten to support a lofty structure.

On the other side of the spectrum, using whole-wheat flour has the opposite problem. Bran is highly absorbent, so you must increase the water in a recipe by 5–10%. Whole-wheat bread will also have a lower profile—all of the stuff (the bran and germ) will get in the way of long gluten chains developing.

So, you want to add whole-wheat to your dough?

Adding whole-wheat flour into doughs is a great way to add flavor and character to your recipes. But when it comes to bread, you run the risk of a flat, deflated end product thanks to the bran and germ slicing through gluten as it is forming. A way around this, taught to me by Master Baker Adam Sellar, is to sift your whole-wheat flour and separate out the bran.

You can then soak this bran in a little of the recipe's liquid and reintroduce it later. This allows two things to happen: the sifted flour is left to adequately develop gluten without interference and the formerly stabby edges of the bran are somewhat neutralized. This way, you get all the benefits of flavor and nutrition from the bran without any headaches or concerns about proper gluten development in your dough.

A BAKER'S TRICK: TOASTING FLOUR

A curious technique in the pastry kitchen is toasted flour. When you toast flour before using it in cakes, cookies, or breads, you bring out new flavor notes via the Maillard reaction (see Color on page 84). In the same way you would roast a hazelnut or almond before using it, flour can benefit from the same process. Simply heat the flour in a pan until it darkens to a mahogany brown and has a nutty flavor—around 10 minutes. But at what cost? When you toast flour, you are scorching each grain, making it impossible for gluten to form—the proteins are denatured and thus unable to form bonds.

So, you should really consider toasted flour as having totally gluten-free properties. This doesn't mean it is safe for people with Celiac disease! But you can use it for recipes that don't strongly rely on gluten, though combining it with a portion of gluten-forming wheat flour is sensible if you plan to use it in cakes and pastries. See it in action in the chamomile and toasted flour chiffon cake on page 151.

DECODING FLOUR

Beyond strength, there are a few other ways to think about flour. Be it color, grain, or type, sometimes it's a case of learning to speak bread. Depending on where you are in the world, flour will be referred to by different names. For example, the T French system uses a mixture of letters and numbers.

The T system classifies flour based on the amount of residue left after burning 1 kilogram (2.2 pounds) of flour. So old-school, but there is a reason. Flour is mainly composed of starch and sugars, which disappear when the flour is burned, leaving behind mineral content, such as bran or ash. Therefore, the lower the T number, for example T45, the softer the flour will be. On the other hand, the higher the T number, which can go up to T170, the less refined the flour will be, and the more it will contain whole wheat.

Flour type	Approx. protein content	T class	Details
Cake flour	7–8%	T45	Mild, neutral, slightly earthy
Rye flour	8–16%	T170 (whole-wheat)	Dense texture, earthy, nutty flavor. Ranges from light to dark. Can be white or whole-wheat
All-purpose flour	9–11%	T55	Mild, neutral, slightly earthy
Buckwheat flour	10–12%		Slightly sweet, nutty flavor
Whole-wheat flour	10–14%	T150	Nutty, earthy flavor, high in fiber and nutrients
Semolina	12–13%		Coarse texture, slightly sweet. Derived from hard durum wheat
Bread flour	12–14%	T65	Mild, neutral, slightly earthy

Low Protein

High Protein

What is 00 flour?

00 flour, popular in Italian baking, refers to how finely flour is ground, rather than a particular grain or strength and it has a variable protein content.

The deal with cocoa

To adapt a dough to a cocoa flavor, you can swap a portion of the flour weight for cocoa powder, starting at about 10%. It will change the flavor of the bake and alter the texture. Cocoa powder is about 25% fat, so it cannot be treated like any other starch (see page 62). It also absorbs more water than flour, so you need to increase the liquid in a recipe by 15%–20% to compensate for this.

MINIMIZING OR MAXIMIZING GLUTEN

Gluten is either the hero or the villain in the story, depending on what you are baking. For bread and buns, gluten is the hero. For tender cakes, it's the villain! No matter what you are making, you should always stop to consider whether you want to minimize or maximize gluten development. Once you know that, you can figure out how to achieve it with the help of other ingredients. Here's a guide on what to look out for.

Ingredient		Minimize gluten	Maximize gluten
Sugar	Sugar is highly hygroscopic, aka water-loving (see All About Sugar on page 29). It competes with the flour for moisture, meaning it draws water away from the proteins, reducing the strength of the proteins network.	Add sugar before or at the same time as the flour.	Hold sugar back from initial mixing.
Fat	Fat inhibits gluten development. Because fat and water do not mix, the water has limited access to the flour if it is combined or coated with fat. Liquid fats like oil help to lubricate the dough and help the dough feel stretchier, improving the extensibility without adding additional water.	Rub fat and flour together or use liquid fat to coat the flour before proceeding with the recipe. Increase the overall amount of fat in the dough to limit the strength potential of the gluten network.	Hold fat back until gluten is somewhat developed.
Whole-wheat flour	Pieces of bran in whole-wheat flour act like little knives, cutting through the dough and literally slicing through strands of gluten. As a result of this, dough made with whole-wheat flour will have less volume.		Sift whole-wheat flour and soak bran, introducing the bran back in later after gluten is developed.
Salt	Improves gluten development, strengthening the bonds between proteins.		Add salt with flour.
pH	A slightly acidic environment is when gluten is happiest, but the gluten strength is reduced by lowering it too much (below 5) or increasing it above 7 (aka making it more alkaline).	Lower the pH of dough to weaken gluten and make the structure more tender, e.g., sour cream or buttermilk for acidic, or baking soda for more alkaline (see How Things Rise on page 74).	Add a small amount of lemon juice or vinegar to your dough to lower pH slightly.
Time	The longer flour and water are left to develop gluten, the stronger the dough will become.	Mix briefly, and do not allow batter or dough to sit for long periods.	Allow the dough to rest or use a preferment (see How Things Rise on page 80).
Alcohol	Alcohol will hydrate flour with a lower percentage of water, reducing gluten development and making a dough more tender or short.	Use a small amount of alcohol in place of the liquid in the dough.	
Add-ins	Add-ins like herbs, nuts, or chocolate chips will get in the way of gluten formation.		Hold back until gluten is somewhat developed.

STARCH

Starch is the unsung hero of flour and it is equally—if not more—responsible for the final structure of baked goods. Just think—flour comprises 70–75% starch compared to the 7–14% protein. If gluten is the best-selling author superstar of flour, then starch is the ghostwriter.

Starch is a carbohydrate and is the food source for yeast in fermented bread (see How Things Rise on page 76) and when hydrated, it will thicken when heat is applied (see Texture on page 94). This thickening process provides the main body and forms the structure for most of the bakes we know and love. That soft crumb of your favorite cake? You've got starch to thank for that. That crispy coating on your favorite fried snack? Starch, we love you!

Starch, however, only comes into its own when there's enough water to interact with. When starch is mixed with water and heated, the granules absorb and swell, creating a mesh network and a thickened consistency. The water is effectively trapped, turning starch from gritty particles to soft ones. This irreversible process is known as gelatinization.

Gelatinization is one of the most important processes that happens again and again in baking. It links shiny bagels to choux pastry, milk bread to chocolate cake. Starch gelatinization begins at 149°F and is complete by 203°F, but we can track its various moves by looking closer at some of our favorite pastries.

ADDING BULK

In baking, bulk refers to the dry ingredients in a recipe. While this is usually wheat flour or sugar, other ingredients add this bulk to recipes without contributing gluten. In some recipes, you might wish to turn to alternative bulkers, like ground nuts or polenta, to help change the character of your bakes. These tend to create a different texture and add depth to your recipes.

Definition: Tangzhong

Tangzhong is a thick, gel-like paste made by heating flour and liquid, which is added to bread dough to increase moisture and create a soft and fluffy texture.

The humble potato

One way to increase the moisture in your dough is by adding your favorite starchy friend: the potato. Like a tangzhong, a cooked potato is a starch sponge stuffed with water. In fact, potato is one of the most effective starches at retaining water because the molecules are bigger and absorb and hold liquid more easily, as well as adding body to your dough, which makes it easier to handle. Since potatoes do not contain gluten, they effectively interrupt the firm gluten network, resulting in a squishier, softer bread, as well as imparting subtle flavor cues. You could also try pumpkin or sweet potato.

Amount of flour

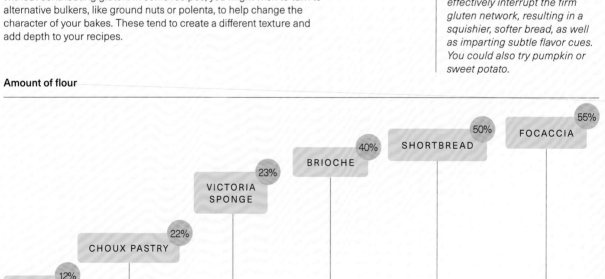

CANELÉ — 12%
CHOUX PASTRY — 22%
VICTORIA SPONGE — 23%
BRIOCHE — 40%
SHORTBREAD — 50%
FOCACCIA — 55%

p.262   p.136   p.140   p.133   p.192   p.280

Low flour content   **High flour content**

STARCH GELATINIZATION IN ACTION

BAGELS

In the case of bagels, starch gelatinization is responsible for that chewy crust. Before baking, bagels are boiled. As the dough hits the water, rapid gelatinization of the outer crust of the bagel occurs. As a result, a supple crust is formed. It is still a bit flexible, but it does set the bagel's shape and reduces outward expansion during the bake, resulting in the dense, chewy middle.

CHOUX

For choux pastry, we gelatinize the flour by cooking it on the stovetop before adding the eggs. This is sometimes referred to as drying out the choux paste. To make sure you've gelatinized it, you can take the temperature of your paste with a probe thermometer. So long as it has reached 185°F, you're in the clear. By gelatinizing the flour, we denature the proteins, which massively reduces the potential for gluten but does not remove it completely.

The choux paste is stretchy but not elastic, i.e., it won't spring back, which works in our favor when baking the choux. The paste expands as the steam evaporates, and the shape is set by the starch and egg proteins setting.

CUSTARD

Starch creates stable, thick, and unctuous mixtures in custard. Crème pâtissière, or pastry cream, gets its texture entirely from starch. Although the eggs coagulate, they mainly contribute flavor rather than texture.

BREAD

Some breads, like squishy milk bread, call for a tangzhong, that is a portion of the recipe's flour to be precooked, aka gelatinized, ahead of time. Pioneered by Yvonne Chen in *The 65-degree Bread Doctor*, she found that using this technique meant you could introduce a higher proportion of hydration into bread.

By pre-cooking the flour, we are essentially trapping hydration by keeping moisture busy with starch, effectively binding the water. This means we can add more hydration while keeping the bread manageable to work with and improving oven spring and texture with the added water and steam power.

CAKES

In cakes, starch gelatinization occurs as the internal temperature of the batter rises while baking. The starch gelatinizes around expanding air pockets as the bake progresses, providing the cake's structure.

PIE FILLINGS

Starch thickens and gels fruit juices as the pie bakes, resulting in sliceable fillings once cool. To go deeper, see Texture on page 94.

RICE PUDDING

In the case of rice pudding, the rice absorbs milk and in turn releases starch into the liquid. This results in a thickened, creamy texture.

BAKER'S PERCENTAGES

There are plenty of ways to make sense of a recipe, but one of the most useful ways is through baker's percentages. If seeing any symbol that remotely refers to math leaves you feeling riddled with anxiety, don't worry. I'm here to guide you through it, and I promise you'll feel good about it afterward. Baker's percentages are a handy way of looking at recipes, breaking down each ingredient and its relative proportion to flour. For example, if we use 70g of water to 100g of flour, we would say the water has a baker's percentage of 70%. In a recipe displayed in baker's percentages, the flour will always be 100%.

An example of a baker's percentage

Brioche	(g)	Bakers %
Flour	285g	100%
Salt	6g	2.1%
Yeast	5g	1.75%
Milk	50g	18%
Eggs	150g	53%
Egg yolk	20g	7%
Butter	170g	60%
Sugar	40g	14%

Baker's percentages are very useful for looking at recipes at a glance and building your own. When building bread recipes, the yeast and salt do not change radically, but the hydration—in the form of milk, eggs, or water—and fat (hi, brioche!) is where things begin to shift. The amount of hydration impacts the texture. A low hydration dough (50–60%) will have a denser, more even crumb with a lot of chew and hold its shape very well. When mixing, it will come together easily and may feel stiff or tight. It's useful for doughs like babka or bagels.

As you increase the hydration, the dough gets wetter and wilder. As a result, it will have a softer, more tender crumb. It can also form erratic, glassy, open-crumb structures like focaccia. It can certainly be more challenging to handle—it will be stickier and take longer to develop significant gluten. What you hydrate the dough with also has an impact and is often where lean doughs become enriched. Lean doughs, such as pizza dough or baguettes, have little to no sugar or fat—just water, salt, and flour. When the dough is enriched, it has been bolstered with sugar, eggs, or fat to create various textures and flavors to make it more fluffy and soft, like brioche and cinnamon buns. Enriched doughs tend to have a higher proportion of sugar for flavor. For more information on how that impacts the dough and the rise, see All About Sugar on page 29 and How Things Rise on page 81.

Lean vs. enriched breads

Enriched

Croissant dough	(g)	Baker's %
Flour	605g	100%
Salt	12g	2%
Yeast	13g	2%
Milk	165g	27%
Butter	30g	5%
Sugar	75g	12%

Lean

Focaccia	(g)	Baker's %
Flour	660g	100%
Yeast	2g	0.3%
Water	545g	83%
Olive oil*	100g	15%
Salt	13g	2%

Yeast in enriched breads

Enriched breads will typically use more yeast than lean breads to accommodate the enriching ingredients, namely sugar. Although sugar at first boosts the yeast, anything above 5% will ultimately slow down the fermentation process because sugar, being highly hygroscopic, steals water from everything, including yeast cells!

* Olive oil is added only during the folding and baking process, so even though focaccia does contain fat, it is closer to a lean bread!

Hydration ranges of baked goods

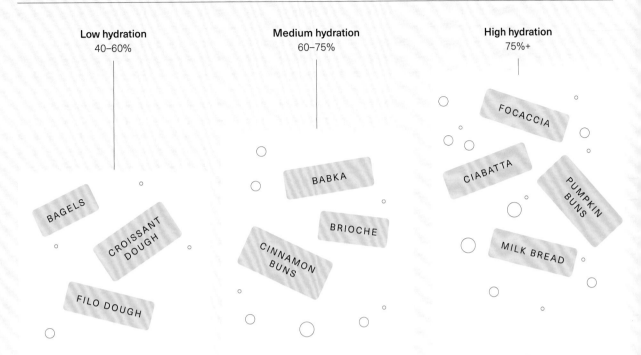

Low hydration
40–60%

Medium hydration
60–75%

High hydration
75%+

FOCACCIA

BABKA

CIABATTA

PUMPKIN BUNS

BAGELS

BRIOCHE

CROISSANT DOUGH

MILK BREAD

CINNAMON BUNS

FILO DOUGH

THE LAST CRUMB

With its delicate balance of protein and starch, flour provides a wonderful and expandable canvas in baking and its ability to bind, stretch, and thicken is instrumental to the success of our cakes, breads, and pastries.

Learning how to minimize or maximize these properties introduces us to a world of textures, though the inherent flavor of grains should also be celebrated. In fact, flour shines the most in our simplest recipes. With the addition of water, yeast, and salt, it impressively houses a cacophony of bubbles in a way that no other ingredient can, and produces textures that are crisp, chewy, airy, and soft at the same time. Flour is the solid foundation that other ingredients can rely on. Without the net of starch or gluten, where would other ingredients be?

Think of it as the designated driver of the friend group, staying steady and keeping all the ingredients in place while allowing them to flourish.

ALL
ABOUT
SUGAR

Sugar and the pursuit of sweet things is almost certainly the first introduction we all had to the world of baking. Stolen spoonfuls of Nutella, winning the bid against your siblings to lick the spoon from the cake mix, the sticky fingers post jam doughnuts from the bakery, chocolate cornflake cakes sold at the school fair. Sugar is so ubiquitous with sweetness that people often think it is a one-note ingredient, only adding flavor to your bakes. But we are selling sugar short.

Whether you realize it or not, sugar is out there holding up cake structures, making your cookies tender while simultaneously making the crusts of those same cookies crispy, improving color, stabilizing foams, and making your ice creams smooth. Heated enough, it will transform into one of baking's most-loved ingredients: caramel (see Color on page 84). It must be exhausting to be sugar. But what exactly is it, and why is it so busy all the time?

This chapter will explore the myriad ways that sugar ingratiates itself in our bakes. From its unique and dominating relationship with water to the extraordinary variety of types, from ones that crunch to ones that flow, we'll see how getting the balance of sugar right is the key to a successful bake.

WHAT IS SUGAR?

Sugar is the generic name for all sweet-tasting carbohydrates in the food world. Think of sugar as the family name, scrawled at the top of an incredibly complex and long family tree, which comprises all sorts of characters. Each branch of this family has its own unique properties and uses, from floral honey to mahogany molasses, chunky pearl sugar to powdered sugar that seems to refuse to obey gravity.

When it comes to baking, it's a good idea to get to know the whole clan, though the most common (and useful for the everyday baker) is sucrose, which comprises the classic table sugar. It comes in many forms, including granulated and coarse sanding sugar, and is usually defined by how finely ground it is.

Beyond sucrose, the other main sugars in baking are fructose, glucose, and lactose. There's also maltose, which comes up less regularly but can still make your bakes sing. Sugars are either a single (monosaccharide) or a pair (disaccharide). This variation gives sugar its varying properties, from the flavor to the way it behaves in bakes.

Intriguingly, sugars are not created equal. They have different levels of sweetening power, meaning some sugars taste sweeter than others when we eat them. This can be exploited for more balanced bakes.

Types of sugar and levels of sweetness

Name	Type	Components	Where to find it
Fructose	Monosaccharide	Fructose	Fruit, honey
Sucrose	Disaccharide	Glucose + Fructose	Table sugar
Glucose*	Monosaccharide	Glucose	Glucose
Maltose	Disaccharide	Glucose + Glucose	Malt syrup, corn syrup
Lactose	Disaccharide	Glucose + Galactose	Dairy

Most sweet ↓ Least sweet

* Also known as dextrose

DEFINING AND REFINING

There are two key forms: refined and unrefined.

Refined sugar is sucrose that has been extracted from one of two sources: sugar beet is grown in cooler climates like the UK, while sugarcane is grown in more tropical climates. They are interchangeable after processing because they both end up as pure sucrose. To refine the sugar, they are first crushed or sliced to release the juice. This then undergoes a series of complex refining processes that results in a mixture of molasses and sucrose. The final process is to separate these. Once the sucrose has been extracted, it is either used as pure white sugar or it undergoes another process to become other products, for example, molasses is added back to make light and dark brown sugars.

Unrefined sugar mainly comes from sugarcane and is rarely derived from beet sugar (see note). It is considered unrefined as the molasses and sucrose are extracted together, rather than the molasses being added back later. Some popular unrefined cane sugars are muscovado, panela, and demerara.

Beet vs. Cane

The main area where the cane and beet sugars vary is the molasses. Beet molasses is not very sweet and is used for animal feed, while cane molasses is the sweet, syrupy stuff we're used to enjoying.

Demerara

A common unrefined sugar derived from cane sugar is demerara. As the sucrose syrup boils down and reduces, you are left with a treasure trove of crunchy crystals. These coarse grains will not melt in the oven, so can be used to decorate baked goods pre-baking to add texture.

THE WORLD OF SUGARS

Sugars can be further subdivided into two major categories: solid and liquid. As well as this, sugars have different acidities, which impact the way they behave and react with other ingredients as well as the flavor. For example, acidic sugars might be paired with baking soda to initiate the chemical reaction that allows bakes to rise (see How Things Rise on page 74), while inverted liquid sugars, like honey or golden syrup, can be used to help prevent crystallization in sugar syrups.

Name	Type	Flavor profile	Water content (approx)	Grain size	pH (approx)	Origin
Powdered sugar	Sucrose with added starch to prevent clumping	Sweet, powdery	0%	Very fine	7	Sugarcane or sugar beet
Pearl sugar	Sucrose	Sweet, crunchy	0%	Large	7	Sugarcane or sugar beet
Coarse sanding sugar	Sucrose	Sweet, neutral	0%	Medium	7	Sugarcane or sugar beet
Granulated sugar	Sucrose	Sweet, neutral	0%	Fine	7	Sugarcane or sugar beet
Light brown sugar	Sucrose and molasses	Sweet, caramel-like	2–4%	Fine, soft	5–5.5	Sugarcane or sugar beet
Muscovado sugar	Sucrose and molasses	Rich, sticky, molasses-like	2–4%	Fine, soft	5–5.5	Sugarcane
Dark brown sugar	Sucrose and molasses	Sweet, rich, molasses-like	2–4%	Fine, soft	5–5.5	Sugarcane or sugar beet
Demerara sugar	Sucrose and molasses	Sweet, caramel-like	2%	Coarse, hard	5–5.5	Sugarcane
Glucose syrup	Glucose	Sweet	20–24%	n/a	4–5.5	Starch (corn, wheat, potatoes)
Corn syrup	Glucose	Sweet	20–24%	n/a	3.5–5.5	Corn
High-fructose corn syrup	Inverted syrup—glucose and fructose	Sweet	20–24%	n/a	3.5–5.5	Corn
Golden syrup	Inverted syrup—glucose and fructose	Sweet, buttery	20%	n/a	5–6	Sugarcane or sugar beet
Honey	Inverted syrup—glucose and fructose	Sweet, floral	15–20%	n/a	3.2–4.5	Bees
Cane molasses	Partially inverted syrup—sucrose, glucose, and fructose	Rich, robust, bittersweet	20–25%	n/a	4.8–5.5	Sugarcane
Maple syrup	Inverted syrup—glucose and fructose	Sweet, earthy, caramel-like	30–35%	n/a	5.5–8	Maple trees
Malt syrup	Malted barley	Sweet, malty, rich	20–25%	n/a	5–6	Malted barley

THE ROLE OF SUGAR

Sugar, granular and liquid alike, is incredibly good at tenderizing baked goods, as well as improving moisture. It also plays a role in color (see Color on page 84), leavening (see How Things Rise on page 68), stabilizing egg foams (see All About Eggs on page 46), and defining the shape of our bakes. Think of sugar as a nosy neighbor—it interferes in everyone's business. Here's an overview of the key interactions to be aware of in baking.

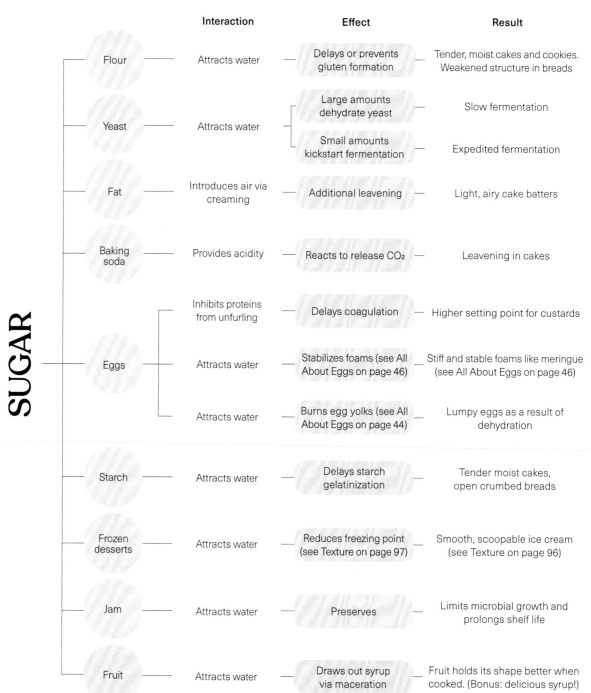

	Interaction	Effect	Result
Flour	Attracts water	Delays or prevents gluten formation	Tender, moist cakes and cookies. Weakened structure in breads
Yeast	Attracts water	Large amounts dehydrate yeast	Slow fermentation
		Small amounts kickstart fermentation	Expedited fermentation
Fat	Introduces air via creaming	Additional leavening	Light, airy cake batters
Baking soda	Provides acidity	Reacts to release CO_2	Leavening in cakes
Eggs	Inhibits proteins from unfurling	Delays coagulation	Higher setting point for custards
	Attracts water	Stabilizes foams (see All About Eggs on page 46)	Stiff and stable foams like meringue (see All About Eggs on page 46)
	Attracts water	Burns egg yolks (see All About Eggs on page 44)	Lumpy eggs as a result of dehydration
Starch	Attracts water	Delays starch gelatinization	Tender moist cakes, open crumbed breads
Frozen desserts	Attracts water	Reduces freezing point (see Texture on page 97)	Smooth, scoopable ice cream (see Texture on page 96)
Jam	Attracts water	Preserves	Limits microbial growth and prolongs shelf life
Fruit	Attracts water	Draws out syrup via maceration	Fruit holds its shape better when cooked. (Bonus: delicious syrup!)

SUGAR

A bug's life

Water movement is the culprit of all spoilage. Why? Well, water is the source of all life. And that life includes all creatures, great and small, including bacteria.

However, sugar is pretty good at preventing this by effectively occupying the water through its hygroscopic—water-attracting—nature. Jams, for example, contain a lot of water, but with the presence of sugar, the water is too busy being entertained to allow mold and bacteria to thrive in the jam.

The problem lies in free water, which acts as a breeding ground for bacteria. This is why frozen or dried items can last indefinitely while fresh items have a short shelf life. It all comes down to water activity and how much water is free to take part in bacteria parties!

THE RIGHT AMOUNT OF SUGAR

There is no strict rule about how much sugar to add to a recipe and it will, of course, always depend on the final product. I am often asked if sugar can be reduced in recipes. And the answer is, annoyingly, it depends! For example, most cake recipes will have a similar result if you reduce the sugar by 20%. But understanding and compensating for these trade-offs is key.

	Not enough sugar	The right amount	Too much sugar
Yeast		Helps kickstart fermentation	Slows down fermentation, and gluten and structure formation
Bread		Adds flavor and tenderness	Prevents gluten fermentation and structure formation
Fruit, as in compotes or jams	Not sweet enough, does not set	Prevents spoilage and mold formation	Overly sweet and thick, cloying texture
Cake	The cake will be dry	The cake will be moist and tender and have a longer shelf life	The cake will lack structure and have a hard, dry crust
Cookies	Cookies will not spread and lack flavor	Cookies will spread and have a soft texture and crisp exterior	Cookies will spread too much, may burn and have an overly chewy/sticky texture
Ice cream	Ice cream will be icy and hard	Ice cream will be soft and scoopable	Ice cream is overly sweet and does not properly freeze

SUGAR AND WATER: A LOVE STORY

No matter what sugar you use, the relationship between sugar and water is one of the most essential in baking, and it underpins a lot of sugar's behaviors. This is because sugar is hygroscopic, aka *loves* water. And when I say love, I mean can't-live-without, standing-outside-the-window-with-a-boombox kind of love. So, when it comes to water, it's like a thirsty sponge constantly reaching out and grabbing hold of water molecules. It just can't get enough.

HOW DOES THIS AFFECT YOUR BAKES?

It's this incredible love story between sugar and water that results in a multitude of consequences in the kitchen, both favorable and less favorable. When you introduce sugar into a mixture, it immediately seeks out the water and bonds with it. On the positive side, this means your bakes will retain moisture. It also has the effect of delaying gluten formation, starch gelatinization, and egg coagulation, which makes your final product more tender. This is why high-sugar bakes like brownies will have soft and gooey textures. On the negative side, sugar attracts water from the other ingredients so strongly that it can dehydrate them. This may prevent the other ingredients from properly functioning or may mean that water is absorbed from the air, leading to dodgy icing or sticky meringues.

It really does vary. A Victoria sponge made with over 50% less sugar will be highly domed, very dense, and dry. Without the delaying properties of sugar, the structure sets too early. And since the sugar is not occupying the water, more is lost as steam, resulting in a loss of moisture.

On the other end of the spectrum, a cake made with double the amount of sugar is also extremely dry. It will collapse in the center because too much tenderizing has weakened the structure. Such a large amount of sugar will also give the cake a rusk-like, dry texture with a thick crust as the sugar returns to its crystallized state after baking.

By replacing some sugar with liquid sweeteners, like honey, you might expect it to help your cake rise more due to its higher water content (see Steam on page 68). However, this isn't the case as honey isn't effective at incorporating air into fat during the creaming process. (See the roasted strawberry Victoria sponge cake recipe on page 140.)

THE DEAL WITH MACERATION

Maceration is the process of mixing sugar and raw fruit for a period of time before cooking or eating, using sugar's hygroscopic nature to great effect. The amount of sugar will vary—from 5–20% of the fruit's weight to spoon onto desserts to 50% for jams. This period of time can be anything from 15 minutes to up to a week. Once sugar is introduced, the moisture in the fruit is drawn out and forms a syrup with the sugar. The sugar, now well-dissolved in the liquid from the fruit, is less likely to stick or burn.

Macerated fruit will also hold its shape better. This is because fruit is made up of a series of cell walls filled with water; the water literally pushes against the cell walls, which defines the shape. As the fruit gets older and water is lost, the fruit will become droopy. The same thing happens when it's cooked; as fruit is heated, the cells break down and the water is released. Since the maceration will have already drawn out a lot of this water, the effect of heating isn't as extreme. This means the cell walls will not break down as rapidly—they have already had time to prepare for this water loss!

This technique can be applied to jams and pies to prevent the overly extreme breakdown of the fruit and to help retain chunks, even after a lot of cooking. It is also a good technique for decorating cakes or pavlovas. You can spoon on the fruit and syrup separately, and the fruit is less likely to weep.

Sugar in cake baking

Perfect amount of sugar

Too much sugar

Not enough sugar

Sugar in frozen desserts

Sugar plays a major role in the texture of frozen desserts. From scoopable ice creams to crunchy granitas, how much sugar we use makes a huge difference. To go deeper into the role of sugar and understand the role of sugar concentration in texture, see Texture on page 97.

Why does honey taste so different?

Honey has an uneven combination of fructose (40%) and glucose (30%). The rest is a mixture of water, pollen, and other impurities.

It's this variable 30% that gives honey its unique, environmentally influenced flavor. White sugar, no matter where it comes from in the world, is always going to taste like white sugar. Honey, for example, Ling Heather or Manuka, is prized for its flavor and medicinal qualities and can only be sourced in specific areas.

SUGAR AND AIR

In the case of eggs and fat, granular sugar introduces air. Because of its crystal-like structure, sugar inherently brings air along with it whenever it is added to a mixture. Although eggs and fat can whip up without any help, sugar helps to stabilize these structures. When creaming butter and sugar, the jagged edges of the sugar cut through the fat and introduce pockets of air, which are captured by the large globs of fat. As the fat loads up on air bubbles, it expands and becomes whiter, resulting in a light, airy mixture that sneaks lightness into our cakes (see All About Fat on page 59 and How Things Rise on page 73). For eggs, the story is slightly different. Sugar draws water from eggs as they volumize, forming a syrup that becomes trapped within strong protein bonds. Air bubbles are also trapped within these bonds, which results in an extraordinary increase in volume known as foams (see All About Eggs on page 45).

SUGAR SWAPS

When it comes to building your own recipes, it's important to be aware of the trade-offs that exist. Although sugars are interchangeable in recipes, there are a few things to be aware of. From accounting for the additional liquid to the level of browning, here's what you need to consider:

Things to consider	Effects
Caramelization and color on bakes	Sucrose and glucose caramelize at around 320°F, but for sugars that contain fructose, like honey, this happens way lower at 230°F. This is why bakes that use honey are often darker in color and can burn more easily. Caramelization and the Maillard reaction are happening concurrently in a double whammy of color! (See Color on page 84.)
Aeration of fat	Granular sugar and butter make the base of most cakes because of the formation of air pockets during the creaming process (see All About Fat on page 59). Because of its water content, liquid sugar does get in the way of these air pockets forming, so swapping in liquid sugar, like maple syrup or honey, will result in a less airy cake.
Texture	Granular sugars are prone to crystallization while liquid sugars, like golden syrup, can help prevent this.
Moisture	Using liquid sugar instead of granular sugar can lead to more tender, loftier bakes thanks to the increased water content. You may need to reduce the overall liquid in the recipe to account for the water in the sugar. For wet mixtures, like cake batter, the additional water is less of an issue. But for drier mixtures, like shortbread, it needs to be taken into account. Liquid sugars tend to be 20–30% water (see the overview of sugars in the baking table on page 28), so either reduce the liquid from the recipe or increase the solids (flour).
Sweetness and flavor	Some sugars are sweeter than others and, compared to sucrose, maple syrup and honey have strong flavors that should be accounted for.
Starch content	Some recipes opt to use powdered sugar in place of granulated sugar, making the most of the added cornstarch or starch. Powdered sugar also dissolves more quickly into other ingredients because of the small particle size.

CRYSTALLIZATION

Sugar has an intrinsic nature to organize itself in a highly structured way. This results in the crystal structure that we know so well. While sugar and water have an impressive love story, it must be noted that there is one thing that it loves more than water: sugar! This means it will happily return to its granular state without much encouragement. This can be a good or bad thing depending on what you are making.

On the good side of things, crystallization can lead to elegant sugared fruit or jewel-like crystallized nuts. On the flip side, crystallization can be a very unwelcome and frustrating event in the kitchen, especially when you're working with syrups.

When sugar is dissolved in water, it becomes a syrup. Crystallization in sugar syrups is the moment when the dissolved sugar seeks to break free from its watery prison and return to that structured, granular form. Like a chain reaction, crystallization spreads rapidly in a syrup, turning your once smooth syrup into a series of chunky sugar crystals. But why?

If given half the chance, sugar will always seek to return to its original state. Stirring or agitating a syrup is a surefire way to see crystallization in action. You see, when sugar crystals are dissolved in water, they are kept separate by the liquid. However, stirring the mixture will cause the sugar crystals to bump into each other, and the temptation becomes too much for the sugar and the crystals reform. The same happens if a small amount of undissolved sugar makes its way into the solution. Once a solution has crystallized, you can either add more water and heat to melt the crystals back down, or you may have to start again completely.

Crystallization is unlikely in sugar syrups with a low proportion of sugar to water since the opportunities for the sugar crystals to interact is relatively low. The higher the concentration of sugar in water, the higher the chance of crystallization. As the water evaporates, there are fewer water molecules between the sugar, thus increasing the opportunity for the crystals to interact and reform.

SYRUPS AND WATER EVAPORATION

A sugar syrup is a mixture of sugar and water. It comes in a variety of concentrations, depending on the use.

Pure water has a boiling point of 212°F. When you add sugar, the boiling point rises, and as the mixture heats, water is evaporated. Another way to think of this is—the higher the temperature, the higher the sugar concentration. The amount of water in the syrup will define how it will behave when combined with other ingredients. This is why you can achieve different results by taking the sugar syrup to different temperatures.

The more water that is evaporated from a mixture, the less it flows once cool. This is because there is less to prevent the sugar from settling back into its hard, crystal structure.

Inverted sugar

A good way to combat crystallization is by using inverted sugars like golden syrup or honey. Inverted sugar is one of those things you don't strictly have to know about, but the fancier the baking books you buy, the more often you'll see it mentioned. Inverted sugar can be made by adding sucrose to a liquid and breaking the bond with an acid.

All this means is that the sucrose has been broken into its component parts— glucose and fructose. Because the molecules have been separated, they are both available to create bonds with water. These smaller crystals also bind more easily with water than sucrose, which helps prevent crystallization. It is sometimes described as "resisting crystallization."

Note

To help prevent crystallization when heating sugar syrups, put a lid on the pot you are heating it in for the first few minutes. The steamy atmosphere will help dissolve any pesky crystals! It's also good practice to check there aren't any undissolved sugar crystals on the sides of the pan—simply wash the sides of the pan with a wet pastry brush before heating.

HELP! My sugar syrup is too hot!

First off, don't sweat it! Add a little water (careful, it may spit) and then reheat the solution. Remember, all the temperature indicates is the sugar/water concentration, so you are in full control and can always course correct it!

It's also good to know that your syrup can be heated to near the correct temperature and then turned off. When you're ready to combine, simply turn the heat back on to get it to temperature. Unfortunately, this doesn't work if you've accidentally got to caramel as the physical structure of the sugar has changed by then.

Note

Much like brown butter (see Color on page 88), sugar syrups are a good opportunity to utilize the lesser-used sense of hearing in the kitchen.

When heating a sugar syrup, the water evaporates rapidly in the 212°F region, and it is noisy. So, rest assured, if you can hear your sugar syrup, it's still quite a way from being ready.

WHAT IS SIMPLE SYRUP?

A simple syrup, which is used to soak cake layers, make granita, or mix into cocktails, is usually 1:1—i.e., equal parts sugar dissolved in water. A syrup for candying fruit may be more like 2:1 sugar to water, depending on the recipe. Suppose you are heating a syrup to make caramel or to reach a particular temperature. In that case, it tends to be a very low concentration of water to sugar because the goal of heating syrup is to evaporate water, and the more water . . . the longer it takes.

GETTING TO KNOW THE TEMPERATURES

When you heat up a sugar syrup, the water evaporates and the mixture undergoes a series of changes. It becomes thicker, and the bubbles turn from rapid and fast-moving to slow. It is incredibly difficult to judge sugar temperatures visually, so a digital thermometer is your best friend here and will help avoid any mistakes. Before digital thermometers were a standard fixture in kitchens, the status of a sugar syrup was tested by scooping out a small amount and dropping it into cold water. The water cools down the syrup quickly and the texture can be ascertained. This is where the common names for the sugar syrup stages come from.

Temp	Name	% of water	% of sugar	
221–235°F	Syrup/thread stage	20–25%	75–85%	Most water
239–244°F	Soft ball	15–20%	80–85%	
244–250°F	Firm ball	10–15%	85–90%	
250–266°F	Hard ball	5–10%	90–95%	
270–293°F	Soft crack	<5%	>95%	Least water
293–311°F	Hard crack	<5%	>95%	
320°F	Caramel	0%	100%	No water

Sugar stages

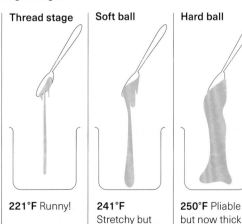

Thread stage

221°F Runny!

Soft ball

241°F Stretchy but still soft

Hard ball

250°F Pliable but now thick

Soft crack

275°F Cannot lift/stretch it out of its container

GRANULAR

SUGAR IN ACTION

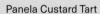
Hazelnut Amaretti

Victoria Sponge

French Meringue

Panela Custard Tart

Financier

DARKEST ←————————————————————————→ **LIGHTEST**

Maple Buttercrunch

Chocolate Peanut
Ice Cream Bars

Toasted Flour Chiffon Cake

Choconut Tart

Golden Syrup Buttercream

Italian Meringue

LIQUID

SALT

It feels fitting to end this chapter on sugar with a mention for its yang: salt. Unlike sugar, which can be added in large quantities in baking, salt remains a relatively small (but mighty) part of any baking recipe.

You'll notice it weaved throughout the chapters for its role in strengthening gluten (see All About Flour on page 19), breaking down the structure of eggs (see All About Eggs on page 41), affecting texture (see Texture on page 97), and slowing down fermentation (see How Things Rise on page 76). Like its sweet counterpart, it has an affinity for water so mirrors its behavior in some ways. But ultimately, salt appears in our recipes for one reason: to season.

Adding salt makes ingredients taste more like themselves and adds character to our bakes. In a genre of cooking that is hinged on sweetness, the balance of salt becomes all the more important. From a finishing of flaky salt on a freshly baked bun or a whisper mixed into honey, salt is the electric shock we all need. With some baked goods, the absence of salt is clearer than others. While a cake without salt in the batter may go unnoticed, bread made without salt is lifeless with muted colors, thanks to salt's important role in slowing fermentation.

When it comes to baking, you can add saltiness through less traditional means—an unusual flavor flourish is always welcome. Fermented pastes, like miso and umeboshi, can make big flavor splashes, while a dash of soy can go a long way, though it should be noted that these bring flavors beyond saltiness and should not be considered replacements. Salty cheese like feta is a surprising, but welcome, addition to a cheesecake, while using salted nuts in your praline paste or brittles will bring them up a notch or two. And if you find that you only have salted butter at home, don't be scared to use it! Your bakes won't be overly salty, but they will have a kick to them that you'll be glad you tried.

If you keep adding salt to sugar, there is a tipping point where the mixture begins to taste more salty than sweet. Finding a harmonious balance between the two makes for an irresistible flavor. The balance between this yin and yang will vary depending on your personal palate. Try it yourself—begin adding salt to sugar (start with 1% salt weight to sugar) and taste until it reaches a perfect tipping point.

A FINAL SPOONFUL

Equipped with the knowledge that sugar is so much more than just sweet, experiment with the different flavors and textures at your (sticky) fingertips: whether it's using maple syrup in your favorite buttercream rather than plain white sugar, or macerating fruit ahead of time to reap the texture (and flavor) benefits, or trying out an unrefined sugar in your favorite cake recipe, there's so much this misunderstood ingredient offers. And if you're not ready to say goodbye to this chapter, skip to Color (see page 84) to learn all about the darker side of sugar: caramel!

3.

ALL
ABOUT
EGGS

The egg is, no doubt, the most versatile and fascinating building block of baking. Eggs are unrivaled shapeshifters. Whether in cake, custard, or cookies, the egg is like the member of the chorus in a Broadway show, always doing the most, helping the rest of the ingredients be the best they can be. Eggs are a total multi-hyphenate and play an essential role in our bakes' structure, volume, color, hydration, and flavor, to name just some of their skills.

In this chapter, we'll explore how foams are created (and maintained), the role eggs play in thickening, and how two opposite characters (the yolk and white) exist harmoniously together.

So how can one little ingredient be responsible for so much? Let's have a closer look.

WHAT'S IN AN EGG?

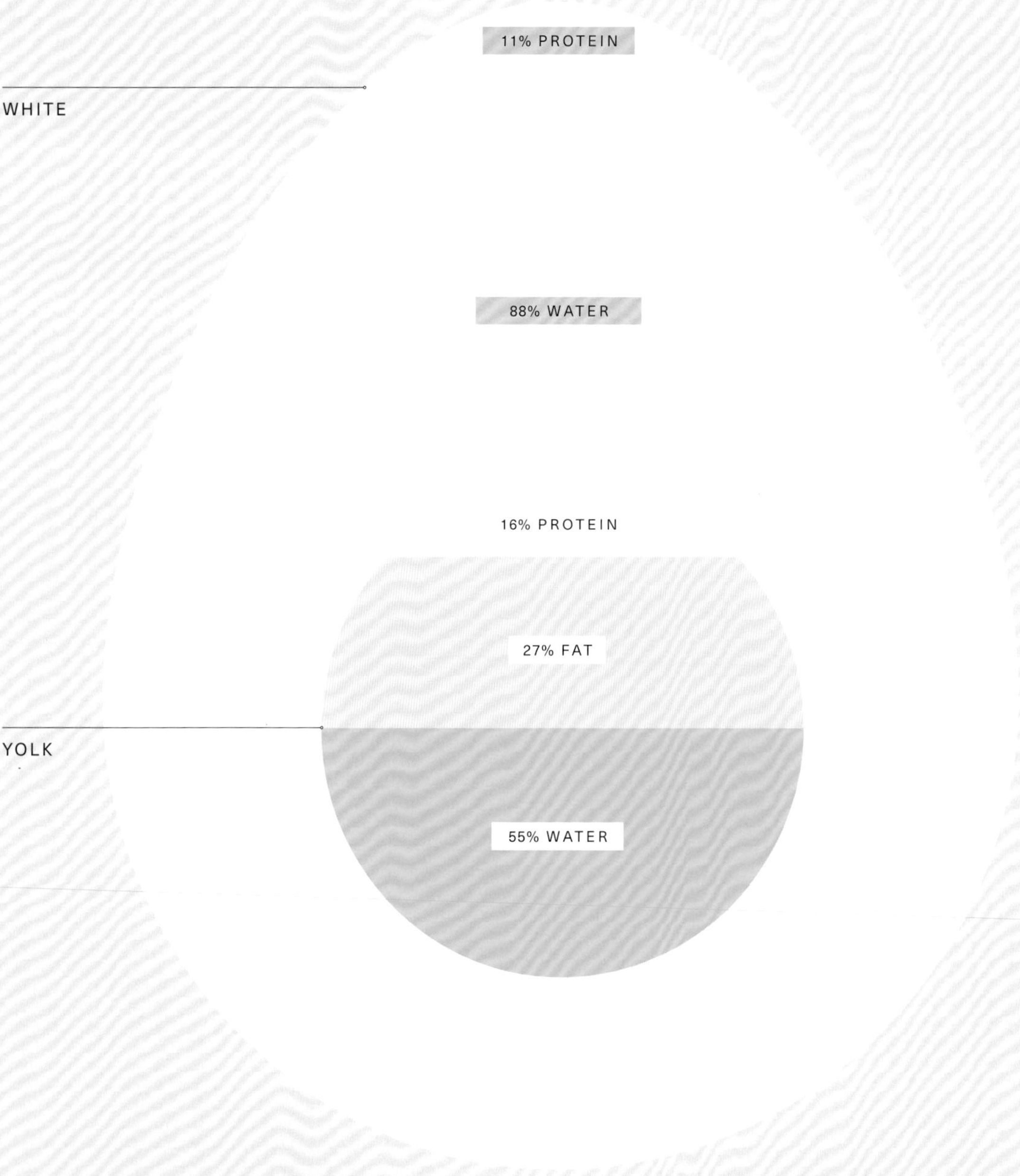

11% PROTEIN

WHITE

88% WATER

16% PROTEIN

27% FAT

YOLK

55% WATER

	WHITE	YOLK	WHOLE EGG
WATER	88%	55%	75%
PROTEIN	11%	16%	13%
FAT	0%	27%	10%

NOTE: APPROXIMATE MEASUREMENTS. THE REMAINING PERCENTAGES ARE MADE UP OF CARBOHYDRATE, MINERAL, AND ASH.

Protein

"Protein" is the catch-all name for molecules made up of lots of amino acids. Each protein involved in baking is different because it contains a unique combination of amino acids. That's why gluten, the protein in bread, behaves so differently to whey (milk proteins) or the proteins in eggs.

Yolks vs. whites in bread

One of the best ways to see how dramatically different egg yolks and egg whites behave is through a loaf of bread.

Q. What do you think will rise higher, a loaf made with egg whites only or egg yolks only?

A. The loaf made with yolks only will rise much higher! Even though whites are better at capturing air, this is only when they are being physically agitated.

Yolks contain the powerful emulsifier lecithin, which helps retain bubble structures by stabilizing the at-odds fat and water in the dough. See page 61 for more about emulsions in baking.

WHOLE EGGS

Whole eggs are approximately 75% water and have two distinct parts: the white and the yolk. Think of the egg as a perfectly balanced partnership, the Lennon/McCartney of ingredients. Both the white and the yolk have their own distinct (though linked) talents, but also have combined powers thanks to their unique molecular structures. Fortunately for us, we get to decide which talents to employ. The egg has been generously designed by nature—crack one open and you can easily separate the yolk and the white and benefit from their independent abilities.

EGG WHITES

Egg whites are roughly 90% water and 10% protein, the latter being responsible for that mucus-like texture of a raw egg white (sorry, were you expecting this baking book to conjure up delicious imagery the whole time?!). These proteins are responsible for all the magic tricks we associate with egg whites and are a mixture of globular and fibrous proteins. Globular proteins, which are dominant in egg whites, are round or spherical in shape and are, to be frank, highly sensitive. It really doesn't take much to affect these. Whether you're whisking them into a voluminous meringue or carefully watching for the wobble while your tart bakes, you're seeing globular proteins at work.

Fibrous proteins, on the other hand, excel in behind-the-scenes organizational tasks. Among the six proteins in egg whites, ovomucin is the fibrous protein responsible for holding the egg white together. If you've ever tried to poach older eggs before, you'll know how fruitless it can be, with wispy and straggling strands going everywhere. This is because ovomucin breaks down over time, resulting in a much thinner white that will struggle to hold its shape.

EGG YOLKS

Yolks are close to 50/50 water and solids, which are predominantly a mixture of fats and proteins. As we know, fat is synonymous with flavor, so yolks are particularly useful in baking, especially in custard, providing flavor, color, and thickening. Like egg whites, yolks can also increase impressively in volume when whipped.

Egg yolks also contain a powerful emulsifier called lecithin. Think of emulsifiers as the peacekeepers of the baking world, with the ability to make bonds between the famously-at-odds oil and water. This is because lecithin molecules have a hydrophilic (aka water-loving) head and a hydrophobic (aka water-hating) tail, which act as a physical bridge between the two. Although famous for its peacekeeping ability in savory preparations like mayonnaise, lecithin also improves the egg's ability to bind ingredients, like in cake batters. Without lecithin, there would be no crème brûlée!

Egg yolks also add that all-important visual appeal to our bakes—the crumb of a citrus cake is even more irresistible with the help of an ultra-orange yolk. The color is determined by pigment molecules called carotenoids that appear naturally in plants and are available to animals entirely via diet. Hens with a varied diet are likely to have more vividly colored yolks. That being said, a good egg is not inextricably linked to the color of the yolk. You can get a perfectly healthy and free-range egg that has a pale yellow hue.

Some farms have learned to game the system. Introducing brightly colored foods, like marigolds or carrots, into the diet of hens results in a superbly bright yolk. Chef Dan Barber has famously gone one step further by feeding his hens a high percentage of puréed red pepper, resulting in a vivid, red yolk.

COAGULATION

"Coagulation" is the fancy word for when egg proteins turn from a liquid structure into a firm or solid structure; this is an irreversible action, so once you start playing around with your eggs, make sure you're ready for action!

Although coagulation is commonly associated with heat, it can occur in a number of ways. This process happens all the time when we bake—it's the same process that thickens custard and provides structure in a cake. Without eggs, your custard will never set and your cake will probably fall down (or have a big hole in it).

In their natural state, egg proteins are just minding their own business, floating around and not interacting with one another. As heat or force is applied, the molecules all start to dance around quite quickly, and the proteins unfurl, aka denature, and connect directly with each other, forming strong bonds.

I like to imagine proteins as grumpy party guests, dotted around a big room with their arms tightly folded. Suddenly the dance floor lights up and an enthusiastic DJ announces a conga line; at first, only a few join in, reaching their arms out and connecting with the other guests, though plenty still keep to themselves. Eventually, the mood takes over and the whole room is up, joined by wiggling arms and legs. The whole room, once dispersed, is suddenly connected in one big mass. That's what happens when egg proteins coagulate.

As these bonds between the formerly distant proteins get stronger and form solid clumps, the water is effectively squeezed out. This results in rubbery, weepy, curdled eggs, the sort you've probably seen in a tragic continental buffet. This is known as over-coagulation. There's a high chance you'll have seen it in action, from a curdled custard to a cracked cheesecake. When it comes to coagulation, we want the proteins to form bonds but only to a point. It's important for the eggs to remain somewhat flexible so liquid can be held in the mesh network. Get this right and you'll reap the rewards in the form of satisfying custard wobbles.

YOLKS VS. WHITES

When it comes to coagulation, the whites and yolks are once again at odds with one another. Consider a hard-boiled egg: when set, egg whites are completely solid—the proteins form together and the water is absorbed. A yolk, however, remains fairly malleable thanks to the interfering fat and the emulsifiers. As a result, whites and yolks provide different structures to bakes. A cake made with all egg yolks will be both more tender and drier (remember, yolks are about 50% water and whites are about 90% water), while a cake made with all egg whites will be moister but lack flavor.

As well as this, the whites and yolks actually coagulate at different temperatures. Whites coagulate at 140–149°F, while yolks are set at 149–158°F. If you heat a whole whisked egg, the coagulation temperature is between 144–158°F.

When eggs are mixed with other ingredients, like milk or cream in custard or sugar in cakes, the temperature threshold for coagulation changes. This is due to the interference of casein (milk proteins, which can't coagulate alone) and sugar. These ingredients are like third wheels, crashing the egg proteins' bonding session. When you combine eggs with other ingredients like milk, cream, or sugar, the setting point rises.

Cooked yolks

Another intriguing way to use yolks is by adding hard-boiled (fully coagulated) egg yolks into your pastry. More popular in typical European baking, this technique results in the shortest pastry out there.

Adding the cooked yolks to the dough interrupts the gluten network, preventing long chains from being made and leading to an unmatched melt-in-the-mouth texture. Though you can achieve something similar by using ground nuts in the pastry, adding cooked egg yolks leads to something lighter and more delicious.

See it in action in my Parmesan and tomato linzer recipe on page 250.

Emulsion

An emulsion is a mixture of two liquids, like oil and water, that don't easily or normally combine. With the help of an emulsifier, like casein (in dairy products) or lecithin (in mayonnaise), emulsions can become permanent or semi-permanent.

Usually, an emulsion has one dominant ingredient, which acts as the host. For example, the water is suspended in fat in butter. Conversely, in milk, the fat is suspended in water. In fact, it also might be useful to note that the famous emulsifier egg yolk is an artful emulsion in and of itself.

The deal with egginess

There's not much I fear more in the kitchen than something tasting eggy. Ugh. Even writing the word makes me shiver. This unpleasant scent is usually a sign of over-coagulated egg whites.

When the whites begin to coagulate at 140°F, sulphur compounds begin to be released. This is totally normal and, at this stage, doesn't release any scent. That story begins to change after 176°F, which is why you need to be extra careful with the cooking of whites only. You can counteract the sulphuric scent by lowering the pH—adding lemon juice or vinegar, for example—but it's much better just to be mindful of the heat.

Why don't cakes, which achieve temperatures of 194°F+, appear curdled?

Well, the sugar radically slows down the coagulation and the excess water is simply evaporated or absorbed by the surrounding ingredients.

As the egg proteins coagulate, along with the stiffening starch or gluten structure, the crumb is formed.

Coagulation comparison

Type of egg	Approx. coagulation temp
White	140°F
Whole egg	144°F
Yolks	149°F
Whole egg + milk	162°F
Yolk + milk	162°F
Yolk + cream	180°F

EFFECT OF SALT

Salt is effective at denaturing egg proteins—a pinch whisked into eggs and left to work will break down the bonds, allowing the proteins to unfurl. The mixture will change color (become darker) and be very runny. This is particularly useful in preparations like egg wash—it goes onto risen pastries like a dream.

EFFECT OF ACID

Adding an acid to eggs lowers the coagulation temperature. This is because acid weakens the hydrogen bonds in proteins, causing them to unfurl and denature. If you make a lemon custard for a tart, even if there is cream present, you will look for a coagulation temperature of around 162°F.

TOUGHENERS VS. TENDERIZERS

When making a recipe, ingredients usually do one of two things: provide structure or softness. This is sometimes referred to as tougheners vs. tenderizers, though I feel the former has unwarranted negative connotations.

Ingredients like flour and coagulated eggs that provide structure usually harden as they bake, meaning your bakes will hold their shape. Sugar and butter, however, interfere with the structure and contribute to softness. (See Texture on page 92 for more information.)

CUSTARD: COAGULATION IN ACTION

A dessert is rarely unimproved by a generous pour of the good stuff, so where better to see coagulation action than the universally loved custard? A simple custard recipe is eggs + dairy + sugar. So, what is happening?

When we make a custard, we are basically creating a series of diversion tactics to keep egg proteins away from each other for as long as possible. Firstly, we are diluting the yolks in dairy, which physically distances the proteins—the fewer opportunities the proteins have to meet once unfurled, the fewer chances they have to bond.

Yolks, as we've learned, have an inherent curdling-defense system in the form of lecithin and fat, so using a majority will mean we are already headed for a smooth custard. Sugar further slows down the process by inhibiting the unfurling of the proteins, while the large globules of fat—in the form of milk or cream—physically block the proteins from bonding. Additionally, tempering helps protect the egg proteins from the effects of heat.

A stirred custard—like crème anglaise—will always be less firm than a baked custard since you are continuously agitating the mixture. By keeping it fluid, you're constantly reorganizing the structure. A baked custard, which is cooked undisturbed, will form a more solid network. Even if it has the same ingredient proportion as a stovetop custard, it will still be firmer. This is why the wobble is actually legitimate when it comes to judging baked custards! Egg proteins will continue bonding even after we remove a baked custard from the oven, so ensuring a level of fluidity (the wobble!) is essential.

By switching up the ratio of fat in the dairy you use, the amount of eggs (see the ratio of eggs to dairy table on page 44), and the ratios of whole eggs, yolks, and whites, you can adjust the final texture of the custard to suit you. Custards made with more fat, e.g., all cream vs. a mixture of cream and milk, will have a thicker texture.

THE DEAL WITH WATER BATH COOKING

When it comes to cooking custards gently, a water bath, also known as a bain-marie, can be incredibly helpful and anxiety-relieving when the threat of curdling seems imminent.

Take crème brûlée, for example, a rich custard made of yolks, sugar, and cream, which has a coagulation point of 180°F. Once mixed together, it is poured into ramekins and baked in a 275°F oven, a temperature somewhat hotter than the custard's max temperature.

Without a water bath, the outside of the crème brûlée would be scrambled eggs before the center was ever cooked. So, we use water's most famous limitation to our advantage: since water cannot rise above 212°F, we are able to cook our custards much closer to their natural coagulation point and achieve a set much more gently than if we were cooking with direct heat. To further encourage a smooth, set custard, it can be worthwhile heating your custard close to its coagulation point before putting it in the oven to avoid heat-shock or separation during the gentle baking process.

What happens when you heat eggs?

1. Egg proteins denature and bond to make a strong mesh network.

2. Adding fat and sugar slows down coagulation by delaying the formation.

3. If you keep heating, the mesh network of proteins tightens and the liquid is forced out—the mixture curdles.

Tempering

In cooking, tempering refers to any process that is temperature controlled. You can refer to tempering chocolate, the process when you carefully raise and lower the temperature of chocolate to help the crystals align neatly, or you can talk about the tempering of eggs when you make custard. To temper eggs, you add a little hot liquid to the eggs, stirring very well, to gently raise the temperature and spread out the egg proteins.

A subtle increase in temperature encourages a gentle unfurling of proteins and helps prevent the mixture from being shocked and curdling when it is introduced into the liquid. This is a similar tactic to a liaison batter (see page 113).

EGGS IN ACTION

SUGAR

WHITES

YOLKS

STARCH

Meringue

Pate À Bombe

Toasted Flour Chiffon Cake

Custard Tart

Mousse

Lemon Curd

Crème Anglaise

Cake

Tuile

Pastry Cream

Financier

Choux Pastry

Brioche

DAIRY RATIO

The relative set of your dessert or dish is also contingent on the proportion of eggs to dairy. Dairy does not have heat sensitive coagulable proteins and cannot be set on its own. The type and texture of dairy also matters. Paired with lemon juice, the coagulation temperature comes right down, as with a lemon tart. For dairy that is already thick, like cream cheese in a classic cheesecake, the amount of eggs tends to be lower to get the ideal texture. So how much egg do we need to set a custard? Let's compare a few classics:

Type of custard	Ratio (eggs to dairy)	Approx. % of egg to dairy	Approx. setting temp	Texture
Crème anglaise	1:8	12%	176–183°F	Pourable, smooth
Pastry cream	1:6	16%	n/a	Firm, smooth (also set with starch)
Crème brûlée/ custard tart	1:4	25%	171–174°F	Wobbly, smooth
Cheesecake	1:4	25%	149°F	Dense, rich, thick (cream cheese is a real outlier)
Quiche custard	1:1.7	58%	158–163°F	Dense, smooth
Lemon Tart	1:2.1	88%	158°F	Rich, dense, smooth

Although less popular, custard can be made with egg whites. The lack of flavor in egg whites is actually its greatest strength, resulting in a beautiful clean taste. For the best results, the fatless whites must be paired with high-fat dairy, to achieve a smooth and melting, rather than firm, texture.

INTRODUCING STARCH

If you mix your eggs with starch, like flour or cornstarch, to make a custard, it is known as a starch-bound custard—the most typical is pastry cream, aka crème pâtissière. Adding starch takes your custard from pourable and flowing to spoonable and thick. Though it's often made with yolks only for richness, color, and flavor, whole eggs can be used, resulting in a milder flavor. Because the set comes from the gelatinization of starch (see All About Flour on page 20), the thickness of the custard is almost identical, whether made with yolks or whole eggs. Though it varies between chefs, I use cornstarch only for pastry cream as it gives a reliable and firm set. The proportion of starch to milk, depending on the final use, is usually 7–10%. If you are baking your pastry cream, like in a pain au raisin, it's sensible to use a higher proportion of starch as it will help the pastry cream remain stable while baking.

As we know, starch gelatinization is a key moment in the lives of many of our pastries. When starch is mixed with water and heated, the granules absorb the water and swell, creating a mesh network and a thickened consistency. As the starch swells (gelatinizes), it interferes with the egg proteins' ability to make a network, further interrupting coagulation. Starch is so effective that our egg mixture can safely boil without any risk of curdling. The resulting custard will be very thick—in fact, with this type of custard the egg has a comparatively small role in the final texture and is mainly there for flavor and color.

Your custard has curdled?

It happens to us all. Before you freak out, take a moment and breathe! It can be saved (to a point) with the help of a blender. Blitz it like there's no tomorrow and, once smooth, pass it through a sieve and let the foam settle. If your mission has been successful, you will be rewarded with a smooth custard. This is for emergency uses only!

Ratio of yolks/whites

The ratio of whole eggs, yolks, and whites can be switched up when it comes to custard. Whole eggs, or whites only, will provide more structure due to the relative proportions of fat and protein, while egg yolks will produce a richer, softer custard.

Beware the burn

When introducing egg yolks, whole eggs, and sugar, be sure to whisk them together immediately. Sugar is highly hygroscopic and it immediately draws the water from the yolk, creating irreversible lumps of chewy gel. I learned this the hard way in my second pastry job on an 11 lb batch of eggs that, tragically, had to be tossed.

Help, my mousseline has split!

If your mousseline cream has split, then do not fear. This is likely due to the fat hardening. Simply warm the mixture over a water bath and whisk like mad. It will come back together as the solid fat melts.

Over-beaten egg whites

Saving over-beaten egg whites is as simple as adding more fresh, unbeaten egg whites.

The unbound proteins and additional water will disperse the bonded proteins, and you will be able to whip the egg whites back to smoothness. Bakers, beware—the saved egg whites are much more likely to over-whip again. For emergency uses only!

Out with the old, in with the new

Remember how the amount of ovomucin protein (determined by the egg's age) influences the egg white's thickness? Well, a thin, older egg white will whip up more quickly and with more volume but this is a false positive—the meringue will be much less stable. Fresh egg whites may take longer to whip up, but they will hold better.

STARCH IN CUSTARDS

Once you have mastered the starch-bound custard, a whole world of fillings is available to you. Adding 20–50% of whipped cream, butter, or Italian meringue can transform your stable custard base into something even richer (and more airy!).

Here are the classics:

- Pastry cream + a little butter = enriched pastry cream
- Pastry cream + lots of butter = crème mousseline
- Pastry cream + Italian meringue = crème chiboust
- Pastry cream + whipped cream = crème légère
- Pastry cream + butter + whipped cream = crème madame
- Pastry cream + whipped cream stabilized with gelatin = crème diplomat

WHEN EGGS MEET AIR

The meeting of eggs and air is true alchemy—show me one person who isn't dazzled by the dramatic transformation of transparent egg whites to floofy, swooping snow-white meringue. This process is known as aeration, and it connects many of our favorite desserts. From a stand-alone role in pavlovas and Eton mess, aerated eggs help sponge cakes to rise and give chocolate mousse its airy, melt-in-the-mouth texture.

As we know, each part of the egg behaves distinctively and it's no different when it comes to aeration. These are all known as foams:

- Whole eggs will increase 5x in volume
- Egg whites will increase 6–8x in volume
- Egg yolks will increase around 3x in volume

Despite effectively having more protein (17% vs. 11%) than whites, egg yolks are half as effective at aerating! When whisked, yolks and whole eggs produce a shiny and flexible foam. Thanks to that powerful emulsifier lecithin, which stabilizes the foam, it is virtually impossible to over-whisk. Whites, on the other hand, are at risk of over-beating.

AERATION IN DETAIL

The process of aeration is not dissimilar to the coagulation process. Instead of agitating the eggs with heat, we physically agitate them with a whisk. As the proteins unfurl and begin to bond, air bubbles are trapped, and the volume increases. As we learned with coagulation, there is a limit. If the proteins get too tightly bound, the water will be squeezed out, and the egg foam goes from smooth, shiny and elastic to dry and chunky. Yuck.

Like custard, which utilizes other ingredients to improve coagulation, egg foams are greatly increased and stabilized by sugar. Unsurprisingly, this also improves the flavor.

EGG WHITES + SUGAR + AIR = MERINGUE

Once an egg white has begun to foam, sugar can be slowly added. It's essential to add the sugar slowly because undissolved grains will wreak havoc later on, coming back to haunt you as weeping droplets. As well as this, sugar added too quickly will overwhelm your egg whites and prevent proper unfurling of the proteins, limiting the volume of the foam.

As the sugar dissolves, it forms a thick syrup with water in the egg whites. The syrup is trapped within the strongly bonded protein network and, as a result, coats the air bubbles.

This makes it hard for the bubbles to merge or the air to escape, so the foam stabilizes. The foam begins as a floppy mixture but will slowly make its way through soft, medium, and then stiff peaks—this is the point where the meringue will stay aloft on its own, pointing its peak proudly into the air.

Once sugar is involved, it becomes virtually impossible to over-whip an egg white. You do, however, need to be aware of the woes of a set meringue. Once a meringue has reached its stiff, glossy status, it's good practice to either use it immediately or to leave it mixing on a very low speed. As long as the mixture is moving, the protein network remains flexible. However, if left, the foam begins to set, turning from fluid and shiny to chunky. This is because egg proteins will continue to bond with each other even after the agitation has stopped, making your meringue hard to combine into another mixture.

THE RATIO OF MERINGUE

Ever wondered what the correct formulation for meringue is? Well, it depends . . . in every kitchen I've worked in, it has been different and ranges massively depending on the final product. From 1:1 to 1:15 to 1:2, as well as having a variety of stabilizers, it's a bit of a minefield. Let's have a look at the lay of the land and the final applications to see how they differ:

Ratios of sugar to egg white for meringues

Name	Ratio	Stabilizer/additions	
Chocolate mousse	1:0.2	None	More soft
Chiffon cake	1:1	None	
Floating islands	1:1	None	
Pavlova	1:1.75	Cornstarch, acid (see note)	
Roulade	1:1.75	Cornstarch, acid (see note)	
Dacquoise	1:2	Nuts	
Meringue nests	1:2	Acid (see note)	
Meringue kisses	1:2	Acid (see note)	More firm

The more sugar, the firmer your meringue will be. So, the rule of thumb is: the more stand-alone the meringue application, the more sugar you need. If your meringue is going to become the backbone of a chocolate mousse or be folded into a chiffon cake, you can use a soft meringue. However, a pavlova or piped meringue decoration will benefit from a higher ratio. Using cornstarch helps promote a marshmallowy, thick texture. As well as this, meringues with more sugar will hold before baking for longer periods of time.

What about acid?

The proteins in eggs make the strongest bonds in the presence of acid. Though it is not essential, adding a squeeze of lemon juice, a little vinegar, or a pinch of cream of tartar will create the most stable meringue.

Foam cakes

The woes of set eggs are evident when you make an egg foam cake, like a genoise sponge. Once the ingredients have been combined, you must use it immediately. If you allow the mix to stand, it will become chunky and deflate as you try to divide it and smooth it into the pans!

What about brown sugar?

Because brown sugar (see All About Sugar on page 27) contains more moisture than white sugar, a French meringue made with brown sugar that is later baked (as in a pavlova, meringue kisses, etc.) will be chewier and more susceptible to weeping.

As an insurance policy, it's sensible to use either a Swiss or Italian meringue technique, as this will make a more stable mixture and circumvent the potential weeping issue.

Baking myth: the clean bowl conundrum

So, if we can whip egg yolks to a voluminous mass, why do we always hear that our mixing bowl needs to be squeaky clean when making meringue?

Consider the example of custard, where we use fat to interfere with the proteins denaturing. In meringue, we want the proteins to denature as fully as possible, so you can see how fat or yolks might be a problem. In reality, a little speck of fat or a greasy bowl is unlikely to mar your lofty meringue goals, though it may slow down the process and your foam might not be quite as strong. However, more than a speck of yolk will cause you trouble. Why? That pesky emulsifier lecithin. In conclusion, don't stress too much if it's a tiny amount, but if there's clearly visible egg yolk, get rid of it or start again.

Baking myth: whisking eggs over a water bath

Contrary to popular opinion, when it comes to cake making, I think that whisking whole eggs over a water bath has a low pay-off to effort ratio. Yes, it allows the foam to form more quickly as heat encourages the egg proteins to denature, but this benefit is not hugely evident in the final baked cake, so I don't see this as an essential step if you're using a powerhouse stand mixer.

However, if you are whisking eggs with a hand mixer or, heaven forbid, fully by hand, you may find it useful to help speed the process up.

EGG YOLKS + SUGAR + AIR

Yolks also have transformative powers when air is introduced, unlocking dishes like ice cream parfaits and flourless chocolate cake. It's definitely something worth getting to know. So, what is happening when we pour hot syrup onto the yolks? Exactly the same as what happens to the whites. The curled-up proteins unfurl and air is trapped in the network, stabilized further by sugar.

Because of the interfering fat molecules, whipped yolks won't achieve stiff peaks and will always be denser than whipped whites, with a lower volume. To get the best results, egg yolks benefit from the assistance of heat to help in the denaturing process, in the form of a hot sugar syrup or a bain-marie.

WHOLE EGGS + SUGAR + AIR

Many of the best recipes begin with whisking whole eggs with sugar— from a genoise cake to baked chocolate tart—to a point known as ribbon stage, the voluminous state where the egg foam has enough body to hold its own weight. Because it is a mixture of whites and yolks, it will never be completely stiff. Instead, an ideal ribbon stage should be incredibly smooth, shiny, and pourable.

While it is possible to whip your whole eggs into a frenzy and achieve an extremely fluffed-up mass in a matter of minutes, the foam will have a chunky texture with lots of visible, irregular-sized bubbles. It will have, in theory, reached the ribbon stage, albeit an ugly and unstable one. We need to go further and seek the ribbon beyond the ribbon.

We can achieve this by mixing the eggs in three stages. First, the eggs are whipped at high speed to fully aerate. After this, the mixing speed is lowered in stages until there are no visible bubbles. This way, we don't lose out on air, but the large, unstable bubbles are split into smaller and smaller bubbles that are very stable. As a result, your whipped egg foam will be easier to work with and less at risk of collapsing no matter what it goes on to become.

Stage 1
Erratic big bubbles

Stage 2
Bubbles are refining

Stage 3
Bubbles are small, even, and strong

TEMPERATURE AND THE EFFECT ON AERATION

As we know, heating eggs helps the proteins fully unfurl or denature, which means they can trap more air and gain volume faster. That means room temperature or slightly warmed eggs will give you the best foam. Fridge-cold eggs are unfairly demonized in baking recipes. You will still get a good and completely usable foam, though it will be a little irregular from the egg proteins that never fully denatured.

To warm your eggs, you have a few options. You can either warm your eggs and sugar together over a bain-marie or you can use a hot sugar syrup.

TYPES OF EGG FOAMS

Name	Type of egg	Type of sugar	Key temps	Action	Examples	
RIBBON-STAGE	Whole egg	Granulated	n/a	Whisk whole eggs with sugar until fully volumized, decreasing speed from fast to slow. Fold in flour and the butter	• Genoise sponge • Baked chocolate tart	Least stable
FRENCH	Egg whites	Granulated	Room temperature	Add sugar slowly to egg whites	• Baked meringue nests • Pavlova • Roulade • Folded into mousses	
SABAYON	Egg yolks	Granulated	158°F	Whisk egg yolks with sugar over a bain-marie until 158°F and very thick	• Tiramisu • Decoration for desserts	
SWISS-FRENCH	Egg whites	Granulated	Heat sugar in oven until 212°F	Whisk the egg whites until foamy like a cappuccino, then add hot sugar all at once, then whip	• Baked meringue nests • Pavlova • Roulade • Meringue-pie topping	
SWISS	Egg whites	Granulated	Heat sugar and eggs until 158°F	Whisk sugar and eggs together, heat over a bain-marie until 158°F, then whip	• Buttercream • Base of crème chiboust • Meringue-pie topping	
PÂTÉ À BOMBE	Egg yolks	Syrup	Take sugar syrup to 244°F	Whisk egg yolks until fully volumized, then slowly pour in 244°F sugar syrup, then whip	• French buttercream • Mousse • Parfait	
ITALIAN	Egg whites	Syrup	Take sugar syrup to 244°F	Whisk the egg whites until foamy like a cappuccino, then slowly pour in 244°F sugar syrup, then whip	• Buttercream • Base of crème chiboust • Meringue-pie topping	Most stable

The importance of stability

Whether we are aerating eggs for a soufflé, cake, roulade, or mousse, we are always striving for stability, whether that is through technique or added ingredients.

An erratically formed, over-beaten or unstable foam will be harder to combine with your other ingredients. However, even a perfectly formed foam can be destroyed with clumsy technique—learning how to properly and effectively fold is an invaluable skill. See more in Technical Overview on page 113.

COOKED EGG FOAMS

Italian meringue and pâté à bombe are examples of cooked egg foams. Using a hot syrup (between 244–250°F) rather than cold granular sugar to create a foam has a few benefits. Firstly, you're pasteurizing/cooking your eggs.

Pouring in the syrup raises the temperature above a safe-to-eat temperature, rapidly denaturing those egg proteins and coagulating the mixture. This means the mixture can hold its structure for longer since it is fixed in place.

As well as this, sugar syrup absorbs extremely quickly and well into the mix, so you don't have any issues with graininess later on. As the mixture is cooked, it is the most stable, but it is also the most dense and will have the least volume. Swiss meringue, which is heated to a much lower temperature, benefits from the stability (but to a lesser extent) and retains more volume.

ONE LAST CRACK

Eggs provide us with the widest range of alchemy in the kitchen. The white and yolk's ability to work together and in direct opposition (think of the meringue failing if the yolk is involved!), make these an extraordinary duo.

Understanding these properties and unique transformative powers—from the lauded ribbon stage to smooth custards to stiff meringues—when you approach a recipe will give you an advantage. Whether it's extra flavor or lift you're looking for, tweaking the eggs—or the way you treat the eggs—will make a big difference.

4.

ALL ABOUT FAT

From toasty brown butter to salted butter cookies to a cake rich with olive oil, fats are the cornerstone of our baked goods. Integral to setting the scene in our bakes—fat IS flavor.

Beyond its own inherent flavors, like peppery, grassy olive oil or rich and creamy butter, fat also plays well with others. It is extremely good at carrying other flavors—aromatic compounds are often strongly soluble in fats, much more so than in water.

This is why citrus zest oils are so zingy and why essential oils—think peppermint—are such potent friends in the kitchen. But it doesn't stop there. When we eat fat, it coats our tongues, making the flavors last longer on our palate.

This chapter will explore the range of fats we rely on to build structure and tenderness in our bakes. We will also use this chapter to explore dairy, whose properties are often inherently linked to the fat content, and take a closer look at special, rule-defying systems like ganache, as well as a brief foray into the world of chocolate. Shall we?

WHAT IS FAT?

Fat is a bit of a contradiction. Despite being considered heavy or rich, isn't it intriguing that fat serves to lighten and lift our bakes? We have fat to thank for the airiness of croissants and puff pastry, as well as the tearable, candy-floss crumb of a freshly baked brioche. Fat is uniquely able to simultaneously offer us ethereally light and flaky textures combined with homely, rounded flavors. Ironically, we often turn to fat to cut through richness. A scoop of ice cream with a sticky toffee pudding or a dollop of whipped cream on top of a baked chocolate tart can go a long way to improve our eating experience.

Heat also impacts the flavor of fat. When fats are exposed to high temperatures, they break down into delicious volatile compounds. This combines the effects of Maillard reactions (see Color on page 84) and lipid degradation, a heat-based reaction unique to fat.

Beyond this pivotal role in flavor, fats work with (and against) the other ingredients to form a range of structures and textures that underpin what makes a good bake. From flakiness to crumbliness, crunchiness to moistness, fat is often pulling the strings. And let's never forget the flavor. As Julia Child said, "With enough butter, anything is good."

TYPES OF FAT

Fats and oils are members of the lipid family, a group of compounds that do not dissolve in water. The two are distinct by their state at room temperature: fats are solid and oils are liquid.

Somewhat confusingly, we can say that all oils are fats, but we wouldn't say that all fats are oils. This is because, when it comes to baking, fats have come to refer generically to both fat and oil. Fats are triglycerides—a glycerol molecule attached to three fatty acid chains. The glycerol molecule stays the same, but the fatty acids switch depending on the fat. The length and angles of these chains give different fats varying properties.

These fatty acids are commonly separated into two categories: saturated and unsaturated. Saturated fatty acids tend to have high melting points—think animal fats like butter and lard—while unsaturated fatty acids, which are usually derived from plants, tend to have lower melting points or be liquid at room temperature—think olive oil or vegetable oil. There are, of course, outliers like coconut oil and cocoa butter, which are plant-based but firm at room temperature.

Butter is the crown jewel of baking fats and probably the one we use the most because of its delicious flavor and versatility. But we shouldn't discount the value of other fats, like oils. One of the best things about baking is the freedom to deploy different fats to get the most out of their inherent properties.

Mouthfeel

One of the words that always strikes my non-foodie friends as strange is mouthfeel. *I get it. It conjures up a slightly odd, perhaps too-medical image.*

But once you get used to thinking about mouthfeel and understand why—crucially— it is distinct from texture, you'll realize how useful a description it can be.

To me, texture refers to how crunchy, soft, or chewy something is. In contrast, mouthfeel explains how we experience things as we eat them. Think of mouthfeel as body—how ice cream coats your tongue or how a perfect segment of mandarin bursts when you bite into it.

THE MELTING POINT

One thing to pay attention to when it comes to fat is the melting point. This is important because it sheds light on why fat improves the eating experience of things we bake: the sensation of fat melting as we eat is crucial for mouthfeel. It also informs the baking process, explaining why some things are baked at a high temperature while others benefit from a lower temperature. Butter, like cocoa butter in chocolate, melts at body temperature, which explains why so many of us find baked goods and chocolate so irresistible. They quite literally melt in the mouth!

Melting temperatures of fat

Solid fat	Melting temperature
Butter	86–95°F
Shortening	117–118°F
Lard	100–109°F
Coconut oil	75–81°F
Cocoa butter	93–100°F

We can also use the changing state of butter to our advantage. Consider a wet brioche dough, rich with softened butter, which hardens in the fridge so we can shape it into buns more easily, or croissants that are able to expand without cracking as they rise.

THE EFFECTS OF FAT

TENDERIZING

By adding fat, which coats the other ingredients, we are weakening the structure provided by gluten (see page 14), starch (see page 20), and eggs (see pages 40 and 92). If you radically reduce the fat in a cake, the texture will become chalky and dry. If you increase it, the crumb will become more and more delicate. Hydrating your pastry with fat-rich yolks gives you a more crumbly, tender pastry. However, adding too much fat will result in a final product that can't hold its shape. It could also become overwhelmingly greasy. Goldilocks, much?

Both solid fats, like butter, and liquid fats, like oils, can be used in our recipes. The more the fat flows, the more tender the final product will be because it is more effective at coating the other ingredients. As well as this, the state matters. Because butter is solid at room temperature, while oil flows, a cake made with oil will be more tender. The same goes for cookies and biscuits. In the case of choux pastry, using oil in place of butter produces a more open choux—it better lubricates the egg proteins, meaning the choux can expand splendidly.

Shortening

Fat is sometimes referred to as shortening, particularly in regard to biscuits, cookies, and doughs. Fat crystals interrupt the continuity and development of long gluten chains.

SPREAD

Anything that melts, like butter or sugar, contributes to the spread and final shape of our baked goods. For example, a cookie with a high butter content will spread a lot in the oven. At the same time, a cookie made with olive oil will still spread. Even though the fat doesn't melt (because it's already a liquid), it strongly interferes with the formation of structure provided by starch, gluten, and eggs (see Texture on page 92).

WHO COATS WHO?

When you make anything with fat and flour, a symbiotic relationship forms. Solid fats, like butter, will get coated in flour, resulting in distinct pockets. Alternatively, if you use a liquid fat like oil, it will coat the flour. This acts like a barrier, and since fat and water don't mix, water simply cannot access the flour and gluten formation is limited.

This is why in enriched bread recipes, like brioche, it is essential to build the gluten before adding the fat, otherwise the gluten will struggle to form. When brioche bakes, the butter (which is evenly dispersed during the mixing process) melts, lubricates the dough around it, and leaves pockets of air bubbles in the gluten structure. Once it cools, all the melted fat re-solidifies in the crumb, yielding a springy yet delicate bread.

Just add oil

Adding a portion of oil to your cakes will make them more tender and have a longer shelf life. Any of your favorite butter cake recipes can be easily adjusted by swapping 10–20% of the weight for a flavorless oil, like vegetable or sunflower oil. This way you can get the best of both worlds—flavor from the butter, and soft texture from the oil.

SIZE MATTERS

Seriously, with fat, size really does matter! Cookies, biscuits, enriched doughs, tart pastry, and cakes rely on the fat to be well distributed in small pieces, resulting in a fine, even crumb. When in large pieces, fat creates flakiness as it bakes, melting into the surrounding dough and leaving a hole in its place—this creates the effect of crisp layers and, in some cases, causes the pastry to rise.

The easiest way to see this in action is through the big three pastries:

Sweet pastry/shortcrust pastry
Butter is evenly distributed in small pieces, resulting in even crumbed and fine textured pastry that snaps/crumbles pleasantly as you eat it.

Examples: Tart pastry

Flaky pastry
Butter is left in uneven chunks and distributed unevenly throughout the dough, resulting in erratic, flaky layers. You can add a series of turns (see How Things Rise on page 70) into flaky pastry dough to make a rough puff, which results in more even, but still quite erratic, layers.

Examples: Pie dough, rough puff

Laminated pastry
Through a series of folds (see How Things Rise on page 70), butter is left in long, uninterrupted layers, resulting in distinct sheets of dough after baking.

Examples: Puff pastry, croissants

State of fat in recipes

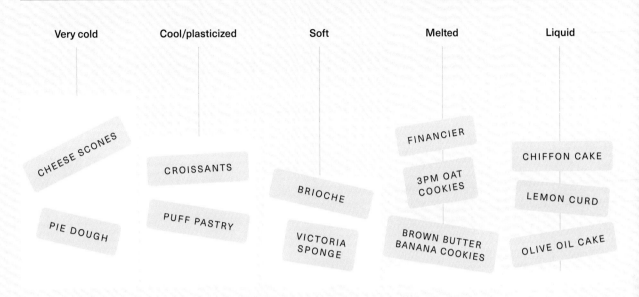

| Very cold | Cool/plasticized | Soft | Melted | Liquid |

CHEESE SCONES

CROISSANTS

FINANCIER

CHIFFON CAKE

BRIOCHE

3PM OAT COOKIES

LEMON CURD

PIE DOUGH

PUFF PASTRY

VICTORIA SPONGE

BROWN BUTTER BANANA COOKIES

OLIVE OIL CAKE

What about peanuts?

Peanuts are not true nuts—they are legumes! Still, you cannot substitute it in recipes 1:1 for butter; peanut butter is only about 50% fat and has so much bulk that it doesn't melt and behave like your average fat.

WHAT ABOUT NUTS?

Nuts are naturally high in fat. When blended, the oils are released, and the nuts happily transform into pastes. Though some of these nut pastes look a lot like butter, you can't substitute them like-for-like in recipes; even the highest-fat nut falls short of butter or oil. Nut pastes must be used in conjunction with traditional baking fats for the best effect.

Another way to make the most of this high-fat content is by replacing a portion of the flour with ground nuts. This will add more tenderness, moisture, and richness to bakes.

Type of nut	Total fat
Macadamias	72%
Pecans	69%
Brazil nuts	63%
Walnuts	62%
Hazelnuts	58%
Pine nuts	58%
Almonds	48%
Cashews	44%
Pistachios	41%

WATER VS. FAT

The proportion of water and fat is also essential in understanding why fats behave differently in baking. This relationship can often be the key to interchanging them successfully, while the fat content is a good way to judge which dairy to reach for. So, what is the effect? Well, baking with fats that contain water will result in a more delicate crumb with more lift—for example, butter, egg yolks, or cream—because the water will contribute to the rise via steam (see How Things Rise on page 68).

For a simple swap, make sure any change in liquid is compensated. Swapping butter for oil, in cakes, for example, may require you to either reduce the fat or increase the hydration elsewhere, since butter contains water, while oil does not. Also look out for any change in pH—acidity, or lack of it, can make a huge difference! The table below is an approximate breakdown of the water and fat content of our go-to baking fats and dairy products. The best way to know what you are working with is to always check the nutritional charts on the packaging.

Name	Approx. water %	Approx. fat %	Other	State at room temp	pH
Butter	15–16%	82–84%	Milk solids	Solid	
Clarified butter/ghee	0%	100%		Solid	
Brown butter (see Color on page 88)	0%	100%	Browned milk solids	Solid	
Whole milk	87%	3.5%	Milk solids	Liquid	6.5–6.9
Cream (UK)	40%	40–50%	Milk solids	Liquid	6.5–7
Cream (US)	60–65%	35–40%	Milk solids	Liquid	6.5–7
Half-and-half	75–80%	20%	Milk solids	Liquid	6.5–7
Sour cream	70%–75%	15–25%		Liquid	4.5–5.5
Ricotta	70–80%	10–15%	Milk solids	Semi-solid	5–6
Crème fraîche	40–48%	40%	Lactic acid	Semi-solid	4.5–5.5
Cream cheese	55%	35%	Lactic acid, stabilizers	Semi-solid	4.5–5
Yogurt	80%–85%	2–6%	Lactic acid	Semi-solid	4–4.5
Buttermilk	90%	0–3%	Lactic acid	Liquid	4–4.5
Mascarpone	40%	45%	Acid	Semi-solid	5–6
Condensed milk	30%	8%	Sugar	Liquid	6–6.5
Oil (olive, vegetable)	0%	100%		Liquid	
Coconut oil	0%	100%		Solid	
Cocoa butter	0%	100%		Solid	
Suet (beef/lamb fat)	0%	100%		Solid	
Lard (pork fat)	0%	100%		Solid	

But what about acidity?

When adding fat in the form of dairy into your bakes, one important factor to consider is the pH (the measure of acidity or alkalinity). Being aware of this tells us what we need to know about the flavor it will impart and its potential role in leavening when baking soda is involved (see How Things Rise on page 74).

In the case of custards, acids lower the temperature that eggs coagulate. In cakes, adding an acidic dairy will aid tenderness through the additional moisture and fat, while weakening the gluten.

The magic of plasticized butter

Plasticizing butter is the action of pounding fridge-cold butter to a malleable state. This allows the butter to become flexible without warming it up much. At this stage, it is perfect for laminating as it can be stretched without smearing (the enemy of great lamination) and melting.

ALL ABOUT BUTTER

Butter is by far the most popular fat in baking. And for good reason—it is delicious. It also has the perfect ratio of fat globules (80–84%) and milk solids (1–2%) with water (15–16%), which gives it a set of unique talents.

As well as expertly capturing air in the creaming process (thank you, fat!), it also contributes to the rise thanks to steam (thank you, water!). But to really get the best out of butter, we must pay attention to its temperature to get the desired results.

Temp °F	Butter state	Texture/consistency	Ideal uses	Notes
Below 32°F	Frozen	Solid, very hard	Grating, puff pastry dough	Hard to incorporate into mixtures, requires grating
32–48°F	Very cold	Solid, hard. It will splinter when pressed	Pie crusts, rough puff, scones	Creates flaky texture
50–55°F	Cold—plasticized	Solid, pliable, bendy	Laminating pastries, puff pastry, croissants	This is the perfect temperature for laminating as it is pliable but doesn't smear
59–68°F	Cool—room temperature	Softened, pliable, still cool	Creaming, incorporating into bun dough	Traps air to create light texture
72–77°F	Softened	Soft and spreadable, but still holds shape	Creaming, good for spreading	Will combine seamlessly into buttercreams and curds
86°F	Butter begins melting	Semi-solid/liquid	Some laminated goods	Easier for mixing, denser texture
95°F	Butter is fully melted	Liquid	Cakes, choux pastry, brownies	Denser texture, not aerated
158°F	Butter destabilizes/splits into component parts	Liquid/milk solids		
212°F	Clarified butter/ghee	Liquid, clear, no milk solids	Frying, cooking at high temperatures	High smoke point, no milk solids or water
248°F	Brown butter	Liquid, browned milk solids suspended in fat	Sauces, frosting, baked goods, caramel	Nutty, toasty flavor and aroma, deeper color, thicker texture

COMPOUND BUTTER

Compound butter is when butter is mixed with another aromatic ingredient. Whether it's herbs, spices, or chocolate, compound butter is one of those secret pastry chef weapons. If you haven't considered using them in your bakes, welcome to the first day of your limitless-possibility-compound-butter-life!

They are particularly brilliant in laminated pastries (see How Things Rise on page 69), with their multiple alternating layers of butter and dough. This is because when the pastry goes into the oven, the flavored butter melts, enriching the dough with flavor. Laminating with compound butter (see page 332) offers the perfect opportunity to flavor and season the pastry from within.

Think of it as a flavor agent on the inside. From a spicy nduja to wild garlic butter (which turned my pastries green) to a citrus butter, the results are always next-level-flavor sort of stuff. See it in action in the recipes (see page 332). However, the road to flavor is not always an easy one.

Compound butter can be more difficult to work with. Since we are literally disrupting the structure, it won't behave as normal. As you add aromatic components to butter, you are physically disturbing the fat/solids/moisture structure.

The chunkier your compound, the more difficult it becomes to work with. When rolling out compound butter, these chunks can disrupt the structure and as the butter stretches out, it will be interrupted. This is where the compound butter can become a trade-off situation: the compound butter is more likely to split/splinter, resulting in less fine or neat lamination due to the physical interruption of the layers from solids. However, getting a gloriously flaky, extremely flavorful, and visually appealing product is still possible.

To mitigate this, you should try to keep the basic structure of the butter relatively similar. This means adding a lot of moisture (like a fruit purée) is not recommended.

You may need to adapt the amount of compound to laminate with, as maintaining the overall fat level is essential for success. For example, if you are using 10% fresh herbs to butter, your recipe will have 10% less fat. So, I like to rebalance my recipes and use more compound butter than plain butter when laminating.

Though you could just mix your aromatics into the dough (it is an easier process), I find the flavor imparted by compound butter via melting in the oven is much more intense, perfumed, and worth the extra work.

A good starting point is up to about 20% flavoring to butter weight. This will vary depending on the strength of the flavoring. Spices, for example, are potent but lightweight. Test and adapt as you go.

Compound butter in action (see page 332 for these recipes)

Roasted garlic butter

Speculoos spiced butter

Chili crisp soy butter

Cocoa butter

AERATION

Some fats, like butter and high-fat cream, are particularly talented at aiding aeration: the process of incorporating air bubbles into a mixture. The two most well-known processes are creaming (as in butter and sugar) and whipping (as in cream).

CREAMING

Creaming is probably the first Hall of Fame–worthy action in baking. From a young age, I was taught that a batch of cupcakes must be earned with hard work. Using a precariously long wooden spoon for my short arms, I would smash together margarine and sugar like my life depended on it.

Of course, I wasn't very effective. My nanny Carole would graciously finish the job, transforming the lumpy fat into a light, airy mixture, and the promise of cake was born. At the time, the creaming process seemed like some kind of punishment, a hoax designed to test my patience. Over time, I've come to understand the point of this delayed gratification.

When we combine solid fats and sugar, we introduce air into the mixture. When these bubbles are incorporated, the fat crystals act as bodyguards, protecting the air bubbles, which produce the crumb structure we know and love. These air pockets also provide a place for other leavening gases, like CO_2, to congregate (see How Things Rise on page 74).

Depending on the recipe, you will often be asked to cream your butter and sugar to different stages. A dense cookie may only require the butter and sugar to be briefly combined before introducing the other ingredients, while a fine-crumbed Victoria sponge will benefit from a 2–3 minute mix to better aerate the fat. There is such a thing as over-creaming your fat, though. Unless I am using it for the base of frosting, I never cream my butter and sugar to the point of being bright white. The fat is so aerated at this stage that it is extremely unstable and, if used in a cake, will likely fall when baked. There are better ways to add more stable vehicles for air bubbles: eggs (see All About Eggs on page 45) and chemical rising agents (see How Things Rise on page 74).

Liquid fats, including melted butter, are extremely poor at aerating, but they make up for this lack of aeration ability in how moist and tender they make cakes. Swapping in liquid fats for solid fats will result in a denser, firmer texture. If this isn't the goal, you can compensate for this lack of aeration via an increase in rising agents, using aerated eggs or the addition of effective steam-producing liquids, like milk, sour cream, or cream.

WHIPPING

Whipping is the process of introducing air into cream until it becomes irresistibly cloud-like.

Cream—a mixture of water, fat, and milk solids—is a rich liquid derived from milk. It comes in varying fat contents:

- Half-and-half (18–20%)
- Heavy cream (US) (35–40%)
- Cream (UK) (40–50%)

Half-and-half doesn't have enough fat to whip—you need at least 30% to achieve the airy mass we know and love.

Before it is agitated, fat and water manage to live within cream in relative harmony, despite being mortal enemies (see Emulsions in Baking, opposite page, for more on this famous rivalry). When you start whisking cream, the large fat globules begin breaking down into smaller droplets. To avoid coming into contact with water, the droplets arrange themselves around the newly introduced air bubbles to keep a safe distance from the water. As a result, the air bubbles are stabilized and everyone is happy— especially us, since the air increases the volume of the cream and turns it from a liquid into a pile of fluff, known as foam.

Unlike oil in mayonnaise, which relies on the help of an emulsifier (egg yolks) for success, cream can whip on its own. This is because milk fat is its own stabilizer. The higher the fat content, the more stable the whipped cream is. If you keep whipping cream, it becomes butter and most of the liquid is squeezed out as buttermilk. This is a unique transformation from an oil-in-water emulsion to a water-in-oil emulsion. If you slightly over-whip your cream, you may be able to save it by adding a little whole milk and folding it in gently, but if it's past the point of no return, just give up and make butter!

From cream to butter

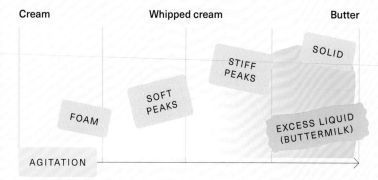

Cream   **Whipped cream**   **Butter**

SOLID

STIFF PEAKS

SOFT PEAKS

FOAM

EXCESS LIQUID (BUTTERMILK)

AGITATION

Oil-in-water emulsion   **Water-in-oil emulsion**

HANDLING HIGH FAT CONTENT

In the UK, we are very lucky to have dairy that is so high in fat that it is able to hold its shape very well when whipped. To compare it, cream in the US is around 36% fat and above, while cream in the UK is around 48% fat. The higher the fat content, the more stable your foam is going to be. On the other hand, it is more susceptible to splitting and is much harder to pipe or decorate with.

Notes

Using a large, wide bowl will help you whip things quicker as it allows you to incorporate more air as you whisk.

Cream will not whip if it is warm. If fat is warm, it is not an effective stabilizer. Make sure it is fridge-cold!

The deal with piping cream

Let me set the scene for you: you've whipped your cream— it's perfect. You put it into a piping bag, ready yourself to decorate your cake, and then 3...2...1... you squeeze, ready for the perfectly smooth cream to appear on your cake. But instead, you get chunky blobs. WHAT?! When you put your cream into a piping bag, you're trapping it in a small space with lots of air. And when you squeeze the piping bag, the cream continues to whip and keeps thickening and aerating every time you touch it.

So, what to do? Firstly, slightly under-whipping the cream is important—it should just hold its shape. Always err on the side of under-whipped—you have to be brave! You can always re-whip, but you can't un-whip!

A CAST OF CHARACTERS

There's a whole cast of characters in colloids: jam, jelly, whipped cream, meringue, cake batter, ganache, and even brioche all come under this umbrella.

There are a few types of colloids that have more commonly known names:

Foams
Meringues and whipped cream are good examples of a foam, which is when gas (air bubbles) are dispersed in a liquid (egg whites/cream).

Gels
Jelly and mousses are examples of a gel, which is when a liquid (fruit purée/dairy) is suspended through a solid (gelatin matrix). Jams are also examples of gels where fruit liquid is trapped in a pectin network.

Emulsions
These are special types of colloids that specifically mix ingredients that do not normally mix, like oil and water. Examples include butter, milk, cream, brioche, and ganache.

Hybrids
A cake mixture is both an emulsion—fat (butter and egg yolks) in water (egg whites)—and a foam, with air bubbles suspended throughout.

Definition

A colloid is a less familiar word in the baking world, but it refers to when one substance is evenly dispersed or suspended in another.

EMULSIONS IN BAKING

OIL VS. WATER

We all know that oil and water don't mix. This is because they have very different molecular structures. Water is like a magnet with a positive and negative side. This is how it makes connections with other molecules. But because fat doesn't carry a positive OR negative charge, it is unable to mix with water. It's not that they are two puzzle pieces that don't quite fit; it's more like water is a puzzle piece and fat is a basketball. They are just completely different entities.

Emulsions are a type of colloid and are mixtures that defy the rules. They are pure alchemy. Butter, perhaps the most famous fat, is an example of a naturally occurring emulsion, a miracle that we probably take for granted every time we spread it on our toast.

UNDERSTANDING EMULSIONS

We can think about emulsions in a few different ways, firstly by type. There are two main categories: oil in water or water in oil. This refers to how the emulsion is organized: either fat suspended in liquid or liquid suspended in fat. In very stable emulsions, the droplets of fat or liquid are very small and evenly distributed. This is usually done with the help of a vigorous whisk or blend, where the immiscible liquids are broken into smaller and smaller droplets and evenly dispersed among one another.

Another way to think about emulsions is their lasting power. Most emulsions we use in cooking and baking—milk, butter, cream, mayonnaise, and ganache—are considered permanent. These systems are so strong and commonplace that we take their alchemy for granted.

One of the ways to stabilize an emulsion is through an emulsifier like egg yolks, as is the case in mayonnaise. Emulsifiers are a bit like disguises. Imagine a fat molecule slipping on an emulsifier invisibility cloak, now able to go unnoticed in a sea of water but still retaining its own unique properties. To learn more about this emulsifying ability of eggs, see All About Eggs on page 39.

It's only when things go wrong—over-whipped cream, an oily brioche, or a split ganache—that we see behind the curtain. Splitting is usually a result of very small droplets beginning to gather together, falling out of rank and causing the emulsion to destabilize and break. This can be caused by a change in temperature or too little (or too much) agitation. Fussy things! To learn about splitting, head to page 64.

What about cocoa powder?

Cocoa powder is a common baking ingredient with an alchemy you may have underestimated. It contains a lot of tiny, evenly dispersed fat particles, which gives it hydrophobic qualities—it repels water. It also has a tiny particle size—this, combined with that hydrophobic nature, makes it very clumpy when it meets liquids. Each tiny particle of cocoa powder individually repels the water, making it hard to combine without a lot of effort. But if you keep working at it, it will turn into a gloriously thick, creamy paste, not dissimilar to the sudden change of yolks and oil to mayo. But it's not an emulsion—that's between two liquids—it's a suspension.

THE ROMEO AND JULIET OF BAKING

Perhaps you've heard that water and chocolate don't mix? That's a lie. Well, a white lie. The first time I melted chocolate over a bain-marie, I remember the fear I felt at a drop of water or steam condensing into my mixture— even the smallest drip could destroy it! And that, actually, is true. A tiny drop of *any* liquid is going to seriously mess with your chocolate and cause it to split apart and seize. However, if you keep adding water, you'll be rewarded with a luscious, smooth mixture.

To understand why chocolate—initially—freaks out when water gets involved, we have to look at what is happening with chocolate in its natural state. Chocolate is a harmonious blend of cocoa mass, sugar, and cocoa butter. It may also have milk solids (for milk chocolate) and additional stabilizers. But let's focus on the holy trinity of flavor (cocoa mass), seasoning (sugar), and fat (cocoa butter). The sugar and cocoa mass are bound by the cocoa butter, holding everything in place in a stable state. No water is present, so chocolate is considered dry even though it melts and acts like a liquid.

Here's where it gets interesting. As we know, when it comes to baking, each ingredient's relationship with water is a really important factor. And the harmonious members of the chocolate society all feel differently about it.

Sugar, as we know, is hygroscopic, aka LOVES water. Cocoa butter is a fat, which means it repels/hates water. Cocoa mass is pretty water-loving, too. These differing relationships with water are where it all goes wrong. A small amount of water gets involved with melted chocolate, and the previously harmonious ingredients ditch each other to form their own relationships with water. Water and sugar get together and form syrupy clumps. Same for the cocoa mass, while the water splits up the mixture even further as it tries to get away from the cocoa butter.

The result? A grainy, miserable split mixture. And there's no going back. But you can go forward. If you keep adding water, the grainy mixture becomes fluid and silky because a new system has formed. Enter ganache!

Ganache ratios

Chocolate:Cream

Dark

Spoonable	2:1
Spreadable	1:1
Whippable	1:2

Milk

Spoonable	2.5:1
Spreadable	1.5:1
Whippable	1:1.5

White*

Spoonable	3:1
Spreadable	2:1
Whippable	1:1

Since white chocolate has little to no cocoa solids, it can also be whipped at a 2:1 ratio into a very thick topping/filling

GANACHE

You can think of ganache as an emulsion or, as food science legend Harold McGee suggests, a combination of an emulsion and a suspension, aka stuff, happily floating about in fluid. In the case of ganache, the stuff is the dry matter like cocoa mass (which swells, hydrated by water) and cocoa fat, which is floating in a syrup made from the water and sugar from the chocolate.

Therefore, adding more water means that the chocolate stops freaking out. Water in small amounts disrupts the fat-dominated chocolate system, but water in large amounts becomes a dominating player and provides a new framework or society for our ingredients to fit into. Instead of the water trying to fit into the fat, the fat relinquishes control and becomes happily suspended in the water.

As a result, you can create interesting and new textures by simply mixing various quantities of chocolate and liquid. You can also add additional sugar, which contributes to flavor and texture. The more fat you add, usually via the liquid (using cream vs. fruit juice, water, wine, plant-based milk, etc.), the thicker the ganache will be. You can add solid fats like butter or coconut oil to increase the fat content. Not all chocolate is created equal though. Depending on the manufacturer, chocolate will have different amounts of sugar, cocoa butter, and milk solids added. This means that you should swap with caution.

To make ganache, chop your chocolate into small pieces (so they can melt easily) and place in a heatproof bowl. Heat your chosen liquid until simmering, then pour over. Let stand for 1–2 minutes to allow the chocolate to melt, then gently whisk until smooth. You can also use an immersion blender to achieve an incredibly strong, smooth, and shiny emulsion. If it splits, don't panic! Turn to page 64 to find out what to do.

WHAT IS TEMPERING?

There are a vast number of brilliant books devoted to the extraordinarily precise world of chocolate work, but I'll try to run you through the headlines in just a few paragraphs. Tempering is the process of melting and cooling chocolate to ensure it sets properly; this means it will be glossy and will snap when broken. If chocolate hasn't been tempered, it will bloom when set, which is when it has those white dots all over it. When chocolate melts, the cocoa butter crystals go through a series of stages: I, II, III, IV, V, and VI. When we temper, we are encouraging cocoa butter to crystallize in the most stable V formation. V formation means the cocoa butter crystals fit together tightly and neatly, resulting in the shiny tempered chocolate we know and love.

We can promote V formation via proper temperature (the chocolate needs to be FULLY melted so it can be reformed, which means all the unstable crystals melt and disappear) and agitation, which means moving it around so all the crystals get in line.

As well as this, these V crystals only form at a certain temperature, which is why you need to temper your chocolate as you go and why we need to cool the chocolate down carefully. We can do this in a few ways, but the simplest is the seeding method. This means adding cold-tempered chocolate to your warm, melted chocolate. This cools it and encourages the melted crystals to get in line!

Once you've reached the right temperature, the chocolate is then rewarmed a bit so that any pesky unstable crystals have the last chance to get in line and it is easier to use. Also, rewarming it slightly means it is easier to work with because properly tempered chocolate will set quickly.

The good thing about chocolate tempering is you can do it over and over again, and the more you do it, the better your tempering skills will be. And don't worry too much, there are worse things in the world than dull chocolate!

THE DEAL WITH SPLITTING

We've all been there. You're right in the midst of mixing up a cake batter, gently whisking a ganache, stirring a custard, or finishing up a buttercream and, suddenly, things go wrong. A previously promising mixture suddenly breaks before your eyes and transforms from glossy to . . . lumpy. Lucky for us, splitting is almost always one of two things:

1) Fixable
2) Unimportant

BUTTERCREAM

Meringue buttercreams are loved equally for their smoothness and stability. To make it, whip up a batch of a cooked meringue—either Italian or Swiss—then add softened butter. The mixture is prone to splitting when you first add the fat. This is resolved simply by trusting the process and continuing to add the remaining butter and whisking. It will come back together. If it still looks split, heat the bowl with a blowtorch or whisk briefly over a bain-marie until it comes together. This advice also works for butter-based custard crème mousseline.

CAKE BATTER

In the case of cake batter, splitting is a result of the breakdown of the emulsion of fat (butter) and water (eggs). This is usually because the eggs have been added too quickly. Trying to force a lot of liquid into fat all at once usually ends in splitting—just think of mayonnaise, which asks you to drip the oil very slowly into the egg yolk to prevent it from breaking. As well as this, the splitting could be a result of rapid temperature change. Cold eggs added to the creamed butter/sugar mixture can result in little bits of butter hardening, which results in a split mixture. In warmer climates, batters tend to curdle less.

Not scraping your bowl properly can also be a culprit. If there is a lot of butter stuck to the bottom of your bowl, you are proportionally reducing the amount of fat that is there to receive your eggs. So, it's a good idea to scrape often to ensure everything is incorporated.

To fix curdled cake batter, you can try warming the bowl gently while stirring, or adding a few spoonfuls of the dry ingredients. But I think curdled cake batter's bark is worse than its bite. In my career, I've made a lot of curdled cake batters and the difference—in my opinion— is not noticeable. So, although it's a good idea to keep all your ingredients at the same temperature, scrape down the bowl, and add the eggs slowly, don't freak out!

GANACHE

No matter what formulation you're working with, there's a chance you have experienced ganache splitting—it's miserable, greasy, and sad. Although it will depend on the recipe you are working with, here's why it happened and how to get past it:

Not enough liquid
There simply isn't enough liquid to suspend the fat— the cocoa mass swells and literally forces the fat out! Add warm water or cream (though if there's too much fat already, the cream will add to the problem) and whisk until smooth.

Chocolate is too hot
Chocolate that is too hot will seize and split up, preventing a smooth emulsion even if your formulation is good. Allow the mixture to cool down before mixing gently.

Chocolate is too cold
Dark chocolate will also not play ball if it's below a certain temperature. Heat the ganache with a blowtorch or over a bain-marie and whisk.

EGGS

Unfortunately, when it comes to eggs, splitting is usually irreversible. This is because the curdling is due to the egg proteins fully coagulating, aka hardening. A quick whiz in a blender might hide the sins if you catch it early, but you can't uncook an egg! See All About Eggs on page 42.

WHIPPING CREAM

If your cream splits when you are whipping it, you can try folding in a little milk to revive it, but know the whipped cream will never be quite as smooth. Otherwise, cut your losses and carry on whipping to make butter!

A DOLLOP TO FINISH

The way that fat interacts with the other ingredients in a recipe is pivotal to the final taste, texture, and appearance. Your choice of fat is important, but it's also down to the way that you use it. From towering sheets of puff pastry that shatter mercilessly as you bite into them to dunkable shortbread cookies, you have the power to deploy fat to get the results you want.

Given that fat = flavor, it's one of the best places to jump off from when tweaking recipes, especially because fats tend to have enough in common to keep a recipe on track while showing you new dimensions of texture and flavor.

From browning the butter to changing up your fat-incorporating technique to swapping butter for an oil, fat is a great place to start exploring, whether it's a brioche or a biscuit, a cake or a cinnamon bun.

5.

HOW THINGS RISE

One of the best examples of baking being magical—but not strictly magic—is how our bakes transform in the oven. Although a crackly brown crust or the bubbling edges of roasted fruit are beautiful sights to see, there's nothing quite like the upward expansion of a croissant, the welcome smile of a muffin top bursting open or the sight of your choux buns puffing up. But what is behind this transformation?

UP, UP, UP!

In baking, three things make our bakes rise:

1.   Steam
2.   Air
3.   Carbon dioxide

These are also known as leaveners, or leavening. The way these three forces are introduced is where it gets interesting. Let's compare three famous bakes: the Victoria sponge, the genoise, and brioche.

Although this may seem like a strange activity, it will help us delve into the why of baking, which is the most exciting place to be. All three of these recipes are a combination of flour, fat, sugar, and eggs. Beyond the ratio of ingredients, the major difference between them is how each one is leavened, i.e., how air is incorporated into the dough.

With the Victoria sponge, the dough is aerated via the creaming of butter and sugar, which creates a network to trap air bubbles, bolstered by chemical-rising agents, like baking powder. In the case of genoise, the air is trapped in the eggs during a long mixing process, producing a foam that sets when baked. With brioche, the air is incorporated via yeast fermentation and trapped in a strong gluten network. Each of these recipes rises when baked, but all for different reasons.

In this chapter, we'll explore all the ways that bubbles find their way into (and out of) our bakes, the joy—and complications—of working with dough that is alive, the impressive effect of layers, and how temperature impacts upward expansion. Let's go deeper.

STEAM

Water is often an overlooked ingredient in baking. As well as adding moisture, it allows for important functions like the development of gluten and starch gelatinization. But its final deed is the all-important transformation from liquid to gas in the form of steam.

When water turns to steam, it expands some 1,600 times in volume. Consider a single quart/liter of water turning into 1,600 quarts/liters of steam—that's equivalent to almost nine completely full bathtubs!

It's no wonder that steam has been used throughout history to power trains, factories, and mills. And as bakers, we get to harness this to rise eclairs, lift pain au chocolat, and elevate cake batters.

Anything that contains water will implicitly help leaven our bakes—all you need to trigger this is heat. That means butter, eggs, milk, dairy, and anything containing water will contribute to the rise. Of course, some of this water may be inseparably bound to starch or gluten, but any water that is not otherwise engaged will transform. This is why bakes weigh less after baking. It's also why oven temperatures are important. Recipes may call for an initial blast of heat at the beginning of the bake. If the temperature of the oven or cooking appliance is not hot enough, the water doesn't turn to steam quickly enough, and we will not benefit from a rapid rise.

THE DEAL WITH LAMINATION

One of the best journeys of pure metamorphosis you can go on in baking is that of laminated pastries. In your hands, two blocks of beige-looking stuff become oohs and ahhs worthy. Few things are more deserving than puff pastry and croissants—both perfect examples of this feat of butter-dough engineering. And these are both achieved by lamination.

Lamination is the process of creating alternating layers of butter and dough. The effect of this is a multi-layered, ultra-flaky pastry that rises—and shatters—impressively. Pastries risen via lamination are excellent examples of steam power in action. In some cases, they are further aided on their upward ascent by yeast (see page 76).

Lamination is achieved by making two separate blocks—one of a simple dough (known as the détrempe) and another of butter. You then enclose the butter into the dough. After this, bit by bit, roll by roll and fold by fold, the butter and dough are spread into fine, distinct layers. So, what is the effect of lamination? When the pastry goes into the oven, the butter melts. This has two purposes:

The melted butter enriches the dough. The steam created by water evaporation forces the layers apart. The dough physically lifts and puffs up, and you're left with an ultra-flaky, crisp, multi-layered pastry.

THE LOCK-IN

So, how do we get our butter into the dough in the first place? Welcome to the lock-in! There are several ways to do this, but here are two of the most popular:

- The French lock-in requires the butter block to be half the length of your dough. Then the edges of the dough are brought together and sealed to create three layers.
- The English lock-in requires the butter block to be two-thirds the length of your dough. Then the butter-less dough is brought halfway across the butter. The other half is then folded on top, creating five layers.

This small change actually creates a significant difference to the layers. Let's have a look at the math.

The French lock-in

1.

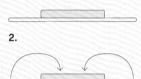

2.

3.

The English lock-in

1.

2.

3.

4.

5.

French lock-in		English lock-in	
3 x double		**3 x double**	
Type	No. of layers	Type	No. of layers
Lock-in	3	Lock-in	5
Double	9	Double	17
Double	33	Double	65
Double	129	Double	257
Total	**129**	**Total**	**257**

So, picking an English lock-in is basically a shortcut to extra layers! So, if ultimate flakiness is what you're after, try an English lock-in next time and get double the layers for the same amount of work.

EXPLAINING TURNS

Making laminated pastries requires you to make a series of turns
and folds in your dough. There are a few ways to do this:

Single turn (a letter fold)

This is the simplest way to fold the dough. You roll
the dough out, then fold it into three, like a letter.

You don't have to roll the dough out as long as you
would for a double turn, meaning you can generally
perform them quicker, especially if you are a beginner.
Issues with lamination often come from accidental
mistreatment of the dough.

Pressing too hard results in the butter breaking up
or smearing, leading to uneven laminations, so single
turns are often recommended. However, you need to
do a lot of single turns to get the number of layers up,
which means you end up working with the dough
more than you would if you were using double turns.

Double turn (a book fold)

This requires you to roll the dough out a bit longer
than for a single turn. You then fold the edges into
the middle, then over on itself again (like a book).

This is a great way to build layers, although it can
result in clunky layers. Also, rolling the dough out longer
can result in the butter getting too warm if you're not
careful, which can negatively impact your layers.

Every time you make a turn in the dough, you must
rotate it 90 degrees to ensure you are rolling it out in
the opposite direction to which it has already been
stretched (see gluten in All About Flour on page 14).

1.   2.

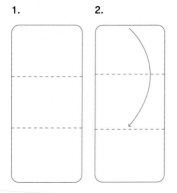

3.   4.

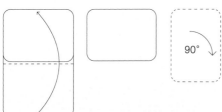

1.   2.   3.

4.   5.

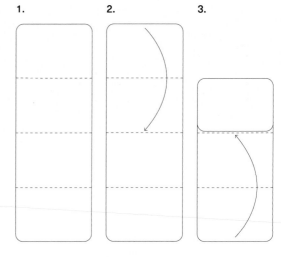

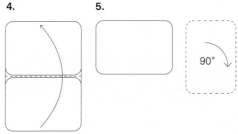

Afterward

After performing a turn, rest according to the recipe. Before you start another turn, don't forget to rotate it
90 degrees to ensure you are rolling it out in the opposite direction to which it has already been stretched
(see All About Flour on page 15).

Fast laminated pastries

While classic laminated pastries are time-consuming and require accuracy and patience for the best results, there are ways to enjoy this technique in a shorter time frame.

Rough puff, aka flaky pastry or blitz pastry, is a quick, semi-slapdash version of puff pastry. Instead of laboring over very symmetrical layers of butter and dough, rough puff approximates this by ensuring chunks of butter are suspended throughout via a series of quick folds.

When baked, these irregular layered chunks leave little buttery pockets behind, which flake apart. Although you don't get as much of a lift, the layers are fantastic, making a brilliant base for tarts, tart tatins, and even mille-feuille.

COUNTING THE LAYERS

When it comes to laminated pastries, how many layers *actually* are there? Is mille-feuille aka "a thousand leaves" accurate or just a red herring? The type of turn (single vs. double), the number of repetitions, and the various combinations can result in a radically different number of layers.

Comparing turns

A		B		C	
Single/double		**Six single**		**3 x double**	
Type	*No. of layers*	*Type*	*No. of layers*	*Type*	*No. of layers*
Lock-in	3	Lock-in	3	Lock-in	3
Single	7	Single	7	Double	9
Double	25	Single	19	Double	33
Single	73	Single	55	Double	129
Double	289	Single	163		
		Single	487		
		Single	1,459		
Total	**289**	**Total**	**1,459**	**Total**	**129**

So, how does the number of layers affect our pastries? Well, it's not just the number of layers but the thickness of the layers that makes a difference. The thicker the layers, the more dramatic the product with very defined layers of dough. The thicker layers will also have a better bite and offer a more substantial mouthfeel. Although hundreds of layers doesn't sound like much compared to thousands, it's still a lot.

The issue with more layers is that they can become so fine that they are easily damaged when rolling out (especially by hand) and don't keep their integrity during baking. Some of the layers, if too fine, may merge into each other, which can end up undoing some of your hard work. You won't get any visual reward for your extra effort.

So, what does this mean? Well, fewer turns = thicker dough = more bite. More turns = thinner dough = fluffier bite! To be honest, with my eyes closed I'm not sure I would be able to tell the difference, but I can imagine the fluffier pastry working better for a chausson aux pommes or a galette, and a pastry with more bite working better for a sausage roll, pie, or mille-feuille.

WHY TEMPERATURE MATTERS IN LAMINATION

If the butter gets too warm while you put folds into your pastry, it will merge into the dough and you will no longer have distinct layers of butter and dough, leading to a poor rise and end result. The way to counteract this is by using your butter at the correct temp (see All About Butter on page 57).

If you bake at the incorrect temperature, water and liquid fat may leak into the pastry. There are two effects here: you may get doughy or bready undercooked layers, or it could taste greasy rather than crisp.

Temperature is even more crucial when laminating yeasted goods like croissants. This is because the ideal temperatures for working with dough and butter are at odds with each other. The ideal temperature for laminating yeasted dough is 39–43°F, straight from the fridge, to help manage yeast activity (see Yeast and Ferments on page 76). But the ideal butter temperature for laminating is 52–57°F. This is the point at which the butter has good plasticity but is not greasy. It does not smudge, but you can bend it. This is key for getting beautiful layers in your pastry.

This means we need to compromise by keeping the dough cool . . . but not too cold! This is why paying attention to the specific resting periods in lamination recipes is essential.

How much butter?

The amount of butter you laminate into a dough makes a difference. Puff pastry is around 50% laminating butter to dough, while croissants is nearer to 30%. The more butter you use, the richer and flakier—and more holey—the lamination will be. If you reduce the butter, you get better definition and shape. This is one of the reasons croissants tend to have a more organized, honeycomb-like structure, while puff pastry tends to be more erratic.

THE DEAL WITH INVERTED PUFF PASTRY

As you continue down the rabbit hole of lamination, you will encounter some curious techniques, like inverted puff pastry. When you embark on the journey of inverted puff, you'll probably wonder, "What on EARTH is this forsaken stuff?" I mean, wrapping the butter *around* the dough? It sounds both ridiculous and amazing.

You see, inverted puff pastry flips the pastry lamination process. First, butter is combined with flour to create a floury/buttery block. This is then wrapped around a dough block. Lamination then continues as normal.

The first turn can be sticky and tricky, but it soon becomes as smooth and supple as any other dough. To me, it's the definition of trust the process.

Compared to standard puff pastry, inverted puff has a dense mouthfeel and shines in its ability to hold a stable shape when baking. This is why it is sometimes favored for mille-feuille and galette des rois. Here's why:

Gluten
Inverted puff has overall LESS developed gluten. When we make the butter dough, we coat a portion of the recipe's flour in fat, preventing the formation of gluten.

Butter stability
Unlike regular puff, the butter layer in the inverted puff is mixed with flour. By mixing butter with a proportion of flour, we are increasing the range of temperatures so that the butter dough is stable. Butter alone becomes greasy and smears very easily (see melting points in All About Fat on page 53), whereas butter tempered with flour is more stable at a higher range of temperatures.

As well as this, butter that has been mixed with flour simply does not crack and splinter as easily during the lamination process. When butter melts, it does so rapidly and unevenly, splitting into component parts (see All About Fat on page 57). When butter mixed with flour melts, it does so more evenly and relatively slowly, resulting in a more even rise in your inverted pastry.

Lower hydration
Inverted puff has a slightly lower hydration than regular puff because a portion of the flour has been moved to the butter block. This means you need less water to make the détrempe. Because the shape of a pastry is also defined by its water content (see Steam on page 68), lower-hydration doughs tend to be stable when baked.

Air in apples

An average apple is 15–18% air. This is why it floats and also why a good apple can be so satisfying to eat: the fresher the apple, the more air it has. And the more air trapped between those fibrous cell walls, the juicier it is. An apple with lots of air will have a fantastic crunch—the cell walls break open and the juice is released. Different varieties have different percentages of air, different sugars, and acidity, giving apples all their wonderful expansive varieties.

AIR

Bakes are often described as being "lighter than air," which is evocative but totally inaccurate. However, the amount of air in something does impact how it interacts with our palates. Many modern baking techniques focus on trapping and retaining air in our bakes—take any recipe and see if you can pick them out. Creaming butter and sugar? That's adding air. Folding in the dry ingredients gently? That's to prevent losing air. Whipping egg whites? Air! Sifting your ingredients? That's right, you're adding air!

Anytime we add air through technique, it is known as mechanical leavening. As well as being their own source of expansion, these pockets serve as safe harbors for other leavening gases like CO_2 (read more on that on page 74).

When heated, these air pockets expand and help our bakes rise. This expansion is not due to the air bubbles getting bigger, it results from the molecules speeding up and pressing against each other and their surroundings.

Imagine a hot air balloon filled with air. As the air heats, the molecules will speed up and bump into each other, which will have the effect of the balloon expanding. On cooling, the balloon deflates as the molecules slow down. This is exactly what is happening in your bakes.

Except, by the time the bake is cooled, the structure has been set, so it doesn't deflate. This is why making sure your bakes are fully cooked is extremely important. If there is any elasticity left—say the eggs have not fully coagulated or the starch has not gelatinized—the bake will shrink or fall. For some bakes, we encourage this rise and fall. Consider the cookie or a baked chocolate tart, which will often settle after an initial lift-off.

Airiest vs. least airy bakes

Not very airy   Very airy!

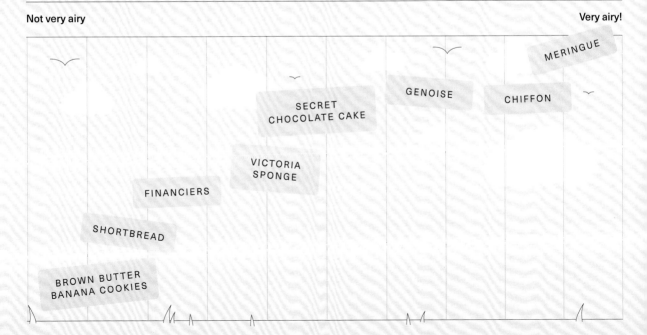

CARBON DIOXIDE

Carbon dioxide, aka CO_2, is an extremely useful leavener. We have CO_2 to thank for fluffy cinnamon rolls, bubbly cake batters, and puffy cookies. Unlike air—introduced by technique and method—and steam—introduced by the inherent ingredients—CO_2 is a bit different. This source of leavening joins the party either via chemical leaveners (aka rising agents, like baking powder and baking soda) or through yeast, the magical microorganism that just wants to eat. Let's jump in.

CHEMICAL RISING AGENTS

Rising agents chemically react with added ingredients, or themselves, to create carbon dioxide (CO_2). As the gas is released, it is trapped in the cells formed by gluten, egg proteins, or fat, aerating and expanding the structure. When heated, this gas expands further, resulting in a light and fluffy structure in our final baked goods. As well as this, rising agents may also affect the pH of the dough, which has the effect of weakening gluten and making cake crumbs more tender.

Rising agents rely on an acid-base reaction. When an ingredient with a high pH (alkaline) meets an ingredient with a low pH (acidic), they react. The by-product of this reaction is water and gas, and it's this gas that rises our bakes. The two main types are double and single action.

Baking soda is a single-action rising agent
Baking soda is alkaline, which means it has a high pH. It will react as soon as it is hydrated and encounters an acid (something with a low pH). This means we need to kickstart the reaction with something acidic: brown sugar, honey, yogurt, or cocoa powder to name just a few. Once it encounters an acid, CO_2 is produced immediately and it does not need heat to initiate a reaction.

This means recipes utilizing this leavening power tend to be baked immediately, especially if they are wet like cake batter. If your recipe is relatively dry, like cookie dough, you don't have to bake it right away because the baking soda only becomes hydrated once the butter melts in the oven. Baking soda is also responsible for the airy holes in honeycomb. It is considered more potent than baking powder and if you use too much, it may taste soapy or metallic.

Modern baking powder is known as a double-action rising agent
Baking powder is a combination of an alkali (like baking soda) and an acid (like cream of tartar). Because it already contains both an acid and an alkali, you don't need to add anything acidic. Think of it as the self-sufficient rising agent, since it reacts with itself once hydrated. It is known as a double-action rising agent because it reacts twice. The initial reaction is when you add a liquid, allowing the alkaline and acid to meet and react. The second reaction occurs in the presence of heat—the baking powder further reacts and creates even more gas.

The rising agent you use will have an impact on your final baked good. Let's take cookies, for example: baking soda only reacts once and is agnostic on temperature. This means it will initially cause the dough to rise but will not continue rising through the baking process. This results in the cookies spreading more. Baking powder will have that initial lift, but will also react a second time as the temperature rises; this coincides with the setting of the starch and protein—the lift is captured, meaning a taller, less-spready cookie.

Yeast and baking powder: a linked history

Before baking powder, cakes were either leavened with eggs or yeast—think genoise or kugelhopf. The invention, in 1843 by Alfred Bird, a chemist living in Birmingham in the nineteenth century, changed the game for cakes. Bird's wife, Elizabeth, was allergic to yeast and eggs, preventing her from enjoying two of life's greatest pleasures: cake and custard. I've always known that dessert is a love story, but this shows just how romantic cake and custard are! Bird's egg-free, cornstarch-based custard powder and baking powder formula are still enjoyed today. Quite the legacy.

The arrival of Bird's baking powder allowed a new type of cake to emerge: a more buttery, richer cake. When cakes relied solely on eggs to rise, the ratio of fat had to be relatively low to make the cake viable, since fat can destroy delicate egg foams and make the batter too heavy. With baking powder, fat can be added in equal quantities to the other ingredients, resulting in a tender yet hefty cake with a rich, flavorful crumb.

This arrival of a new type of cake coincided with the reign of Queen Victoria, hence the name Victoria sponge cake. As well as this, the cake could be made almost instantly, whereas before, it would have taken several hours for the cake to rise via yeast. Thanks, Alfred!

Lye

Lye is also known as caustic soda aka sodium hydroxide and has a pH of 14, very alkali, which also makes it quite dangerous to use. Much like a strong acid, strong alkalis can cause burns.

In traditional bagel and pretzel making, the risen dough is boiled in a lye solution, which helps provide those thin, chewy crusts. Baking soda can be used to approximate this safely.

QUANTITIES

When it comes to rising agents, there can be too much of a good thing. Adding these strategically—and with restraint—will result in the best rise:

The properly balanced recipe has a light, fluffy crumb with a flat-ish top. The cake with no rising agents is exceptionally dense, even though there is some implicit rise from the air from creaming and inherent steam. The cake with double-rising agents will be explosive as the reaction results in more gas than it is possible to capture.

SO, HOW MUCH TO USE?

A generally accepted quantity of baking powder to flour is 1½–2 teaspoons (6–8g) per 1 cup plus 3 tablespoons (150g) flour, which is a suitable ratio for cakes. For biscuits and cookies, ¼–⅔ teaspoons (1–3g) per 1 cup plus 3 tablespoons (150g) flour would be more suitable.

When there is an acidic ingredient in the recipe, like lemon juice, brown sugar, or an acidic dairy like sour cream, you can also use baking soda to add lift. To fully neutralize, you need around ½ tsp per 1 cup (240g) acidic dairy (yogurt, buttermilk, etc.) or ¼ tsp per 1 tablespoon (15ml) strong acid like lemon juice.

A combination of both baking soda and baking powder can also be used. A general rule of thumb is 1 teaspoon (4g) baking powder and just under ½ teaspoon baking soda per 1 cup plus 3 tablespoons (150g) flour. Please note that all of these are approximate and you should experiment and tweak!

Common baking ingredients pH

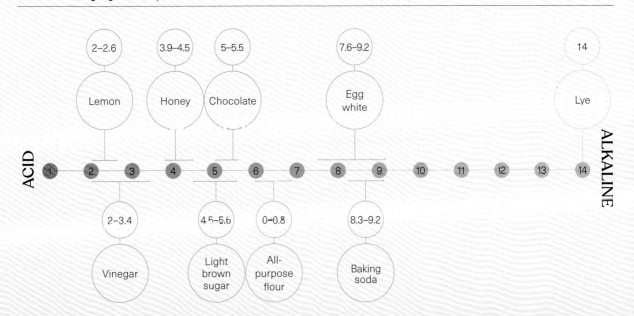

YEAST AND FERMENTS

Yeast is a small but mighty ingredient that literally breathes life into your doughs. Add yeast to a simple flour and water mixture and watch it work. Doughs become tender, airy, and soft, expanding and lifting. It's what transforms puff pastry from crisp and shattering to croissants, which are tender and flaky.

To understand why this happens, it's important to know what yeast actually is. Yeast is a tiny, diverse microorganism that feeds on sugar (usually the starch in flour) and produces CO_2 as a by-product. This gas causes the dough to rise as it is trapped in a mesh network of gluten (see All About Flour on page 23). This process is known as **fermentation.**

To make things when reading bread books, sometimes I like to replace the word *ferment* with *eat*. It's always helpful to me to imagine yeasts as little Pac-Men, nibbling their way through doughs and batters and being satisfied with their meal, burping out gas.

The warmer it is, the more active yeasts become. Temperature strongly affects the fermentation rate. This is why some recipes will ask you to warm up your liquids before adding them to the dough, to kickstart the activity, or to keep the dough somewhere warm.

This also means that it will take longer for your doughs to rise in the winter than in the summer if you are allowing them to proof (another word for rise) at ambient temperature. You might therefore see different results than the recipes suggest. When I'm recipe developing in my warm kitchen, doughs rise within the hour, but if it's mid-winter and the oven is off, it might take 2 or even 3 hours.

Yeast activity

Yeast is dormant	32–36°F
Yeast activity increases	36–77°F
Yeast activity is optimal	77–90°F
Yeast cells begin to die	113°F
Yeast is dead	140°F

But it's not only CO_2 that we get. Yeast also produces ethanol and flavor compounds. Specifically, these are a bunch of organic compounds like esters, aldehydes, and alcohols. Non-specifically, it's the things that make your bread taste like . . . well, bread. These compounds are aromatic and give bread the tangy and fruity notes we know and love.

How many times can bread rise?

Yeast is TOUGH. A dough can be deflated several times and re-shaped before the yeast can no longer rise the dough. Studies have suggested you could still have success upward of 10 times, before diminishing returns. But just because you CAN . . . doesn't mean you should!

Salt

In baking, salt is essential for flavor, but it also has a key role in controlling fermentation. It does this by attracting moisture away from the yeast cells. Without water, yeast cannot perform its metabolic functions, so salt keeps our microbe colony in check, slowing it down but not inhibiting it completely.

Note

If you're waiting for your dough to rise and it doesn't look very active, perhaps you will be thinking your yeast is dead, or you haven't added the right amount.

Try moving it to a warm place before ditching it completely—it may just need a kick of warmer temperature!

Commercial yeast

The fresh and dry yeast you can buy at the supermarket is generally a single strain of yeast. It was isolated, laboratory grown, and tailored over the years to be extremely efficient in rising dough. Commercial yeast comes in either fresh (like a moist cake) or dry form, e.g., active dry yeast. Some dry yeasts must be activated in warm water before use, while others can be added straight to the dough. The main difference here is the method of production. Yeast that requires activation has usually been given a protective coating (of dead yeast cells!) to improve its shelf-life. This coating literally needs to be melted to free the yeasts.

Wild yeast

Wild yeast, like sourdough, contains a whole gang of yeasts. These are populated from the air around the starter and any yeasts naturally present in the flour. These yeasts aren't as reliable, efficient, or speedy as their commercial counterparts. When it comes to leavening sourdough, it isn't *just* yeast that's responsible for rising the dough. Crucially, sourdough also contains LAB—lactobacteria. These naturally occurring lactobacillus are responsible for fermenting the dough, producing CO_2, and for the sour flavors associated with the bread. In fact, when it comes to sourdough, these lactobacteria actually outnumber yeast. But this interactive effect of the yeast and the LAB gives a compounded effect of fermentation in the form of bread structure and flavor. That's why sourdough bread has so much depth in its flavor compared to commercially risen yeast.

The breadmaking journey

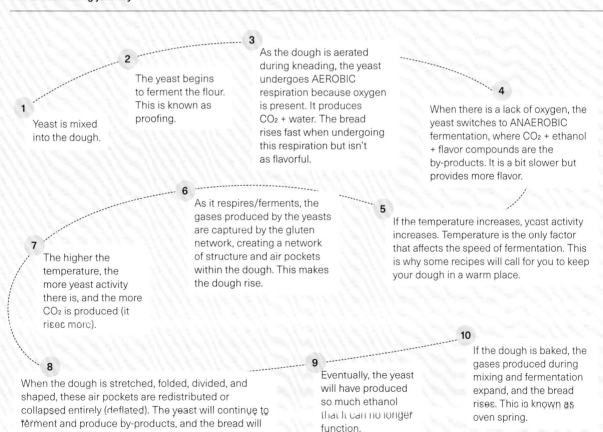

1 Yeast is mixed into the dough.

2 The yeast begins to ferment the flour. This is known as proofing.

3 As the dough is aerated during kneading, the yeast undergoes AEROBIC respiration because oxygen is present. It produces CO_2 + water. The bread rises fast when undergoing this respiration but isn't as flavorful.

4 When there is a lack of oxygen, the yeast switches to ANAEROBIC fermentation, where CO_2 + ethanol + flavor compounds are the by-products. It is a bit slower but provides more flavor.

5 If the temperature increases, yeast activity increases. Temperature is the only factor that affects the speed of fermentation. This is why some recipes will call for you to keep your dough in a warm place.

6 As it respires/ferments, the gases produced by the yeasts are captured by the gluten network, creating a network of structure and air pockets within the dough. This makes the dough rise.

7 The higher the temperature, the more yeast activity there is, and the more CO_2 is produced (it rises more).

8 When the dough is stretched, folded, divided, and shaped, these air pockets are redistributed or collapsed entirely (deflated). The yeast will continue to ferment and produce by-products, and the bread will rise again as CO_2 is captured in the gluten network.

It will continue to do this until it runs out of nutrition and there's nothing left for the yeast to process, getting continuously sourer.

9 Eventually, the yeast will have produced so much ethanol that it can no longer function.

10 If the dough is baked, the gases produced during mixing and fermentation expand, and the bread rises. This is known as oven spring.

WORKING WITH YEAST

Although a gram of yeast might seem like a small amount, it contains an estimated 5–20 billion cells! The more yeast in a dough, the quicker it will rise. But quick isn't always a good thing.

When you think about bread, the most important thing to remember is that you are trying to balance gluten development with fermentation. This means trying to make sure you have enough structure to capture the gases produced by yeasts. This is why it's important to always make sure you have fully developed your dough before moving onto the bulk fermentation stage.

If the yeast ferments the flour before a strong gluten network has been established, you will end up with a sticky dough that isn't strong enough to hold on to the little bubbles of carbon dioxide created during fermentation. The dough warms up when we develop gluten, like in a mixer or when kneading. Particularly in summer, when yeast is more active, we have to be careful that we don't let it warm up too much. To combat this, we can use fridge-cold liquids (or even chill our flour) for our dough, as well as take strategic rests to give the dough a break.

If we add a lot of yeast to our dough, it will ferment more quickly, but there will be nowhere for the gases to go. If anything, it is a better idea to REDUCE the amount of yeast that a recipe suggests—a slow rise makes it more likely that your dough will be developed enough to capture all the spoils of fermentation. Most recipes you find will take this into consideration and balance convenience with flavor.

HOW MUCH YEAST TO USE?

The amount of yeast in a recipe will depend on what other ingredients are in the dough.

There are two main categories of yeasted bread: lean and enriched.

Lean doughs
These refer to your typical sandwich loaf, pizza, or baguette and have little to no sugar or fat added, just water, flour, yeast, and salt, which helps control the rate of fermentation.

Lean doughs tend to have a relatively low amount of yeast, just 1% of the flour weight. In a lean dough, salt moderates the rate of fermentation by stealing water away from the yeast.

Enriched doughs
When the dough is enriched, it means it has been bolstered with sugar, eggs, or fat to create various textures and flavors to make the dough more fluffy and soft, like brioche and cinnamon buns.

Enriched doughs tend to have a higher quantity of yeast, closer to 2% or 2.5%. This is increased to accommodate the enriching ingredients, namely sugar. Although sugar at first boosts the yeast, anything above 5% will ultimately slow down the fermentation process. Sugar, being highly hygroscopic, steals water from everything, including yeast cells. As a result, enriched doughs generally benefit from a slightly higher proportion of yeast to function.

Yeast enemies

There are also compounds that are particularly fatal to yeast—cinnamon drastically inhibits yeast, so should be added to bread doughs with caution. There are also enzymes in milk that can affect yeast activity.

Some recipes may suggest that you scald then cool the milk to prevent interference with yeast activity, but this is no longer always essential. Most widely available milk has undergone thorough pasteurization (a process whereby the milk is heated sufficiently so enzymes are deactivated), so it's less likely to cause an issue.

YEAST NOTES

To me, the absolute best thing you can do when it comes to yeast is to treat it like a precious jewel or, even better, a pet that you love! If you take care of your yeast, it will take care of you:

- Once yeast enters your home, make sure you don't leave it open on the shelf at room temperature for months and then suddenly expect it to do the heavy lifting for you months down the line. Once opened, move it into the fridge.

- Read the instructions. I know it's annoying, but you will save yourself a world of pain if you check if it needs to be mixed into the dry ingredients first or if you need to bloom (activate) it in warm liquid first.

- Fresh yeast can be both helpful and anxiety-relieving because you know it is going to work—if it looks and smells fresh, you are good to go. If you can find it, use it! You need approximately double the amount of fresh yeast to dry yeast.

- When making dough, it's a good idea to keep the yeast away from the salt and sugar to mitigate the potential interference with fermentation. This is a simple fix—just scale the ingredients separately and give them a little distance when measuring into the mixing bowl.

- Aiming for a dough temperature of 73–77°F will help kickstart yeast activity. This can be achieved by warming your liquids slightly before incorporating them.

PROOFING

Proofing is the stage when we allow the yeast to get to work, consuming sugars in the dough and converting them to CO_2, making the dough rise. This usually happens twice when we make a dough and typically happens at room temperature or in a warm environment. The first proof, after mixing, is sometimes called bulk fermentation. The second proof takes place after shaping and just before baking.

In an ideal world, proofing should take place in a 77–81°F environment with 80% humidity. This temperature is ideal for yeast activity as the humidity allows the skin of the dough to remain supple for maximum expansion. It's basically a spa holiday for your dough! If the skin gets dry during proofing, it may rip as it expands.

Professional bakeries will have special equipment and entire rooms dedicated to these dough spas, but the average household isn't so well equipped. Homes in the UK typically have an ambient temperature of 64–70°F and around 70% humidity, so when it comes to proofing, you've got a few options:

- Ensure the dough is covered to prevent a skin from forming. A wet kitchen towel or cloth over the bowl is helpful.

- Lightly cover pastries with plastic wrap to prevent skin from forming.

- Proof dough under a large container to limit airflow or in a deep container that you can put a lid on and then easily lift out to bake.

MAKESHIFT PROOFING CHAMBER IN YOUR OVEN FOR PASTRIES

1. Around 15 minutes before you are going to proof your pastries, boil the kettle.

2. Pick a shallow baking pan and place it in the bottom of your oven.

3. Pour boiling water into this pan and place your temperature probe on the top shelf of the oven. After 15 minutes, check the temperature probe— it should be 77–86°F.

4. You will see condensation/steam on the oven door. This is great, but I still recommend using the plastic wrap to prevent any skin from forming on the pastries.

5. As you proof your pastries, you can top up the pan with warm water to keep the ambient temperature around 77–80°F, checking the temperature probe every now and then.

6. DO NOT LET IT GET TOO HOT as it may melt your butter layers, resulting in bready pastries.

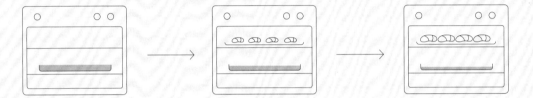

COLD PROOFING

Cold proofing is a technique we can apply to any dough. Rather than keeping our dough at room temperature for the entire process, we simply move it to the fridge after the first rise for a long, cool rest, usually overnight. Allowing the dough to have the first rise at room temperature is important because you need to let the yeast establish itself in the dough.

Cold proofing really pays off in the flavor department. This is because in cool environments yeast activity slows right down. This is a good thing because when the yeast isn't busy stuffing its face with sugar and producing CO_2, it gives a helping hand in the flavor department.

During cold fermentation, starches are further broken down into sugars and flavors are made, with yeast providing some useful enzyme action to coax those flavors out. This helps provide new dimensions for your bread. Between 12 and 24 hours is optimal—the dough can develop unpleasant flavors after this.

As well as this, during the cold proof the gluten becomes fully hydrated, creating an even stronger gluten network. This provides an even more dramatic and noticeably improved structure to your bread.

PREFERMENTS

When you make dough, time is an ingredient. The longer you ferment your dough, the more the yeast gets to work, producing flavor compounds along the way. Spending more dedicated time on the fermenting stage is a great way to improve the overall aroma of your dough. A preferment can help you achieve this. A preferment is a portion of flour, liquid, and yeast from your recipe that you mix ahead of time. There are many names for preferments—biga, poolish, sponge, pâté fermentée—the list goes on. The reality is, they are all sort of . . . the same. All the variations achieve the same goal: an improved flavor and texture.

Types of preferments

Biga

A biga is a type of stiff preferment that, usually, is proportionally 50% water to the weight of flour.

Poolish

A poolish is a type of wet preferment that is usually equal parts (i.e. 100%) water and flour.

Maybe you're thinking—why not just proof the WHOLE dough for longer instead of just a small portion? Well, that's a good question. It's possible that if you do that the whole dough may over-ferment, producing overly yeasty aromas and running out of juice by the time it hits the oven. Making a preferment is like giving your dough a kickstart, allowing you to build layers of flavor and complexity.

While you do lose time by prefermenting the flour, you can actually gain some of that back during the mixing process and rise. The prefermented dough will have well-developed gluten (see All About Flour on page 14) and an aromatic flavor profile. This makes the actual mixing process shorter since you already have the beginnings of a strong structure, which goes to improve the texture and fluffiness later on.

Enriched doughs, like brioche or anything with sugar, eggs, or fat, can be slow to rise (see How much yeast to use? on page 78). This is because it takes longer for the yeast to actually reach its food source (the flour) to begin fermenting it. Plus, sugar is a real water hog (see All About Sugar on page 29) and steals moisture from the yeast which, in turn, slows down the rate of fermentation.

By prefermenting some of your dough, you have circumvented this issue. You have fermented some of your flour without the interference of other ingredients. As well as this, your yeast is already active and ready to take charge, so your next rise will be shorter.

JUDGING PROOF

Judging proof is always one of the hardest things to do when you start making yeasted doughs. A degree of guesswork and repetition is required to feel confident. But visual cues are always the best. The dough should look noticeably puffed and will jiggle. When lightly pressed with a floured or wet finger so as not to tear the dough, the dough should fill back in slowly. Some doughs may never double in size, so always refer to the directions in the recipe.

THE FINAL RISE

There is no greater delight than watching your dough rise to the occasion, but that also means there's no bigger tragedy than extracting a flat, greasy pancake from the oven that was supposed to be a cake. Though many parts of baking can be viewed and understood through the lens of science, the alchemy of rising agents is probably the clearest. Paying attention to your rising agents, treating your yeast with love and care, and keeping an eye on the thermometer will help you reap the results you deserve. And, for goodness sake, please check the expiration date of your baking powder!

6.

COLOR

At some point in every baker's life, you simply learn to love the color beige. Although it might not seem particularly exotic at first, coming to appreciate the extraordinary range of browns is actually about recognizing the transformation of color in our bakes. From the copper tones of caramel sauce to the darkly burnished bronzes of your bread crust and the pale golden crumb of a Victoria sponge, each hue tells a story.

Color can, and should, be added after baking with artfully placed fruit, splashes of jam, decorations/garnishes, and vibrant buttercreams. Or it may be influenced by a key ingredient, like cocoa powder or molasses. But this chapter investigates the naturally occurring magic that connects color, texture, and flavor.

You see, when it comes to baking, color represents change. It's the visual cue we follow to know if something is done, it gives us clues about the flavor and even helps us taste the food before it comes anywhere near our mouths or noses. I hope by the end of this chapter, you'll learn to love brown as much as I do!

MAILLARD REACTION VS. CARAMELIZATION

The two main culprits for color are the Maillard reaction and caramelization. It's the mixture of these two processes that gives our bakes a golden gleam and adds those all-important flavor dimensions to our food. However, the distinction between the two is often misunderstood. Something may appear caramel colored but that, rather confusingly, does not always mean caramelization! By understanding how this duo works together, we can better inform our choices when baking—from deciding on oven temperatures to the ingredients that we use.

The Maillard reaction is the official term for browning, named for Louis Camille Maillard, a French chemist who first described the process in 1912. It's the chemical reaction that occurs between amino acids and a reducing sugar (e.g., whey protein and lactose in milk), which produces color, aroma, and flavor compounds. The burnished tops of your pastéis de nata? Maillard reaction! The crust of your bread? Maillard reaction! Your egg-washed pastries? You guessed it . . . Maillard reaction!

Although it can happen at room temperature (over very long periods of time, in a non-desirable way), this reaction occurs rapidly from 284°F and takes place in almost all forms of cooking and baking. Whether it's rice pudding or muffins, each reaction creates unique flavors because the proteins and sugars reacting are all different. Milk is very susceptible to Maillard browning as it contains large amounts of whey (protein) and lactose (sugar), so bakes that use milk will brown more readily and quickly when baking.

Unlike the Maillard reaction, **caramelization** is not a reaction between two compounds. Caramelization occurs when sugar is heated. It doesn't need to react with anything else to take place.

When sugar is heated and melts, it begins to decompose. It first breaks down into glucose and fructose. As we continue heating it, it breaks down further into a range of new molecules that are collectively known as caramel. These are a mixture of color and flavor molecules that are responsible for the visual appeal of caramel, as well as those nutty, buttery, and toasty caramel notes. Though these molecules start out as desirable, if you continue cooking the caramel, those flavor notes will continue warping and transforming, becoming intensely bitter and burned, with hardly any sweetness remaining.

Different sugars undergo caramelization at different temperatures. Sucrose caramelizes at around 320°F. Glucose is just behind at 302°F. But fructose begins at 221°F. This is why bakes that use honey, which is high in fructose, are often darker in color and susceptible to burning.

Over time, caramel has come to describe a color and a flavor as well as the official term for the compound itself. This leads to confusion about how things brown. White chocolate that is cooked slowly until blonde, for example, is often called caramelized white chocolate, even though no caramelization has taken place.

Egg wash

Egg wash is probably the most well-known example of Maillard reactions. Want a shiny, golden crust on your galette or loaf of bread? Egg wash! Depending on the desired final color of your baked goods, you can adapt the egg wash

Egg yolks contain more proteins than whites and yield a darker crust, while egg whites will result in a lighter, shiny crust. Adding cream to yolks will yield the darkest, richest color. Oh, and a pinch of salt will help break down the egg proteins and, made ahead of time, produce an egg wash that is easy to spread. Adding milk can also improve the browning (and brushability) of the wash.

The progression of Maillard reactions and caramelization

< 230°F	Maillard reaction occurs, but more slowly
221–230°F	Fructose caramelizes
230–284°F	Maillard occurs but more slowly and reactions at lower temperatures result in less aromatic and visual browning cues
284–356°F	Maillard occurs rapidly, resulting in typical browned flavor compounds
320–338°F	Caramelization of sucrose begins.
392°F	Caramelization occurs but sugar is at risk of burning, eventually reaching the point of no return—pyrolysis

When sugar turns to caramel, there is no sugar available to react with proteins for Maillard

THE QUESTION OF WHEN

Although WHY? is my favorite question in the kitchen, WHEN? is also important. One of the biggest decisions we make when creating a recipe is WHEN to put flavors into bakes.

You have two options—either put your ingredients through these processes prior to the final cooking or ensure your final cooking method will result in the development of flavors.

Caramelization is a great example of thinking about the when because it occurs at high temperatures. Take a custard tart, for example, which is baked at a much lower temperature than what is required for caramelization or significant Maillard reactions to take place, to prevent curdling (see All About Eggs on page 40). So, adding as much flavor as possible before the bake is essential to ensure you have banked as much flavor as you can.

Browning from (mostly) caramelization   Browning from (mostly) Maillard

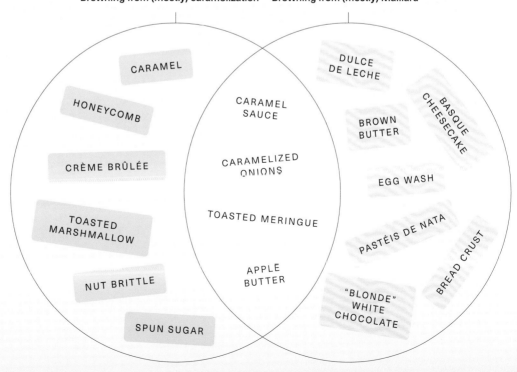

CARAMEL

HONEYCOMB

CRÈME BRÛLÉE

TOASTED MARSHMALLOW

NUT BRITTLE

SPUN SUGAR

CARAMEL SAUCE

CARAMELIZED ONIONS

TOASTED MERINGUE

APPLE BUTTER

DULCE DE LECHE

BASQUE CHEESECAKE

BROWN BUTTER

EGG WASH

PASTÉIS DE NATA

BREAD CRUST

"BLONDE" WHITE CHOCOLATE

THE STORY OF CARAMEL SAUCE

Caramel sauce is the perfect example of Maillard and caramelization coming together to make a perfect, complex, and irresistible flavor profile. To begin with, sugar (or sugar and water) is heated to 320°F, where the sugar turns to caramel. We continue heating the caramel until a deeper, darker amber is reached (depending on the chef, this can be dangerously dark—at Ottolenghi, I was taught by Verena Lochmuller to wait until I saw black spots) before carefully adding cream. Once added, the cream—and sometimes butter—rich with lactose and whey proteins, immediately undergo Maillard reaction alongside the caramelized sugars, resulting in a perfect blend of flavor and color.

Caramel sauce lives and dies on the depth of your burnt sugar flavor. Suppose you haven't taken your caramel sauce dark enough. In that case, you can improve the flavor by intentionally overheating a batch of sugar. You have to make it almost unpalatably dark, but a small amount of almost-too-burnt sugar will greatly improve a one-note sweet sauce.

Playing around with the sugar, butter, and cream ratio will give you different results. Here's two to get you started:

Caramel ratios

Firmer: best for piping and fillings

50% Sugar	20% Butter	30% Cream

Pourable: stays soft in the freezer; best for swirls

50% Sugar	50% Cream

Note: Do not exceed 221°F

A tale of two brown things

Perhaps you're wondering what the difference between fudge and butter caramels is?

Well, in browned milk preparations, like fudge or dulce de leche, you never get the mixture hot enough to caramelize the sugar. The sugar is there for flavor, structure, and to bulk. In caramels, like butter caramels, you are caramelizing the sugar at a high temperature and then using dairy to mitigate the texture.

CARAMELIZATION TYPES

Caramel has an unfair reputation for being a bit of a diva. I admit, there are things that can go wrong, but this is a small price to pay for a world of flavor that caramel unlocks. Although there are plenty of tricks, I find that my caramel always turns out best when I approach it with confidence.

There are two ways to make caramel: dry and wet. Both methods will end up with the same result but have pros and cons relating to color and flavor.

A dry caramel
This is made by adding sugar to a dry pan and stirring until it has melted and is an amber color. It is difficult to achieve a light caramel using the dry method and it must be carefully watched to prevent accidental burning. A dry caramel can be stirred without any risk of crystallization.

A wet caramel
This is made by mixing sugar with 25–30% of its weight in water until it looks like wet sand. This is then heated through various stages of water evaporation until caramel compounds begin to form. You get the slightest hint of blonde at around 284°F, but a clear golden color by 320°F. You must avoid stirring or you risk immediate crystallization.

Which is better? Judging caramel is usually a case of personal preference (I like to wait until I see a few dangerously dark spots!), but a wet caramel gives you the highest degree of control over the color. However, it is more susceptible to crystallization because (as you learned in the chapter All About Sugar on page 32) sugar LOVES itself. We love a self-confident queen!

The deal with caramelized honey

Caramelized or burnt honey crops up in recipe books and menus. Made simply by heating honey until darkened, it—in theory—increases the complexity of the honey. But should it be done?

I think honey should be treated a bit like olive oil. In kitchens, there are two sorts of olive oil— olive oil for cooking and olive oil for finishing. The olive oil you use for cooking doesn't have to be extra-virgin or the best you'll ever buy—in fact, it 100% shouldn't be. Cooking olive oil needs to be affordable and also a team player. You don't want something extremely perfumed just to soften onions in.

Honey is similar. In your pantry, you should have two types: a generic one for general use (that will likely be heated, used in cake batters or syrups, etc. and thus burn in the oven), and one for a final flourish. The final flourish honey should stand out and should not be heated. EVER. So, although burnt honey is absolutely a thing, it should never be done to an artisan, small-batch honey that has been carefully preserved and purposefully never heated above 122°F. This action destroys all the nutritious and delicious bits, automatically turning your very special honey into something very generic.

THE INTERSECTION OF SOUND AND COLOR

We're used to using our sight, taste, and touch when baking, but a surprising relationship exists between sound and color. Whether in caramelization or during the Maillard reaction, the first step to achieving golden colors is to get rid of all the water. The reactions required to build those toasty flavor compounds just cannot be created in the presence of water due to the limit on temperature (water boils at 212°F). This is why roasted food tastes different from boiled or poached food.

During my first job in NYC, I was attempting to multitask, making a wet caramel and conversing with Chef Dominique himself. As we chatted, I kept turning around to check the temperature. Without looking, Chef Dominique said, "You've got lots of time! Don't worry." Amazed by this magic trick, I asked, "How did you know that without looking?" He replied, "I can still hear it!" Since then, I've never underestimated the power of sound in the kitchen.

As rapid water evaporation occurs, as in a wet caramel or when browning butter, the process is pretty noisy until suddenly . . . it all goes Björk levels of quiet. That's when it's time to pay attention, because most of the water has evaporated, and color changes are imminent.

EFFECT OF PH ON BROWNING

You know how good things come to those who wait? Well, there are ways to get those good things a bit quicker. Intriguingly, we can impact the browning of our baked goods by altering the pH. A pH number tells you how acidic or alkaline a substance is: a low pH means it is acidic, while a high pH means it is alkaline. Seven is considered neutral.

When it comes to the Maillard reaction, a high pH/alkaline environment encourages the all-important amino acid chains to be broken down into separate proteins, accelerating the reaction and resulting in deeper browning. And fast. Baking soda, with a pH of 9, is an accessible alkali (also known as a base) in the pastry kitchen. As well as providing leavening, recipes with baking soda result in deeper colors—a pinch can hurry the famously slow caramelized onion process along.

This high pH is also the reason why boiled-then-baked goods, like pretzels and bagels, have an unmistakably unique, dark crust. In professional production environments, bakers are known to use a lye solution to treat the dough, either by immersing, boiling, or spraying. Lye, aka caustic soda, aka sodium hydroxide (see page 75), has a very high pH of 14, which radically increases the Maillard reactions.

Much like a strong acid, strong alkalis can cause burns, so it's not advisable to do this at home (even if some particularly enthusiastic online forum members think differently). Fortunately, baking soda can be used as a safe alternative, though its effects are less potent.

On the other end of the scale, it should be noted that highly acidic batters may not brown well. This is why it's important to neutralize acidic ingredients, for example, sour cream in cake batter, with alkalis like baking soda, to ensure the color of your bake isn't affected. (See the common baking ingredients pH table in How Things Rise on page 75.)

BROWN BUTTER TECHNIQUE

Brown butter is a shortcut to flavor town and the easiest way to see the Maillard reaction in action. It adds a unique richness with a "How did you do that?!" quality to your food. To make it, add butter to a pan over medium heat and listen for the water to stop evaporating.

Once it's quiet, pay attention to the pan and start checking the color, occasionally stirring and scraping the pan to release the browned milk solids that are gathering. If you don't agitate them, they'll burn really quickly before the butter has reached the desired color. So, what is the right color?

It depends. For cakes, cookies, or biscuits, I like to go dark! The brown butter needs to stand up against the other flavors, so I aim for it to be as distinct as possible. I also like to leave all the flecks of brown/burnt milk solids in for extra flavor hits. In some kitchens, the chefs prefer to sieve all of this out, but I'm not one of them.

There will be some carryover cooking because once heated up, fat can hold and retain heat extremely well. So, once you have your desired color, get it off the heat before it accidentally heads into bitter territory. Remember, you can always heat it back up and brown it more if you need to. And don't forget that the final weight of brown butter will be about 20–25% less than the original quantity of butter, so always do more than you need.

OXIDATION

On some occasions, there are unwelcome color changes in the kitchen. Ever seen a beautiful bowl of sliced apples turn brown before your eyes? Or mixed up a batch of shortcrust pastry and come back to find it an unappealing shade of gray? There's only one process to blame: oxidation.

Fruit, like apples, undergo unwanted discoloration known as enzymatic browning. Enzymes are the molecules responsible for ripening fruit. When the fruit is cut and the flesh is exposed to the air, the enzymes begin rapidly oxidizing, resulting in a brown color. For example, the amount of damage (i.e., cuts) to an apple will also define how much it oxidizes. Grating apples, for example, will ensure a dramatic onslaught of enzymatic activity. It's a similar process (but in wheat enzymes), that causes our pastry to turn an unappetizing gray after several days in the fridge, even if it's well-wrapped. The solution for both is the same: acid.

Steaming—when there is no color

Both the Maillard reaction and caramelization process require high temperatures. Steamed bread will not take on any dark colors and will be a creamy, slightly yellow color when cooked. Pure white steamed buns, like bao and mantou, will often use bleached flour. Although beautiful, bleached white flour has very little nutritional value and has lost much of its flavor.

Shortcut to Maillard flavors

A great way to experience intense Maillard flavors is by browning/toasting white chocolate. Despite its name, white chocolate has very little chocolate (if any) in it—it is mainly milk solids, cocoa butter, and sugar. This means that when you heat it, it will turn golden as it undergoes Maillard reactions. This results in complex, toasty flavors. See it in action on page 222 (blonde rice pudding) and on page 215 (milky panna cotta). The same technique can be applied to milk powder—bake in a medium oven until golden, or toast in a dry frying pan.

Introducing acid in some form, like lemon juice or vinegar, reduces enzymatic activity, as well as bolstering flavor. It's worth noting that oxidized dough has a bark worse than its bite. A gray dough, so long as it doesn't smell rancid, will still bake up golden brown. For fruit, you do have another option: salt. Despite being slightly alkaline, immersing your quick-to-oxidize sliced fruit in salt water inhibits the enzymes in the same way an acid does. Just immerse your fruit in about 2 cups (500g) water with 1 teaspoon salt for 10 minutes. Any lingering salt flavor can easily be rinsed off before using.

HOW FERMENTATION AFFECTS COLOR

When I learned about fermentation, I was surprised to find out how significantly yeast activity impacts the color of bread. A telling sign of both underfermented and overfermented dough is a pale crust that never properly browns, no matter if your oven is working well and your baking time is correct.

When the dough is underfermented, it means there has not been enough time for the starch to break down properly into the sugars and proteins that take part in the Maillard reaction. Your dough will brown but in a more lackluster fashion.

Overfermented dough also has the same issue, but for different reasons. If the dough has fermented too much, it means the yeast has digested every last bit of sugar available and, once again, a poor Maillard reaction will take place. As well as improving the color and texture, an overnight cold fermentation process is the easiest way to guarantee that you will fully benefit from the Maillard reaction.

The use of salt in fermented doughs assists with keeping this balance in check. Because salt slows down yeast activity, it helps ensure that there is enough sugar left over to undergo Maillard reactions during the bake.

A FINAL SPLASH

Only in a baking book would an entire chapter on color only explore the varieties of brown. You are, of course, encouraged to pair these browns with flashes of color through a range of decors—think generous heaps of cream, extraordinarily arranged fresh berries, or a dusting of powdered sugar, to name a few.

But embracing the small differences between the deep bronzes and mahoganies, the ombre of a pie crust, and the hints of blonde on a shortbread will give you a deeper appreciation of the extraordinary flavor enhancing reactions taking place. A browned crust not only looks inviting, but it is a symbol of flavor, a promise of crunch.

7.

TEXTURE

Crunchy, creamy, chewy, tough, smooth, airy, tender, snappy, moist. Texture is a key pillar of a well-baked good. Think of the crisp bread crust that gives way to a soft, creamy crumb; the shortbread that melts in the mouth; the crunch of a caramelized choux bun; or a tender bun interspersed with chewy candied peel.

For me, texture can be the make or break for a great dessert: I'm much more accepting of something that lacks flavor but has great texture than the other way around. Whether it's a squelchy strawberry, rice pudding with too much bite, a dry sponge cake, a soggy sausage roll, or ice cream laden with ice crystals, a poor texture can be seriously off-putting. To get it right, careful attention needs to be paid from start to finish, from the selection of ingredients to the temperature of the oven and even the cooling process.

Texture is an intriguing topic of contradictions. Something can be tender and moist, like cake, but also tender and dry, like a cookie. So, what are the factors? In this chapter, we'll delve into the ingredients that influence texture and the techniques that impact the final character of the bake.

TOUGHENERS VS. TENDERIZERS

As we've seen in All About Flour, Sugar, Eggs, and Fat—our most common baking ingredients all play a role. Although there are quirks to each ingredient, one way to split up ingredients is to categorize them as either tenderizers or tougheners. When we bake, it's like a tug of war between the tenderizers and the tougheners—an imbalance throws it all off.

Playing around with the ratio of these will lead to different textures. Tenderizers will weaken the structure while tougheners will harden your bakes. To get deeper into each ingredient and their role, refer back to the chapters above.

Crust and crumb

One of the most common (and enjoyable) textures we come across in oven-baked goods is the classic contrast of crust and crumb. This textural interplay perfectly shows how baking techniques and methods impact the final product.

Because ovens cook food by transferring heat from the outside inward, our baked goods will form a crust. Alternatively, steaming a cake batter will give you a cohesive texture without forming a crust as there is not a high direct heat source. See this in action in my steamed plum buttermilk sponge recipe on page 155.

To learn more about this process, see the Technical Overview section on page 104.

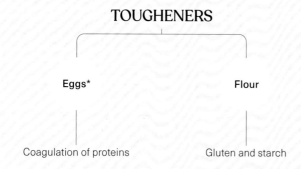

TOUGHENERS

Eggs*	Flour
Coagulation of proteins	Gluten and starch

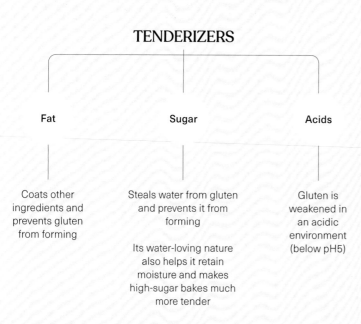

TENDERIZERS

Fat	Sugar	Acids
Coats other ingredients and prevents gluten from forming	Steals water from gluten and prevents it from forming Its water-loving nature also helps it retain moisture and makes high-sugar bakes much more tender	Gluten is weakened in an acidic environment (below pH5)

*Whole eggs and whites are considered more toughening than yolks because of the lower amount of fat. But yolks are still considered tougheners because they will harden (i.e., coagulate) and provide structure.

Alternative hydrocolloids

Among the slightly lesser-known hydrocolloids are agar agar, carrageenan, and xanthan gum, which offer distinct thickening properties. Agar agar and carrageenan, derived from seaweed, are widely used in East Asian and Irish cooking, respectively, and are often utilized as substitutes for gelatin in plant-based recipes, while xanthan gum is commonly enlisted in gluten-free recipes to help mimic the flexibility of gluten.

THICKENERS

One of the most important ways we alter texture when baking is the transformation of a liquid to a semi-solid. A simple way to think about this is to consider how something flows. From custard to jam, marshmallows to panna cotta, we often seek to alter the texture in baking, turning liquids from thin and flowing to dense and firm.

Hydrocolloids is the official name for substances that form a gel with water. Some well-known hydrocolloids include gelatin, pectin, and starch, which we'll cover in detail in the coming pages.

Depending on the product, the route to thickening may either be through coagulation, freezing, fat, acid, volumizing with air, gelling or, simply, a reduction in water. It may also change depending on whether your goal is to stabilize (as in cheesecake), improve the texture (as in crème anglaise), or completely gel (as in panna cotta).

Other than the products that rely on a straightforward reduction of water, all of these thickening agents do the same thing: immobilize water.

How things thicken

	Primary thickener	Secondary thickener	Result
Crème anglaise	Egg yolks	Fat	Thin, creamy, smooth
Baked custard	Egg yolks	Fat	Firm, creamy, smooth
Burnt cheesecake	Eggs, fat	Flour	Dense, rich, creamy*
Pastry cream	Starch	Eggs	Thick, unctuous, smooth
Sugar syrup	Sugar		
Jam	Pectin	Sugar, reduction of water	Thick, goopy, sticky
Compote	Reduction of water	Pectin	Thick, goopy, flowing
Posset	Acid	Fat	
Panna cotta	Gelatin	Fat	Creamy, slightly bouncy
Jelly	Gelatin	Sugar	Springy
Marshmallow	Gelatin, air	Sugar	Springy, chewy
Cheesecake	Fat, eggs	Starch	Thick, creamy, smooth
Pie filling	Starch	Pectin	Viscous, smooth
Whipped cream	Air	Fat	Light, dissolving, smooth
Meringue	Egg whites	Air, sugar	Dense, dissolving, smooth
Ice cream	Air/freezing	Fat, eggs	Firm, smooth, melty

*Flour stabilizes by reducing weeping of liquid

STARCH

When it comes to texture, we can draw similarities between egg proteins and starch: both are made up of long chains that unravel, creating a series of slings or pockets that can hold gas, air, or liquid.

Starch is a naturally occurring carbohydrate in plants. It's usually tasteless and pure starch, more often than not, is white or white-ish. It is starch's ability to thicken that makes it our friend in the kitchen. Different starches have varying strengths—literally—and weaknesses. But they are all linked with one necessary process: gelatinization (see All About Flour on page 20 for more information).

When starch is mixed with water and heated, the granules absorb the water and swell. Some of these swollen starch granules burst, leaking out amylose. It's a combination of the two that provides a mesh network: the water is trapped inside, and you get a thickened consistency.

Of the starches, wheat flour is the most common in the kitchen. However, it's important to note that wheat flour is only 75% starch compared to corn, tapioca, potato, and arrowroot, which are almost 100% starch. This results in different setting temperatures. Flour thickens nicely at around 149°F, but the other starches won't thicken fully until above 185°F and up to 203°F, when they reach their full thickening potential.

Another consideration when picking starch is clarity. Visually, a pure starch will appear clear when set, while wheat flour will be cloudy because the gluten proteins appear opaque.

SO HOW MUCH STARCH DO YOU NEED?

How much starch to employ in a recipe is directly related to your final product and what you are trying to gel. For example, when considering how much starch to use for fruit in pie fillings, each will need different amounts thanks to the varying levels of water and pectin.

Since flour is only 75% starch, it is less effective at gelling liquids. As a rule of thumb, you need 1.5x more to set the same amount of liquid as pure starch.

Amount of starch in proportion to weight

Recipe	Amount of starch
Pastry cream	7–10%
Standard bechamel (for lasagne)	8%
Thick bechamel (for pastry fillings)	15%
Basque cheesecake	2–4%
Pie fillings—juicy fruits (berries, etc.)	4–8%
Chicken pie filling	5%
Pie fillings—firmer fruits (apples, etc.)	1–3%

The deal with nuts

One thing that links all thickeners—and gives them their special properties—is size. Both starch and protein are large and complex molecules that rearrange to trap water, resulting in thickening. Although this rearrangement of molecules is effective, you can also achieve very good results by adding a naturally thick ingredient to a recipe. Ingredients high in fat, like butter or cream, can do the trick.

Nuts are particularly useful for this—a nut butter can be an effective way to add body to a sauce or custard (but cannot replace fat completely, see All About Fat on page 55). Ground nuts are also very potent thickeners, being high in fat and with a strong ability to absorb liquid, but at a cost: the resulting gel will be very flavorful (great!) but also very textured.

PECTIN

Pectin is a type of starch found in fruit, mainly in the cell walls and core. It is responsible for holding the cell walls of the fruits together and is often thought of as the glue. This function extends to an ability to thicken, stabilize, and gel.

Though it is sometimes used in other ways, the best place to see pectin in action is during the fruit-preserving and jam-making process. Most fresh fruits have a water content of 85–93%. As fruit is heated, the cell walls break down, and the water is released. This process begins at 140°F. The longer and more strongly the fruit is heated, the more liquid it becomes. So, having a plan of how to entertain all that water is essential. This is where pectin comes in.

Once the pectin is extracted, it begins to create a network capable of holding liquid and making a gel. But pectin relies on the backup of two ingredients to do its best work. Firstly: sugar. Ever the pursuant of water, sugar assists the pectin gelling process by attracting water away from pectin and forming a syrup. This occupation of water allows the pectin mesh to form uninterrupted.

Secondly: acid plays a key role here. Pectin molecules carry a negative charge. As we know, like-charges repel each other, meaning that pectins may struggle to interact properly. When we add acid—usually in the form of lemon juice if the fruit itself is not acidic enough—it neutralizes some of these negative charges, allowing the pectin molecules to interact with each other and create the bonds essential for gelling.

STALE BAKES

When you think about staling—when our bread and pastries seemingly dry out, sometimes a mere few hours after baking—the first culprit that comes to mind is probably water loss. Although this is true, this is only part of the story. We also need to look at starch!

As we've learned, gelatinization (see All About Flour on page 20) is an important step in every baked good's life. Starch gelatinization occurs at 149°F (for wheat), where water enters the starch molecules and they swell, creating a gel. This gel network—along with the structure provided by gluten, air bubbles, sugar, fat molecules, and all the rest—creates the final interlocking structure of cakes and bread. Basically, the starch and water don't waste any time in teaming up.

As your cake cools, the starch molecules start to feel a bit weird about how quickly they declared being best friends with water and try to revert back to their pre-baked state—i.e., hanging out with other starch molecules only.

As a result, the previously happily swollen starch molecules re-arrange themselves to be a tightly packed network (rather than a lovely bouncy one) and eventually become so dense that crystals are formed. At this point, water feels really left out (fair enough), and with nothing holding it in place, it evaporates, resulting in a dry product, aka staling.

Fortunately, it can be reversed. Warming in the oven is your friend! You can literally melt these starch crystals (and the butter, too!) by gently heating in a 350°F oven for 4–5 minutes. To take it a step further, place a dish of boiling water next to it to increase the humidity of the oven. This steaminess further helps the BFF's starch/water to rejoin. Good as new. For stale lean bread, like baguettes, spray or sprinkle with water before reheating in the oven for a bit of extra oomph and to replace some of that lost water.

LESSONS OF FROZEN DESSERTS

There is much to be understood about texture through the lens of frozen desserts. From semifreddos to churned gelatos, there are very few things as universally loved as ice cream (or ice cream adjacent desserts, for the purists out there).

Ice cream's texture is key: it is the perfect interplay of air, fat, sugar, and temperature. Ever put a slightly melty tub of ice cream back into the freezer only to come back to it days later and find it . . . crunchy? And not in a fun way . . . Let's get into why that happens.

WHY ICINESS HAPPENS

If left to its own devices, water freezes at 32°F into a hard, icy block. This happens because the low temperature causes the molecules to slow down so much that they settle into place, forming crystals as they line up. But these aren't nice, smooth crystals; quite the opposite—these are jagged, stabby crystals with pointy tips that crunch when you eat them. As well as this, you'll know from making ice cubes that water goes from clear to cloudy. That's because water will freeze as soon as it passes the 32°F threshold. Since this will be from the outside inward, impurities and air bubbles get pushed to the middle.

The typical way to prevent this is by churning our ice cream bases. Churning is the process of agitating a mixture while lowering the temperature, which hardens the mixture.

FORMULATING FROZEN DESSERTS

Most churned frozen dessert formulations have common ingredients. A liquid base (milk/cream/fruit purée) enriched with egg yolks, sugar, and additional flavorings, which can be anything from infusions to jammy ripples to solid chunks of chocolate.

For no-churn frozen desserts, it's a bit different. Without the help of a churning motion to break down ice crystals as they form, these recipes must be balanced perfectly. As well as this, any air needs to be added into the mixture before freezing. Fortunately, there's a team of ice-fighting ingredients at your disposal. Let's go deeper into each ingredient:

Fat
Fat is usually provided by cream or egg yolks and is essential because it coats ice crystals, preventing them from expanding and creating those jagged networks. It is also essential for mouthfeel, melting as it hits our palate, coating our mouths pleasantly, and adding its own flavor. Since fat is such a good carrier of flavors, our experience of eating a frozen dessert changes depending on the proportion of fat to other ingredients. Fat-free sorbet has an immediate, intense flavor that is very clean, while ice cream tends to have more of a slow release.

When you freeze cream, the water and fat will separate, clumping together in their respective tribes. As the water freezes, the jagged crystals literally splice through the milk fat—brutal, right? From a texture perspective, it takes much longer to go solid because it is only half water. So, at 32°F only half of the mix will be frozen, so it will be semi-solid. It's not until you get to temperatures of -22°F that over 90% of the mix will have been converted into solids, so the cream will be as solid as ice.

The magic of condensed milk

A lot of no-churn recipes call for condensed milk because it is, to put it inelegantly, full of stuff.

This stuff, meaning sugars, milk solids, and fat, helps create a smooth frozen texture as it interrupts the rough, ice crystal structure that water forms below 32°F.

There can be, of course, too much of a good thing. Overly fatty mixes may split when agitated, leaving chunks of solid butter throughout the ice cream. Since no-churn ice cream is not agitated after the initial mix, the risk of the emulsion breaking is smaller, so it can have a higher proportion of fat than a standard churned ice cream.

Milk solids
These are basically the leftovers once all the liquid is removed from dairy. The solids refer to a few things: fat, as above, but also protein (whey, casein), lactose (a sugar), and a small number of minerals. Solids are important in ice cream because they reduce iciness by absorbing water. This prevents water from freely moving to hang out with other water and form chunky ice crystals. Fruit solids, basically fibers, are also key and have the same role.

Sugar
This is also a key part of the story. Beyond sweetness, sugar has several roles. Firstly, it adds body aka solids (as mentioned above). Crucially, sugar determines the ice cream's softness or scoopability by depressing, i.e., lowering, the freezing point. This is why it is also known as an antifreeze.

Freezing point depression is a term you often hear in ice cream making. The temperature at which a liquid turns into a solid is the freezing point. With water, that's 32°F. So, depressing the freezing point means it needs to be colder for a liquid to turn into a solid. How much the freezing point is depressed aligns with how soft or scoopable the ice cream is when frozen.

Sugar effectively lowers freezing points because it totally disrupts the structure. Sugar, dissolved in water, prevents water from making the hydrogen bonds required to become solid by literally getting in the way. Without hydrogen bonds, liquid water cannot form ice crystals! Instead of forming hydrogen bonds with other water molecules, they form hydrogen bonds with sugar. Sugar molecules physically interrupt the structure, holding the mixture together but preventing ice crystals from getting bigger and, therefore, crunchier on the palate. The less sugar there is, the larger the ice crystals will be.

Fruit solids
Since sorbet usually is fat-free, we can't rely on butterfat or lactose's ability to temper those crystals. That means we need a higher proportion of solids (in the form of fruit fibers) and sugar to get a non-icy product, predominantly sugar. For context, sorbet needs 20–30% sugar in the final product, while ice cream has 10–12%.

Salt and alcohol
It's worth noting that salt is also an antifreeze, but it can't be added in large amounts due to its potent flavoring abilities. Alcohol is also an antifreeze. Ethanol, the compound found in wine, beer, spirits, etc., doesn't freeze solid until -173°F, so adding a portion of booze into your frozen desserts can also provide softness.

JUDGING SUGAR CONCENTRATION

For ice creams and sorbets, the sugar concentration of your base is key because, beyond sweetness, it defines softness and scoopability once frozen. One way to find out how much sugar is dissolved in a liquid is through a tool called a refractometer, which measures brix. The brix tells us how dense the liquid is with sugar (1% sugar = 1 brix, etc.). This is handy if you are working with market fruits as the sugar in each crop can change from year to year. You simply purée your fruit and then add sugar until it reaches that magic 25–30% sugar content, which gives you a thick, creamy sorbet. Less accurate, but still legit, is the egg trick.

A fresh egg is filled with air, so when there's around 25% sugar concentration, the egg will float and a 1-inch section of the shell should be visible from above. This is helpful and though it won't tell you if you've got too much sugar, it will indicate you're in the right place.

The egg test

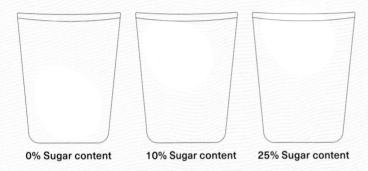

0% Sugar content   10% Sugar content   25% Sugar content

NO ICE CREAM MACHINE? NO PROBLEM

Ice cream machines work by churning/aerating mixtures while freezing them to break down ice crystals. Let's be honest, having an ice cream machine at home isn't practical for most of us. Fortunately, there are other options. As well as the no-churn recipes, a food processor or blender is a very useful tool.

With the motorized blending action, food processors do a good impression of a piece of professional equipment called a Pacojet. A Pacojet produces ice cream and sorbet by finely shaving frozen blocks of the ice cream/sorbet base into very thin sheets, essentially puréeing it without melting it. We can approximate this by freezing sorbet or ice cream bases and blending them until smooth.

If you don't have a food processor, you can use the old-school, totally equipment-free no-machine method—freezing your base in a home freezer, removing it every 30 minutes, and agitating it with a fork until it is smooth and almost entirely frozen. Basically, you're acting as the lo-fi churn in an ice cream machine. This process takes about 4 hours, compared to 15–20 minutes in a machine.

TEXTURE VIA TECHNIQUES

THE LESSON OF PÂTÉ SUCRÉE AND PÂTÉ SABLÉE

In one of my first jobs, the recipes for pâté sucrée, or "sweet pastry," and pâté sablée, or "sandy pastry," were kept in the same folder but on two pieces of paper. The ingredients looked pretty similar—fat, sugar, flour, and eggs—but the methods differed. If the recipe called for sablée, I'd rub the flour and fat together until breadcrumbs formed before adding the wet ingredients and mixing until just combined.

For sucrée, I'd cream together the butter and sugar before adding the wet ingredients and carefully paddling in the dries. This was one of my first great lessons in seeing how a list of the same ingredients could be expressed differently. Sablée, with the rubbed-together fat and flour, was a crumbly, shorter pastry. Sucrée was snappier, crisper, and did not crumble. What was this sorcery? Technique!

Consider brioche and pie dough. The fat-to-flour ratio is very similar, but the expression of these ingredients is very different. In the case of pie dough, we are minimizing the development of gluten and further interrupting the network with irregular-size pieces of fat throughout, resulting in a crispy, flaky, rich dough.

For brioche, we are developing a strong gluten network that the butter can be evenly spread across, resulting in a tender, fine-crumbed dough. The development of gluten is one of the best examples of how technique impacts texture. To learn more, see All About Flour on page 14.

ADDING CONTRAST

When we think about how to approach texture, one of the most important things to consider is contrast. Many of our favorite desserts and baked goods rely on dynamic variation between two elements. Consider a crème brûlée, whose crackled caramel crust and rich, just-set custard are greater as a team.

When you sit down for a plated dessert at a restaurant, see if you can spot all the textural elements at play. Something creamy (ice cream, custard, a ganache), something more substantial (a cake, some pastry, could be poached fruit) and something crunchy (a crumb, a brittle). Desserts like fruit crumbles have stood the test of time because of their inherent make-up of creamy/crunchy/tender.

Plenty of classic baked goods have built-in elements of contrast. Take the crisp pavlova with its pillowy center or chocolate fondant with its melting middle. Other recipes benefit from adding ingredients with an inherent texture. Think of nuts or chocolate chips strewn through a cookie or cake batter, or demerara sugar sprinkled on top of a muffin before baking, a flicker of crunchy sea salt atop a caramel or whole grains mixed through a soda bread.

GELATIN

Gelatin is one of the most common settling agents in the pastry kitchen. In fancy French patisseries, there's rarely an element in the display case that isn't supported by gelatin, be it mousses, jellies, or glazes. So, what is it, and how does it work? Simply put, gelatin is a protein derived from animals and is made up of chains of amino acids. The thing about amino acids? They are BFFs—they are truly obsessed with each other. At room temperature, they stick together in a strong formation.

Adding gelatin to a hot liquid warms up the bonds between the amino acids, which then loosen and move away from each other. As these amino acids break apart, they create bonds with other liquids, and the proteins are dispersed throughout the liquid. As the liquid cools, the BFF amino acids seek each other out again and create a formation. Only this time, there are other things trapped within the mesh—this is what a gel is. If you reheat the gel, it will become liquid again and can be reset multiple times. This gel is enhanced by the hygroscopic—water-loving—sugar (see All About Sugar on page 29).

GELATIN TIPS

There are a few things to look out for:

- Always bloom your gelatin before using. For sheet gelatin, this means soaking in cold water until soft. For powdered gelatin, this means soaking in cold water so there are no granules left. Undissolved gelatin is gritty and unpleasant.

- Beware of enzyme action! Since gelatin is a protein, any fruit that contains the protease enzyme will break it down and wreak havoc with the set. These fruits include kiwi, pineapple, figs, and papaya. Ginger is also a tricky area.

- Acidity can also interfere with the gelling ability as it may denature the proteins involved with the setting.

HOW MUCH TO USE

A safe starting place for fruit juice and jellies is 1 leaf or 3g powdered gelatin per 100g/7 tablespoons of liquid, with 10–20% sugar. For preparations using dairy and cream, like panna cotta, I begin with 0.4–0.5 leaf, or 1.25g/⅓ teaspoon powdered gelatin, to set 100g/7 tablespoons of liquid.

So, what on earth is going on? FAT! When gelatin sets, it prevents liquids from moving around freely. When we use cream, which can be up to 50% fat, there is less water for the gelatin to hold. So, we need at least 50% less gelatin. A good starting point for curds, custards, and anything with components beyond liquid is 0.5–1% of the weight in powdered gelatin. Due to the complicated nature of sheet gelatin, it is easier to calculate the amount of gelatin to use in powdered (grams) then convert.

Approx. setting guidelines

Ingredient	Non-dairy liquids	Dairy liquids
Leaf of gelatin (or)	1	0.4–0.5
Powdered gelatin	3g/1 teaspoon	1.25g/⅓ teaspoon
Liquid	100g/7 tablespoons	100g/7 tablespoons
Sugar	10–20%	10–20%

A note on sheet gelatin

Gelatin remains a murky topic due to its seemingly endless variations (Powdered? Leaf? Bovine? Fish? Bronze? Platinum? ARGH!) and the inconsistency of its notation throughout pastry books. Some pastry books refer to sheets by number (but what size?) and some will refer to sheets by weight.

Both of these have problems. Let's start with sheet size. Gelatin sheets in professional kitchens are double the length of those sold in supermarkets. Many books will not take this into account.

Now, weight. Sheet gelatin comes in many different blooms: titanium, bronze, silver, gold, and platinum. These blooms represent different strengths and qualities (namely clarity), with titanium being the weakest and platinum being the strongest. So, you need more bronze gelatin to set the same amount of liquid as you would with gold gelatin.

Rather confusingly though, four sheets of bronze will set the same amount of liquid as four sheets of platinum. This means you can generally swap like-for-like between the blooms when using sheets without any serious issues. This is because the sheets are produced at different thicknesses, which are pretty imperceptible to the eye. However, a bronze sheet weighs almost 100% more platinum. Due to this difference in weight, the sheets are interchangable, even though they look the same.

WHEN ACID MEETS DAIRY

Some desserts are set entirely by acid. Creamy desserts, like posset, are made by adding acid to dairy, which leads to the coagulation of the proteins, resulting in a lush, softly set cream. But if you add lemon juice to heated milk, you'd get ricotta. So, why doesn't that happen with posset? Fat and sugar!

Although the acidified proteins clump up, the fat in the dairy gets in the way of those clumps, while the sugar keeps the texture smooth, again interfering with the network of proteins. Hence, the final smooth result, similar to the behavior of dairy and sugar in custard (see All About Eggs on page 42).

How to build your own posset
Note: the more acidic the juice, the less you need to set it.

Cream	100g/7 tablespoons
Sugar	25–35g/2–3 tablespoons
Acidic juice (e.g., lemon juice, passionfruit juice, lime juice)	20–30g/1 tablespoon plus 1 teaspoon–2 tablespoons
Butter (optional for richness)	20g/1 tablespoon plus 1 teaspoon

ONE MORE SQUEEZE

Whether it's a chewy crust or a crunchy crumb that you desire, or whether you're looking for a custard that dollops or one that pours, perfecting the texture of your bakes can be as simple as adjusting your technique!

Keeping an eye on the balance of tenderizers and tougheners will also help you achieve the desired outcome. It's usually not a single ingredient that makes the difference, but rather it's a master class in teamwork. From delicate crumbs to buttery flaky pastry, the unique combination of ratios and techniques will deliver the best textures in baking. Remember, you are in control!

8.

TECHNICAL OVERVIEW

Good technique underpins our recipes in baking. A perfectly mixed cake will still fall if it's taken out of the oven too early, and many techniques can only be earned with practice and persistence.

The first time you pipe an eclair, it probably won't look perfect, but that's OK—it's all part of the journey. From understanding what baking actually is, to lining techniques that will make sure your pastry never shrinks, to the magic of infusions, this chapter will explore the techniques, temperatures, and theory that really matter.

When I bake, I think of it like a house being built. The recipe is the architectural plan and the mixing process is the first hint of the layout taking shape on the empty plot. Once it goes into the oven, every ingredient acts as a different tradesperson, each having a unique ability and contribution to the final house, working one-by-one but also side-by-side. First, the fats come in to lay the foundation, followed by the rising agents or yeasts, which build the walls. Next, the proteins—both eggs and flour— raise the roof, while the starch installs all of the fixtures. The browning of the proteins— the Maillard reactions—come in to put the finishing touches to it all.

SO, WHAT ACTUALLY IS BAKING?

Baking is the process of heat transfer from a source—like an oven element—to the surface and then to the center of a dough or batter. As the heat travels through it, it undergoes a magical transformation, resulting in a distinct crust and crumb. Depending on the ratio of ingredients and the baking technique, there may be more than one texture in the final baked good, as well as variety in color, crumb size, and firmness.

Watch a cookie go into the oven and you'll notice a few things. Firstly, it will spread. Next, it will start bubbling and rise up a little, creating satisfying cracks and craters on top. Finally, it will settle and brown. But what is actually happening? Whether you're baking a cookie, eclair, or brioche bun, the same reactions happen in a specific order. However, the proportion of ingredients, plus the oven temperature, will impact the outcome.

The baking process

Start	Dough/batter goes into the oven
86°F	Fats melt and release the air trapped within the crystal network, resulting in the expansion (rise). The fat enriches the surrounding ingredients, lubricating the structure. The baked good might spread as the fat melts
122°F	Rising agents activate: yeasts have a final burst of activity before dying, rapidly releasing CO_2. Chemical-rising agents undergo reactions and release CO_2. Air and gases already existing within the structure of the batter or dough begin to expand, causing your baked good to rise
176°F	Proteins coagulate—i.e., turn from a liquid to a solid, hardening the structure. This is predominantly and most noticeable with egg proteins, but it also happens with gluten, the trusty flour protein. If your recipe is made with high-protein flour, it will likely have a firmer crust
149–203°F	Starch fully gelatinizes, setting the structure for the baked good. Starch molecules absorb water from the surrounding structure and swell. Baked goods with high levels of water, like cake, will have high levels of starch gelatinization, resulting in soft crumbs, while baked goods with low levels of water, like shortbread, will be set predominantly by hardening gluten proteins and be crunchy
248°F (surface temp)	A crust begins to form as steam and moisture are lost from the structure and Maillard reactions occur
320°F (surface temp)	If sugar is present on the outside, caramelization will occur
Finish	Baked good is removed from the oven

Cooling bakes

The right way to cool your bakes will vary from recipe to recipe; for cakes, the best practice is usually to remove from the oven and let cool in the pan for 10–15 minutes on a cooling rack until you can safely handle it. Then remove the pan and let it cool completely on the rack.

Doming

Doming is a result of the outside of the cake cooking and setting faster than the center, which continues to expand long after the edges have set. Some bakers use cake strips—an insulated collar that wraps around pans—to try to prevent this.

What's the crack?

One of the most frustrating things that can happen to bakes is when they crack. This is particularly prevalent with custards or anything that relies on egg coagulation to set, like cheesecakes or airy egg foam cakes (see All About Eggs on page 40). Cracking is always a result of overcooking— the egg proteins bond too tightly and separate. But it can also happen if you cool your custards too quickly. If there is a rapid temperature change, the outside of the custard will cool down much more quickly than the inside.

As it cools, the proteins begin to settle and contract while the hot middle continues to cook and expand. These opposite tensions can result in a fissure. The best way to counteract this is to avoid overcooking your custards and cool them down gently at room temperature before moving to the fridge.

As for chiffon and egg sponge cakes, make sure to bake at the correct temperature. If the temperature is too high, the outside of the cake will set before the center has even warmed up and the middle will end up bursting out, causing cracks.

THE RISE AND FALL

Whenever we bake, several reactions happen simultaneously. A good recipe will ensure these happen at the right time and in order. When the gases release, for example, there should be enough hardening egg or gluten proteins to capture the gases. If a recipe is poorly balanced, it might expand rapidly and then fall. This also explains why many recipes will warn against opening the oven door: by opening the door, you risk a drop in temperature. If this happens before the starch and proteins have begun to set or have set properly, the structure will fall, releasing all the gases and air generated during the baking process.

If a cake is underbaked, it will fall as it cools because the structure is not set and might be gummy and unpleasant to eat. This is either a result of poor recipe formulation or a poor bake—the batter not reaching a high enough temperature for the starch, egg, and flour proteins to coagulate.

THE DEAL WITH CARRYOVER COOKING

Carryover cooking is when your baked good continues to cook even after it has been removed from the heat source. This is why recipes might ask you to remove a custard tart from the oven while it is still wobbly or a few degrees cooler than the desired cooking temperature. This is because a lot of baked goods will retain enough heat to continue transferring it into the parts where it is cooler, i.e., from the fully cooked edges to the center.

This is particularly important to consider when you are baking something very temperature sensitive, like custards. It's possible that the residual heat could be enough to curdle the custard. Visual cues like the wobble (the custard is just set around the edges but still jiggly in the middle) are essential to avoid this.

Cut into a cake while it's still steaming and you'll know how fragile it is: Crumbaggedon! As our bakes cool down, several processes also occur: the fats and proteins resolidify, and the sugar and starch molecules recrystallize, which makes our cakes firm up. For more information on how this leads to staling, check out Texture on page 95.

WHAT TEMPERATURE?

The optimal baking temperature will vary depending on what you are making, but the goal is always the same: to cook evenly and thoroughly without burning or drying out.

Higher temperatures suit recipes that rely on butter to lift (see How Things Rise on page 69), like puff pastry or croissants, while lower temperatures suit recipes that are sensitive to curdling, like baked custards. Some recipes may require the oven to be preheated to a higher temperature and then turned down partway through the bake. This is a useful technique for things like choux pastry, which benefits from an initial blast followed by a longer drying-out period.

If your oven temperature is too high, the outside of your bakes will border on burned before the middle has had a chance to cook. If it's too low, it may be heavy.

Let's not forget that oven temperatures really do vary from oven to oven. An oven thermometer is the best way to keep things accurate and avoid disappointment from a bake that didn't line up with the recipe's directions.

HOW DO I KNOW IT'S READY?

Learning exactly when your baked good is ready can take some practice. Recipes should give you a reliable timeframe, but all our ovens are different, and there are times when you'll have to use your intuition.

Color
The progressing color of your baked good as it undergoes Maillard reactions (see Color on page 84) can give you a clue as to whether it's ready or if your oven is at the wrong temperature. Taking visual cues from your baked good will help you know if you need to course correct. If your cake is darkening too much on the edges while the middle is still totally liquid, you may need to adjust your oven or cover your bake with foil to mitigate the color. It can be hard to use color to judge anything made with cocoa powder effectively, as it is already a dark brown.

Spring
For cakes, a crust that springs back merrily when pressed, but feels relatively firm, is a good indication that it is ready. It may also pull away slightly from the sides of the pan as the starch and egg set and contract. Pair this with other cues to confirm it is done. For cakes, a skewer or toothpick inserted in the middle that comes out clean or with just a few crumbs barely hanging on is a pretty good way to go. For cookies and flourless cakes, the key to fudgy centers is underbaking—if it springs, you've gone too far!

Temperature
So, the saying goes, "When in doubt, stab it with a thermometer." Internal temperature can be a reliable indicator of doneness for many bakes but should always be deployed with the other cues.

A level of common sense is required here. Jams, for example, should always be tested by spooning a small amount onto a cold plate and chilling in the freezer for 2 minutes—this will give you a clear indication of how it will be when it cools. And custard will always depend on the formulation and ratio of eggs to dairy (see All About Eggs on page 44).

Wobble
The irresistible wobble of custard or cheesecake can be a good indicator that it's time to take it out of the oven. A perfectly baked custard or cheesecake will have a slight jiggle in the center when gently shaken, but the edges will be set.

Bubbles
In the case of fruit pies, success often relies on the filling properly thickening. The best way to judge this is to see if the filling is bubbling—this is a sign that it has reached a high enough temperature to thicken properly.

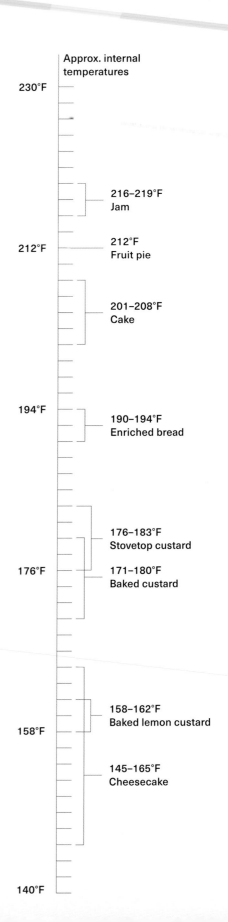

Approx. internal temperatures

230°F

216–219°F
Jam

212°F — 212°F
Fruit pie

201–208°F
Cake

194°F — 190–194°F
Enriched bread

176–183°F
Stovetop custard

176°F — 171–180°F
Baked custard

158–162°F
Baked lemon custard

158°F

145–165°F
Cheesecake

140°F

Toothpick

The toothpick test is a good way to check for doneness in some cakes. Insert a toothpick into the center and see if it comes out clean or with a few dry crumbs. If so, it's ready! If the toothpick is covered in wet batter, it needs more time. However, it should be noted that in some cases, like a flourless chocolate cake, a clean toothpick may indicate it is overbaked.

Your own baking intuition

There will be times that you have to break free from a recipe. This could be due to personal preference or could be because your oven behaves radically differently to the one it was developed in. Don't forget that you are always in control! Like a bit more color on your shortbread? Leave 'em in a few extra minutes! Your roasted fruit still rock hard even though the timer has gone off? Keep going till they look right to you! You've got this.

Cooking methods

While most sweet recipes will have you preheating your oven, there are a few other cooking techniques worth being familiar with.

	Description	Pros	Best for
Baking	Cooking food by dry heat, usually in the oven	Exposed to heat from all angles, goods will bake evenly and a crust will form	Breads, croissants, cakes, cookies, pies
Broiling	Cooking food under a direct high heat source in the oven	Intense direct high heat produces strong browning and caramelization reactions	Crème brûlée, baked Alaska
Deep frying	Immersing food in hot oil until crispy and golden brown. The temperature will change depending on what you are frying—usually in the range of 320–356°F	Crunchy, crisp crust with a tender center	Doughnuts, beignets, crullers
Poaching	Cooking food in liquid below boiling point until tender on a stovetop or in the oven	Gentle cooking that softens the fibers of food while enhancing moisture, flavor, and tenderness	Under-ripe or bland fruit, meringues for floating islands
Roasting	Cooking food by dry heat in an oven, often with fat	The surface crisps and flavors intensify, undergoing browning and caramelization reactions	Roasted fruit
Steaming	Cooking food by exposing it to steam until cooked through	Gentle cooking that undergoes no browning or caramelization	Steamed puddings, bao buns

LINING TART CASES AND BLIND BAKING

If I had to choose a subject that confounded me—and so many other bakers at the beginning of their baking journeys—it's the question of pastry shrinkage. It happens to us all. But there was a real turning point for me.

At my first job in New York, I was sent downstairs to help line tarts. I got to the basement to see Christian, the sous chef, surrounded by hundreds of mini tart rings. He asked if I knew how to line tart cases, to which I replied, "Yeah, of course" (which was half-true). Chef Christian walked to the freezer and produced sheets of ultra-thin, rolled-out sweet pastry. I had never seen pastry prepared like this—it was genius! Rather than cutting out circles and then lining a single piece, Chef Christian took a knife and cut perfectly-sized strips and circles.

Then, using these two pieces, he masterfully placed them in the ring and gently fused them together . . . and, BEHOLD: the perfect tart case appeared.

After the hundreds were lined, they took a snooze in the freezer for 20 minutes while the oven preheated. Just as we were about to load them in, I had a brainwave. "Chef," I said, "what about the baking beans?!" so sure that I had saved us all from imminent shrinkage doom. He looked at me for a moment and then, without replying, loaded all of the tart shells into the oven, shut the door, and said, "Just wait and see!" And so, I did. Not one of the tart cases shrank, nor did the bases billow. What magic was this? I had lived in fear of shrinkage, and I had always used baking beans. Seeing this made me question everything. So, what is really going on when our pastry shrinks?

Issue	Solution
Poor formulation Sometimes it really is as simple as this. The recipe, ingredients, and methods are always at the heart of your baked goods. Sometimes recipes just have too many tenderizers (see Texture on page 92), and your fate is set before it even goes into the oven. The pastry will likely shrink whatever you do.	Use a reliable recipe with a good balance of tenderizers and tougheners for a pastry that eats well but doesn't melt too much in the oven. Too much fat or sugar will prevent the pastry from setting.
The elastic factor Pastry contains flour, which means it contains gluten. When you make sweet pastry, you really want to limit the gluten formation as much as possible. Although elasticity is a favorable characteristic in pizza dough, it's really not something we're after for pastry. Some gluten is necessary and will be formed while making the sweet pastry, but minimizing it is favorable. Most sweet pastry recipes will contain a large amount of butter and some sugar, which help keep the gluten at bay.	Err on the side of undermixing—when you add the flour, you can always incorporate any dry bits by hand. Mechanical mixers are great but very efficient at developing gluten, so you should proceed with caution. Rest and chill the dough adequately before lining/baking, allowing the gluten to relax.
Dodgy lining This is, above all, the biggest culprit for shrinkage. During baking, the butter in the pastry will melt before the crumb has a chance to set, which means the pastry is in a bit of a sensitive situation. Therefore, it is important to make sure there is nowhere for the pastry to shrink to! If there are any gaps or holes, the pastry will move to fill them in while in its soft state, resulting in shrinking sides. It's as simple as that. This is why a good lining technique is essential.	Line with care. The more you squish, squash, and pull your pastry, the higher the chances that it will shrink later. As well as putting pressure on the dough, you're essentially leaving unsupported gaps for it to melt into. Imagine the gluten in your pastry has a memory (it's elastic!), so if you don't treat it with care from the outset, it might be payback time when it comes to baking. Find which lining technique works for you and check as you go. If you are using a tart ring, just lift up the base and see if it goes right to the edges. It's those pesky corners that will give your pastry room to shrink, so don't give it even a millimeter to do so!

What is blind baking?

Blind baking is when you pre-bake your tart or pie crust before adding the filling. This process helps to ensure a crisp base (no soggy bottoms!) in your finished tart. It will depend from recipe to recipe, but as a rule of thumb, if your filling is very wet or has a shorter bake (less than 45 minutes–1 hour) it is sensible to blind bake.

LINING TECHNIQUES

Method A aka "the classic"
Take a single piece of pastry, slightly larger than your pan, and lay it across, gently pressing it into the edges of the pan. Check that it has gone all the way into the corners.

Method B aka the "omg why didn't I think of that sooner?"
Roll out your dough. First, use the pastry ring to mark bottoms. Then measure the width of your pastry ring and mark strips to the same width. Chill the pastry for 30 minutes. Once firm, cut out the bottoms and place in the tart rings on a baking sheet. Then pick up the strips and coil into the tart rings. Use your fingers to fuse the edge pieces and bottoms together. Chill for 10 minutes, then pick up each tart ring and look at the bottom to check there are no gaps.

Method C aka the "screw-the-rules method"
Freeze your pastry block, grate it, and then press the bits of grated pastry into the pan, trying to work as evenly as possible.

Method D aka "just try and stop me"
Take the freshly mixed, still-soft pastry and squish it directly into your pan or tart cases.

BAKING BEANS

Baking beans, in the form of raw rice, coins, ceramic beads, or anything heavy and heatproof, are used to weigh down pastry as it bakes. Placed into a tart case, with parchment paper or foil acting as a barrier, their role is to prevent the bottom of a tart from rising up. Halfway through blind baking, once the pastry has been set, the weights are removed to allow the pastry to color.

But why does pastry rise up? As the butter melts and produces steam, the pastry sometimes puffs up as air tries to escape. Also, if there are any gaps in your lining, the air trapped here will expand, and this will also make your pastry lift. Provided you have lined your tart case well and there is no air trapped under the case, baking beans are not strictly necessary when making small tart cases. For larger tart cases, which are more likely to have billowy bases, weighing down the center is sensible.

When working with flaky pastry, like pie dough or pâte brisée, baking beans are essential.

EGG WASHING

Egg wash plays a clear role visually—the proteins undergoing Maillard reactions result in the shiny, mahogany crusts we love (see Color on page 84 for more details).

It can also play a more practical role. Once your tart is blind baked—and this is especially useful if you are filling it with something very liquid like custard—it is sensible to brush the case with egg wash and then return it to the oven to create a protective seal. Some chefs even do this two or three times. This is an effort to create a liquid-tight barrier between the wet filling and the pastry shell.

The deal with docking

Docking is a technique of—for lack of a better word—stabbing your pastry with lots of little holes (using a fork) before baking. These effectively act as a series of vents, so the steam produced during baking can escape. This can be helpful when baking butter- and moisture-rich pastry, like puff pastry, but it is not essential when working with sweet or shortcrust pastry.

INFUSING

One of the best ways to level up your bakes is through infusions. In baking, an infusion refers to the process of steeping an aromatic ingredient, such as herbs, spices, or tea leaves, in a liquid, such as water, milk, or cream. The liquid is passed through a sieve, leaving the flavor behind. The liquid can then be used to add a subtle or intense flavor—depending on your method and desire!—to custards, ice creams, and cakes. From adding a vanilla pod to your custard (see page 342) to the chamomile-infused chiffon cake (see page 151), you'll see the way infusions open up a world of flavor.

Deciding between a hot and cold infusion, as well as the proportion of ingredients and time, has a major impact on the intensity and flavor of the final infusion:

- A hot infusion means heating up your liquid and adding your flavorings, then letting the liquid cool for 30 minutes–1 hour, depending on the desired strength.
- A hot/cold infusion means heating up your liquid, adding your flavorings, then allowing it to cool in the fridge for 8–24 hours.
- A cold infusion means introducing your liquid and flavoring without any heat. A cold infusion usually takes 24–48 hours and should be done in the fridge, especially for dairy.

Temperature has a huge impact on the flavor of infusions. Ever tried to make a cup of tea and impatiently poured the kettle before it was ready? Then you'll know that heat is the key to a fast, highly flavored infusion. But it isn't that simple. A hot infusion may result in the release of astringent, bitter flavor compounds and your mixture is often highly pigmented as a result. A cold infusion, though much more time-consuming, can often result in a cleaner flavor that suits sensitive infusions with flavor compounds that may be damaged by hot or boiling liquids. Some flavor-carrying oils may also be dulled or modified by heat, so leaving them unchanged will let us enjoy the flavors.

There is a simple way to speed up infusion time that is not heat related: increasing the surface area. This is why commercial teabags are filled with powdered leaves and why we grind coffee before using it. By tearing (e.g., herbs), chopping up (e.g., peels), or lightly smashing (e.g., coffee beans and spices), we are going to increase the strength and speed of the infusion.

As well as this, volatile bases, like alcohol, will infuse more quickly and strongly. Toasting your aromatic ingredient before adding it to a liquid will also improve the infusion. Don't forget to always reweigh your liquid after infusing as it will have reduced—you will need to top up with fresh liquid.

Here are a few ideas for infusions with approximate ratios—these should be experimented with to suit your own tastes!

INFUSIONS

Citrus zests

1–3% of liquid weight

Beware that some more acidic peels, like lemon, may split dairy. So, if using in this context, it's best to add to warm or cool, but not hot, dairy.

Coffee beans

2% (finely ground) of liquid weight
5% (whole beans) of liquid weight

Using crushed whole beans will impart a lot of flavor without adding color.

Elderflowers (fresh)

10–15% of liquid weight

A pinch of citric acid or a few lemon peels can go a long way in making elderflower infusions pop!

Fresh herbs (mint, basil, lime leaves)

5–10% of liquid weight

For the cleanest flavors, I prefer cold infusions for herbs. Once infused, blitz herbs into the liquid and proceed or remove before using.

Fruit pits (noyaux)

2–5% of liquid weight

You can make an infusion using pits of plums and apricots—be aware that pits contain amygdalin that converts to cyanide after eating. There's little to no risk of this if you're just using the pits for infusing as the toxins are very diluted throughout the entire recipe.

Ginger (fresh)

5% of liquid weight

Slice or grate. Warning, ginger can curdle dairy!

Lemongrass

10% of liquid weight

Bash stalks slightly.

Loose-leaf tea (chai, green tea, hibiscus)

1–2% of liquid weight

Tea leaves tend to go astringent in hot infusions, so limit infusing time to 20 minutes (hot). Cold infusion should not have this issue.

Nuts

15–20% of liquid weight

Roasting the nuts before adding to hot cream is essential for the best flavor.

Oils/extracts (rose water, orange blossom, peppermint)

2–3 tsp per 1 quart/liter

Go carefully as these can be very strong. No need to steep—simply add to the recipe as required.

Spices—whole (star anise, cardamom, cinnamon)

1–5% of liquid weight

The strength of the infusion really varies among spices.

Vanilla pods

1–2 per 1 quart/liter

Vanilla extract

2–4 tsp per 1 quart/liter

Split and scrape the pod for the best results. You can also play around with toasting or burning the vanilla beans before infusing.

FOOD PROCESSORS

A food processor is a useful—though sometimes bulky—tool in the kitchen, which uses a motor and rotating blades to chop, purée, and emulsify food. While it is not an essential piece of equipment, it opens the door to some handy processes. The blades create a vortex that pulls the contents of the container toward them. Thanks to this action, you can mix smooth cake batters (it's great at creaming: see All About Fat on page 59); blitz together butter and flour for short pie doughs and cookies; blend nuts to a paste; produce frozen desserts; and even whip up a brioche at record speed.

One of the best tricks in the kitchen is making small batches of enriched dough or brioche in the food processor. Thanks to the brute force and speed of the blades, as well as the more compact bowl, there is maximum contact and impact between the dough, the blade, and the bowl itself. This intense dough mixing session results in rapid gluten development, some 10x faster than if you were to use a stand mixer.

The resultant dough will have a different crumb than one made traditionally—it won't rise as high and the crumb will be more erratic, but its speed is worth the trade-off.

To read about how food processors make a good alternative to ice cream machines, see Texture on page 98.

WATER BATHS

I have to confess that reading the words *water bath* used to make my eyes glaze over. I'd even avoid recipes that would ask for it. But when I finally realized what a bounty of benefits water bath cooking brings, I decided to get over it. Water bath cooking is the process of partially submerging the baking dish or container in water for the baking process. So, what makes this technique so effective? (Before we continue, it should be noted that a water bath may also be referred to as a bain-marie. Whichever term is used, it may be referring to a heatproof bowl set over a simmering pot of water to aid gentle cooking or melting.)

Let's take cheesecake, for example. Heat exchange, which happens when you put something in the oven, is quite different between water and your cheesecake vs. air and your cheesecake. The water absorbs some of the heat from the oven, allowing the temperature to be regulated, resulting in a gentler and more even bake. As water has a maximum temperature of 212°F, it gently turns to steam during the cooking process. As well as this, a symbiotic relationship forms between the water and the cheesecake that is submerged in it. As the cheesecake heats up, some of the heat is transferred to the water, and vice versa, minimizing temperature fluctuations. Leaving the cheesecake in the water bath while it cools also helps regulate the temperature for extra smoothness.

So, why do some gentle cooking recipes require a water bath and others don't? Custard tarts, for example, are never baked in a water bath. Instead, they are baked in a low oven—around 250°F oven. So, would this work for cheesecake? Yes—a lower temperature would work, but it would take a very, very long time. Cheesecake is usually a lot deeper than a custard tart, and we are not heating up our filling to give it a head start during the mixing process for cheesecake. It might seem overcomplicated, but a water bath really is the only way to guarantee gentle cooking at a reasonable pace.

RPM Speeds (approx.)

Equipment	RPM
Blender	17,000–30,000
Food processor	1,700
Hand mixer	700–1,200
Stand mixer	40–200

Baking materials

Your choice of baking pan—whether glass, silicone, stone, or metal—significantly impacts your baking results due to differing heat transfer abilities.

Glass and stone are insulators, leading to longer baking times and a higher risk of overcooking or burning. Silicone is a poor heat conductor, potentially hindering browning, though some contain metal powder to improve this. Metal, a superior heat conductor, is typically the best option for baking.

Dark metal pans promote quicker browning and baking than light-colored ones like aluminum, as they absorb heat faster. Be prepared to adjust baking times accordingly based on your equipment collection!

Piping

If you intend to use various piping tips with the same mixture, follow these steps:

- *Load all of the mixture into a piping bag without fitting a piping tip.*
- *Take this filled piping bag and insert it into a second piping bag that has your desired piping tip already attached to it.*
- *To switch between piping tips, you can simply remove the filled inner bag from the second bag with the piping tip and replace the piping tip as needed.*
- *This method allows for quick and hassle-free interchange of piping tips while using the same mixture.*

Thank you to Holly Cochrane, food stylist for this book, who showed me this!

Liaison batter

To retain maximum airiness in your baked goods, it's often a good idea to employ a liaison batter. This is a practical strategy when combining ingredients of contrasting densities—such as egg foam and melted butter in a genoise sponge cake (page 131).

To address this density gap, merely whisk a small amount of foamy egg into the melted butter. This liaison batter integrates more smoothly into the foamy egg mixture. Think of it like tempering a mixture, like you would eggs for custard (see page 42).

PIPING

Piping is a skill that, I'm afraid, has no shortcuts: it's something that can only be earned with time. If you are really keen to improve, practicing with a readily available and cost-effective ingredient like vegetable shortening is a worthwhile task. Whether you're piping decor on a tart or choux paste for eclairs, the most important factor for good piping is even pressure and avoiding air bubbles.

When you fill a piping bag, it's important to do your best to squish and squash it to remove as many air bubbles as possible. When you are piping and there is a gap in the flow, it will be imprinted *forever* in your choux or leave an annoying hole in your buttercream decor.

Remember that most things—like choux—can be scooped up and repiped many times over, so don't be afraid of trying it a few times until you're happy.

Although I don't use them all the time, having various piping tips is useful. These are a really good thing to put on gift lists! I like to have wide star tips for piping cookies, narrow/many-toothed star tips for eclairs, a St Honoré tip for fancy piping (though you can fake this by just cutting your piping bag at an angle) and, of course, a Bismarck tip for doughnuts and filling everything.

FOLDING

Air is an undercelebrated factor in baking. I've come to realize that a lot of the technical troubles that we come across in baking relate to the successful—or erroneous—introduction of air into our bakes. From the improper lining of tart cases to overly enthusiastic folding techniques, air can sometimes make or break our bakes.

I see folding as the final frontier of many recipes. From a chocolate mousse to a genoise sponge cake, a recipe can live or die on your folding technique. Most often utilized when incorporating dry ingredients, like flour, to a light, airy base, like whisked eggs, good technique goes a long way.

Folding is when you methodically and gently cut through mixtures while adding well-sifted dry ingredients in several parts. It can also be used when mixing together two ingredients that need to stay airy, like chocolate ganache and whipped cream. For best results, use a capital D motion, slicing through the foam's center and using the bowl's edge to guide the utensil. I always prefer to use a wide, flat spatula, though some chefs swear by the virtues of a metal spoon or even a balloon whisk.

Once a fold is complete, turn the bowl 45 degrees and repeat. Poor folding technique is often the culprit in heavy, flat sponge cakes. Moving your ingredients to an extra-wide bowl and increasing the surface area can be really helpful in promoting good technique since you don't have to dig deeply into the mixture to fold it, thus breaking fewer bubbles each time you fold.

HOW TO BUILD A BAKE

So, you want to develop your own recipes? Best. News. Ever!

Building and developing your own recipes requires creativity, patience, and a bit of perseverance. The easiest way to start on this path is to mix and match similar ingredients in tried-and-tested recipes: changing almonds for hazelnuts, swapping light for dark brown sugar, substituting in seasonal fruit, altering the fat, or adding spices are good places to begin. These are all additions you can make without drastically altering the structure. I love thinking of recipes as balanced equations—a harmonious blend of fat, sugar, eggs, and flour.

It all depends on what your goal is, but when it comes to judging the range of potential variations, you need to think about what you want from the outcome before you get your scales out and your oven on. Do you want your cookies to spread more? Try increasing the fat and sugar. Do you want your dough to be easier to work with? Try increasing the flour. Do you want your pastry to be less flaky? Try reducing the butter and leaving it in smaller pieces. Do you want your dough to be richer? Try hydrating with fatty egg yolks or dairy. And you know what, if it doesn't quite work out, just think of it as a data point for your next bake.

I always try to keep the overall balance of hydration and fat consistent—keeping an eye on this will help maintain the texture but let you experiment with flavor. If you are building a recipe that relies on the set from eggs, like a baked custard, playing around with the ratio of eggs to dairy will ensure a consistent set.

Learning to deeply understand the role of each ingredient, why it reacts (and if it hasn't, why it hasn't) with the help of the reference sections and the charts, you'll get a good idea of what can change and how much, what is crucial, and what is not. The matrix at the back of the book (see page 344) is also filled with ideas about how to mix and match the recipes. And although knowledge is power, I'll never underestimate the importance of trial and error. Some days there will be disasters, no matter how perfect something looks on paper! Learning to troubleshoot or doing a post-mortem will often give you the insight you need to make adjustments.

What to look out for

Ratios and scaling

Is there an obvious ratio or scaling error? If your baked good is too dry, perhaps there are too many tougheners in there. And if it doesn't have enough structure, there are too many tenderizers (see Texture on page 92).

Temperature

Is your oven temperature accurate? An oven that runs too hot or too cool can lead to uneven or undercooked baked goods (see the baking process table on page 104). Invest in an oven thermometer to check your oven's temperature accuracy if you aren't confident it is right.

Rising agents

Check the efficacy of your rising agents. From expired yeast to old baking powder, you may not be to blame for flat buns or dense cakes (see How Things Rise on page 74).

Mixing process

Evaluate your mixing process. Did you overmix or undermix? Or did you not adequately rest the dough? Overmixing can lead to tough, chewy baked goods, while undermixing can result in uneven textures or dry pockets throughout, while lack of resting may result in warped shapes.

THE NEXT STEPS

So, what now? Turn that oven on!

Whether you want to create your own or just be a better baker, the recipes I've included in the next section of this book will take you through a series of flavors and techniques. Perhaps you have your sights set on a lofty choux tower or maybe you just want to make something great to dunk in tea. I hope you'll dip in and out of them as you please, learning as you go.

Every recipe in this book has been developed on the basis of the foundational rules for each ingredient, making room for each one to shine, with notes on which techniques are exhibited should you want to remind yourself of what is happening when you check the wobble of your tart. By referencing the techniques, you'll realize how much your skill set expands every time you bake.

If you're new to baking, I recommend starting out on the Afternoon recipes before jumping to the Day or Weekend sections so you can hone those skills. Trying out a shorter recipe will help you nail a technique before moving on to the more complex version: beginning your lamination journey with flaky cheese and pickle scones (see page 183) or rough puff pastry (see page 128) will kickstart your journey toward perfect croissants (see page 306) or a spectacular apricot custard mille-feuille (see page 270).

Whether you've got an afternoon, a day, or a weekend to delve into them, I hope you'll use these recipes as a way to explore the world of ingredients and techniques at your fingertips, marking off when you've coagulated eggs or when you've whipped air into your fat or when you've hit the perfect sugar temperature. And though there is plenty to get stuck into, I also hope you'll take to the other books on your shelf and be able to look at the recipes in a new light. Spying where the sugars differ or where the fat is center stage and having a complete understanding of why the eggs are whipped for 17 minutes (or realizing you don't need to!). It's the foundational rules that prop up our recipes.

Remember, you can change the flavor, but you can't change how flour will react when you add water. And that's a wonderful thing.

ON TO THE RECIPES ⟶

BASE RECIPES

Meringues 118

Tart pastry 119

Milk bread 122

Bun dough 123

Classic puff pastry 124

Inverted puff pastry 125

Rough puff pastry 128

Pie dough 129

Suet pie dough 130

Sablé Breton 130

Genoise sponge 131

Brioche 133

Brioche variations 135

Choux 136

Craquelin 137

MERINGUES

·

MAKES 10½ OZ / 300G
MERINGUE

Techniques

Egg foam	pg.45
Sugar syrup	pg.33

100g/about 3	egg whites
200g/1 cup	granulated sugar

To get a stiff meringue, you need a ratio of at least 170g/6 oz sugar to 100g/3½ oz egg whites, but 2:1 sugar to egg whites is the most common. Recipes may give you different ratios, but the techniques are always the same. Remember to not stop whisking the whites until you are ready to start folding or they will begin to set and become chunky. Once you have reached stiff peaks, turn the mixer down to low and keep it moving but slowly.

Total: 10–20 mins

5–10 mins	15–20 mins	15–20 mins	15–20 mins
French meringue	Swiss meringue	Swiss-franc meringue	Italian meringue

French meringue

1   Whisk the whites on high speed until generously foamy, then turn the mixer down to medium speed (to avoid sugar explosions!) and add your sugar, bit by bit. Turn the speed back up, then whip to stiff peaks, 2–3 minutes. Use as directed in recipe.

Swiss meringue

1   In the bowl you are going to make the meringue in, whisk the egg whites and sugar. Place the bowl over a simmering saucepan of water and whisk until the mixture is 154–158°F—it will be lovely and warm to the touch and there won't be any crystals of sugar if you rub a bit of the mixture between your fingers. Remove from the heat and whisk on high speed until cool and thick, stiff peaks have formed, about 10 minutes. Use as directed in recipe.

Swiss-franc meringue

1   Preheat the oven to 400°F.

2   Place the sugar on a low, wide baking sheet and heat it in the oven for 7–10 minutes. Remove from the oven and set aside.

3   Whisk the egg whites on high speed until generously foamy, then start adding the warmed sugar bit by bit. Continue whipping for 8–10 minutes, until very stiff and the meringue is cool. Use as directed in recipe.

Italian meringue

1   In a saucepan, dissolve the sugar in a third of its weight of water to make a syrup. Make sure there aren't any sugar crystals on the edge of the pan otherwise it can create crystallization issues later on. Alternatively, cover the pan with a lid for the first 3 minutes of cooking.

2   Heat on high and bring the syrup up to 244°F. While the syrup is heating, whisk the egg whites on high speed until somewhat foamy. Turn the speed down and drizzle the hot syrup into the egg whites. Turn up the speed and whip on high until stiff, shiny, and cool, about 10 minutes. Use as directed in recipe.

Soft peaks
Egg white peak only just holds its shape when the whisk is lifted up

Medium peaks
Egg white peak holds its shape but droops slightly when the whisk is lifted up

Stiff peaks
Egg white peak points directly into the air when the whisk is lifted up

TART PASTRY

·

MAKES 1 LB 2 OZ/500G PASTRY
ENOUGH FOR APPROX 10–12 SMALL TART CASES

Total: 1 hr 30 mins

10 mins	50 mins	30 mins
Mix	Roll out, line & chill	Blind bake

Techniques

Creaming	pg.59
Rolling out	pg.108
Lining a tart	pg.108

90g/6 Tbsp	butter, cold
90g/¾ cup	powdered sugar, sifted (actually do this!!! It is essential there are no lumps. Don't try to skip this, even though it's tempting, I know)
50g/1	whole egg
230g/1¾ cups plus 1 Tbsp	all-purpose flour
30g/⅓ cup	almond flour
1g/¼ tsp	flaky sea salt

Classic tart pastry

This tart pastry will be your new go-to. It is delicious, crisp, and never shrinks. It's impossible to get a bad result with this pastry. You can swap out the almond flour for a different nut or use this quantity to swap in another flour, like rye or buckwheat, or just use more all-purpose flour.

1   Cube your butter into 1-inch chunks and mix on low speed with the sifted powdered sugar using the paddle attachment of a stand mixer until well combined. Do not aerate.

2   Scrape down the sides of the bowl and add the egg. It will appear split and curdled but persevere until it comes together a little, about 30 seconds. Scrape down the sides of the bowl.

3   Mix the dry ingredients together—the all-purpose flour, almond flour, and salt—then pour them into the mixer and mix on low speed until it comes together. That's it!

4   You can now use the pastry as directed in the recipe. You can store your tart pastry in well-wrapped portions to roll out later, or roll out into thin sheets now (I like to roll out the dough while it is still soft). Pastry will keep for 3 days well-wrapped in the fridge or 30 days wrapped in the freezer.

Techniques

Rubbing in	pg.99
Lining a tart	pg.108

230g/1¾ cups plus 1 Tbsp	all-purpose flour
75g/⅔ cup	powdered sugar
1g/¼ tsp	flaky sea salt
155g/⅔ cup	butter, cold
40g/2–3	egg yolks

Rich tart pastry

This is a step-up from the classic pastry. It has a higher proportion of butter and uses all egg yolks to make it even richer. The mixing method creates a sandy, cookie texture. Note that it's harder to work with because of the higher fat content.

1   To make by hand, mix the dry ingredients together. Add the butter, cut into ¾-inch cubes, and rub into the dry ingredients completely until it looks like breadcrumbs. Add the egg yolks and stir together (a round bladed knife is good here) until a dough forms.

2   To make in a stand mixer, mix the dry ingredients together using the paddle attachment. Add the butter, cut into ¾-inch cubes, and beat on low speed until breadcrumbs form, 3–4 minutes. Add the egg yolks and mix until a dough begins to form. Turn onto a clean surface and finish the mixing by hand, ensuring there are no dry bits.

3   You can now use the pastry as directed in the recipe. You can store your tart pastry in well-wrapped portions to roll out later, or roll out into thin sheets now (I like to roll out the dough while it is still soft). Pastry will keep for 3 days well-wrapped in the fridge or 30 days wrapped in the freezer.

Note

You can also make your pastry in a food processor. Pulse the butter and dry ingredients until crumbs form, then add the yolks.

Continued →

TART PASTRY
Continued

·

MAKES ABOUT 1 LB/450G PASTRY
ENOUGH FOR 1 X 8-INCH/20CM TART CASE

Total: 1 hr 30 mins

10 mins	50 mins	30 mins
Mix	Roll out, line & chill	Blind bake

Techniques

Rubbing in	pg.99
Rolling out	pg.108
Lining a tart	pg.108

250g/2 cups	all-purpose flour
1g/¼ tsp	flaky sea salt
Ground black pepper, to season (optional)	
125g/½ cup plus 1 Tbsp	butter, cold
25–50g/ 2–3 Tbsp	water (you can also use 1 egg yolk and 30–50g/2–3 Tbsp water for a richer pastry)
1g/¼ tsp	white wine vinegar

Savory shortcrust pastry

This simple ratio of 2:1 flour to butter will give you a rich crust that is highly adaptable and worth having up your sleeve. By completely crumbing in the butter, you get a rich, snappy, and melty pastry.

1   Place all the dry ingredients into a large bowl with the black pepper, if using. Add the butter, cut into ¾-inch cubes. Using your fingertips, breadcrumb the butter completely into the flour. Drizzle in the water and vinegar (with the egg yolk, if using), mixing lightly with a knife until a dough forms. You may not need to use all of the liquid.

2   You can now use the pastry as directed in the recipe. You can store your tart pastry in well-wrapped portions to roll out later, or roll out into thin sheets (I like to roll out the dough while it is still soft). Pastry will keep for 3 days well-wrapped in the fridge or 30 days in the freezer.

Techniques

Rubbing in	pg.99
Lining a tart	pg.108

125g/½ cup plus 1 Tbsp	butter, cold
250g/2 cups	all-purpose flour
10g/1 Tbsp	granulated sugar
1g/¼ tsp	flaky sea salt
100g/7 Tbsp	water (you can also use 1 egg yolk and 50–75g/3–5 Tbsp water for a richer pastry)

Monique's flaky sweet shortcrust pastry

This version of shortcrust pastry leaves some of the butter in larger chunks for a flakier finish. As a result, you need a bit more liquid to make it come together. This adaptation of the classic was shown to me during a trip to France. It makes a great base for fruit tarts. If you want to make it savory and use it for quiches or any kind of savory tartlet, just omit the sugar. Thank you, Monique!

1   To make a flaky version, cut the cold butter into ½-inch pieces. Place into a large bowl along with the dry ingredients and roughly work the butter into the dough. You want most of the pieces to still be large, among the crumbs.

2   Add the egg yolk, if using. Drizzle in half of the water and toss lightly. Press the mixture together gently with your fingertips.

3   As a dough clump forms (sometimes there is a formed dough on top with dry bits below), remove it from the bowl and place it into a clean container. Taking the pastry out in stages means you are less likely to overwork it. Continue drizzling the remaining water on the dry bits left in the bowl and gently working it into the flour/butter until it clumps together and you can add it into the container.

4   Press the clumps together, then flatten into a disc to make it easier to roll out later.

5   Wrap well and chill for at least 1 hour, but up to 3 days, before rolling out and using as required. Freezes well for 3 months.

TO LINE A PASTRY CASE

For a tart ring

1   Place the soft pastry in between two sheets of parchment paper and roll until it's around ⅛ inch thick. Use your chosen tart ring to mark the size of the bottom and use a ruler to mark a long strip the width of your chosen tart ring or case. Chill until firm, about 30 minutes.

2   When firm, cut the bottom out and place in the tart ring on a lined baking sheet. Take the strip and place around the edge of the tart ring. Do your best to keep it really delicate. Once it is tight to the edges, press it into the bottom to join the two pieces of pastry.

3   If your strip or bottom gets too warm, you can put it back into the fridge. You want your pastry to be firm while you handle it.

4   Place the lined tart case into the freezer until the pastry is firm, around 30 minutes, or in the fridge for 1 hour.

For a small or large fluted tart case

Option 1
1   Press the soft pastry directly into the case, using your fingers to press it right into the edges and keep it as even and thin as possible. Chill until firm, 30 minutes–1 hour in the fridge.

Option 2
1   Roll out the soft pastry to ⅛ inch between two sheets of parchment paper. Chill in the fridge for 30 minutes, until firm. Trim the pastry so it is larger than the tart pan you are lining. For small tart cases, you may want to use a circular pastry cutter.

2   Remove the paper and drape the pastry into the tart case, gently pressing it into the edges and bottom.

3   Place the lined tart case into the freezer until the pastry is firm, around 30 minutes, or in the fridge for 1 hour.

To blind bake

1   Preheat the oven to 375°F. Place parchment paper in your chilled and lined tart(s).

2   If baking a large tart, fill with weights—baking beans or raw rice work well. For small tarts, baking beans are optional.

3   For small tart cases (3¼ inch/8cm): Bake for 15–18 minutes. For large tart cases (8 inches/20cm): Bake for 25–30 minutes, until dry, then remove the weights and bake for 5–10 minutes, until golden.

4   You also have the option to seal the pastry. Brush with egg wash (see page 343), then return to the oven for 5 minutes, until golden. You can repeat this several times. This is a particularly useful technique for wet fillings, like a custard tart.

5   Baked tart cases can be kept in an airtight container for 3 days. Refresh in a 350°F oven for 5–10 minutes before using.

Notes

The uncooked tart case can be made in advance and kept in the fridge for 2 days. Trim before filling by cutting the edge with a sharp knife.

See the Technical Overview section (page 108) for more details on how to line tart cases successfully.

Reserve any remaining pastry or offcuts for later use. They can be re-rolled once and used for another tart before they misform. The rest can be baked as cookies.

MILK
BREAD

·

MAKES 1 LOAF OR 8 BUNS

Techniques

Starch gelatinization	pg.20
Gluten development	pg.14
Fermentation	pg.76

Equipment
9 x 5 x 2½-inch/
24.5 x 14.5 x 6cm loaf pan

Tangzhong

50g/3 Tbsp	whole milk
20g/3 Tbsp	bread flour
50g/3 Tbsp	water

Dough

55g/¼ cup	whole milk
50g/1	whole egg
230g/1¾ cups	bread flour
4g/1⅓ tsp	dry yeast
25g/2 Tbsp	granulated sugar
5g/1 tsp	fine salt
20g/1½ Tbsp	butter, softened

Plus
Egg wash (see page 343)

This classic milk dough bread has a relatively high hydration and is low in fat. The result is a super airy, squishy bread that bakes perfectly as a loaf or buns. Use as burger buns at your next bbq. Why is it so squishy? Look no further than the magic of a tangzhong aka pre-gelatinized flour (see All About Flour on page 20).

Total: 2 hrs 50 mins

10 mins	20 mins	1 hr	1 hr	20 mins
Make tangzhong	Mix dough	Proof	Shape & proof	Bake

1   To make the tangzhong, off the heat whisk the milk, flour, and water together.

2   Cook over medium heat, whisking/stirring all the time, until it thickens. It will be very thick. Take off the heat and move it into the bowl of a stand mixer, allowing it to cool slightly. Too hot and you risk harming the yeast, so if you can comfortably touch it, that is good.

3   In the stand mixer, first add the liquids on top of the warm tangzhong, followed by the dry ingredients. Mix on medium speed for 6–8 minutes, until medium gluten development is reached—this is when you can pull on the dough and it stays together, but it is still quite fragile. You can take it further than this, but this is the minimum requirement before adding the butter.

4   Add the soft butter 1 teaspoon at a time with the mixer running. Mix until very smooth— another 6–8 minutes—and full gluten development is reached. This is when you can pull a thin, almost translucent layer with the dough. If you have not reached it by this stage, rest the dough for 5 minutes, then mix for another 5 minutes. Continue until you get that full gluten development.

5   Remove from the bowl and use your hands or a bench scraper to form it into a round shape. Use the work surface to help create some surface tension so it has a smooth surface. At this point, you can press it down and put it into the fridge to cold proof and shape the next day. Otherwise, move into a clean bowl, then let rest and rise for 1 hour, covered, or until puffy and doubled.

6   To make buns, divide your dough into 60g/2¼-oz pieces and shape them into smooth balls. For a loaf, divide the dough into three 170g/6-oz pieces and roll into even rectangle shapes, ½ inch thick. Roll each piece of dough up into a sausage, then nestle into the loaf pan. Loosely cover and proof at room temperature until puffy, around 1 hour.

7   Meanwhile, preheat the oven to 425°F.

8   When proofed, brush gently with egg wash. This is your opportunity to add any desired toppings (a mix of black and white sesame seeds is good for buns). Immediately turn the oven down to 375°F and bake the buns for 12–14 minutes, until golden or 18– 22 minutes for the loaf.

BUN DOUGH

·

MAKES 1 LB 5 OZ/600G DOUGH, ENOUGH FOR ABOUT 10 BUNS

Techniques

Starch gelatinization	pg.20
Gluten development	pg.14
Fermentation	pg.76

145g/½ cup plus 2 Tbsp	whole milk
50g/1	whole egg
270g/2 cups plus 2 Tbsp	bread flour
4g/1⅓ tsp	dry yeast
40g/3 Tbsp	granulated sugar
5g/1 tsp	fine salt
70g/5 Tbsp	butter, softened

Techniques

Starch gelatinization	pg.20
Gluten development	pg.14
Fermentation	pg.76

Tangzhong

120g/½ cup	water
25g/3 Tbsp	bread flour

Dough

35g/2½ Tbsp	whole milk
50g/1	whole egg
245g/1¾ cups plus 3 Tbsp	bread flour
4g/1⅓ tsp	dry yeast
40g/3 Tbsp	granulated sugar
5g/1 tsp	fine salt
70g/5 Tbsp	butter, softened

Note

The water in the tangzhong can be replaced with equal parts milk and water or all milk. This makes the buns brown a little more and become slightly more tender.

This bun dough is the jumping off point for all the enriched doughs in this book. It has a 75% hydration, which is on the high side, and 25% butter, which puts it firmly in the rich—but not too rich—camp. You don't have to make it with a tangzhong, but I love borrowing this technique from its less rich sibling: the milk bread.

Total: 2 hrs 40 mins

20 mins	1 hr	1 hr	20 mins
Mix dough	Proof	Shape & proof	Bake

1   Follow the directions below, omitting the tangzhong.

Tangzhong bun dough

The tangzhong version of the classic bun dough makes use of the pre-gelatinized starch technique to sneak a bit more hydration into the recipe. This dough will be fluffier and have a better shelf life, too.

Total: 3 hrs

10 mins	20 mins	1 hr	1 hr	30 mins
Make tangzhong	Mix dough	Proof	Shape & proof	Bake

1   To make the tangzhong, off the heat whisk the water and flour together.

2   Cook over medium heat, whisking/stirring all the time, until it thickens. It will be very thick. Take off the heat and move it into the bowl of a stand mixer, allowing it to cool slightly. Too hot and you risk harming the yeast, so if you can comfortably touch it, that is good.

3   In the stand mixer, first add the liquids on top of the warm tangzhong, if using, followed by the dry ingredients. Mix on medium speed for 8–10 minutes, until medium gluten development is reached—this is when you can pull on the dough and it stays together, but it is still quite fragile. You can take it further than this, but this is the minimum requirement before adding the butter.

4   Add the soft butter 1 teaspoon at a time with the mixer running. Mix until very smooth—6–8 minutes—and full gluten development is reached. This is when you can pull a thin, almost translucent layer with the dough. If you have not reached it by this stage, rest the dough for 5 minutes, then mix for another 5 minutes. Continue until full gluten development is reached.

5   Remove from the bowl and round it a few times on the work surface so it has a smooth surface. At this point, you can press it down and put it into the fridge to cold proof and shape the next day. Otherwise, move into a clean bowl, then let rest and rise for 1 hour, covered, or until puffy and doubled. Shape the dough as directed in the recipes.

CLASSIC PUFF PASTRY

·

MAKES 1 LB 2 OZ/500G PASTRY

Techniques

Lamination	pg.69

Détrempe (dough block)

200g/1½ cups	bread flour or all-purpose flour (see note)
7g/2 tsp	granulated sugar
5g/1 tsp	fine salt
45g/3 Tbsp	butter, softened
85g/⅓ cup	water
2g/½ tsp	white wine vinegar

Butter block

160g/¾ cup	butter, cold

I'm obsessed with layers and lamination—there's nothing like watching your pastry successfully puff up in the oven. Puff pastry is actually very forgiving, though it is relatively time-consuming, so it's a great place to begin your layers journey. After a while, I promise all the rolling out will feel like meditation!

Day 1   Total: 6 hrs 10 mins

10 mins	10 mins	1 hr 10 mins	1 hr 10 mins	1 hr 10 mins	2 hrs 10 mins	10 mins
Make détrempe	Make butter block. Lock in	Single turn. Rest	Double turn. Rest	Single turn. Rest	Single turn. Rest	Roll out dough

The dough

1   For the détrempe, put all of your dry ingredients into a bowl and mix. Breadcrumb the soft butter into the dry ingredients using your fingertips. Create a well in the middle of your dry ingredients and slowly pour in the water and vinegar, bit by bit, mixing with a fork so you are combining the liquid/dry ingredients carefully. You can also make this in a stand mixer.

2   Once everything is combined, turn onto your work surface and squish together until just combined—don't overwork it at this stage. Pat into a 6 x 10-inch rectangle and rest in the fridge, wrapped in plastic wrap, for at least 2 hours, until firm and cool.

The butter block

3   Do not make your butter block until you are ready to laminate. The most important thing about your butter is that it is pliable but not greasy or smeary. It is at its most plastic and pliable (and the ideal temperature) as soon as you've bashed it into shape!

4   Make your butter block by cutting the fridge-cold butter into strips. Then lay the strips out as a square on a piece of parchment paper. Fold the paper around the butter in an approximate 8 x 10-inch shape, leaving some room on each side.

5   Using a rolling pin, bash the butter into shape. Once it is pliable, use a rolling motion to spread it into an even block. It will be pliable and bendy but still cold when you're done! It is now ready to use. If it feels soft or greasy, pop it in the freezer for 3 minutes and then check again. If it is too cold and is cracking when you bend it, leave it out for 1 minute and check again.

Locking in your butter

6   To lock in your butter, roll your détrempe so it is double the width of your butter block. Use your butter block to measure the size. You want the edges to be able to fold back over and cover the block completely.

7   When you are satisfied it is the right size, unwrap the butter and stick it into the middle of your dough. Bring the edges in and pinch it together in the middle. Your butter is now in!

8   Now turn your dough 90 degrees and press down on your dough several times decisively with your rolling pin—it should leave an imprint as well as helping to lengthen the dough and fuse the layers together. You're now ready to laminate (see page 70).

Note

You can use either bread flour or all-purpose flour for puff pastry. Bread flour will have more crunch and, I think, a more wild puff in the oven. All-purpose flour will be more tender.

INVERTED PUFF PASTRY

·

MAKES 1 LB 2 OZ/500G PASTRY

Techniques

Lamination	pg.69

Détrempe (dough block)

200g/1½ cups	bread flour or all-purpose flour (see note on page 124)
7g/2 tsp	granulated sugar
5g/1 tsp	fine salt
45g/3 Tbsp	butter, softened
85g/⅓ cup	water
2g/½ tsp	white wine vinegar

Butter block

160g/¾ cup	butter, cold
60g/½ cup	bread flour

Inverted puff pastry is the definition of "trust the process." Instead of wrapping dough around butter, we wrap butter around dough! The first turn can be a bit messy, but it quickly becomes very enjoyable to work with. The result is a pastry that rises more neatly and has better bite!

Day 1 — Total: 6 hrs 10 mins

10 mins	10 mins	1 hr 10 mins	1 hr 10 mins	1 hr 10 mins	2 hrs 10 mins	10 mins
Make détrempe	Make butter block. Lock in	Single turn. Rest	Double turn. Rest	Single turn. Rest	Single turn. Rest	Roll out dough

The dough

1   Make the détrempe according to the classic puff pastry instructions (see page 124).

2   To make the butter block, mix the butter and flour until completely combined.

3   Smear the butter/flour mix onto parchment paper and squash into an approximately 6 x 16-inch rectangle—use your détrempe to measure it. The détrempe should be two-thirds the size of the butter block.

4   Let chill—around 30 minutes to 1 hour is usually sufficient. It should be firm and cool but pliable.

Locking in your butter

5   To lock in your butter, ensure your détrempe is two-thirds the size of your butter block. Use your butter block to measure the size. When you are satisfied it is the right size, check the butter block is pliable (if not, roll over it a few times with your rolling pin) and then unwrap it, leaving it on its paper. Stick your dough on top, so it covers two-thirds.

6   Now perform your English lock-in, which is a bit like a single/letter fold. Bring the top third down over the middle, then bring the bottom third up, using the paper to help you. The butter will likely crack and look awful but don't worry! Just go with it and remember—trust the process.

7   Rotate 90 degrees and roll out the block to three times its length—you can do it in between paper and use as much flour as you need. Try to keep it in shape.

8   Brush off the excess flour—you are now ready to laminate (see page 70)!

Continued →

Before you start rolling out, here are a few things to be aware of:

- Decide how many turns and what combination you want to do (see page 70). Your options are:

    - 6 x single

    - 2 x single, 2 x double

    - 3 x double

    (see How Things Rise on page 71 for the impact.)

- You always want to turn the dough 90 degrees so you are alternating the direction you are rolling in. The dough can only stretch so far in one direction, so you need to switch it up each time.

The lamination

1   To start the lamination, dust your work surface. Place the locked-in dough in front of you and press down on the dough/smack the dough decisively with the rolling pin—this helps soften the butter and makes the dough more plastic, while lengthening it slightly.

2   Roll out the dough to 3 times its length, aiming for a thickness of ¼–½ inch. Mine is about 20 x 8-inch.

3   Perform a single or double turn. If you use a lot of flour to help you roll it out, make sure you brush off the excess with a pastry brush before adding the turn.

4   Wrap the dough well and make a note of the turn you have performed. Chill the dough for 1–2 hours, minimum.

5   Remove the dough from the fridge and turn it 90 degrees so it looks like a book. Roll out the dough to 3 times its length, approximately ¼–½ inch thick, and keep adding in your turns. Wrap the dough well and make a note of how many turns you have performed.

6   Once all of your turns are in, it's time for a nice long final rest before the final roll out—I like 2 hours or overnight. At this stage, puff pastry can be wrapped well and frozen for 3 months. Thaw overnight in the fridge.

The final roll out

7   Roll your puff pastry out to ⅟₁₆–⅛ inch thickness, taking plenty of rest breaks to get the best shape. Continuously lift your pastry up and off the table to see if it shrinks back. If it shrinks back, the gluten is too fired up. Just put it into the fridge to rest and return 20 minutes later. If you are baking sheets, measure them against your baking pans to make sure they will fit.

8   When you are rolling out your pastry, it's important to think about what your final product will be. Your puff will rise approximately six to eight times its height so keep that in mind when you are picking your final roll-out thickness.

9   If you are cutting a shape, for example a circle for a galette, you must allow the puff to relax before doing so. At least 30 minutes is essential (otherwise you'll end up with an oval).

The bake

10 Puff pastry needs to be baked hot! Preheat the oven to 425°F.

11 Make sure your puff is nice and cold when it goes in. It is the cold pastry going into the hot oven that creates the steam and layers.

12 Depending on the thickness, your puff will need anywhere from 30–50 minutes to fully bake. I like to start it at 425°F and then lower to 400°F after the first 15 minutes.

13 If you do get your puff out of the oven and realize it isn't fully baked then ... get it back in! Don't worry—it happens to us all. As long as it is still warm, you can continue baking.

Note

I like to store my uncooked pastry in sheets in rolled-out form for ease. Here you can freeze them (they last for up to 3 months well-wrapped!) or keep them in the fridge, depending on when you're planning to bake them.

To caramelize and compress your puff pastry

1   Preheat the oven to 425°F. After rolling out the pastry and cutting it to the exact size, line the baking sheet with paper, then sprinkle with 20g/2 tablespoons granulated sugar. Place the pastry on top, then sprinkle 30g/3 tablespoons granulated sugar on top. Lower the heat to 400°F and bake for 15 minutes—it will probably shrink a bit, but don't worry. This is normal!

2   After 15 minutes, place a piece of parchment paper on top followed by a heavy baking sheet. I use a standard baking sheet with a heatproof baking dish filled with baking beans to weigh it down.

3   Bake for an additional 30 minutes.

4   After 30 minutes, check to see if it is baked—you may want to go for another 5–15 more minutes. Remove the baking sheet if you are struggling to get caramelization in the center of the pastry—it should be gleaming and golden!

5   You can bake your puff up to 2–3 days in advance and keep well-wrapped before using for mille-feuille, or vanilla slices!

ROUGH PUFF PASTRY

·

MAKES 1 LB 2 OZ/500G PASTRY,
ENOUGH FOR 2 X 8 X 1½-INCH TARTS

Techniques

Lamination	pg.69

95g/6 Tbsp	water, ice-cold
10g/2 tsp	white wine vinegar
165g/¾ cup	butter, cold
160g/1⅓ cups	all-purpose flour
75g/½ cup plus 1 Tbsp	bread flour
5g/1⅓ tsp	flaky sea salt

This pastry never fails to amaze me at how much it puffs up given how quick the mixing process is. For more crunch, I use a mixture of bread flour and all-purpose flour, but you can play around with the flour here. Whole wheat, for example, makes a great addition.

Total: 1 hr 20 mins

20 mins	1 hr
Mix pastry & perform folds	Chill

1 Measure the water and vinegar, chop the butter into ¾-inch cubes and put them all into the freezer for 20 minutes or the fridge for 1 hour, at least, along with the measured flours.

2 Put the flours and salt into the bowl of a stand mixer and mix with the paddle attachment until all is combined.

3 Add the cubed butter and mix on low speed until the butter is in irregular-size pieces. You want some to be breadcrumb style and some to still be large—around ½ inch.

4 Immediately add the cold water/vinegar and mix until it looks hydrated, about 20 seconds. You will still have dry bits at the bottom of the bowl.

5 Move the pastry onto a clean surface and add flour if you need to underneath.

6 Roll the pastry out to be 16 inches long and perform a double fold. This is when you fold both edges into the middle and then fold it over itself again.

7 Roll the pastry out to be 16 inches long again and perform two more double folds immediately, adding flour when you need to.

8 Chill in the fridge for 1 hour before using. Pastry will keep for 3 days well-wrapped in the fridge or 30 days in the freezer.

PIE DOUGH

·

MAKES 1 LB 7 OZ/640G DOUGH,
ENOUGH FOR A DEEP 9-INCH DOUBLE-CRUSTED PIE

Techniques

Lamination	pg.69

60g/¼ cup	water
60g/¼ cup	crème fraîche
280g/2¼ cups	all-purpose flour
6g/1¾ tsp	flaky sea salt
25g/2 Tbsp	granulated sugar
210g/¾ cup plus 3 Tbsp	butter, cold

I use a variation of my rough puff to make pie dough. The only difference is what I hydrate the dough with. For pie dough, I go for extra richness and tenderness by using a portion of crème fraîche to hydrate the dough and add a little sugar; whereas rough puff is more classic, being hydrated with water (and a little vinegar) only and no sugar.

	Total: 1 hr 50 mins
20 mins	1 hr 30 mins
Mix pastry & perform folds	Chill

1 Whisk the water and crème fraîche together and set aside in the fridge or freezer to chill.

2 Mix together the flour, salt, and sugar and whisk to distribute everything evenly.

3 Cut the butter into small cubes/rectangles, add to the flour, and toss to coat. Coating the butter in flour will help protect it from the warmth of your hands and getting melty, which can negatively impact the flake-factor of your pie dough.

4 Squish the butter into flat pieces, one by one.

5 Now it's time to add the liquid. Pour in half and toss the dry ingredients around the bowl until you can't see the liquid anymore. Now add the rest and squish together. Tip the dough onto your work surface.

6 Squash everything together as best you can and then, adding flour if you need to, roll out the dough and perform a single turn (see page 70). You'll see chunks of butter turn into long, thin pieces—it's quite satisfying!

7 Press the dough back together—adding more flour if you need—then perform two more single turns until the dough is evenly combined but you can still see big, lovely marble-y streaks of butter.

8 Divide the dough into 300g/10½-oz pieces (perfect for top and bottom crusts for a deep 9-inch pie!), then wrap. Put into the fridge for at least 1½ hours for it to firm back up. The pie dough can be kept frozen, well-wrapped, for 30 days.

9 To roll the pastry out, flour your surface enough to prevent any sticking, then roll the pie dough out to ¹⁄₁₆–⅛ inch thickness. This is way thinner than you think is going to work. Trust me. I've made a lot of pie doughs that are too thick because I simply haven't trusted the process but you do want to go quite thin here. You'll still get a fantastic chubby edge as you fold the dough in on itself anyway during lining, so don't worry about losing any drama. Pastry will keep for 3 days well-wrapped in the fridge or 30 days in the freezer.

SUET PIE DOUGH

·

MAKES 1 LB/450G DOUGH, ENOUGH FOR 1 X DOUBLE-CRUST
LATTICE PIE IN AN 8-INCH/20CM SQUARE BAKING PAN

Techniques

Rubbing in	pg.99

160g/1⅓ cups	all-purpose flour
30g/¼ cup	whole wheat flour
4g/1¼ tsp	flaky sea salt
80g/6 Tbsp	butter, cold
80g/6 Tbsp	shredded suet or butter
80g/⅓ cup	water, very cold
2g/½ tsp	white wine vinegar

This is a slight adaptation on the classic pie dough that uses suet to great effect. The result is a rich, tender, melt-in-the-mouth pie dough that is perfect for savory pies (see chicken pie on page 173).

Total: 1 hr 20 mins

20 mins	1 hr
Mix pastry & perform folds	Chill

1   Mix the flours and salt together, then add the cold butter, cut into approximately 1-inch pieces, and press each piece between your fingers to create thin, flat strips. If you are using all butter, rub half of the butter into the flour to make fine crumbs before adding the larger pieces and flattening into flat strips.

2   Add the suet and briefly mix before adding the water and vinegar, bit by bit, and forming a rough dough.

3   Turn the dough out onto your work surface and roll out to be about ½ inch thick. Fold into three like a letter to add layers of flakiness and then wrap. Chill for 1 hour before rolling out. The pastry will keep for 3 days well-wrapped in the fridge or 30 days in the freezer.

SABLÉ BRETON

·

MAKES 10½ OZ/300G DOUGH, ENOUGH FOR 30 THIN COOKIES
OR 8–10 COOKIE CRUSTS BAKED IN A CUPCAKE PAN

Techniques

Creaming	pg.59

85g/6 Tbsp	butter, softened
40g/3 Tbsp	granulated sugar
40g/3 Tbsp	light brown sugar
15g/about 1	egg yolk
120g/1 cup	all-purpose flour
3g/¾ tsp	baking powder
3g/1 tsp	flaky sea salt

This is an extra rich, extra crumbly shortbread-adjacent dough that is made crackly and lighter with the addition of baking powder. It makes fantastic sandwich cookies or chunky bases for fruit tarts.

Total: 1 hr 15 mins

15 mins	1 hr
Mix	Chill

1   In a mixing bowl, cream together the softened butter and both the sugars until light and fluffy.

2   Gradually add in the egg yolk, mixing well after each addition. Scrape down the sides of the bowl to ensure the yolk is incorporated.

3   Sift in the flour, baking powder, and flaky sea salt. Fold in the dry ingredients until just combined.

4   Wrap the dough and chill for at least 1 hour or up to 3 days. It can also be rolled out between two sheets of parchment paper to the correct thickness and chilled before cutting and baking.

GENOISE SPONGE

·

2 X 6-INCH CAKES OR 1 X 8-INCH CAKE

Techniques

Egg foam	pg.45
Folding	pg.113
Liaison Batter	pg.113

Equipment

2 x 6-inch/15cm or
1 x 8-inch/20cm pan(s)

220g/4–5	whole eggs, at room temperature
100g/½ cup	granulated sugar
70g/½ cup plus 1 Tbsp	all-purpose flour
35g/⅓ cup	cornstarch
45g/3 Tbsp	butter

This basic, plain airy sponge cake is perfect for layer cakes. It is quite dry, so it is strong enough to be soaked with syrup. Sandwich together with jam and whipped cream for a classic treat.

Total: 1 hr 10 mins

25 mins	25–30 mins	15 mins
Mix	Bake	Cool

1   Preheat the oven to 375°F. Line the pan(s) with parchment paper.

2   Whisk the eggs and sugar on the highest speed for 5 minutes. The eggs should be almost white and the mix will look shiny. If it doesn't, don't stop high-speed mixing until you get to white, shiny territory. Lower to medium speed and whisk for 3 minutes, then finally decrease to low speed and whisk for 10 minutes, until you can see no visible bubbles.

3   Sift the flour and cornstarch together three or four times.

4   Melt the butter—ideally you want it at around 122°F. To achieve this, I melt it in a pan and then once it is half melted, I take it off the heat. The residual heat should be enough to melt the rest and it will be at a good temperature. Set aside.

5   Pour your ribbon-stage eggs into a large bowl. It is easier to fold more gently if the bowl is large.

6   Sift the dry ingredients once again onto the egg mixture, folding very gently with a slicing motion (I like to do a capital D shape—slice through the middle or edge then go around and under!). You can do this in two or three stages, waiting until there is only a small amount of flour visible before adding the next lot. Try not to deflate the mixture.

7   Make a liaison batter by whisking 2–3 tablespoons of the flour/egg mixture into your melted butter. It should look smooth and emulsified.

8   Fold the liaison batter back in, in one go. Divide between the pan(s), then drop from an 8–12-inch height to break any large bubbles.

9   Bake for 25–30 minutes, until risen and golden. You can stab the sponge with a knife to check it comes out clean.

10 Drop the pans(s) again from an 8–12-inch height when the cake(s) comes out of the oven, then invert onto a cooling rack and let cool in the pan. Once cool, wrap and freeze for 30 days or use within 2 days.

BRIOCHE

·

MAKES 1 LB 9 OZ/700G OR 1 LOAF

Techniques

Gluten development	pg.14
Fermentation	pg.76

Equipment
9 x 5-inch/24 x 12cm loaf pan

285g/2¼ cups	bread flour
6g/1 tsp	fine salt
5g/1¾ tsp	dry yeast
50g/3 Tbsp	whole milk
150g/3	whole eggs
20g/1	egg yolk
170g/¾ cup	butter, softened (68°F is great), cut into small pieces
40g/3 Tbsp	granulated sugar

Plus
Egg wash (see page 343)

Brioche is the yardstick by which all other enriched breads are measured. Famously rich with eggs and butter, this recipe uses an additional yolk for extra lift, color, and richness. To really make it shine, it has 60% butter and is about 70% hydrated. Brioche can be used for bread-and-butter pudding (see page 212) or used in place of the dough in recipes like French toast cinnamon buns on page 254.

Day 1		**Total:** 5 hrs 30 mins	Day 2	**Total:** 3 hrs 35 mins
30 mins	1 hr	4–24hrs	3 hrs	35 mins
Mix dough	Move onto baking sheet & proof dough	Move into fridge & rest	Shape & proof	Bake

1   Place the flour in the bowl of a stand mixer fitted with the dough hook attachment, adding the salt and yeast separately on top. Add the milk, eggs, and egg yolk and mix on low speed until no dry flour remains, about 1 minute. Increase the speed to medium and mix for 3 minutes, then let the dough rest for 3 minutes. Repeat this on-off mixing and resting until the dough is evenly combined and has reached medium gluten development.

2   With the mixer running on medium speed, add one-third of the butter, a few pieces at a time, ensuring the butter is incorporated fully before adding the next, 3–4 minutes. Add the sugar and mix until completely incorporated (the dough will suddenly look wetter). Start adding the butter again, piece by piece, and scrape down the bowl as needed until it's all incorporated, about 5 minutes.

3   Increase the speed to medium-high and mix the dough until it pulls away cleanly from the sides of the bowl and full gluten development is reached, so that it is able to be gently stretched into a thin sheet without tearing, about 8 minutes.

4   Scrape the dough onto a clean, unfloured work surface. Using clean hands, slide your hands under the left and right sides of the dough and lift it up from the middle until the dough releases from the work surface, then slap the bottom half of the dough down onto the work surface, quickly stretching the top half up and folding it over the bottom half (it will be sticky at first but don't worry, this process will reduce that as you work; do not add flour). Repeat this slap-and-fold motion, rotating the dough as you work, until the dough is smooth and less sticky, 5–10 slaps.

5   Transfer the dough to a baking sheet lined with parchment paper, cover with plastic wrap, and let the dough proof at room temperature until it is visibly puffed, about 1 hour.

Note

For a less rich brioche, try playing around with the butter percentage. Try halving the butter for a demi-brioche, which is still enriched but not quite as hefty.

Continued ⟶

BRIOCHE
Continued

6 Press the dough down into an 8 x 12-inch rectangle, then cover and place in the fridge. The dough will proof more in the cold and the butter will solidify. Chill for at least 4 hours or up to 24 hours.

7 To bake a loaf, line the loaf pan, then roll the rectangle up into a sausage, pinching to close, and place into the pan. Alternatively, for a brioche Nanterre, flour a work surface, then divide the dough into 70g/2½-oz portions and shape into balls using your hands. Nestle into the loaf pan.

8 Proof at room temperature for 2½–5 hours for a classic loaf or 2–3½ hours for the Nanterre shape. It will double in size and be very puffy. Loosely cover with plastic wrap to prevent a skin from forming. If desired, brush gently with egg wash before placing it in the oven.

9 Preheat the oven to 425°F.

10 Place the loaf in the oven, lower the temperature to 400°F and bake until deep golden brown and to an internal temperature of 190°F, about 35 minutes. If the loaf is darkening too much, cover with foil during the bake. If the loaf doesn't reach the correct internal temperature, continue to bake, checking the temperature every 5 minutes. Let cool in the pan for 5 minutes, then carefully remove from the loaf pan and let cool completely on a cooling rack, about 1 hour.

11 Brioche is best on the day it's baked, but leftovers can be stored in an airtight container for 3 days or refrigerated for up to 7 days. It will also keep well in the freezer for 1 month.

Note

If you use flour to help you shape the brioche, don't forget to dust it off with a pastry brush to ensure the dough adheres properly to itself.

BRIOCHE VARIATIONS

•

MAKES 1 LOAF

Techniques

Gluten development	pg.14
Emulsification	pg.61
Fermentation	pg.76

Lower hydration brioche

285g/2¼ cups	bread flour
6g/1 tsp	fine salt
5g/1¾ tsp	dry yeast
115g/½ cup	whole milk
50g/1	whole egg
80g/6 Tbsp	butter, softened, cut into small pieces
25g/2 Tbsp	granulated sugar

Food processor brioche

175g/1⅓ cups	bread flour (can sub all-purpose flour for a cakier texture)
25g/2 Tbsp	granulated sugar
3g/½ tsp	fine salt
3g/1 tsp	dry yeast
100g/2	whole eggs
25g/2 Tbsp	whole milk
70g/5 Tbsp	butter, cold, cut into small pieces

Lower hydration brioche

MAKES 1 LOAF/500G

This variation on the classic brioche dough has a lower hydration with less egg and butter. Good for baked goods that benefit from better definition, more complex shapes, and less oven spring, like babka.

Day 1		Total: 5 hrs 30 mins		Day 2	Total: 3 hrs 35 mins
30 mins	1 hr		4–24 hrs	3 hrs	35 mins
Mix dough	Move onto baking sheet & proof dough		Move into fridge & rest	Shape & proof	Bake

1   Mix, proof, rest, shape, proof, and bake according to the brioche instructions on pages 133 and 134.

Food processor brioche

MAKES 1 LOAF/400G

A small-batch, lower fat content brioche that can be mixed in a food processor. Good for beignets and buns. Using cold butter here helps keep the temperature of the dough down, since the food processor can transfer a lot of heat to the dough.

	Total time 1 hr 10 mins
10 mins	1 hr
Mix dough	Proof dough

1   Place the flour, sugar, salt, and yeast into the bowl of a food processor with the eggs and milk. Using the blade attachment, process until a rough dough forms, 30 seconds–1 minute. Scrape down the edges of the bowl.

2   Turn the food processor on and add the cold butter, in small pieces, one by one. Continue processing for another 1–2 minutes, until the dough comes together and full gluten development is reached. It will be shiny and slick. If your dough has overheated, it may not appear to have reached full gluten development—remove it from the bowl anyway and allow it to rest.

3   Perform a few slaps and folds on a floured work surface until it is a cohesive, shiny dough. Move into an oiled container and let rise for 1 hour, or until very puffy.

4   Shape and proof as the recipe requires.

CHOUX

·

MAKES ABOUT 12¼ OZ/350G DOUGH,
ENOUGH FOR 15-20 LARGE CHOUX BUNS

Techniques

Starch gelatinization	pg.20

40g/2½ Tbsp	whole milk
65g/¼ cup plus 1 tsp	water
55g/¼ cup	butter
4g/1¼ tsp	granulated sugar
75g/½ cup plus 1 Tbsp	bread flour or all-purpose flour (see notes)
110–130g/2–3	whole eggs
2g/⅓ tsp	fine salt

Total: 30 mins

10 mins	10 mins	10 mins
Heat milk, water & butter	Add flour, cook & cool	Add eggs

1   Heat the milk, water, butter, and sugar together. Bring to a rolling boil and stir to make sure the sugar is dissolved.

2   Sift the flour several times to prevent lumps and add to your boiling liquid.

3   Turn the heat down and stir rapidly until a smooth paste forms and a dry film is formed. If you have a probe thermometer, check that it reaches 185°F.

4   Move the paste into a bowl and either spread it out to cool down or paddle on low speed if using a stand mixer.

5   Meanwhile, whisk the eggs with the salt—this makes them easier to combine as the salt will break down the eggs slightly.

6   When you can touch the paste comfortably for 10 seconds, start to add the eggs. I do this in three or four additions, mixing well between each.

7   The paste should be smooth and shiny. If you lift up a spatula, it should slowly drop off—it needs to be thick but pipeable. If it is really stiff, you can add a little more egg (10g at a time).

8   The choux paste is now ready to use. Use and bake as directed in the recipe. Choux paste can be stored in the fridge for 1–2 days.

Choux notes

You may need more eggs than the recipe states to get to the consistency required. See the recipe for details.

Using bread flour will create a more defined choux with a slightly crisper crust. This is good for crullers, eclairs, and anything that needs to have a defined shape. For buns, all-purpose flour will work well.

When you put the choux into the piping bag, do your best to squish and squash it to remove as many air bubbles as possible. Air bubbles and gaps may come back later to bite you when piping, plus these gaps will be imprinted into the choux. And if the choux is piped unevenly, remember this will bake into the final shape, so it's important to try to be as even as possible. Choux can be repiped as many times as you like, so feel free to practice.

When it comes to choux, the freezer is your friend. You can either bake your choux, then freeze the baked shells and refresh in a 375°F oven for 5 minutes when you want to fill, or you can pipe your choux and bake from frozen. Choux paste can also be frozen and then defrosted overnight and used. It may oxidize (see Color on page 88).

CRAQUELIN

·

MAKES 8 OZ/225G CRAQUELIN,
ENOUGH FOR 20 LARGE CHOUX BUNS

Techniques

Rolling out	pg.108

Plain

75g/5 Tbsp	butter, softened
75g/⅓ cup	light brown sugar
1g/⅛ tsp	fine salt
75g/½ cup plus 2 Tbsp	all-purpose flour

Cocoa

75g/5 Tbsp	butter, softened
75g/⅓ cup	light brown sugar
1g/⅛ tsp	fine salt
60g/½ cup	all-purpose flour
15g/3 Tbsp	cocoa powder

Think of craquelin as a crisp, sugary outfit for your choux buns. Placed on top before baking, it melts in the oven, leaving your choux with a thin coating of cookie-like crust. It also hides any lumps and bumps in your choux, making them appear more even and uniform.

Total: 15 mins

5 mins	10 mins
Mix	Roll out & chill until needed

1   Mix together (not cream—you don't need any air in this) the soft butter, sugar, and salt. Stir in the flour. If you want to make a cocoa craquelin, stir in the cocoa powder. Bring the dough together with your hands.

2   Roll out to a ¹⁄₁₆–⅛ inch thickness between two sheets of parchment paper and chill until it is needed.

3   When ready to use, cut the craquelin approximately the same size as the piped choux. It's best to warm the craquelin up slightly with your hands before cutting, otherwise it will crumble or crack. Craquelin can be re-rolled over and over again and stored in the freezer indefinitely.

Note

The recipe can easily be halved.

AN AFTERNOON

Cakes

Roasted strawberry Victoria sponge	140
Coriander and panela cake with honey cream cheese and apricots	143
Marble cake with chocolate frosting	144
Ricotta, marmalade, and hazelnut chocolate-chip cake	147
Apricot and rosemary polenta cake	148
Chamomile and toasted flour chiffon cake	151
Upside-down sticky pear and walnut cake	152
Steamed plum buttermilk sponge cake	155

Tarts & pies

Lemon curd meringue tarts with blackberries	156
Choconut tart	159
Passionfruit posset flower tarts	160
Brown sugar custard tart	163
Sablé Breton fruit tarts	164
Tomato and fennel tarte Tatin	167
Any galette	168
Chicken pie with rich pastry	173
Leek and mustard tart	174

Breads

Spiced pumpkin buns	175
Festive buns	179
Earl Grey scones	180
Flaky cheese and pickle scones	183

Cookies & confections

Brown butter banana cookies	184
Chocolate, peanut, and coconut twice-baked cookies	187
Amarettis	188
Golden syrup crunch cookies	189
Salted vanilla shortbread	192
Salted double-chocolate shortbread	193
3pm oat cookies	194
Miso walnut double-thick chocolate-chip cookies	197
Fruity marshmallows	198
Maple pretzel buttercrunch	201
Pickled pineapple pâte de fruit	203

Desserts

Plum and mascarpone karpatka	204
Caramel poached oranges with sabayon and langues de chat	207
Lemon Basque cheesecake with sticky lemons	208
Orchard turnovers	211
Bread-and-butter pudding with caramel mandarins	212
Panna cotta with burnt white chocolate and soy	215
Baked lemon custard brûlée	216
PBJ Paris brest	218
Crullers	221
Blonde rice pudding with pears and hazelnuts	222
Granitas	224
Jam ripple parfait	227
DIY mint Viennese ice cream cake	228

ROASTED STRAWBERRY VICTORIA SPONGE

SERVES 8–10

Techniques

Creaming	pg.59
Rising agents	pg./4
Whipping	pg.60

Equipment

2 x 8-inch/20cm cake pans

Roasted strawberries

200g/7 oz	strawberries
20g/2 Tbsp	granulated sugar

Cake

200g/¾ cup plus 2 Tbsp	butter, softened (68°F is great)
5g/1⅓ tsp	flaky sea salt
245g/1¼ cups	granulated sugar
65g/¼ cup	heavy cream
160g/about 3	whole eggs
35g/about 2	egg yolks
4–8g/1–2 tsp	good quality vanilla extract
90g/6 Tbsp	whole milk
245g/2 cups	all-purpose flour
17g/4¼ tsp	baking powder
25g/2 Tbsp	granulated sugar

Whipped cream

200g/¾ cup plus 2 Tbsp	heavy cream
40g/3 Tbsp	crème fraîche (optional)
15–20g/ 1½–2 Tbsp	granulated sugar (optional)

Plus

Powdered sugar, to decorate (optional)

This Victoria sponge breaks the mold of the classic equal parts sugar/flour/butter/ eggs. I made over 30 cakes to get the ratio just right. By replacing some of the butter with egg yolks and adding cream, we get an extra-moist cake with good structure and lots of flavor. Reducing the butterfat also allows the other flavors, like the milkiness of the cream, to come through, providing a wonderfully rich and tender backdrop for your whipped cream and fruit. Roasted strawberries could be swapped for jam, but the rich syrup is unbeatable.

Total: 3 hrs 10 mins

40 mins	15 mins	30 mins	1hr 15 mins	30 mins
Roast strawberries	Mix cake	Bake	Cool	Assemble

1   Preheat the oven to 350°F.

2   To make the roasted strawberries, rinse the strawberries briefly and halve. If they're small, just leave them whole. Toss with the sugar on a baking sheet. Roast for 30–40 minutes, until soft, syrupy, and slightly shrunken. The strawberries will turn a deeper shade of red. You can keep cooking them for up to 1 hour. Let them cool and move into a container with all the syrup. You can store them in the fridge for 3–5 days.

3   Preheat the oven to 375°F and line the pans. Set aside.

4   To make the cake, cream the soft butter with the salt and sugar for 2 minutes on medium speed using a stand mixer. This is enough for the butter and sugar to aerate slightly and become a little paler, but not so much that it is whipped. It is better to err on the side of caution—we don't want too much air at this stage!

5   Mix together the cream, whole eggs, egg yolks, vanilla extract, and milk. Set aside. Sift together the flour and baking powder. Set aside.

6   Starting with the liquid, alternate adding the liquid and dry ingredients into the creamed butter and sugar, in around three batches, scraping down as necessary.

7   Divide the mixture between the two pans, 475–500g/1 lb 1 oz–1 lb 2 oz per cake. Sprinkle one cake with the 25g/2 tablespoons sugar. This will be your top.

8   Bake for 25 minutes, then check if the sponge is golden and bouncy and pulling away from the sides slightly. Bake for an additional 5 minutes if it doesn't look or feel ready. Let cool in the pan for 10 minutes, then remove and cool completely on a rack.

9   To make the filling, whip the cream with the crème fraîche, if using, and granulated sugar, if using, to very soft peaks, then set aside.

10 Spread the whipped cream filling over the unsugared sponge cake, leaving a 1-inch border so it doesn't splurge too much, followed by generous dollops of the roasted strawberries and their syrup. You may not need to use it all. As a splurging insurance policy, you can pop your assembled cake in the fridge or freezer to firm up the cream a bit.

11 Place the sugared sponge cake on top. Sprinkle with powdered sugar, if desired. Serve with any extra roasted strawberry syrup.

CORIANDER AND PANELA CAKE WITH HONEY CREAM CHEESE AND APRICOTS

•

SERVES 8-10

Techniques

Poaching fruit	pg.107
Creaming	pg.59

Equipment

8-inch/20cm square pan

Poached apricots

5	apricots
250g/1¼ cups	granulated sugar
500g/2 cups plus 2 Tbsp	water
1	chamomile teabag
25g/2 Tbsp	lemon juice

Cake

3g/2 tsp	coriander seed
160g/¾ cup	butter, softened
1g/¼ tsp	flaky sea salt
200g/¾ cup plus 3 Tbsp	dark brown or panela sugar
155g/3	whole eggs
200g/1½ cups	all-purpose flour
14g/3½ tsp	baking powder
50g/3 Tbsp	whole milk
75g/5 Tbsp	heavy cream or crème fraîche

Honey cream cheese frosting

75g/5 Tbsp	butter, softened
90g/¼ cup	honey (can sub granulated sugar)
1–2g/¼–½ tsp	flaky sea salt
240g/8½ oz	full-fat cream cheese

Plus

Edible fresh flowers or herbs, to decorate (optional)

Coriander seed is an unsung flavor hero in baking, providing intriguing "can't put my finger on it" citrusy notes. Paired with panela, a rich unrefined cane sugar, it's a surprisingly complex combination for tea time. If you can't find panela, you can use any dark brown sugar for this. This is actually the bake I brought to meet my publishers when I submitted the proposal for this book, so I'll always be grateful for this cake!

Total: 2 hrs 40 mins

20 mins	15 mins	35 mins	1hr 10 mins	20 mins
Poach apricots	Mix cake	Bake	Cool	Assemble

1   Preheat the oven to 375°F. Line the pan with parchment paper.

2   To poach the apricots, halve the apricots, setting the pits aside for other uses (see the noyaux cream recipe on page 270). Poach the apricots according to the instructions on page 336.

3   Grind the coriander seed and set aside.

4   To make the cake, first cream the soft butter with the salt and sugar for 2 minutes on medium speed using a stand mixer. This is enough for the butter and sugar to aerate slightly and become a little paler, but not so much that the mixture is whipped. It is better to err on the side of caution. Whisk in the eggs.

5   Sift together the dry ingredients, then beat them into the butter/sugar along with the coriander seed using the paddle attachment until well combined, about 1 minute. Finally, stir the milk and cream together, then paddle this into the butter/flour mixture.

6   Pour the mixture into the prepared pan and bake for 30–35 minutes or until the cake is springy and a skewer comes out clean. The internal temperature should read above 205°F on a probe thermometer. Let cool in the pan for 10 minutes, then remove and let cool completely on a cooling rack.

7   For the cream cheese frosting, whip the butter until smooth and airy, 3–4 minutes. Scrape down the butter from the sides of the bowl, then add the honey and salt. Whip for another 3–4 minutes on high speed until very airy, scraping down the bowl as necessary. Stir in the cream cheese on medium-low speed until well combined and smooth—you can finish off with a fast whip to ensure it's all combined.

8   To finish, swoop the frosting over the cake and decorate with the poached apricot halves. Decorate with flowers or herbs, if using. Keep any leftovers in the fridge for 2–3 days.

 Notes   If your panela sugar is lumpy, whiz it in the blender before using.

The aromatic oil in coriander can contain up to 85% of linalool, which is used to synthesize blueberry flavor.

MARBLE CAKE WITH CHOCOLATE FROSTING

·

SERVES 8–10

Techniques

Creaming	pg.59
Ganache	pg.63
Emulsification	pg.61

Equipment
8-inch/20cm square pan

Cake

120g/½ cup	butter, softened
1g/¼ tsp	flaky sea salt
75g/⅓ cup	light brown sugar
95g/½ cup	granulated sugar
70g/about 1	whole egg
	or 70g/1 egg plus
	1 yolk
155g/1¼ cups	all-purpose flour
2g/⅓ tsp	baking soda
4g/1 tsp	baking powder
125g/½ cup	sour cream
30g/6 Tbsp	cocoa powder
30g/2 Tbsp	whole milk

Chocolate frosting

20g/2 Tbsp	light brown sugar
75g/5 Tbsp	heavy cream
75g/2½ oz	dark chocolate
90g/6 Tbsp	butter, softened
15g/3 Tbsp	cocoa powder
2g/½ tsp	flaky sea salt
	(optional)

Plus
Sprinkles (optional)

Marble cake is such a crowd-pleaser. Team that up with the best chocolate frosting in the world, which is the love child of ganache and buttercream, then all you need is sprinkles and it's a real party. This is a cute single-layer cake that you can serve up as nibbly mini pieces at a party—a "go back for one more" kind of recipe.

Total: 1 hr 30 mins

20 mins	25 mins	25 mins	20 mins
Mix cake	Bake & make ganache	Cool	Finish frosting & decorate

1   Preheat the oven to 375°F. Line the pan with parchment paper.

2   To make the cake, cream the soft butter with the salt and sugars for 2–3 minutes on medium speed using a stand mixer. This is enough for the butter and sugar to aerate slightly and become a little paler, but not so much that it is whipped. It is better to err on the side of caution. Whisk in the whole egg and yolk, if using, until completely incorporated.

3   Sift together the flour, baking soda, and baking powder, then stir these into the butter/sugar. Finally, stir in the sour cream.

4   Divide the batter in half, about 360g/12¾ oz each, then stir the cocoa powder and milk into one half.

5   Alternate blobs of each batter into the lined pan then, using a knife, swirl the batters together to create a marble pattern.

6   Bake for 25 minutes or until the cake is bouncy and a skewer comes out clean. Let cool in the pan for 10 minutes, then remove and let cool completely on a rack.

7   Meanwhile, to make the chocolate frosting, whisk the sugar into the cream, then heat until simmering. Chop up the chocolate into small, approximately ½-inch pieces and put into a bowl. Pour the cream over and let stand for 1 minute before whisking to a smooth ganache. Allow to cool in the fridge or at room temperature until the ganache reaches room temperature or 64–68°F.

8   Beat the butter until smooth, then stir in the cocoa powder. Beat until smooth and shiny, then add the ganache, a third at a time. Whip and beat until smooth—it should be very shiny and lush. Taste and check the seasoning, adding the salt if needed.

9   To finish, spoon the frosting over the marble cake and decorate in swoops. Add sprinkles, if desired. Keep any leftovers in the fridge for 3–4 days but bring up to room temperature before enjoying.

RICOTTA, MARMALADE, AND HAZELNUT CHOCOLATE–CHIP CAKE

·

SERVES 8

Techniques

Baking with nuts	pg.55
Creaming	pg.59

Equipment
8-inch/20cm loose-bottomed cake pan

340g/12-oz jar	marmalade with shreds
165g/¾ cup	butter, softened (68°F is great)
Zest of 1	orange
165g/¾ cup plus 1 Tbsp	granulated sugar
250g/2¼ cups	ground hazelnuts
70g/¾ cup	almond flour
3g/¾ tsp	baking powder
155g/about 3	whole eggs
330g/1⅓ cups	ricotta
2g/½ tsp	flaky sea salt
100g/½ cup plus 1 Tbsp	dark chocolate chips (⅛ inch)

Topping
Strained marmalade from above

90g/6 Tbsp	orange juice
45g/¼ cup	granulated sugar

This cake is based on a recipe passed on to me by Nichola Gensler. We'd make this at the bakery on Saturdays and it was always a hit. I've increased the fat slightly and used a mixture of hazelnuts and almonds, as well as adding chocolate chips. As someone who grew up eating Jaffa Cakes by the fistful, this is nicely reminiscent of it. It's Nichola's brilliant marmalade glaze that really sets this cake apart though. I'll be forever grateful for it.

Total: 3 hrs 15 mins

15 mins	50 mins	10 mins	2 hrs
Mix cake	Bake & make glaze	Cool	Glaze cake & let cool completely

1   Preheat the oven to 350°F. Line the pan with parchment paper.

2   Heat the marmalade and strain through a sieve, retaining the marmalade and shred separately. Set aside.

3   To make in a food processor, blitz the butter, orange zest, granulated sugar, ground nuts, almond flour, and baking powder together, then add the eggs, one by one, and blitz until smooth. Pour the mixture into a larger bowl, then fold in the ricotta, salt, marmalade shred, and chocolate chips.

OR

To make in a stand mixer, cream the butter, orange zest, and granulated sugar together. Add the eggs and beat with the paddle attachment until combined. Scrape down the sides of the bowl. Next, stir in the ground nuts, almond flour, and baking powder. Finally, fold in the ricotta and salt, along with the marmalade shred and chocolate chips.

4   Pour into the cake pan, smooth the top, and bake for 50 minutes, until springy to touch and very deep golden. Let cool in the pan for at least 10 minutes before adding the glaze.

5   To make the glaze, heat the strained marmalade with the orange juice and sugar in a saucepan. Bubble for 1 minute, then allow to thicken, until it can coat the back of a spoon, at about 86°F.

6   Pour the glaze over the still-warm cake and let completely cool in the pan for 1–2 hours. You can put it into the fridge to help the top set. This cake lasts in the fridge for 3–4 days.

APRICOT AND ROSEMARY POLENTA CAKE

·

SERVES 6–8

Techniques

Baking with nuts	pg.55
Creaming	pg.59
Caramelization	pg.84

Equipment
8-inch/20cm cake pan

Cake
20g/2 Tbsp	polenta or medium cornmeal
100g/7 Tbsp	whole milk
110g/2	whole eggs
115g/½ cup	butter, softened
110g/½ cup	granulated sugar
140g/1½ cups	almond flour
40g/¼ cup	medium cornmeal
3g/¾ tsp	baking powder
3g/1 tsp	flaky sea salt

Apricot topping
30g/2 Tbsp	butter
30g/2 Tbsp	granulated sugar
4–5g/¼ oz	rosemary, fresh whole needles
4	apricots, halved and pitted

Plus
Crème fraîche, to serve

This combination marries the highly aromatic, menthol, and piney scents of rosemary with mellow corn. The apricots sit somewhere in between. Their piquancy has been gentled by cooking in caramely, slightly browned butter, but they are still bright. These flavors dance happily with each other but are grounded by the butteriness of almond. Perfect with tea.

Total: 1hr 40 mins

15 mins	5 mins	10 mins	10 mins	40 mins	20 mins
Cook polenta	Cool & blend	Cook apricots	Mix cake	Assemble & bake	Cool & serve

1   First, cook the polenta. Heat the milk to simmering and add the polenta. Whisk over medium-low heat until thickened, then continue to whisk for a few minutes, until creamy and smooth—taste it and check for hard lumps. Once it is tender, let cool.

2   Once cooled, mix the polenta with the eggs and set aside.

3   To cook the apricot topping, melt the butter, add the sugar, and heat until bubbling and browning slightly. Finely chop half of the rosemary, add, and bubble for 30 seconds or so, then place the apricot halves into the pan, cut-side down. Add the rest of the large pieces of rosemary around the apricots. Cook for 8 minutes over low heat—check and see if the apricots have colored a little. The butter/sugar should be dark in spots like a dark caramel. Turn off the heat.

4   Preheat the oven to 375°F. Line the cake pan with parchment paper.

5   Meanwhile, for the cake, cream the butter and sugar together for 2–3 minutes, until slightly lightened. Scrape down the sides of the bowl, then add the eggs/polenta mixture slowly until well combined.

6   Mix the dry ingredients together—the almond flour, cornmeal, baking powder, and salt—then stir them into the butter/sugar mixture.

7   Pour into the cake pan and smooth out. Nestle the apricots in the batter, cut-side up then pour the rosemary/butter/caramel over the top.

8   Bake for 25–30 minutes. It will be deep golden and if you poke it with a skewer, only a few moist crumbs should hang on.

9   Let cool in the pan before serving slightly warm with a spoonful of crème fraîche. The cake will last in an airtight container for up to 3 days.

Note

You can substitute the almond flour for 110g/¾ cup plus 2 tablespoons almond flour and 30g/¼ cup ground hazelnuts, which are DELISH if you have them.

Notes

Use all-purpose flour in place of toasted flour for a classic plain chiffon. This cake will also roll well if baked in a 9 x 13-inch/23 x 33cm swiss roll pan for 15–20 minutes, until firm but springy.

To make the cake easier to remove later, you can add a circle of parchment paper to the bottom of the pan.

CHAMOMILE AND TOASTED FLOUR CHIFFON CAKE

•

SERVES 6
(1 X 6-INCH CHIFFON CAKE—
DOUBLE THIS RECIPE FOR AN 8-INCH CAKE)

Techniques

Maillard reaction	pg.84
Making meringues	pg.46
Toasting flour	pg.18

Equipment

6-inch/15cm loose-bottomed aluminum pan (do not use non-stick!)

60g/¼ cup	whole milk
1	chamomile teabag
20g/3 Tbsp	all-purpose flour, to toast
40g/⅓ cup	all-purpose flour
160g/3	whole eggs
30g/2 Tbsp	vegetable oil
1g/¼ tsp	flaky sea salt
20g/1 Tbsp	honey
5g/1 tsp	good quality vanilla bean paste or ½ vanilla pod, scraped
40g/3 Tbsp	granulated sugar

Dusting

50g/¼ cup	granulated sugar
1	chamomile teabag

Honey cream

200g/¾ cup plus 2 Tbsp	heavy cream
25g/1 Tbsp	honey
1g/¼ tsp	flaky sea salt

Plus

Chamomile flowers, to decorate (optional)

Toasting flour changes the flavor and impacts how it interacts with other ingredients, making it perfect for airy cakes like chiffon, which don't predominantly rely on gluten for structure. A little of the flour goes a long way. This cake has a wonderful flavor and is a perfect tea-time snack with a little honey whipped cream on the side. Chiffon cake has a fragile structure that requires it to cling onto the edges of a pan and be cooled upside down for success—avoid non-stick pans at all costs!

Total: 3 hrs 15 mins

30 mins	1 hr 10 minutes	1 hr 30 mins	5 mins
Infuse milk & toast flour	Mix cake batter & bake	Let cool	Dust with sugar & serve with whipped cream

1   Preheat the oven to 350°F.

2   Heat the milk until boiling, then add the teabag. Let cool completely. Press the teabag to extract as much chamomile flavor as possible. Re-measure the milk and make sure it is 60g/¼ cup.

3   Put the 20g/3 tablespoons of flour into a frying pan and toast over medium heat. Once it starts coloring, turn the heat down and keep it moving. Cook until dark golden in color. It will take 7–8 minutes. Let cool completely, then strain the toasted flour through a sieve into a bowl with the remaining flour.

4   Separate the eggs. Whisk the oil into the flour, followed by the chamomile milk. Then add the egg yolks, salt, honey, and vanilla.

5   Whisk the egg whites and sugar to a French meringue with medium peaks according to the instructions on page 118. Add 2–3 tablespoons of meringue to the yolk/flour mixture and whisk until combined. Then fold the rest of the meringue into the mixture in thirds, trying not to deflate the mixture too much.

6   Pour the batter into the cake pan, tapping the pan a few times on the counter to burst any large bubbles and to level the batter, and bake for 50–55 minutes—it will be risen and springy. Turn the cake upside down as soon as it comes out of the oven to cool. You may need to balance it on some pans to give it some height!

7   Let cool for at least 1 hour. To demold, carefully run a sharp knife or offset spatula around the edge of the pan. Gently push the cake out or lift the pan off.

8   For the dusting, whiz the granulated sugar up with the chamomile tea from the teabag, then dust this over the cake. Finish with chamomile flowers, if using.

9   For the honey cream, whip the cream until it is as thick as the honey. Add the honey and salt, then whip until thickened and smooth—don't over-whip it! It should just be soft. Serve dolloping spoonfuls with slices of the cake. Leftover cake will last at room temperature in an airtight container for up to 3 days.

UPSIDE-DOWN STICKY PEAR AND WALNUT CAKE

·

SERVES 6-8

Techniques

Caramelization	pg.84
Baking with nuts	pg.55

Equipment
8-inch/20cm springform pan

Walnuts
60g/⅔ cup	walnuts

Goo
240g/1 cup plus 2 Tbsp	light brown sugar, packed
80g/6 Tbsp	butter
120g/½ cup	heavy cream
3g/1 tsp	flaky sea salt

Cake
400g/14 oz	pears (about 2 small)
100g/7 Tbsp	butter, softened
100g/½ cup	dark brown sugar, packed
25g/2 Tbsp	granulated sugar
100g/2	whole eggs
90g/¾ cup	all-purpose flour
15g/2 Tbsp	buckwheat flour
8g/2 tsp	baking powder
½ tsp	ground cinnamon
1–2g/¼–½ tsp	flaky sea salt
20g/2 Tbsp	toasted walnuts from above
45g/3 Tbsp	whole milk
35g/2 Tbsp	heavy cream

Plus
Ice cream, to serve

I was never a fan of upside-down cakes until I realized one very important detail: they MUST be eaten warm. This is the sort of thing to serve at the end of lunch. The cake comes together in less than 5 minutes in a food processor, too! I'm always surprised at how far a small amount of buckwheat flour goes. Just a large spoonful in this recipe lifts it and creates the most delicious potent flavor. If you don't have any open, you could sub with more ground walnuts or flour.

Total: 1hr 35 mins

20 mins	15 mins	50 mins	10 mins
Toast walnuts, prep pears & goo	Mix cake	Bake	Cool & remove from pan

1   Toast the walnuts in a frying pan over medium heat for 5–8 minutes or for 15–20 minutes in a 400°F oven until toasty and golden. Set two-thirds aside and roughly chop—you want a mixture of sizes with some halves and larger pieces.

2   To make the goo, in a saucepan combine the sugar and butter. Bring to a boil and bubble for 1–2 minutes, until darkened. Whisk in the cream and salt and bubble for 1 more minute, until thickened. Reserve half for serving.

3   Line the bottom of the springform pan with parchment paper that extends about 1 inch up the sides of the pan. This will prevent the liquid from seeping out.

4   Pour the other half of the goo mixture into the pan. Sprinkle with half of the chopped toasted walnuts.

5   Peel, halve, and core the pears, then slice them into ¼-inch pieces. Arrange the pears in concentric circles, slightly overlapping, in the pan. Tuck the remaining roughly chopped walnuts into any gaps.

6   Preheat the oven to 375°F.

7   To make the cake in a stand mixer or by hand, cream together the butter and sugars. Add the eggs, one by one, scraping down the sides of the bowl as you go. Sift together the dry ingredients and beat into the butter with the paddle attachment. Grind the remaining toasted walnuts and stir in. Finally, stir in the milk and heavy cream.

OR

To mix in the food processor, blitz the walnuts with the granulated sugar until finely ground, then add the dark brown sugar and butter and blend until aerated and smooth. Add the eggs, one by one, scraping down the bowl as you go. Sift together the flours, baking powder, cinnamon, and salt, then add to the bowl. Finally, add the milk and heavy cream.

8   Spread the cake batter evenly over the pears. Bake for 45–50 minutes or until a skewer comes out clean. Let cool in the pan for 5–10 minutes. Place a plate underneath, then flip the cake over. Carefully remove the pan and paper. Serve warm with the reserved goo and ice cream. Leftovers should always be reheated!

Note

If your cake mixture splits as you mix it, see All About Fat on page 64 for tips.

STEAMED PLUM BUTTERMILK SPONGE CAKE

·

SERVES 3–4

Techniques

Steaming	pg.92

Equipment

1-quart/1-liter pudding basin or oven-safe bowl

Stewed plums

170g/6 oz	plums
1	bay leaf
1	cinnamon stick
40g/3 Tbsp	granulated sugar
10g/2 tsp	lemon juice
25g/2 Tbsp	water

Cake

Butter, for greasing
Demerara sugar, to dust

60g/¼ cup	butter, softened
80g/6 Tbsp	granulated sugar
3g/1 tsp	flaky sea salt
50g/1	whole egg
110g/¾ cup plus 2 Tbsp	all-purpose flour
1–2g/⅛–¼ tsp	baking soda
3g/¾ tsp	baking powder
110g/7 Tbsp	buttermilk
4g/1 tsp	good quality vanilla extract

Plus

Vanilla crème anglaise (see page 342), to serve

Steamed desserts are such a great way to end a meal. Because they take a bit of time, it's the perfect dessert to serve when you have a lazy lunch with friends—just pop it on when you sit down for your meal and don't stress because steamed desserts are pretty difficult to overcook. The stewed plums could be changed for peaches, apricots, or even subbed for jam—this is a no-stress dessert that has an impressive reveal.

Total: 1hr 30 mins

15 mins	15 mins	1 hr
Cook plums	Prep pudding basin or bowl & mix batter	Steam cake

1   For the plums, cut the plums into six, removing the pits. Set them aside (see the noyaux recipe on page 270 for how to use them). In a small saucepan, combine the bay leaf, cinnamon stick, granulated sugar, lemon juice, and water. Heat over medium heat, occasionally stirring until the sugar has dissolved. Add the plums to the saucepan and stir gently to coat them.

2   Bring the mixture to a gentle simmer, decrease the heat to low, and cover the saucepan with a lid. Steam for 4–5 minutes. If the plums are still firm, cook for a further 2 minutes. You want the plums to be tender but to hold their shape. Remove the saucepan from the heat and let the plums cool in the syrup for a few minutes.

3   For the cake, grease the pudding basin or bowl with butter and dust with demerara sugar. Strain the plums and put 100g/3½ oz in the bottom of the basin with 2 tablespoons of the syrup. Save the rest for serving.

4   In a mixing bowl, cream together the butter, sugar, and salt until light and fluffy.

5   Beat in the egg. Sift in the flour, baking soda, and baking powder and fold until just combined. Stir in the buttermilk and vanilla extract until the mixture is smooth.

6   Pour the mixture into the pudding basin, over the plums, cover it with a layer of parchment paper and foil, and secure with cooking twine.

7   Place the pudding basin into a large pot, set on a trivet (e.g., a tart ring) so it isn't sitting directly on the bottom. Fill with enough water to reach halfway up the sides of the basin. Cover the pot with a lid and bring the water to a boil.

8   Decrease the heat to low and let the cake steam for 1 hour or until it is firm and cooked through—check it has reached a 207°F internal temperature (just stab a probe thermometer through the foil!).

9   Carefully remove the pudding basin from the pot and let it rest for a few minutes before removing the parchment paper and foil.

10   Turn out onto a plate. Serve with the additional plums, plum syrup, and some vanilla crème anglaise.

11   The cake is best enjoyed immediately. Store leftovers in the fridge for 2–3 days and reheat before eating.

LEMON CURD MERINGUE TARTS WITH BLACKBERRIES

·

MAKES 6 SMALL TARTS

An absolute classic, these little tartlets zing with the addition of blackberries. The flavor of the lemons is bolstered by using a zippy extra-virgin olive oil but you could play around with the fat here. Though the meringue is best made last minute, the curd and cases can be made in advance.

Techniques

Blind baking	pg.109
Thickening with starch	pg.94
Egg coagulation	pg.40
Swapping fats	pg.56
Making meringues	pg.46

Equipment

6 x 3¼-inch/8cm tart rings

Tart cases

½ x recipe	tart pastry (see page 119) or rich tart pastry (see page 119)
125g/4½ oz	blackberries, halved

Olive oil lemon curd

110g/7 Tbsp	lemon juice
Zest of 4	lemons
90g/½ cup	granulated sugar
35g/about 2	egg yolks
12g/2 Tbsp	cornstarch
80g/6 Tbsp	butter, chopped
1–2g/¼–½ tsp	flaky sea salt
35g/2½ Tbsp	olive oil (if it's a super-strong flavored oil, you might want to decrease to 25g/1¾ tsp!)

Swiss meringue

60g/2	egg whites (from above)
120g/½ cup plus 2 Tbsp	granulated sugar

Plus

Edible fresh flowers (optional)

Total: 3 hrs 10 mins

1 hr	1 hr 30 mins	30 mins	10 mins
Mix, line & bake tart cases	Make lemon curd & set	Make meringue	Decorate & finish

1. For the tart cases, line and blind bake 6 x 3¼-inch/8cm tart cases according to the instructions on page 121. Place 2–3 blackberry halves in the bottom of each tart case.

2. For the lemon curd, combine the lemon juice and zest in a saucepan and whisk in half the sugar. Heat over medium heat until simmering. Meanwhile, whisk the egg yolks, the other half of the sugar, and the cornstarch together. Temper the egg yolk mix with the lemon juice by gently pouring it in and whisking at the same time, and then return it all to the stovetop. Heat over low-medium heat and whisk constantly until it thickens.

3. Once it has boiled for 1 minute, remove from the heat and let cool for about 10 minutes, until it is about 140°F, before whisking in the butter and salt. Check for seasoning. Finally, whisk in the olive oil. It should be shiny and fluid.

4. Let cool for a minute or two, then pour into the tart cases, about 50g/1¾ oz per case. You can do this while warm or you can make it in advance and spoon in later. Level the cases. Allow to set in the fridge, about 1 hour.

5. For the Swiss meringue, make according to the instructions on page 118, whisking to stiff peaks.

6. To assemble, spoon 1–2 heaped tablespoons of meringue onto the curd. A dollop looks good here. If using a blowtorch, gently move it back and forth over the meringue to toast. Or if you don't have a blow torch and want it warmed up, heat in a 375°F oven until lightly toasted. Decorate with the remaining blackberry halves and edible flowers, if using. Let cool a little before eating.

7. While the blowtorched lemon meringue tarts will last for a couple of days in the fridge, they are best enjoyed immediately.

CHOCONUT TART

·

SERVES 8

Techniques

Making custard	pg.42
Ganache	pg.63
Emulsification	pg.61

Equipment
8 x 1½-inch/20 x 3.5cm tart pan

Crust (you can also use the cocoa crust on page 248)

130g/4½ oz	dark chocolate, chopped
130g/1½ cups	toasted coconut flakes
1–2g/¼–½ tsp	flaky sea salt

Chocolate crémeux

100g/7 Tbsp	whole milk
190g/¾ cup plus 1 Tbsp	heavy cream
55g/about 3	egg yolks
50g/2½ Tbsp	barley malt syrup
190g/7 oz	milk chocolate, finely chopped
30g/2 Tbsp	butter
1g/¼ tsp	flaky sea salt

Plus
Very dark chocolate (85%+)

This no-bake tart base is inspired by my sister Adrienne—for her wedding, she requested salty chocolate coconut clusters as favors for all the guests. You can play around with the chocolate in this tart—both elements work well with milk or dark.

Total: 5 hrs

30 mins	15 mins	4 hrs	15 mins
Make & chill crust	Make crémeux	Pour into case & allow to set	Finish & serve

1 For the crust, melt the chocolate over a bain-marie. Slightly crush the coconut flakes (you need to be able to press them into a tart case without leaving gaps), then stir them into the chocolate, followed by the salt. Mix well, then taste, adding salt if required. If you can't find toasted coconut flakes, toast raw coconut flakes at 325°F for 10–15 minutes until very golden.

2 Put a circle of parchment paper on the bottom of the tart pan to help easily remove the tart later. Press the crust into the tart pan, trying to make sure there are no holes. There should be a fairly robust ¾-inch-thick crust on the edges.

3 Chill completely in the fridge or freezer. Before proceeding to the next step, check for gaps and fill in with extra melted chocolate, if required.

4 To make the crémeux, first make a crème anglaise: Heat together the milk and cream in a saucepan until simmering. Meanwhile, whisk the egg yolks with the barley malt syrup. Carefully pour one-third of the milk/cream over the egg yolks while whisking to temper the eggs (see page 42 in All About Eggs). Pour this back into the saucepan and stir over low heat until it thickens; it should read around 180°F on a probe thermometer and should coat the back of a spoon or spatula when it is lifted out of the mixture.

5 Pour the custard through a sieve over the finely chopped milk chocolate, butter, and salt. Let rest for 1 minute and then whisk until smooth. Pour this into the prepared tart case.

6 Allow to chill completely, at least 4–6 hours.

7 To finish, grate very dark chocolate on top using a fine grater. Store in the fridge and serve in thick slices. This will keep well in the fridge for 3 days, if it lasts that long.

Note

The final grating of chocolate works best if it's very bitter, but you could dust with cocoa powder or omit if you prefer. The crémeux is extremely lush but takes its time to set up. Patience is key. If you don't have barley malt syrup, dark brown sugar or maple syrup make good alternatives here.

PASSIONFRUIT POSSET FLOWER TARTS

·

MAKES 6 SMALL TARTS

I'm always caught between rustic bakes and gilding the lily. These are definitely in the latter camp. These tarts look beautiful with fresh passionfruit spooned on top, but the whipped ganache petals take them to the next level.

Techniques

Blind baking	pg.109
Thickening with acid	pg.101
Whipping cream	pg.60
Using gelatin	pg.100

Equipment
6 x 3¼-inch/8cm tart rings

Tart cases

½ x recipe	tart pastry (see page 119) or rich tart pastry (see page 119)

Whipped vanilla ganache

½	gelatin leaf (see page 100; I use Dr. Oetker Platinum) (optional)
300g/1¼ cups	heavy cream
½	vanilla pod, scraped or 8g/1½ tsp good quality vanilla bean paste
Pinch of fine salt	
120g/4¼ oz	white chocolate, finely chopped

Posset

30g/2 Tbsp	passionfruit juice (about 3 passionfruits)
10g/2 tsp	lime juice
200g/¾ cup plus 2 Tbsp	heavy cream
60g/¼ cup plus 1 Tbsp	granulated sugar
40g/3 Tbsp	butter
1g/¼ tsp	flaky sea salt

Plus

2–3	passionfruits, to serve

Total: 3 hrs 35 mins

1 hr	20 mins	2 hrs	15 mins
Make pastry, line & blind bake	Make ganache	Make posset. Fill & chill tarts	Finish

1   For the tart cases, line and blind bake 6 x 3¼-inch/8cm tart cases according to the instructions on page 121.

2   To make the vanilla ganache, bloom the gelatin, if using, in cold water for 10 minutes, then squeeze out. Heat the cream with the vanilla and salt until simmering, then whisk in the bloomed gelatin, if using. Pour this over the white chocolate and whisk until smooth. Pour into a container and allow to chill completely.

3   To juice the passionfruit for the posset, spoon out the flesh, discard the seeds, and place into a blender. Blitz until liquefied, then strain through a fine sieve to remove any seeds.

4   To make the posset, mix together the passionfruit and lime juices and set aside. Heat the cream and sugar together, then continue to simmer for 3 minutes to ensure the sugar is fully dissolved. Turn off the heat, then whisk in the juice, followed by the butter and salt. Pour this mixture into the tart cases, about 50g/1¾ oz per case, and put into the fridge to chill completely, around 2 hours.

5   To finish, whip the ganache until soft peaks form, being careful not to over-whip. This can take less than 1 minute in a stand mixer on medium speed. Either spoon blobs on top of each tart or transfer into a piping bag and cut a ½-inch hole or fit with a round tip. Pipe blobs around the edge of the tart cases. Add a spoonful of passionfruit pulp to the middle of each.

6   These tarts are best enjoyed on the day they are made but can be stored in the fridge for up to 3 days, though the tart cases will soften.

 Notes   The gelatin in the ganache is optional, but it helps to stabilize this mixture and prevent it from splitting when it is whipped.

You can use whipped cream to decorate instead of ganache—whip 400g/1⅔ cups of heavy cream with 40g/3 tablespoons granulated sugar and the vanilla above to soft peaks.

BROWN SUGAR CUSTARD TART

·

SERVES 6–8

Techniques

Blind baking	pg.109
Egg coagulation	pg.40

Equipment
8 x 1½-inch/20 x 3.5cm tart pan

Tart cases

½ x recipe	rich tart pastry (see page 119)

Egg wash (see page 343)

Custard

75g/⅓ cup	whole milk
400g/1⅔ cups	heavy cream
75g/⅓ cup	panela sugar (you can use dark brown sugar here if you don't have any)
1g/¼ tsp	flaky sea salt
120g/6	egg yolks

Custard tart is always a crowd-pleasing classic. An easy way to update it is by playing around with the sugar. I love using brown sugar—the more flavor the better; panela, an unrefined cane sugar, or a dark muscovado shine here. The final torching of the top creates a dramatic aesthetic and extra toasty notes, but isn't essential.

Total: 3 hrs 30 mins

1 hr	20 mins	35 mins	1 hr 30 mins	5 mins
Make pastry, line & blind bake	Make custard	Bake custard	Remove from oven & chill	Torch & serve

1 For the tart case, line and blind bake the pastry, according to the instructions on page 121, sealing four times with egg wash. You want the pastry to be a tiny bit thicker than ⅛ inch so it can withstand the custard filling.

2 Preheat the oven to 275°F.

3 To make the custard, in a medium saucepan, heat the milk and cream with the sugar and salt. Whisk until simmering and the sugar is dissolved, about 176°F.

4 In a separate bowl, whisk the egg yolks until combined. Carefully pour one-third of the hot cream over the egg yolks, whisking constantly to temper the yolks. Whisk the rest of the hot cream in. Strain the mixture through a sieve into a measuring cup.

5 Pour the warm custard mixture into the tart case.

6 Bake until the internal temperature of the tart is 171–174°F or the tart is mainly set around the outside. There should be a 2-inch wobble in the center. It will continue cooking once you take it out of the oven. Start checking after 15–20 minutes, but it may take up to 35 minutes.

7 Let cool completely to room temperature before serving, around 1 hour 30 minutes. You can also chill in the fridge and serve cold, but the pastry might become soggy. If desired, torch the top of the tart once cool. Leftovers can be stored in the fridge for 3 days.

Notes

This classic baked custard can also be baked in ramekins as crème brûlée or crème caramel.

If your panela sugar is lumpy, whiz it in the blender before you use it.

SABLÉ BRETON FRUIT TARTS

·

MAKES 8 TARTS

Techniques

Starch-bound custard	pg.44

Equipment
Cupcake or muffin pan

1 x recipe	sablé Breton (see page 130)
½ x recipe	crème mousseline (see page 338)

Seasonal fruit, such as raspberries or thinly sliced gooseberries

Plus
Chopped pistachios, edible fresh flowers, to decorate (optional)
Clear apricot jam, to glaze (optional)

These are little freeform fruit tarts that you can decorate however you like. The recipe can be scaled up or down and you can really let your artistic side free. Berries and firm plums work well here, but try to avoid very juicy fruits, which can make the bottoms soggy at an alarming rate.

Total: 2 hrs 40 mins

15 mins	1 hr	15 mins	40 mins	30 mins
Mix sablé Breton	Rest & make pastry cream	Bake cookies	Cool	Finish mousseline & assemble

1   Lightly grease the cupcake pan. Roll out the sablé Breton dough to ½–¾ inch thick between two sheets of parchment paper. Chill until firm, around 30 minutes, then cut 8 x 1¾-inch rounds (or whatever size fits in your cupcake pan). Each should weigh about 25g/¾ oz per bottom.

2   Preheat the oven to 375°F. Bake for 15–17 minutes, until evenly golden. Let cool completely before removing from the pan as the cookie is very fragile while warm.

3   To finish, pipe generous 30g/1 oz blobs of mousseline cream onto each bottom. Decorate each blob with fruit and nuts or flowers, if using. Brush the fruit with warmed apricot jam as a shiny glaze, if you like.

TOMATO AND FENNEL TARTE TATIN

·

SERVES 4

Techniques

Lamination	pg.69
Caramelization	pg.84

Equipment

8-inch/20cm oven-safe frying pan (e.g., a cast-iron pan)

Tart crust

½ x recipe	rough puff (see page 128) or you can use classic puff pastry (see page 124), or savory shortcrust pastry (see page 120)

Filling

1	fennel bulb (about 350g/12¼ oz)
250g/9 oz	cherry tomatoes
30g/2 Tbsp	butter
30g/2 Tbsp	light brown sugar
15g/2 tsp	honey
3g/¾ tsp	flaky sea salt
1g/½ tsp	black pepper
4g/2 tsp	fennel seeds, plus extra to garnish
½–1 tsp	chile flakes
10g/2 tsp	light soy sauce (optional)

A tarte Tatin is a feast for the eyes and one of the most glorious things you can serve up for lunch or dinner. And there's nothing quite like the heart-fluttering post-bake reveal. I'm not fussy about what pastry to use, as long as you get the cook of the filling right. It's a total showstopper.

Total: 2 hrs 30 mins

1 hr	20 mins	30 mins	30 mins	10 mins
Make pastry	Rest	Roll out pastry & make filling	Bake	Cool & garnish

1   Preheat the oven to 425°F.

2   For the tart crust, roll out your pastry to ⅛ inch thick and into a circle large enough to cover the frying pan. Set aside in the fridge.

3   For the filling, slice the fennel lengthwise (top to bottom) into ½ inch slices. Reserve and chop the fronds. Halve some of the tomatoes—this will help fit all the tomatoes in.

4   Melt the butter in the ovenproof frying pan over medium heat. Add the brown sugar and honey and stir to dissolve. Place the fennel in the pan face-side down. Turn up the heat and cook for 10–12 minutes or until the pan-facing side of the fennel is deeply browned and the sugar is melty and caramelized. Flip the fennel over occasionally to check. Don't be afraid to go dark.

5   Sprinkle with the flaky salt, black pepper, fennel seeds, and chile flakes, then add the cherry tomatoes into the gaps and cook for 5 minutes, or until the tomatoes start to blister and soften. Add the soy sauce for an extra umami flavor, if you like.

6   Place the pastry over the top of the fennel and tomato mixture, tucking the edges down around the sides of the pan. Cut a few vent holes in the top.

7   Bake for 25–30 minutes, or until the pastry is golden brown and cooked through. Once cooked, remove the pan from the oven and allow it to cool for a few minutes before turning it out onto a plate or serving dish.

8   Serve hot, garnished with the reserved fennel fronds and more fennel seeds.

ANY GALETTE

·

SERVES 4–6

Techniques

Lamination	pg.69
Thickening with starch	pg.94

Filling

500g/1 lb 2 oz	seasonal fruit
25–100g/ 2 Tbsp–½ cup	granulated sugar, depending on taste
7g/2⅔ tsp	cornstarch or all-purpose flour, (optional)

Pinch of fine salt, scraped vanilla pods, spices, zests, etc. (optional)

Galette base

½ x recipe	pie dough (see page 129)

Plus

Egg wash (see page 343)

12–25g/ 1–2 Tbsp	demerara sugar

The galette is my easy go-to, sweet or savory, crowd-pleaser; crispy, flaky, buttery pastry with seasonal roasted fruit or veggies. What's not to love? Think of it as a free-form/flat pie—it is endlessly adaptable and can be made in advance, which is always handy. It can also be eaten hot or cold and easily carried to a friend's house on the sheet it was baked on. When it comes to serving sweet versions, ice cream, whipped crème fraîche, custard—or all three—are all great options.

Total: 2 hrs 50 mins

20 mins	1 hr	30 mins	1 hr
Make pastry	Chill pastry & prepare filling	Roll out galette & decorate	Bake

Fruit galette

If you are using particularly juicy fruit, you might want to toss it with cornstarch or flour, but it isn't essential. Using a mixture of plums, blackberries, and other soft fruits is always a treat.

1   For the filling, cut the fruit in the desired way. Apricots and plums, for example, are nice in halves, while peaches are better in slices. Place the sliced fruit in a bowl and toss with the sugar and cornstarch/flour, if using. This is your opportunity to add salt, vanilla pod seeds, spices, zests, etc. Because the sugar will begin to draw the water out of the fruit, it's best to do this only 15–20 minutes max before you are ready for it to go into the oven.

2   Preheat the oven to 425°F.

3   Roll the dough to about ⅛ inch thick—you can either roll it into a rectangle or into a circle, depending on what shape of galette you want. For a circle, I go to 11 inches.

4   Arrange the fruit in a fun pattern or just lump it on, leaving a 1½-inch border.

5   Fold the pastry border over itself to create a crust, folding the pastry where it overlaps. Egg wash the galette and sprinkle with the demerara sugar.

6   Decrease the oven to 400°F and bake the galette for 40–60 minutes, until golden and bubbling. Check the bottom is cooked—you may want to bake for another 10 minutes or so, with foil covering the top. Let cool slightly before serving.

7   You can also bake it ahead of time and reheat in a 350°F oven for 10–15 minutes.

Veg galette

Techniques

Lamination	pg.69

Filling

150g/½ cup plus 2 Tbsp	ricotta
30g/about ½	whole egg (use the rest for Egg wash; see page 343)
25g/¼ cup	grated Parmesan cheese
3g/1 tsp	flaky sea salt
Zest of 1	lemon
1	garlic clove, grated
20g/1 cup	finely chopped soft herbs, like basil or dill
5–10g/1–2 tsp	lemon juice
Black pepper, to taste	

Zucchini

400g/14 oz	zucchini
2g/½ tsp	flaky sea salt
9g/2 tsp	olive oil

Galette base

½ x recipe	pie dough (see page 129)

Plus

Drizzle of olive oil
Radicchio leaves

You could put the veg straight onto the pastry bottom, but an herby ricotta mix is good with almost everything.

1   For the filling, mix together the ricotta, egg, Parmesan cheese, salt, lemon zest, grated garlic, finely chopped herbs, and lemon juice. Add black pepper to taste.

2   For the zucchini, cut into ¼-inch-thick rounds, then place into a colander and toss with the salt. Allow to drain for about 30 minutes—the water will be drawn out. Carefully squish the water out, then add the olive oil and toss.

3   Preheat the oven to 425°F.

4   Roll out the dough to about ⅛ inch thick—you can either roll it into a rectangle or into a circle, depending on what shape of galette you want. For a circle, I go for 11 inches.

5   Spread the ricotta mixture over the bottom, then arrange the zucchinis on top, leaving a 1½-inch border. Drizzle with a little olive oil.

6   Fold the pastry border over itself to create a crust, folding the pastry where it overlaps. Gently brush the galette with egg wash.

7   Decrease the oven to 400°F and bake the galette for 40–60 minutes, until golden in places. Check the bottom is cooked—you may want to bake for another 10 minutes or so, with foil covering the top. Let cool slightly before serving with radicchio leaves.

8   You can also bake it ahead of time and reheat in a 350°F oven for 10–15 minutes.

CHICKEN PIE WITH RICH PASTRY

·

SERVES 2–3

Techniques

Rubbing in	pg.99
Thickening with starch	pg.94

Equipment
8 x 5-inch/20 x 15cm rectangle pie dish

Chicken
13g/1 Tbsp	olive oil
200g/7 oz	bone-in, skin-on chicken thighs
400g/1⅔ cups	chicken stock
½	onion, chunked
½	celery stick, chunked
3	sprigs of tarragon

Filling
50g/1¾ oz	smoked bacon, cut into ¾-inch lardons
15g/1 Tbsp	butter
1	leek, sliced into ½-inch thick rounds
1	carrot, diced into ½-inch pieces
½	celery stick, diced into ½-inch pieces
15g/2 Tbsp	all-purpose flour
35g/2½ Tbsp	dry sherry
35g/2½ Tbsp	heavy cream
A good grating of nutmeg	
8g/¼ oz	tarragon leaves, finely chopped

Pie crust
1 x recipe	suet pie dough (see page 130)

Egg wash (see page 343)
Caraway seeds (optional)

This recipe is a collaboration between myself and the talented food stylist, chef, and writer extraordinaire Rosie Mackean. We had so much fun creating this ultimate chicken pie—her rich filling works perfectly with the suet-enriched pastry.

Total: 3 hrs 30 mins

20 mins	50 mins	30 mins	40 mins	1 hr	10 mins
Make pie crust	Chill crust & make filling	Chill filling	Roll out pie crust & fill pie	Bake	Cool & serve

1   To cook the chicken, heat the oil in a large pot or frying pan over medium heat. Season the thighs with salt and black pepper on the skin side, then place skin-side down and cook for 10–15 minutes, until golden brown. Flip and fry for 1 minute.

2   Pour in the chicken stock, carefully scraping up any gold on the bottom of the pan into the stock; the skin should be above the liquid level. Next, add the onion, celery, and tarragon sprigs. Simmer for 20 minutes.

3   Remove the chicken and strain the stock, discarding the onion, celery, and tarragon. Set aside 225g/¾ cup plus 3 tablespoons of the intensely flavored stock.

4   For the final filling mix, wipe out the pan, then cook the lardons over medium-low heat until golden, about 10 minutes. Add the butter and chopped vegetables and cook for another 10 minutes, until the leeks have wilted. Add the flour, stir for 1 minute, then add the sherry—it will look like a sticky goo.

5   Add the reserved stock gradually while whisking, a quarter at a time, waiting for it to bubble before adding the next lot. Simmer for 3–4 minutes, then turn off the heat and add the heavy cream, nutmeg, and season with some salt and black pepper.

6   Flake in the cooked chicken without skin, bones, and gristle. Transfer to a flat dish and cool completely.

7   Before using, stir the chicken mixture, then add the chopped tarragon (because it's a soft herb, it will lose flavor each time it's cooked!).

8   For the pie crust, preheat the oven to 400°F. Roll out the pie dough to ⅛ inch thick and about 10 x 16 inches. Cut in half. Grease your pie dish and lay one half into the dish—trim any excess around the edges so you have about 1 inch of overhang. Place into the fridge while you create the lattice. For the lattice, cut 4 x 2-inch wide strips. Cut two of these in half, so you now have six strips. Fill the pie dish with the chicken mix—about 650g/1 lb 7 oz should do it—and then create the lattice, interweaving the strips. Trim any excess from the lattice strips and fold over the bottom crust overhang, crimping with your finger and thumb in a wavy pattern. Brush gently with egg wash and add caraway seeds to the crust, if desired.

9   Bake for 50 minutes–1 hour, until bubbling and golden. Let stand for 10 minutes before serving. Your pie can be assembled 24 hours in advance and stored in the fridge (add 10 minutes to the cooking time) or baked from frozen (add 20 minutes extra to the cooking time and watch the color!).

Note

You could also use pie dough, rough puff, or any of your favorite pastry recipes for the top.

LEEK AND MUSTARD TART

·

SERVES 6

Techniques

Egg coagulation	pg.40
Lamination	pg.69
Maillard reaction	pg.84

Equipment
8-inch/20cm loose-bottomed fluted tart pan

Tart case

½ x recipe	rough puff pastry (see page 128) or you can use savory shortcrust pastry (see page 120) or pie dough (see page 129)
Egg wash	(see page 343)

Savory custard

65g/¼ cup	heavy cream
65g/¼ cup	crème fraîche
65g/¼ cup	whole milk
110g/2	whole eggs
30g/2 Tbsp	Dijon mustard

Filling

600g/1 lb 5 oz	leeks
3	garlic cloves
40g/3 Tbsp	butter
2	bay leaves
Parmesan rind (optional)	
½	vegetable stock cube or 1 tsp vegetable stock paste
A grating of nutmeg	
50g/½ cup	grated hard cheese, such as Gruyere or Cheddar

I'm averse to the "q" word . . . isn't it in desperate need of a rebrand? This is not your average q***** so let's just call this a savory tart: crisp, flaky pastry and rich custard with buttery leeks, spiked with mustard. It also has a gorgeously browned top; it's the sort of tart you'll wish you had leftovers of (but you probably won't, because it really is so inhalable).

Total: 4 hrs 50 mins

20 mins	1 hr 20 mins	1 hr	30 mins	40 mins	1 hr
Make pastry	Rest	Line & blind bake	Make fillings	Fill quiche & bake	Let cool

1   For the tart case, roll out the pastry using firm strokes of the rolling pin, turning it a quarter turn between each roll to keep it in an even shape. Roll it to ¹⁄₁₆–⅛ inch.

2   Line your tart pan. Roll the pastry up onto the rolling pin and drape over the case. Tuck carefully into the corners and press into the sides. Go over it several times with floured fingers if you need to—it's got to be super-tight to the pan. Trim the overhang with scissors so it only has ¾ inch left. Dock with a fork all over—sides and all. Chill in the fridge for 1 hour or the freezer for 30 minutes.

3   To blind bake, preheat the oven to 400°F. Press foil into the tart, ensuring it is tight to the edges (foil gets into the edges best, but please note foil does not work for sweet pastry, it will stick, but it works fabulously for flaky pastry). Pack with raw rice or baking beans. Bake the case for 30 minutes, until it looks very dry when you peak inside. Remove the rice/beans and bake for another 20–30 minutes, until golden brown and fully baked. Brush the baked case with egg wash (fill in all the docked holes!) and return to the oven until magnificent looking—about 10 minutes.

4   For the savory custard, blitz all the ingredients together and strain through a sieve. Season with black pepper and salt. If you like it more tangy, add more mustard.

5   For the filling, rinse the leeks and cut the thick green part off. Slice into thin rounds and reweigh—you should have around 400g/14 oz. Slice the garlic thinly or grate finely. Heat the butter in a pan until foaming, then add the leeks, garlic, bay leaves, and Parmesan rind, if using. Sauté over medium heat for 15 minutes, until wilted. Add the crumbled stock cube or paste and nutmeg. Taste and check if it needs salt—add as required.

6   To assemble the tart, put all of the leeks into the tart case, removing the rind, if using, and bay leaves, then pour in the custard. Sprinkle the cheese on top.

7   Bake at 375°F until the internal temperature reaches 163°F. Start checking around 20 minutes in, but it could take up to 40 minutes. Check in a few spots—it's OK if the middle is still a bit gooey or not quite up to temperature as carryover cooking will take care of that, trust me.

8   Wait for 1 hour before cutting or chill overnight, then reheat the slices before serving—10 minutes in a 350°F oven should do it. If desired, trim the crust with a sharp knife.

Notes

Any leftovers can be kept in the fridge for 3 days and reheated.

SPICED PUMPKIN BUNS

·

MAKES 12 BUNS

Techniques

Fermentation	pg.76
Gluten development	pg.14
Adding cooked starch to dough	pg.20

Equipment
8-inch/20cm square baking dish

Dough
150–200g/ 5¼ –7 oz	pumpkin (I like kabocha squash)
130g/½ cup plus 1 Tbsp	whole milk (see Note on page 176)
50g/1	whole egg
4g/1½ tsp	dry yeast
300g/2⅓ cups	bread flour
5g/2¼ tsp	medium curry powder
12g/1 Tbsp	granulated sugar
6g/1 tsp	fine salt
40g/3 Tbsp	butter, softened
10g/½ cup	cilantro, finely chopped
15g/½ oz	green onions, finely chopped
Egg wash (see page 343)	
2–4g/1–2 tsp	nigella seeds or cumin seeds, to sprinkle

Chile maple butter
150g/½ cup plus 2 Tbsp	butter
2–2½ tsp	chile flakes, depending on your tolerance
2g/½ tsp	flaky sea salt
50g/3 Tbsp	maple syrup

Not your average pumpkin spice, these super-soft buns are bolstered with curry powder and laced with green onions and cilantro. The chile maple butter, folded into the dough "Parker House roll"-style before shaping, adds sweetness and kick.

Total: 4 hrs 20 mins

1 hour	35 mins	1 hr	1 hr 20 mins	25 mins
Roast & cool pumpkin	Make dough	Bulk ferment & make maple butter	Shape & proof	Bake

1 Preheat the oven to 400°F. Cut the pumpkin in half. Place face-down on a baking sheet lined with parchment paper. Bake for 40 minutes, until very soft. A knife should easily pierce the flesh.

2 Allow to cool until you can handle it safely but it's still warm, about 20 minutes. Remove the flesh and smoosh with a fork until smooth—you need 100g/3½ oz.

3 If you are using your pumpkin purée while hot, add cold milk, then the egg in the bowl of your stand mixer. (If you did step 1 in advance and your pumpkin purée is cold, warm the milk to 140°F, then add to the pumpkin, followed by the egg.) Mix briefly.

4 Next, add the yeast, followed by the flour and curry powder, finally adding the sugar and salt.

5 Mix on medium-high speed in the stand mixer for 8–10 minutes, until medium gluten development is reached. Rest for 5 minutes. Add the butter and mix for 5 minutes.

6 Add the chopped cilantro and green onions. Continue mixing for 3–10 minutes on high speed, until it pulls away from the sides of the bowl and full gluten development is reached. Scrape down as needed. If the dough doesn't come together in this time, rest for 5 minutes, then mix for another 5–10 minutes. The dough will be smooth and fully developed.

7 Move into a lightly oiled bowl (use about 1 teaspoon and spread it all over) and cover so it doesn't dry out! Let rise for 45 minutes–1 hour, until it doubles. This dough is quite active so you shouldn't have to wait too long.

8 To make the chile maple butter, melt the butter until foaming and add the chile. Turn off the heat, then stir in the salt and maple syrup. Whisk as it cools. Use when the butter is cooled but not solid.

9 Tip the proofed dough onto a well-floured surface. If your dough is very active, you might want to press it flat onto a baking sheet and then place in the freezer for 20 minutes so it is easier to work with.

Notes

A pumpkin or squash with low water content and dense flesh will make the most flavorful bun.

Continued ⟶

SPICED PUMPKIN BUNS
Continued

10 Press down into a rectangle 16 x 9½ inches and about ½ inch thick. Divide into thirds, about 5 inches in width each. Brush 30–40g/1–1½ oz of the cooled chile maple butter onto each section of dough. Reserve the rest of the chile maple butter for serving.

11 Fold the rectangles in half lengthwise. Cut the folded dough into four equal pieces. You should now have 12 buns. To finish, tuck the edges of each bun under itself to meet. Nestle the buns into a lined 8-inch/20cm square baking dish.

12 Let proof, covered, for 45 minutes–1 hour. The buns should be kissing each other by now.

13 Preheat the oven to 400°F.

14 Brush the buns generously with egg wash and sprinkle with nigella seeds. Try to get into the little divots between the buns.

15 Bake for 20–25 minutes, until golden. To double-check they are baked in the middle, check with a temperature probe that they are above 199°F.

16 Let cool for at least 5 minutes in the dish and then move onto a cooling rack. Wait at least 15 minutes (if you can!) before enjoying. Serve with the remaining chile maple butter.

17 These buns will stay fresh for 2 days at room temperature, wrapped tightly.

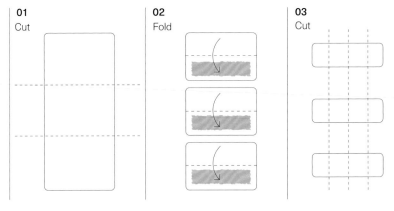

01
Cut

02
Fold

03
Cut

Note

Depending on the pumpkin you use, the dough can behave differently. This is because the water content varies between pumpkins. If the dough looks very dry and stiff, you can add an additional 30–50g/2–3 tablespoons whole milk during the mixing process.

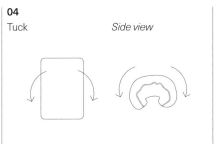

04
Tuck   *Side view*

05
Nestle

FESTIVE BUNS

·

MAKES 9 BUNS

Techniques

Fermentation	pg.76
Gluten development	pg.14
Starch gelatinization	pg.20
Sugar syrup	pg.33

Equipment

8-inch/20cm square pan

Tangzhong

20g/3 Tbsp	all-purpose flour
100g/7 Tbsp	water

Dough

85g/½ cup plus 1 Tbsp	golden raisins
100g/3½ oz	white chocolate
25g/2 Tbsp	whole milk
20g/1 Tbsp	honey
50g/1	whole egg
200g/1½ cups	bread flour
4g/1⅓ tsp	dry yeast
10g/1 Tbsp	granulated sugar
1	vanilla pod, scraped or 8g/2 tsp good quality vanilla extract
4g/⅔ tsp	fine salt
Zest of 1	orange
60g/¼ cup	butter, softened
Egg wash (see page 343)	

Glaze

60g/¼ cup	orange juice
60g/¼ cup	granulated sugar

Plus

Ground pistachios, to decorate

Notes

If making hot cross buns, mix 100g/¾ cup all-purpose flour with 1 teaspoon granulated sugar and 90–105g/6–7 tablespoons water and whisk well until you get a pipeable mixture. Transfer to a piping bag and pipe crosses on the proofed buns.

This bun recipe also lends itself well to spices—saffron would work marvelously.

The combination of orange, pistachios, raisins, and white chocolate makes a distinctly festive bun that can be enjoyed all year round. Add a cross and you've got an alternative hot cross bun that might make the original jealous. The classic tangzhong bun dough has been adapted to include honey and orange zest, as well as plenty of mix-ins.

Total: 4 hrs 30 mins

30 mins	1 hr 30 mins	2 hrs	20 mins	10 mins
Mix dough	Bulk ferment	Shape & proof	Bake	Remove from oven & glaze

1   To make the tangzhong, off the heat, whisk the all-purpose flour and water together.

2   Cook over medium heat, whisking/stirring constantly, until it thickens. It will be very thick. Take off the heat and move it into the bowl of a stand mixer, allowing it to cool slightly. Too hot and you risk harming the yeast, so if you can comfortably touch it, that is good.

3   Soak the raisins by covering in boiling water for 10 minutes, then drain before using. Chop the chocolate into ½-inch pieces.

4   In the bowl of a stand mixer, add the milk, honey, and egg on top of the warm tangzhong, followed by the bread flour, yeast, sugar, vanilla, salt, and zest. Mix and add in the butter according to the instructions on page 123.

5   Once full gluten development is reached (this is when you can pull a thin, almost translucent layer with the dough), add the raisins and chocolate and mix for 1–2 minutes, until well combined.

6   Remove from the bowl and round it a few times on the work surface so it has a smooth surface, then transfer to a clean bowl. Let rest/rise in a bowl, covered, for 1 hour or until puffy and doubled.

7   Divide into nine 70g/2½ oz pieces and shape into rounds with the curve of your hand—this can be tricky because there is so much filling, but just persevere! Nestle into the pan. Cover and proof for 1–1½ hours or until very puffy.

8   Preheat the oven to 375°F. Gently brush the buns with egg wash and then bake for 16–20 minutes or until golden and the internal dough temperature reading is around 194°F.

9   While the buns are baking, prepare the glaze. Heat the orange juice and sugar together until bubbling and then let cool.

10 Brush the warm buns with the glaze and sprinkle the ground pistachios on top. The buns can be stored in an airtight container at room temperature for 3 days.

EARL GREY SCONES

·

MAKES 5-6 SCONES

Techniques

Rubbing in	pg.99
Rising agents	pg.74

Equipment

2½-inch round or fluted cutter

Scones

220g/1¾ cups	all-purpose flour
6g/2 teabags	Earl Grey, finely ground
30g/2½ Tbsp	granulated sugar
16g/4 tsp	baking powder
2g/⅓ tsp	fine salt
75g/5 Tbsp	butter, cold
130g/½ cup	crème fraîche
Egg wash (see page 343)	

Plus

Crème fraîche
Raspberry rhubarb jam (see page 335)
Stewed plums (see page 155)

I think people often fear scones—we've been told so many times to avoid overworking the dough for fear of producing rocks, but please don't be scared to work the dough. I think most errors actually come from underworking! Your enemy is dry bits and I promise these won't be heavy—there's plenty of rising agents in there to lighten things up.

Total: 1 hr 15 mins

10 mins	30 mins	15 mins	20 mins
Mix scones	Cut & rest	Bake	Let cool

1   Line a baking sheet with parchment paper.

2   In a large mixing bowl, whisk together the all-purpose flour, Earl Grey, granulated sugar, baking powder, and salt until well combined.

3   Cut the cold butter into ½–¾-inch pieces, then rub into the flour mixture using your fingertips until it resembles coarse breadcrumbs, about 5 minutes.

4   Add the crème fraîche to the mixture and stir until just combined. You can use a round-bladed knife to cut through the dough to stir it together.

5   Lightly dust a clean surface with flour and transfer the dough to it. Knead the dough gently by folding it over on itself several times until it is smooth and no dry bits remain, about 1 minute. Then, using a rolling pin or your palms, flatten it into a 1-inch-thick dough. You want to make sure the dough is evenly combined and there are no dry bits or areas where the dough isn't in one piece, otherwise it will split open during baking.

6   Using a 2½-inch round or fluted cutter, cut out scones decisively from the dough and place them upside down on the prepared baking sheet. You can re-roll the scraps. They often turn out a bit oddly shaped but are still very delicious.

7   Rest the scones for about 20 minutes while you preheat the oven to 425°F.

8   Brush the tops of the scones with a little egg wash and bake in the preheated oven for 12–14 minutes or until they are golden brown. They should be towering.

9   Once baked, remove the scones from the oven and transfer them to a wire rack to cool. Serve with crème fraîche, jam, and plums.

10   Store for 2 days in an airtight container, though you will lose crispness.

FLAKY CHEESE AND PICKLE SCONES

•

MAKES 6 LARGE SCONES

Techniques

Lamination	pg.69

Equipment
2½-inch cutter

210g/1⅔ cups	all-purpose flour
30g/¼ cup	dark rye flour
10g/2½ tsp	baking powder
4g/1¼ tsp	flaky sea salt
2g/1 tsp	black pepper
100g/1 cup	grated Cheddar cheese
110g/½ cup	butter, very cold
75g/2½ oz	pickles, drained and chopped
120g/½ cup	buttermilk (see Note)
Egg wash (see page 343)	

The humble cheese scone is given the flaky treatment. The addition of rye flour and pickle chunks in the layers gives these scones a deli sandwich energy that would be welcome at any picnic. Working fast and having a light touch here is key for the flakiest scones possible.

Total: 1 hr 15 mins

5 mins	5 mins	5 mins	15–45 mins	25 mins	20 mins
Mix	Add folds	Shape & cut	Rest	Bake	Let cool

1   Get everything cold. And I mean cold. If you have time, put your dry ingredients in the freezer for 20 minutes before mixing. Your butter must be fridge-cold and firm to the touch.

2   Combine all the dry ingredients in a bowl, plus half the grated Cheddar cheese.

3   Cut the butter into ¾ inch cubes. Using the paddle attachment or your fingertips, work the cold butter into the dry ingredients, along with the chopped pickles for about 30 seconds. Only go so far that the butter is in irregular-size pieces. You need some larger bits of butter to get the layers later.

4   Now, add the buttermilk in a steady stream and mix until it is looking just hydrated—there can still be dry bits.

5   Tip onto a clean surface and push together, scraping all the dry bits into the middle.

6   Roll to approximately 16 inches long, sprinkle with half of the leftover cheese and perform a single fold—that's when you bring the top down two-thirds and then the bottom over the middle third, like a business letter!

7   Turn 90 degrees and roll to 16 inches long, then sprinkle with the rest of the cheese and perform another single fold. Use a knife or a bench scraper to cut the folded edge—this will give you the best layers possible.

8   Pat the dough into a rectangle around 1 inch high. Trim the edges (you can bake these as snack scraps!) and pat down slightly to get the dough back into proportion. Cut into six large squares. Place on a baking sheet lined with parchment paper and put into the freezer for 15 minutes or the fridge for 45 minutes.

9   Preheat the oven to 425°F.

10   Gently brush the tops of the scones with egg wash, if desired. Bake for 12–15 minutes (watch the color), then turn the oven down to 375°F and continue cooking for 5–10 minutes, until the scones are golden and well baked. Transfer to a cooling rack to cool, then serve warm.

Note

If you don't have buttermilk, mix 115g/½ cup whole milk with 5g/ 1 teaspoon white wine vinegar and then put in the fridge to curdle for about 5 minutes. It will appear thickened but a bit split.

BROWN BUTTER BANANA COOKIES

·

MAKES 9–10 COOKIES

Techniques

Browning butter	pg.88

125g/½ cup	dark rum
90g/⅔ cup	raisins
80g/6 Tbsp	brown butter, melted (see page 88)
75g/6 Tbsp	granulated sugar
75g/6 Tbsp	light brown sugar
75g/2½ oz	very ripe, gooey bananas (peeled weight)
150g/1¼ cups	all-purpose flour
3g/½ tsp	baking soda
⅛ tsp	ground allspice or ground cloves
40g/½ cup	rolled oats
1–2g/¼–½ tsp	flaky sea salt

This little egg-free cookie comes together very quickly. Soaking the raisins in rum for a few hours takes the flavors to the next level, but you could just as easily soak them in boiling water for 10 minutes to speed things up. These cookies are my homage to Milli Taylor's famously good Brown Butter Banana Bread—all the comforting flavors in a miniature package. As ever, the blacker and gooier the bananas you begin with, the better!

Total: 2 hrs 45 mins

2 hrs	20 mins	10 mins	15 mins
Soak raisins in rum	Brown butter	Mix dough	Bake

1   To soak the raisins, pour the rum over them and cover. Let rest for at least 2 hours but they will keep for up to 1 month in the fridge. To speed this up, you can warm the rum to about 140°F before pouring it over.

2   Preheat the oven to 350°F.

3   In a mixing bowl, mix the melted brown butter, granulated sugar, and brown sugar until combined.

4   Add the mashed banana to the bowl and stir until combined.

5   Sift in the flour, baking soda, and ground allspice or ground cloves. Add the oats and flaky salt, then mix until just combined. Fold in the drained rum raisins.

6   Line a baking sheet with parchment paper.

7   Scoop 60g/2¼ oz balls of dough onto the lined baking sheet—try to keep them as round and even as possible. Leave space between the cookies to allow space to spread.

8   Bake for 12–14 minutes, or until the edges are golden brown.

9   Remove from the oven and let the cookies cool on the baking sheet for a few minutes before transferring them to a cooling rack to cool completely. The cookies will last in an airtight container for 3 days.

Note

Cloves and bananas share a flavor compound, so a little pinch will help take the banana-y flavor to the max!

CHOCOLATE, PEANUT, AND COCONUT TWICE-BAKED COOKIES

•

MAKES 16–20 COOKIES

Techniques

Creaming	pg.59

80g/6 Tbsp	butter, softened
80g/6 Tbsp	granulated sugar
110g/2	whole eggs
200g/1½ cups	all-purpose flour
2g/½ tsp	baking powder
3g/1 tsp	flaky sea salt
80g/½ cup plus 10g/1 Tbsp	roasted salted peanuts
3g/1½ tsp	espresso powder
100g/3½ oz	milk chocolate, chopped into ¼-inch pieces
75g/¾ cup	dried shredded coconut

Plus

| 100g/3½ oz | dark or milk chocolate, chopped, to melt and dip (optional) |

Salty, rich and toasty, these biscotti-inspired cookies have been formulated so they're just on the dentist-approved side of crunchy. The tenderizing effect of the butter is evident. The coffee in the dough should be pretty imperceptible after baking—just offering a bit of balance with its pleasant bitterness.

Total: 1 hr 40 mins

20 mins	40 mins	10 mins	30 mins
Mix dough	Form dough & bake at higher temp	Remove from oven to cool slightly	Slice & rebake

1   Preheat the oven to 350°F.

2   Cream the butter and sugar until well mixed and a little bit fluffy, 2 minutes. Scrape down the side of the bowl and add the eggs.

3   Mix the flour, baking powder, salt, peanuts, espresso powder, and chocolate chips together. Paddle the dry ingredients into the butter mixture. A wet dough will form.

4   Fill a clean baking sheet with the dried shredded coconut. Move the dough onto the sheet and divide by eye into two. Roll and press the dough into two 2-inch-wide rectangular logs. Make sure these are well formed with no big holes. Press the dried shredded coconut into the surface of each log, ensuring it is covered. Move them to a clean, lined baking sheet, ready to bake.

5   Bake the logs for 25–30 minutes. They will spread and rise slightly, be pale golden brown, and crack on the surface. Remove from the oven and let cool on the baking sheet for 20 minutes.

6   Slice the logs into ¾-inch-thick pieces on the diagonal using a serrated knife.

7   Decrease the oven temperature to 325°F.

8   Lay the wedges back on the baking sheet and bake for an additional 25 minutes, flipping halfway through. Transfer to a cooling rack to cool.

9   This will give you a tender, but crisp, cookie. You have the option to bake for longer if you want them harder but note they do harden further as they cool.

10 If desired, melt the dark or milk chocolate over a bain-marie until liquified. Dip the cookies (either the bottoms or in half vertically) into the chocolate, then allow to set on a lined baking sheet. Store in an airtight container for up to 2 weeks.

AMARETTIS

•

EACH RECIPE MAKES 18–20 AMARETTIS

Techniques

Baking with nuts	pg.55

140g/1 cup	hazelnuts
70g/½ cup	blanched almonds
2g/1 tsp	ground ginger
1g/½ tsp	espresso powder
120g/½ cup, plus 1 Tbsp	light brown sugar, packed
1–2g/¼–½ tsp	flaky sea salt
40g/1½ oz	dark chocolate
60g/2	egg whites
50g/6 Tbsp	powdered sugar, to roll

These squishy, crunchy cookies make wonderful gifts. You can bake them until they're crunchy or keep them soft—both are perfect. You can use pre-ground nuts for this recipe if you don't have a food processor.

Total: 1 hr 20 mins

20 mins	10 mins	30 mins	20 mins
Mix dough	Shape	Form dough & bake	Let cool

Hazelnut amaretti

1   Preheat the oven to 375°F. Line two baking sheets with parchment paper and set aside.

2   Blitz the nuts in a food processor until roughly chopped. Add the ginger, espresso powder, sugar, salt, and dark chocolate and whiz until it is all finely ground. Transfer to a mixing bowl, add the egg whites and mix together until a dough forms. Let rest for 10 minutes for the liquid to absorb.

3   Divide the dough into 18–20 pieces and roll into golf ball-size balls (20–25g/¾–1 oz). Roll in the powdered sugar, then place on the lined baking sheets, pinching with your fingers to create indents. You can also roll them into little crescent shapes—this dough feels (and looks) like play dough. You can also leave in a ball shape.

4   Bake the amaretti for 12–14 minutes, until they have puffed up and cracked and are golden around the edges (but still soft inside). You can also bake them until completely hard, around 25 minutes, if desired.

5   Let cool completely on the baking sheets. Keep in an airtight container for up to 10 days.

100g/¾ cup	shelled pistachios
110g/¾ cup	blanched almonds
2g/1½ tsp	coriander seed
120g/½ cup plus 2 Tbsp	granulated sugar
Zest of 1	lemon
1–2g/¼–½ tsp	flaky sea salt
60g/2	egg whites
50g/6 Tbsp	powdered sugar, to roll

Lemon pistachio amaretti

1   Preheat the oven to 375°F. Line two baking sheets with parchment paper and set aside.

2   Blitz the nuts and coriander seed in a food processor until finely ground. Add the sugar, lemon zest, and salt, then blitz until everything is finely ground. Add the egg whites and blend until a dough forms. Let rest for 10 minutes for the liquid to absorb.

3   Divide the dough into 18–20 pieces and roll into golf ball-size balls (20–25g/¾–1 oz). Roll in the powdered sugar, then place on the lined baking sheets, pinching with your fingers to create indents. You can also roll into little crescent shapes—this dough feels (and looks) like play dough. You can also leave in a ball shape.

4   Bake the amaretti for 12–14 minutes, until they have puffed up and cracked and are golden around the edges (but still soft inside). You can also bake them until completely hard, around 25 minutes, if desired.

5   Let cool completely on the baking sheets. Keep in an airtight container for up to 10 days.

GOLDEN SYRUP CRUNCH COOKIES

·

MAKES 15–16 SANDWICH COOKIES

Techniques

Creaming	pg.59

Equipment
2-inch round cutter
Piping bag

1 x recipe	sablé Breton (see page 130)

Golden syrup buttercream

150g/½ cup plus 2 Tbsp	butter, softened
20g/3 Tbsp	powdered sugar
75g/¼ cup	golden syrup or light corn syrup
3g/1 tsp	flaky sea salt

A simple sandwich cookie that makes the most of the sablé Breton's crumbly, rich texture. Because the filling is mainly butter, it has low moisture, which means these cookies last surprisingly well. If you prefer your filling with a bit more body, you can keep them in the fridge! Just don't blame me for the weird looks you get when you have guests for tea and you tell them you keep your cookies cold.

Total: 2 hrs 30 mins

15 mins	45 mins	15 mins	30 mins	45 mins
Mix sablé	Roll & chill dough	Cut & bake	Cool & make buttercream	Sandwich & chill

1   Preheat the oven to 375°F.

2   Roll out the sablé Breton dough to 1/16–1/8 inch thick between two sheets of parchment paper.

3   Chill for 30 minutes in the fridge, until firm, then cut out 2-inch rounds. You can re-roll this dough and chill it to cut more. Transfer the rounds to a baking sheet.

4   Bake on a baking sheet lined with parchment paper, leaving 1¼–1½ inches between the rounds to allow for spreading, for 12–13 minutes, until evenly golden all over. Remove from the oven and transfer to a cooling rack to cool completely.

5   To make the buttercream, beat the butter for 1 minute, until very smooth, then add the sugar. Beat for about 1 minute, until well combined and lightened. Finally, add the golden syrup and salt and beat well for about 2 minutes.

6   Move into a piping bag and cut a ¼-inch hole in the tip. Pipe the buttercream in an even spiral on half the cookies (12–15g/1/3–½ oz per cookie), then top with the other half of the cookies.

7   To firm up the buttercream, chill in the fridge for at least 30 minutes. The cookies last well in an airtight container for 1–2 days, but become softer over time.

SALTED VANILLA SHORTBREAD

·

MAKES 20 LARGE COOKIES

Techniques

Creaming	pg.59

240g/1 cup plus 1 Tbsp	butter, softened
120g/½ cup plus 2 Tbsp	granulated sugar
260g/2 cups plus 1 Tbsp	all-purpose flour
100g/⅔ cup	fine semolina
3g/1 tsp	flaky sea salt
1	fat vanilla pod, scraped or 5–10g/ 1–2 tsp good quality vanilla bean paste

Plus

zest of ½–1	pink grapefruit
15g/1 Tbsp	pink grapefruit juice
100g/¾ cup	powdered sugar (depending on brand, you might need more or less)

This is the only shortbread recipe you'll ever need! It uses the classic ratio (1:2:3 sugar, butter, flour) but the addition of fine semolina adds a flavor and texture note you'll never look back from. If you can't find semolina, using more all-purpose flour works well, too.

Total: 3 hrs 50 mins

10 mins	2 hrs 10 mins	20 mins	40 mins	30 mins
Mix	Roll & chill	Cut & bake	Let cool	Glaze

1 For the shortbread, cream the butter with the sugar. You want it to be light but not ultra-fluffy or white—1 minute should do it. Mix the dry ingredients together, then stir them into the butter mixture with the vanilla until no dry bits remain. Roll into an approximately 3-inch wide log and wrap.

2 Chill the dough in the freezer/fridge so you can cut it neatly. Around 2 hours in the fridge or 30–40 minutes in the freezer. You can also store it well-wrapped in the freezer for 30 days or the fridge for 3 days.

3 Preheat the oven to 350°F. Slice the chilled log into ½-inch rounds and place on two large baking sheets. Bake for 15–17 minutes, then let cool completely on a cooling rack.

4 To glaze, mix together the grapefruit zest and juice and the powdered sugar—the glaze should be thick but still run off the spoon, like thick honey. You may need to add a little more sugar/juice to get it just right. Spoon over the cooled shortbread rounds. Let rest for 20–30 minutes to harden. Store in an airtight container for up to 1 week.

SALTED DOUBLE-CHOCOLATE SHORTBREAD

·

MAKES 16 SMALL COOKIES

Techniques

Creaming	pg.59

100g/7 Tbsp	butter, softened
50g/¼ cup	granulated sugar
45g/¼ cup	fine semolina
110g/¾ cup plus 2 Tbsp	all-purpose flour
15g/3 Tbsp	cocoa powder
3g/1 tsp	flaky sea salt
75g/scant ½ cup	dark chocolate chips

I've played around with the proportion of cocoa to flour here and think that this treads the line of bitterness really well. I didn't remove any flour to make room for the cocoa—this means the mix is slightly drier than others, but this gives the cookie more of a bite after baking. I wish I had more to say about this, but this is a properly chocolatey cookie that, to be honest, would probably always be my first pick. Make sure you use some really nice dark chocolate chips to make the most of it.

Total: 3 hrs 20 mins

10 mins	2 hrs 10 mins	20 mins	40 mins
Mix	Roll & chill	Cut & bake	Let cool

1 Cream the butter with the sugar. You want it to be light but not ultra-fluffy or white—1 minute should do it.

2 Mix the dry ingredients together, then stir them into the butter mixture, along with the chocolate chips. Mix until just combined. You can finish mixing it by moving it onto your work surface and kneading gently, working in any dry bits that remain.

3 Roll into a log approximately 1½ inches in width and wrap. Chill in the freezer/fridge so you can cut it neatly. Around 2 hours in the fridge or 30–40 minutes in the freezer. You can also store it well-wrapped in the freezer for 30 days and the fridge for 3 days.

4 Preheat the oven to 350°F. Slice the chilled log into ½-inch rounds and place on a baking sheet. Bake for 15–17 minutes, then let cool completely on a cooling rack. Store in an airtight container for up to 1 week.

3PM OAT COOKIES

·

MAKES 18–20 ASSEMBLED
COOKIES

Techniques

Rubbing in	pg.99

Equipment

2½-inch fluted cutter

150g/1⅔ cups	rolled oats
100g/¾ cup	all-purpose flour
3g/½ tsp	baking soda
3g/1 tsp	flaky sea salt
50g/¼ cup	light brown sugar, packed
85g/6 Tbsp	butter, cold and cubed
85g/6 Tbsp	butter, melted and cooled slightly
5g/1 tsp	malt vinegar
150–175g/ 5¼–6¼ oz	dark chocolate, chopped

There aren't many things I love more in this world than cookies. I come from a long line of cookie lovers. The Lamb Family—we are cookie people. This particular cookie is the lovechild of the infamous IKEA Havreflarn and the British Hobnob. Like so many of us on this little island, I get a real hankering for a cookie in the afternoon, so I've fondly named these my 3pm oat cookies. Flaky, crunchy, chocolatey. Put the kettle on!

Total: 2 hrs 5 mins

20 mins	25 mins	20 mins	30 mins	30 mins
Mix cookie dough	Roll & chill	Cut & bake	Cool	Sandwich with chocolate. Leave to set

1 Mix together all the dry ingredients in a bowl, then rub the cold cubed butter into the dry ingredients.

2 Once the melted butter has cooled down, mix in the malt vinegar. Pour the butter/vinegar mix into the dry ingredients and mix together to form a dough.

3 Squash the cookie dough in between two sheets of parchment paper and roll it out to about 1/16 inch thick. You want it to be quite thin as you will be sandwiching the cookies together later and so two cookies actually = one cookie in this case.

4 Let the cookie dough chill for about 20 minutes in the fridge. You want it to be pliable but chilled. Line a baking sheet with parchment paper. Cut out the cookies and place them on the sheet. I use a 2½-inch fluted cutter—they will weigh around 10g/⅓ oz each. You can squash all of the offcuts together and re-roll ad infinitum!

5 Bake at 375°F for around 10 minutes. If the cookies aren't golden by then, leave them in for 1 minute longer at a time. Allow to cool completely on a cooling rack before sandwiching with chocolate.

6 As the cookies are cooling down, melt your dark chocolate over a bain-marie until liquified. Put a small spoonful (ish) of cooled chocolate onto a cookie—you can spread it a little bit to the edges to encourage the chocolate to squish out of the edges when you sandwich it with another cookie. If the chocolate doesn't splurge out of the edges a bit, add a little more chocolate! Repeat with the other cookies and melted chocolate.

7 Now allow to set and chill. I put mine in the fridge because I am impatient. You now officially win 3pm. Keep your cookies in an airtight container for up to 5 days.

MISO WALNUT DOUBLE-THICK CHOCOLATE-CHIP COOKIES

·

MAKES 5 HUGE COOKIES

Techniques

Caramelization	pg.84
Creaming	pg.59

Miso walnuts

50g/3 Tbsp	mirin rice wine
40g/3 Tbsp	granulated sugar
50g/3 Tbsp	white miso
100g/1 cup	walnuts, toasted

Cookies

90g/6 Tbsp	butter, softened
80g/6 Tbsp	light brown sugar
80g/6 Tbsp	granulated sugar
50g/1	whole egg
220g/1¾ cups	all-purpose flour
3g/½ tsp	baking soda
4g/1¼ tsp	flaky sea salt, plus a sprinkle on top
260g/9¼ oz	dark chocolate, chopped

Unashamedly thick cookies inspired by the Levain Bakery in New York—thick and gooey in the middle (when warm) and crisp on the edge. A winner! When I lived in the city, I would travel 70 blocks just to get one of these. Compared to other cookies, these have a relatively low butter and sugar content in relation to the other ingredients and an extremely high proportion of mix-ins, which you can change to suit your mood. Don't decrease the quantity though—they play an important role structurally! The baking time is variable—it's up to you how dangerously gooey you want them. The addition of miso walnuts, a technique shared with me by friend and mentor Ayako Watanbe, brings an extra complexity.

Total: 1 hr 10 mins

20 mins	10 mins	20 mins	20 mins
Make miso walnuts	Mix cookies	Bake	Cool

1 To make the miso walnuts, heat together the rice wine, granulated sugar, and white miso over medium heat. When boiling, add the toasted walnuts and mix together, cooking for 2 minutes more over low heat, until thickened. Remove from the pan and let cool completely before using.

2 To make the cookies, cream the butter with the sugars until well combined but not aerated—it should look a little fluffy.

3 Add in the egg, scraping down as needed to make sure it's evenly combined. Sift the dry ingredients together, then fold them into the emulsified butter/egg mixture. Add the walnuts and stir to break them up a bit before mixing in the chocolate.

4 Form into loose 180g/6⅓-oz balls, keeping them looking and feeling airy!

5 At this stage you can chill or freeze the dough overnight for extra-tall cookies if you like, or you can bake right away. I didn't notice a super significant difference to the final baked texture.

6 Preheat the oven to 375°F. Line a baking sheet with parchment paper.

7 Spread the balls of dough on the baking sheet. Bake for 18 minutes (though you could do 16 minutes or up to 20 minutes to suit your taste!). Sprinkle a little extra salt on top, if desired, then let cool completely on a cooling rack. Ideally enjoy while still a little bit warm, but they are just as good completely cooled! The texture will change from gooey to more firm.

Note

You can, of course, make these into smaller portions! Just adjust the baking time accordingly—I suggest 9–12 minutes for half portions.

FRUITY MARSHMALLOWS

·

MAKES 16–20
MARSHMALLOWS

Techniques

Sugar syrup	pg.33
Using gelatin	pg.100
Egg foam	pg.45

Equipment

8-inch/20cm square pan

7	gelatin leaves (see page 100; I use Dr. Oetker Platinum)
60g/2	egg whites
70g/5 Tbsp	any fruit purée, e.g., black currant or passionfruit (see Note)
Pinch of flaky sea salt	
1g/¼ tsp	citric acid (optional—helps add acidity)
50g/3 Tbsp	water
150g/¾ cup	granulated sugar
125g/6 Tbsp	liquid glucose

Plus

Cornstarch and powdered sugar, to dust

An airy, squishy marshmallow is always a welcome gift. Use this as a base to make your own formulas.

Total: 2 hrs 40 mins

10 mins	10 mins	10 mins	2 hrs	10 mins
Bloom gelatin	Make syrup	Whip marshmallow	Pour into pan & let cool	Cut and dust

1   Bloom the leaf gelatin in a little cold water for 10 minutes. Squeeze out and put in the bowl of a stand mixer with the egg whites and fruit purée. Add the salt and citric acid, if using.

2   Mix together the water, sugar, and glucose in a saucepan. Heat until it reaches 244–250°F. Meanwhile, whisk the egg whites on medium-low speed until foamy. When the sugar reaches the correct temperature, decrease the whisk speed to low and gently drizzle/pour the syrup down the side of the mixer bowl. Once it is all incorporated, increase the speed to medium-high and whisk for 10 minutes, until the mixture is fluffy and volumized and only just warm to the touch.

3   Pour into a square pan lined with greased parchment paper and allow to set completely at room temperature.

4   To cut, dust your board with a mixture of 40/60 cornstarch and powdered sugar, then turn out the marshmallows from the pan and remove the paper. Dust the top and then cut the marshmallow mixture into squares: 1½ x 1½ inches is a cute size. Make sure you wipe your knife in between cuts—if your knife isn't super-sharp, you might also want to oil your knife. Once cut, dust each mallow.

5   Store in an airtight container at room temperature for up to 7 days, in the fridge for 2 weeks, or the freezer for 3 months.

Note

For plain marshmallows, reduce the amount of fruit purée to 30g/2 tablespoons and use water instead and reduce quantity to 30g.

MAPLE PRETZEL BUTTERCRUNCH

·

MAKES ENOUGH FOR 10-12 PIECES

Techniques

Sugar syrup	pg.33
Maillard reaction	pg.84
Tempering chocolate	pg.63

Toffee

170g/¾ cup	butter
50g/3 Tbsp	water
100g/⅓ cup	maple syrup
125g/½ cup plus 2 Tbsp	granulated sugar
2–3g/¼–½ tsp	baking soda
1–2g/¼–½ tsp	flaky sea salt

Chocolate

125g/4½ oz	dark chocolate, chopped into pieces (to melt)
50g/1¾ oz	dark chocolate, finely chopped into pieces

Toppings (swap these to suit your tastes)

30g/1 oz	salted pretzels
Flaky sea salt	

It takes a little bit of patience to get the candy to the right temperature (too low and it'll stick to your teeth, too high and it'll break them), but you'll be rewarded with an utterly charming homemade gift that will disappear in seconds.

Total: 1 hr 40 mins

20 mins	1 hr	20 mins
Make brittle	Let cool	Temper chocolate & decorate

1   In a high-sided medium saucepan, melt the butter. Then stir in the water, maple syrup, and granulated sugar. Heat over medium heat, bringing it to a boil. Without stirring, bubble until the mixture darkens and reaches 293°F, the hard crack stage, for about 10 minutes.

2   Remove from the heat, then stir in the baking soda and salt. Stir well. Pour onto a silicone mat or well-greased paper, then spread out until ¼ inch thick. Let cool completely for 1 hour.

3   To temper the chocolate, melt the 125g/4½ oz chocolate over a bain-marie until it reaches about 104°F. Take it off the heat and stir well to cool slightly, about 30 seconds. Agitation is key.

4   Add the finely chopped chocolate, about 15g/½ oz at a time, waiting about 1 minute between each lot, stirring until completely melted and the chocolate reaches around 86°F. Agitate the mixture a LOT—moving the chocolate around a lot ensures you have enough friction to get the crystals in line to properly temper.

5   At this point, the chocolate will be really shiny and thick and it may even begin to set on your spatula! Check if the chocolate is tempered by dipping in your spoon and popping it to one side. After 2 minutes, check if it has set and is shiny.

6   Warm the chocolate back to 90°F (pop it over a bain-marie for about 10 seconds—chocolate heats up quick!) so you can use it. If you take it further than 93°F, you'll have to retemper it (eye roll—chocolate is so annoying!).

7   To finish with the toppings, working quickly, spread the tempered chocolate on one side of the toffee and sprinkle with the pretzels, plus a little salt. BE QUICK. Tempered chocolate sets soooo fast. Allow it to set. Flip it over and spread the bottom with the rest of the chocolate. Let cool for about 1 hour.

8   Break into pieces and enjoy. Lasts for 30 days in an airtight container.

Notes

I use a bitter 70% dark chocolate.

This recipe will temper more than you need probably, but anything you don't use you can scrape onto some parchment paper and reuse!

PICKLED PINEAPPLE PÂTE DE FRUIT

·

MAKES 50-60 CANDIES

Techniques

Setting with pectin	pg.95
Sugar syrup	pg.33

Equipment
8-inch/20cm square pan

520g/1 lb 2 oz	canned pineapple chunks (drained weight)
70g/3 Tbsp	honey
110g/½ cup	cider or white wine vinegar
24g/2 Tbsp	powdered pectin (avoid apple)
480g/2 cups plus 6 Tbsp	granulated sugar
2g/½ tsp	flaky sea salt

Pepper sugar

3–5g/1–2 Tbsp	Szechuan peppercorns, depending on tolerance
100g/½ cup	coarse sanding sugar
1g/¼ tsp	citric acid (for sour candy flavor, optional)

Growing up, I was obsessed with sour gummy candies and jelly tots. As an adult, it's seemingly more acceptable to move onto pâte de fruit or pectin fruit jellies (even though they're definitely the exact same thing). Think of them as a very firmly set jam. These make great gifts and are highly snackable.

Total: 2 hrs 35 mins

25 mins	2 hrs	10 mins
Cook mixture	Pour into pan & set	Cut & finish

1   Line the square pan with parchment paper.

2   Blend the pineapple with the honey and vinegar. Transfer to a saucepan and heat over medium heat to around 122°F.

3   Mix the pectin with 70g/6 tablespoons of the granulated sugar, then whisk into the pineapple mixture.

4   Heat until simmering, whisking all the time. Add the remaining granulated sugar in three batches, whisking well, finishing with the salt. Whisk constantly while heating over medium heat until the mixture reaches 223°F, 6–10 minutes.

5   Pour into the lined pan. Allow to set completely at room temperature for around 2 hours.

6   For the pepper sugar, grind the Szechuan peppercorns finely, then mix with the coarse sanding sugar. Strain through a sieve to remove any very large husks of peppercorn. Taste and check it is a little sweet, numbing, and spicy. Add more ground peppercorns to taste. Add the citric acid, if using.

7   Turn out and trim the pâte de fruit (these offcuts are your snack!).

8   Cut the pâte de fruit into the desired shape (I like 1½ x ½-inch rectangles), then dust in the pepper sugar.

9   Let rest on a cooling rack to dry the edges slightly—you can enjoy them immediately but for the best results let rest overnight or for at least 4 hours at room temperature. Pâte de fruit should be stored in an airtight container at room temperature for up to 1 week.

Note

You can cook the pâte de fruit up to 226°F for an even firmer set.

PLUM AND MASCARPONE KARPATKA

·

SERVES 10-12

Karpatka, aka Polish Mountain Cake, is a choux-based cake that perhaps isn't a cake at all. Although its origins are unclear, Karpatka seems to be a variation on the mille-feuille or vanilla slice/Napoleon (known as Kremplta in Poland), but instead of puff pastry, you get wild 'n' wiggly, tender-crisp choux. This choux recipe deviates slightly from the norm in that it has baking powder in the base. This encourages additional lift and a pleasingly irregular shape to the final cake.

Total: 3 hrs 10 mins

1 hr	1 hr	10 mins	1 hr
Make bases	Make custard & fillings	Build	Chill

Techniques

Starch gelatinization	pg.20
Egg coagulation	pg.40

Equipment
2 x 8-inch/20cm round pans

Choux base
65g/¼ cup	whole milk
65g/¼ cup	water
65g/¼ cup	butter
15g/1 Tbsp	granulated sugar
90g/¾ cup	all-purpose flour
4g/1 tsp	baking powder
150g–175g/ 3–4	whole eggs
3g/1 tsp	flaky sea salt

Stewed plums
250g/9 oz	plums, pitted
70g/4½ Tbsp	water
60g/¼ cup plus 1 Tbsp	granulated sugar
1 spent	vanilla pod (optional)
5g/1½ tsp	cornstarch

Mascarpone custard
300g/1¼ cups	whole milk
75g/1	whole egg and 1 egg yolk
60g/¼ cup plus 1 Tbsp	granulated sugar
30g/¼ cup	cornstarch
8g/2 tsp	good quality vanilla extract
250g/1 cup plus 2 Tbsp	mascarpone, at room temp

Plus
Powdered sugar, to dust

1   For the choux, preheat the oven to 400°F. Make the choux according to the master choux method on page 136, adding the baking powder in with the flour.

2   Line the two pans with parchment paper at the bottom only. Spread 200–225g/7–8 oz of choux paste in each pan, leaving the top slightly rough and wavy and using an offset spatula to help. If you only have one pan, bake one at a time.

3   Bake for 35–40 minutes, until well peaked, golden, and crisp. Let cool completely in the pans on a cooling rack, then remove.

4   For the plums, cut the plums into six. In a small saucepan, combine the plums with 50g/3 tablespoons of the water, the sugar, and vanilla. Heat over medium heat, occasionally stirring so the plums are well coated. Bring the mixture to a gentle simmer, decrease the heat to low, and cover the saucepan with a lid. Steam for 4–5 minutes. If the plums are still firm, cook for a further 2 minutes. Mix the cornstarch with the remaining water to create a slurry, then stir into the hot liquid. Bring to a bubble so it thickens. Pour into a clean container and let cool.

5   For the mascarpone custard, heat the milk until simmering. Meanwhile, whisk together the whole egg, egg yolk, sugar, cornstarch, and vanilla. Pour the hot milk over the egg mixture while whisking constantly to temper, then return the custard to the stovetop. Cook for 3–4 minutes over medium heat, until boiling, whisking the whole time. Pour into a clean container, then set aside to cool and gelatinize—make sure you put plastic wrap or parchment paper on the surface so it doesn't form a skin. You want it to be totally cold and firm before continuing with this recipe.

6   Beat the mascarpone until smooth—it does have a tendency to be a bit lumpy, so you just have to be prepared to work it. Once that's ready, set aside and beat the custard until smooth and no longer jelly-like. The easiest way to do this is in a stand mixer bowl if you have one.

Note

You can also use your favorite jam in the middle of this! Thanks to Marta Beimin, who makes the most stunning Karpatkas, for inspiring the juicy stewed plums in this recipe!

7 Now, fold/mix the two together—it should make a very thick cream. You can also do this in your stand mixer with the paddle attachment. Chill it in the fridge until ready to use.

8 To assemble, line one of the cake pans with acetate or parchment paper. This will help you get a smooth edge. Place your less cute choux disc in the bottom. Pile in half of the mascarpone custard, then spread the stewed plums on top. Top with the other half of the custard. Place the most mountainous choux disc on top. Allow the cake to settle/reset by resting it in the fridge for at least 1 hour.

9 Before serving, remove the cake from the pan and dust with powdered sugar. It will keep in the fridge for 3 days and will get softer over time.

CARAMEL POACHED ORANGES WITH SABAYON AND LANGUES DE CHAT

•

SERVES 4

Techniques

Making caramel	pg.86
Egg foam	pg.45

Caramel poached oranges

500g/1 lb 2 oz	oranges or mandarins
200g/1 cup	granulated sugar
110g/½ cup	water
75g/⅓ cup	sweet wine aperitif/ sweet wine (I use Lillet)

Langues de chat

40g/3 Tbsp	butter, softened
55g/7 Tbsp	powdered sugar
Zest of ½	orange (optional)
30g/1	egg white
45g/⅓ cup	all-purpose flour
10g/1 Tbsp	cornstarch
Pinch of flaky sea salt	

Sabayon

45–50g/about 3	egg yolks
30g/2 Tbsp	granulated sugar
75g/⅓ cup	sweet wine aperitif/ sweet wine (I use Lillet)
Pinch of fine salt	

Plus

Toasted sliced almonds, to decorate

This dessert came about after a glorious day at the Lillet Orange Festival in Bordeaux. Although I'd made sabayon before, our wonderful host Sophie blew me away when she told me it could be grilled. I'm a total sucker for a Maillard reaction. I'll always be transported back to that sunny weekend in Bordeaux when I tasted this dessert. Merci, Sophie!

Total: 1 hr 15 mins

30 mins	20 mins	15 mins	10 mins
Poach oranges	Make langues de chat	Make sabayon	Assemble & serve

1 To prepare the oranges, remove the peel and pith and slice into ½-inch rounds. Set aside.

2 To make the poaching syrup, put the sugar in a pan with half of the water and stir until it is all dissolved. If the sugar grains are on the pan's edge, use a pastry brush dipped in water to remove them or it can cause the mixture to crystallize when heating. Alternatively, place a lid on the pan for the first 3 minutes of heating. Heat the sugar/ water over high heat until you get a dark caramel, 5–8 minutes. If preferred, you can make this as a dry caramel (see Color on page 86).

3 Once the mixture is a dark golden, turn off the heat and add the remaining water and the sweet wine, bit by bit—it will splutter, split, and seize! Just add little bits at a time and, if it doesn't all dissolve, heat gently while whisking. Bring the liquid back to a boil, then add your fruit. Simmer for 1 minute, then pour into a heatproof container to cool completely. The oranges can be made 3 days in advance, kept in the fridge.

4 For the langues de chat, by hand or in a stand mixer, mix the butter and powdered sugar together until well combined, as well as the zest, if using. Add the egg white, little by little—it can be a bit hard to combine, so do it slowly. If you add too much and it splits apart, you can warm up the bowl slightly, then beat it until it comes together. Finally, stir in the dry ingredients.

5 Preheat the oven to 375°F. Pipe long thin cookies onto parchment paper, then bake for 5–7 minutes or until just turning golden at the edges. Let cool on the sheet. The cookies can be made in advance and kept in an airtight container for 3 days.

6 For the sabayon, whisk the egg yolks with the sugar over a bain-marie over medium-high heat until frothy. Once a foam begins to form, whisk in the sweet wine and salt and keep whisking until it is thick and can hold its own shape, about 10 minutes. As soon as it is ready, remove from the heat so it does not overcook. The sabayon should be used immediately while warm.

7 To serve, spoon the caramel oranges into individual bowls/dishes—a coupe shape works well—with a spoonful of caramel syrup. Spoon the sabayon on top. If desired, prepare the dessert in heatproof bowls, then grill for 30 seconds–1 minute, until the sabayon is browned in spots. Decorate with toasted sliced almonds. Serve with the langues de chat. This dessert can also be chilled and served cold—the sabayon will set into a very light mousse.

Notes

The caramel poaching technique can be used for other fruits —you may need to add more liquid to cover larger fruits like peaches. Check for readiness by piercing the fruit with the tip of a sharp knife. There should be no resistance.

Turn the poaching liquid into a sauce by adding equal parts heavy cream, then bring to a boil and reduce until thick.

LEMON BASQUE CHEESECAKE WITH STICKY LEMONS

·

SERVES 8

Techniques

Maillard reaction	pg.84
Egg coagulation	pg.40
Liaison batter	pg.113

Equipment

8-inch/20cm round pan

600g/1 lb 5 oz	full-fat cream cheese
200g/1 cup	granulated sugar
200g/4	whole eggs
130g/½ cup	sour cream
50g/3 Tbsp	lemon juice
130g/½ cup	heavy cream
25g/3 Tbsp	all-purpose flour
6g/1¾ tsp	flaky sea salt

Sticky lemons

2	medium lemons, cut into ¹⁄₁₆–⅛-inch slices
100g/½ cup	light brown sugar, packed
100g/7 Tbsp	boiling water

Basque cheesecake is cheesecake for people who love cheesecake but don't like the fuss or stress associated with water baths. The mix is simple and baking it at a high temperature creates a dreamy browned crust that plays beautifully with the soft center. The bittersweet sticky lemons are the perfect foil to the silky creaminess of the cheesecake.

Total: 3 hrs

20 mins	40 mins	2 hrs
Make cheesecake mix & prep lemons	Bake	Chill & decorate

1 Preheat the oven to 450°F.

2 For the cheesecake, mix the cream cheese in a stand mixer with the paddle attachment until evenly combined, then paddle in the sugar until it has dissolved fully. Check with your fingers! It should feel totally smooth.

3 Now, add the eggs, one by one, scraping down the sides of the bowl to make sure they're combined. Finally, add the sour cream, lemon juice, and heavy cream.

4 Sift the flour and add the salt into another bowl, then whisk in a few spoonfuls of the cheesecake batter. This is a liaison batter to help the flour incorporate easily into the cheesecake. Ensure it's smooth before adding it back into the rest of the cheesecake batter. Mix the two batters together, scraping down the sides to make sure it's evenly combined.

5 Prepare the pan by taking two pieces of parchment paper and laying them on top of each other at a perpendicular angle, then pressing them into your baking pan. It should comfortably cover the pan and have a slight collar. You can trim it if it's too dramatic. Pour in the cheesecake mixture and tap against your kitchen counter to level the mixture.

6 For the sticky lemons, put the lemon slices into a shallow baking dish. Sprinkle the sugar over the top, followed by the boiling water. Wrap with foil.

7 To bake, put the lemons and cheesecake into the oven at the same time. Bake for 25–35 minutes, until the top of the cheesecake is well browned and the internal temperature reads 140–144°F. This temperature will increase 41–50°F as it cools thanks to carryover cooking. Let cool and then put in the fridge until totally cold. The cheesecake lasts well in the fridge for 3–5 days but is best enjoyed at room temperature.

8 For the sticky lemons, remove the foil once the cheesecake is out and place back into the oven for 5 minutes to brown slightly. Let cool, then store in the fridge until ready to use. You can also rewarm, then add a little boiling water to the syrup to create a sauce— just add 1 large spoonful at a time until it becomes spoonable. Serve alongside the cheesecake.

Note

You can sub the all-purpose flour for gluten-free flour.

ORCHARD TURNOVERS

·

MAKES 6 TURNOVERS

Techniques

Lamination	pg.69

Pie dough

½ x recipe	pie dough (see page 129)

Sweet apple and pear mixture

200g/7 oz	sweet apples such as Fuji, peeled and cored
200g/7 oz	pears, peeled and cored
20g/1½ Tbsp	butter
1	bay leaf
20g/2 Tbsp	light brown sugar
Zest of 1	lemon

Tart apple quince mush

150g/5¼ oz	tart apples such as Granny Smith, peeled and cored
100g/3½ oz	quince
20g/1½ Tbsp	butter
20g/2 Tbsp	light brown sugar
2g/⅓ tsp	fine salt
10g/2 tsp	lemon juice

Whipped cream (optional)

250g/1 cup	heavy cream
25g/2 Tbsp	granulated sugar

Plus

Egg wash (see page 343)
Granulated sugar, to sprinkle

All the best bits of autumn wrapped in flaky pastry. I made this turnover as an ode to UK orchards, which are brimming with apples, quinces, and pears come October. This is an unfussy filling—you can swap the fruits around for whatever you've got access to. Celebrate your local orchard (or farmers market)!

Total: 3 hrs 20 mins

15 mins	1 hr	20 mins	15 mins	30 mins	45 mins	15 mins
Make pastry	Chill & make fillings	Roll & fill	Chill	Bake	Cool	Fill with cream & serve (optional)

1 For the sweet apple and pear mixture, cut the peeled and cored apples and pears into wedges. For a medium-size apple, I get about 8 slices per apple. Melt the butter with the bay leaf in a pan. Add the apples and pears, then sprinkle the sugar and lemon zest on top and cook gently over medium heat, flipping occasionally, for 5–8 minutes, until the apples have softened a bit. You don't want them to turn to mush at this stage. Remove from the heat and let cool.

2 For the tart apple quince mush, core and cut the tart apple into ½–¾-inch cubes and peel and grate the quince, avoiding the core. Add the butter to a frying pan and heat over high heat, swirling until it is browned. Add the light brown sugar, followed by the salt, apple cubes, grated quince, and lemon juice. Cook until browned, 2–3 minutes. The mixture should look a little caramelized. Transfer to a clean bowl to cool.

3 Preheat the oven to 400°F. Roll out your pie dough to an 8 x 12-inch rectangle, about ⅛ inch thick, and cut into six equal 4-inch squares. Use around 1 heaping tablespoon (20–25g/¾–1 oz) of the tart apple mix per square, then place three pieces of the sweet apple and pear on top. If there is buttery apple/pear goo left over from cooking, you can drizzle a bit of this on, too.

4 It might be a bit hard to close the turnovers because there's so much filling, but it's so worth it! I'd always rather fight to close my turnovers than not have enough apples inside. Fold the square of pastry over into a triangle and press together. At this stage, you can crimp the edge with a fork to try to keep it closed, but I LIKE it open! Don't worry if it doesn't close completely, either. You can give it another squish after chilling.

5 Place on a baking sheet. Chill the turnovers in the freezer for 15 minutes. Once chilled, press the edges together further. It should be easier now if there are any big gaps.

6 To bake, place on a baking sheet lined with parchment paper and brush the turnovers with egg wash then sprinkle generously with granulated sugar. This will create your sugary crust. Bake for 25–30 minutes, until puffed and golden.

7 To finish, if making the whipped cream, wait until cool, then gently pry open the turnovers. Whip the cream and sugar to very soft peaks, then pipe your whipped cream into the turnovers. Eat within 3 hours. They can be kept in the fridge for 2–3 days.

Note

You can freeze turnovers before or after baking. If baking from frozen, add 5–10 minutes to the baking time. If refreshing baked turnovers, thaw at room temperature, then re-crisp for 10 minutes at 350°F.

BREAD-AND-BUTTER PUDDING WITH CARAMEL MANDARINS

·

SERVES 6

Techniques

Egg coagulation	pg.40
Caramelization	pg.84
Making custard	pg.42

Equipment
9 x 5 x 2½-inch/24.5 x 14.5 x 6cm loaf pan

Spiced custard

130g/½ cup plus 1 Tbsp	whole milk
300g/1¼ cups	heavy cream
1	orange, peel only
½	lemon, peel only
1	cinnamon stick
1	vanilla pod, split (optional)
70g/6 Tbsp	granulated sugar
90g/about 5	egg yolks (or about 1½ whole eggs, for less richness!)

Bread base

375–400g/ 13–14 oz	brioche or any enriched bread, cut into ¾-inch slices
70g/5 Tbsp	melted or brown butter (see page 333)

Plus
Demerara sugar, to sprinkle
Vanilla crème anglaise (see page 342) or whipped cream
Caramel poached mandarins (see page 207)

There comes a time every once in a while when you really need to be comforted by a pudding. And I know no better comforter than bread-and-butter pudding, an absolute classic. My version uses a spiced custard and works so well with a helping of caramel mandarins and extra custard on the side. Pro tip: if you can be patient, toasted bread-and-butter pudding is kind of life changing.

Total: 2 hrs 35 mins

30 mins	10 mins	10 mins	50 mins	45 mins	10 mins
Infuse milk	Prepare custard	Build pudding	Bake	Serve or cool	Slice, toast & serve (fried pudding)

1   First, make the custard infusion. Heat the milk and cream with the citrus peels, cinnamon, and vanilla, if using. Bring to a boil, then remove from the heat and cover, allowing it to infuse for at least 30 minutes but up to several hours. You can also do this the night before and allow to infuse in the fridge.

2   To prepare the custard, add the sugar to the infused milk/cream mixture and heat until steaming. Meanwhile, place the egg yolks in a heatproof bowl. While whisking the egg yolks, pour in the hot milk/cream mixture and whisk well. Strain the mixture through a sieve to remove the peels, cinnamon stick, and vanilla, if using. Set aside.

3   Line your loaf pan with parchment paper. To prepare the bread base, brush one side of each brioche slice with the melted or brown butter. Let cool slightly, then cut the bread into 1-inch squares.

4   Pile the brioche squares loosely into your lined loaf pan. It's nice if there are pockets for the custard to settle into.

5   Now pour in the custard. Go slowly, filling in all the gaps and ensuring each piece of bread gets a soaking. If the ones on the top miss out, that's OK—they'll just be extra crisp.

6   Sprinkle with demerara sugar.

7   Preheat the oven to 350°F. If using a water bath, place the loaf pan in a larger baking dish with high sides and fill halfway with boiling water. You can skip this step, but you will get the best results with a water bath. However, please make sure your loaf pan is watertight first!

8   Bake for 40–50 minutes or until a probe thermometer inserted into the middle of the pudding reads at least 165–167°F. Start checking after 40 minutes.

9   Either turn out and serve immediately or let cool completely, then cut into thick slices and toast in a skillet over medium heat with lots of butter, 1–2 minutes per side.

10   Serve with vanilla crème anglaise or whipped cream, plus the caramel poached oranges in their syrup. Leftovers can be stored in the fridge for 3 days.

PANNA COTTA WITH BURNT WHITE CHOCOLATE AND SOY

•

SERVES 6

Techniques

Using gelatin	pg.100
Maillard reaction	pg.84

Equipment

6 x small molds (I use 3¼ x 2-inch/
8.5 x 5cm dariole molds)

Burnt white chocolate

100g/3½ oz	white chocolate

Panna cotta

3½	gelatin leaves (see page 100; I use Dr. Oetker Platinum)
1 x 350g/ 12-oz can	evaporated milk
170g/⅔ cup plus 2 tsp	whole milk
1 x 397g/ 14-oz can	condensed milk
3g/1 tsp	flaky sea salt

Plus

Light soy sauce, to serve (optional)

On our first shoot day for this book, I accidentally gave the totally wrong instructions to Holly, our wonderful food stylist, for the blonde chocolate—the oven temperature was off by 86°F. Instead of a gorgeous golden white chocolate, Holly ended up with a burnt white chocolate the color of mahogany. We figured we'd taste it anyway—I LOVED it; ultra complex and umami. I developed this recipe in honor of that and the result is a uniquely rich and addictive dessert. The addition of soy sauce is optional, but you should definitely try it.

Total: 3 hrs 10 mins

40 mins	10 mins	10 mins	2 hrs	10 mins
Bake the white chocolate	Bloom gelatin	Make panna cotta	Allow to chill & set	Demold & serve

1   Preheat the oven to 350°F.

2   For the burnt white chocolate, break up the chocolate and put in a baking dish with a piece of parchment paper or a silicone mat underneath. Bake, stirring every 10 minutes, until very dark, like dark milk chocolate. It feels wrong and it will be lumpy but persevere! It will take anywhere from 25 to 40 minutes. Depending on your oven, it could take longer or shorter. Let cool completely.

3   As it's cooling, press it back together with a spatula or spoon so it forms one cohesive lump. This makes more than you need, but you can store any extra and store for 3 months in an airtight container.

4   For the panna cotta, bloom the gelatin sheets in cold water for 10 minutes, then squeeze them out.

5   Heat the evaporated milk and whole milk until simmering. Turn off the heat and whisk in the gelatin. Finally, whisk in the condensed milk and salt.

6   Pour the mixture into molds, 150–160g/5¼–5¾ oz per portion. Allow to set completely in the fridge, for at least 2 hours, or up to 3 days in advance.

7   To demold each dessert, dip into 176°F water for 5–6 seconds. Dry the mold, then place a plate on top. Turn it over and wiggle the mold. The panna cotta should release. If not, repeat.

8   Finish with a grating of the burnt white chocolate and a dash of soy sauce, if using.

Note

This recipe uses no added sugar because there is already sugar in the condensed milk. For a classic base/ jump-off point for developing your own recipes, use the instructions above but heat together 375g/1½ cups heavy cream, 375g/1½ cups whole milk, and 120g/½ cup plus 2 tablespoons granulated sugar to 3 leaves of gelatin with 2g/¼ teaspoon fine salt. You can add vanilla and flavorings to this base.

BAKED LEMON CUSTARD BRÛLÉE

·

SERVES 4

Techniques

Making custard	pg.42
Egg coagulation	pg.40
Caramelization	pg.84

Equipment
4 x ramekins
Blowtorch

Peel of 4	unwaxed lemons (thick strips with a vegetable peeler)
125g/½ cup	heavy cream
145g/¾ cup	granulated sugar
210g/4	whole eggs
125g/½ cup plus 2 Tbsp	lemon juice

Plus
Granulated or demerara sugar, to sprinkle

Caramel and lemon is an underrated combination—the tang of the ultra-smooth custard plays so well with the bitterness of the caramel. The custard can be made in advance and brûlée'd when you're ready to serve.

Total: 4 hrs 20 mins

40 mins	30 mins	3 hrs	10 mins
Make custard	Bake	Cool & chill	Brûlée & serve

1   Preheat the oven to 275°F. Arrange the ramekins in a large baking dish with high sides for the water bath.

2   Heat together the lemon peels, heavy cream, and half the sugar until simmering. Remove from the heat and set aside for 30 minutes to infuse.

3   Whisk together the eggs and the remaining sugar very well, followed by the infused cream and the lemon juice. Strain through a fine sieve. Use a spoon to remove any bubbles or foam from the top of the mixture. This can be a painstaking process but it's important!

4   Divide the lemon custard among the ramekins. Boil the kettle, then pour the boiling water carefully into the baking dish until it reaches halfway up the sides of the ramekins.

5   Bake until there is around 1 inch of good wobble in the center of your custards. You don't want to overbake them as this leads to potential cracks later down the line, so just watch out for that. I start checking after 20 minutes and then every 5–10 minutes after that. Remember it's better to underbake than overbake in this case!

6   Remove from the oven and carefully transfer each ramekin to a cooling rack. Allow to cool for 1 hour before transferring to the fridge for at least 2 hours or overnight.

7   Just before serving, sprinkle the top of the custard with a thin, even layer of granulated or demerara sugar. Caramelize the sugar using a blowtorch. You can do several layers if you prefer a thicker crust. Allow the caramelized crust to cool and harden for 5 minutes before serving. If you don't have a blowtorch, preheat the broiler to high, then place the custard dishes on a baking sheet and broil for 1–2 minutes, until the sugar caramelizes and turns golden brown. Cool and harden as above.

Note

This custard can be used to make a lemon tart. For a large tart, I recommend heating up the lemon custard to 131–140°F before transferring it to the tart case and baking until set but still wobbly.

PBJ PARIS BREST

•

MAKES 8 PARIS BREST

Techniques

Starch gelatinization	pg.20
Piping	pg.113
Starch-bound custard	pg.44
Making jam	pg.95

Equipment
Piping bag
3–inch and ¾–1-inch cutter

1 x recipe	choux (see page 136)
½ x recipe	craquelin for choux (see page 137)

Peanut butter pastry cream

350g/1½ cups	whole milk
45g/about 3	egg yolks
85g/7 Tbsp	granulated sugar
30g/¼ cup	cornstarch
90g/⅓ cup	dark-roast smooth peanut butter
2g/⅓ tsp	fine salt

Caramelized peanuts

20g/4 tsp	water
75g/6 Tbsp	granulated sugar
100g/⅔ cup	roasted salted peanuts

Plus

1 x recipe	nut praline paste (see page 334), you can sub for loose-textured natural peanut butter
250g/9 oz	raspberries
125g/⅓ cup	good quality jam or make your own, e.g., raspberry rhubarb jam (see page 335)

I love giving unfancy flavor combinations fancy makeovers—peanut butter and jelly has never looked so elegant.

Total: 4 hrs 15 mins

45 mins	30 mins	2 hrs 30 mins	30 mins
Make choux & craquelin	Pipe & bake buns	Cool. Make fillings	Finish buns

1   Draw 8 x 3¼-inch circles on parchment paper to use as a guide, then flip over and place on a large, flat baking sheet.

2   Transfer the choux paste to a piping bag fitted with a ½-inch round tip (you can also cut a ½-inch hole if you don't have a tip). Smoosh the paste to try to reduce those pesky air bubbles.

3   For the flower shape, staying inside the lines of each circle, pipe 1-inch choux blobs at 12, 3, 6, and 9 o'clock. Pipe smaller blobs to fill in the gaps. You should have eight small choux blobs and each will weigh around 30g/1 oz. Alternatively, pipe a two-layered circle just inside the line.

4   Cut circles of craquelin using a 3-inch cutter. Cut out the center using a ¾–1-inch cutter. Lay a craquelin ring on top of each flower, about 15g/½ oz.

5   Preheat the oven to 475°F.

6   Place the choux inside the oven and turn it down to 425°F. Bake them for 15 minutes, then turn the oven down to 375°F and bake for another 10–15 minutes. If you need to turn the sheet, do so only in the last 10 minutes. Remove from the oven and place the sheet on a cooling rack to cool completely, about 1 hour.

7   For the peanut butter pastry cream, heat the milk on the stove until simmering. Whisk the egg yolks, sugar, and cornstarch together. Once the milk is bubbling, pour a little over the egg yolks to temper them before adding to the remaining milk and returning the whole mixture to the stovetop. Cook—whisking all the time—until the mixture is thick and bubbling. Whisk in the peanut butter and salt, then pour into a clean container, cover, cool, and chill completely in the fridge. This can be made 2 days ahead of time.

8   Make the caramelized nuts according to the instructions on page 334.

9   To assemble, very carefully cut the top off the choux rings using a serrated knife. If you used the flower/blob shape, be careful not to accidentally pull apart the bottom layer. If the top layer breaks, it isn't as much of an issue—you can just place it back on.

10 Pipe a ring of jam in the bottom of each choux ring (about 10g/⅓ oz), followed by a ring of praline paste or peanut butter (5–10g/¼–⅓ oz). Lightly chop the caramelized peanuts and arrange a few in the bottom.

11 Beat the peanut butter pastry cream until smooth, then move into a piping bag fitted with a fluted tip. Pipe five swirls (about 85g/3 oz) on each ring, leaving a gap in between each blob.

12 Fill the raspberries with jam using a piping bag, then place them in between the blobs, jam-side down. Dip a small spoon in boiling water and create little divots in the top of each peanut custard blob. Spoon a little praline paste/peanut butter into each. Decorate the blobs with a few chopped caramelized peanuts.

13 Finish by placing the top of the choux ring back on each.

CRULLERS

·

MAKES 8

Techniques

Deep-frying	pg.107
Starch gelatinization	pg.20
Piping	pg.113

Equipment
Piping bag

1 x recipe	choux (see page 136)
1½–2 quarts/ 1.5–2 liters	vegetable oil, to deep-fry

Black 'n' blue glaze
60g/⅓ cup	blackberries/ blueberries mix
3g/½ tsp	fine salt
200g/1⅔ cups	powdered sugar
10–20g/2–4 tsp	lemon juice
10–20	mixed blackberries and blueberries, to decorate (optional)

Spicy hibiscus sugar
15g/⅓ cup	dried hibiscus flowers
2g/1 tsp	chile flakes
150g/¾ cup	granulated sugar

Vanilla cinnamon glaze
200g/1⅔ cups	powdered sugar
50g/3 Tbsp	whole milk
½ tsp	ground cinnamon
2–3g/¾–1 tsp	flaky sea salt
4g/1 tsp	good quality vanilla extract

Airy with slightly gooey insides, crullers are the cool sister of the doughnut family. Try tossing in different flavored sugars or switching up the glaze. You can also try using different nozzles to mix up the final look of the cruller—the wider the tip, the more dramatic the final result. How about piping different squiggles—alphabet crullers, anyone?

Total: 1 hr 35 mins

20 mins	20 mins	25 mins	30 mins
Make choux	Pipe cruller rings & prepare glaze	Fry cruller in batches & remove to drain	Dip in glaze, allow to set & serve

1   Cut out 8 x 4-inch squares of parchment paper. Transfer the choux paste to a piping bag with a fluted tip—I use a ½–¾-inch fluted tip with lots of teeth to encourage even expansion—and smoosh the paste to try to reduce pesky air bubbles.

2   Pipe 3–3¼-inch rings (about 40g/1½ oz) of choux onto the parchment paper squares.

3   Pour the vegetable oil into a large saucepan. The oil should be at least 2 inches deep and there should be 2 inches between the oil level and the top of the pan.

4   Heat to 356°F. When the oil is hot, slide the crullers into the oil with the paper on, face-side down—a maximum of three or so at a time or as many as you feel confident to do. There's no rush. Use heatproof tongs to remove the paper as it naturally releases from the crullers. Monitor the oil temperature to ensure it stays at 356°F for the best results. Cook for 3–4 minutes, then flip and cook for another 3–4 minutes.

5   Remove the crullers from the oil using a slotted spoon and let drain on a cooling rack. Dip in your chosen glaze or toss in sugar, then allow to set on the rack.

Black 'n' blue glaze

1   Smoosh the blackberries, blueberries, and salt together.

2   Add the sugar, stirring well. Add lemon juice until the consistency is thick but pourable.

3   Once set on the cruller, decorate with the extra blueberries and blackberries, if using.

Spicy hibiscus sugar

1   Blitz the hibiscus and chile together, then combine with the granulated sugar.

Vanilla cinnamon glaze

1   Whisk all the ingredients together. Check the consistency is pourable but still thick.

BLONDE RICE PUDDING WITH PEARS AND HAZELNUTS

·

SERVES 4

Techniques

Starch gelatinization	pg.20
Maillard reaction	pg.84

Blonde white chocolate

200g/7 oz	white chocolate

Poached pears

200g/1 cup	granulated sugar
400g/1⅔ cups	water, white wine, or brewed chamomile tea, or a mixture

Lemon peels, pink peppercorns, green cardamom pods, vanilla pods—whatever you like!

2	Comice pears
20g/4 tsp	lemon juice

Rice pudding

700g/3 cups	whole milk
100g/7 Tbsp	heavy cream
80g/6 Tbsp	granulated sugar
1	vanilla pod, scraped
120g/½ cup plus 2 Tbsp	long-grain white rice
Pinch of flaky sea salt	
30g/about 2	egg yolks
100g/3½ oz	blonde white chocolate (see above and method)

Plus

75g/½ cup blanched hazelnuts, to serve

I've long been obsessed with rice pudding and getting the perfect texture whether hot or cold. After a lot of failures, I realized the key to controlling the liquid absorption was by par-cooking the rice, and the best texture comes from vigorous whisking to help release the starch. As an added bonus, stirring in egg yolks at the end means instant custard—what's not to love? A final richness is added with the blonde chocolate here.

Total: 2 hrs 25 mins

1 hr	10 mins	45 mins	30 mins
Toast white chocolate	Roast hazelnuts	Poach fruit	Cook rice pudding

1   To make the blonde white chocolate, preheat the oven to 275°F.

2   Break up the chocolate and put in a baking dish. Bake, stirring every 10 minutes, until golden. It will seem lumpy at first but persevere! It will take around 1 hour of regular stirring. Once it reaches a pale golden, remove it from the oven and let cool completely in the dish. You can break it up into pieces and store in an airtight container for 2 weeks.

3   Turn the oven temperature up to 425°F, then roast the hazelnuts for about 10 minutes, or until well toasted and dark brown. Roughly chop, once cool.

4   To make the poached pears, first prepare your poaching liquid. Heat the sugar, your chosen liquid, and your flavorings of choice in a pot large enough to immerse the pears fully. Bring to a simmer.

5   Peel your pears and add to the poaching liquid with the lemon juice. Ensure the liquid stays at a very gentle simmer—if the pears are bobbing around, you can put some parchment paper on top (a cartouche) to keep them immersed fully. Poach for around 45 minutes—check after this point and see if you can easily pierce the pear with the tip of a knife. If not, keep poaching. Try not to let the pears get mushy.

6   Take off the heat and let cool in the syrup. If you are poaching and the pears accidentally get a bit too soft, remove from the syrup to cool separately. Store the poached pears for up to 1 week in the fridge.

7   To make the rice pudding, heat the milk, heavy cream, sugar, and scraped vanilla seeds together gently—bring to a gentle simmer to begin infusing.

8   Meanwhile, bring a pot of water to a boil. When rapidly boiling, add the rice and cook for 2 minutes (up to 3 minutes for an extra-tender final pudding), boiling hard. Drain the rice and add to the simmering milk, and stir.

9   One way to follow the the progress of your rice pudding is to monitor the reduction in weight. To do this, note the weight of the rice/milk mixture, then multiply by 0.8 to get the desired final weight.

Note

Don't add the egg yolks if your rice pudding is above 185°F—you might risk scrambling the eggs!

10 Bring to a boil while whisking and then lower to simmering—199–201°F. Cook for 30 minutes, whisking vigorously every 10 minutes to help it cook evenly and release the starch. Try not to let it boil.

11 After 30 minutes have passed, check how tender the rice is—it should be very tender and perfectly cooked, if not, cook for another few minutes. When you are satisfied with the texture, turn off the heat and whisk for about 1 minute to help release the starch.

12 Check the weight of the mixture—it should have reduced by about 20% and approximately match the desired weight you noted down earlier. It should still look quite loose and wave when you shake the pan. Check the temperature of the rice—it should be 162–167°F after whisking.

13 Add a pinch of salt and the yolks then whisk until totally incorporated and slightly thickened. Cut the blonde white chocolate into small pieces and stir them in. Check the seasoning, adjusting as needed. Serve with the sliced and cored poached pears and toasted hazelnuts.

GRANITAS

•

SERVES 6

Techniques

Freezing	pg.96
Sugar syrup	pg.33

Simple syrup

100g/½ cup	granulated sugar
100g/7 Tbsp	water

Cucumber-jalapeño granita

225g/8 oz	cucumber (not peeled)
1	jalapeño (about 15g/½ oz—you can scale this up or down, depending on how spicy it is!)
1g/¼ tsp	flaky sea salt
40–60g/ 2½–4 Tbsp	lime juice
60g/¼ cup	simple syrup (see above)

Tart apple granita

250g/9 oz	tart apples such as Granny Smith, cored and peeled
100g/7 Tbsp	water
25g/2 Tbsp	lemon juice
50g/¼ cup	granulated sugar
2g/½ tsp	flaky sea salt

Pink lemonade granita

125g/4½ oz	raspberries
70g/5 Tbsp	lemon juice
80g/⅓ cup	simple syrup (see above)
1g/¼ tsp	flaky sea salt

Mocha granita

50g/¼ cup	light brown sugar
25g/¼ cup	cocoa powder
250g/1 cup	brewed coffee (French press/cafetière coffee works well here)
1g/¼ tsp	flaky sea salt

Granita is a very forgiving dessert that is a refreshing end to any meal. Unlike ice cream, where ice crystals are the enemy, we WELCOME ice crystals with granita. The only thing you need to be careful of is how much sugar is in it. If there's too much sugar, the freezing depression point of the liquid will become too low, meaning you never get ice crystals—you'll just get slush. Granitas can be savory or sweet, or a bit of both. A low, wide container is ideal—you wouldn't want the mix to be deeper than ½–1 inch. Here are a few formulations to get you going.

Total: 2 hrs 30 mins

10 mins	45 mins	30 mins	30 mins	30 mins	5 mins
Blend ingredients together	Freeze	Check & scrape	Scrape	Scrape	Scrape & serve

Simple syrup

1   Heat together the sugar and water until boiling and all the sugar is dissolved. Cool before using. Simple syrup can be stored in the fridge for 2 weeks.

Cucumber-jalapeño, Tart apple, or Pink lemonade granita

1   Blend all the ingredients together in a food processor or blender until well combined. Taste and check—tweak as necessary (add more acid, more salt, sugar, etc.).

2   Pour into a wide baking dish and put into the freezer.

3   After 45 minutes, check it and start scraping any ice crystals that have formed, especially from the edges.

4   After this, check every 30 minutes, scraping as you go. At first it will be a bit slushy. As you continue to scrape, it will become more granular. Finally, it will be like beautiful little tiny snowflakes!

5   To make ahead of time, cover and store in the freezer for up to 1 week. Bring to room temperature for 5–10 minutes, then rescrape before serving.

Mocha granita

1   Whisk the sugar and cocoa powder into the coffee, then heat together until the sugar is dissolved. Add the salt and whisk well.

2   Cool, then pour into a wide dish and put into the freezer.

3   After 45 minutes, check it and start scraping any ice crystals that have formed, especially from the edges.

4   After this, check every 30 minutes, scraping as you go. At first it will be a bit slushy. As you continue to scrape, it will become more granular. Finally, it will be like beautiful little tiny snowflakes!

5   To make ahead of time, cover and store in the freezer for up to 1 week. Bring to room temperature for 5–10 minutes, then rescrape before serving.

JAM RIPPLE PARFAIT

·

SERVES 6

Techniques

Whipping egg yolks	pg.47
Sugar syrup	pg.33
Whipping cream	pg.60

Equipment

8½ x 4½ x 2½-inch/22 x 11 x 6cm loaf pan

1–2	vanilla pods, scraped or 15g/1 Tbsp good quality vanilla bean paste
90g/about 5	egg yolks
50g/¼ cup	granulated sugar
25g/1 Tbsp	honey
15g/1 Tbsp	water
265g/1 cup plus 2 Tbsp	heavy cream
150g/½ cup	good quality jam or make your own, e.g., raspberry rhubarb jam (see page 335)

Parfait is a great way to dip your toes into the world of frozen desserts before you commit to an ice cream machine. A combination of airy, cooked yolks and whipped cream, it has a melt-in-your-mouth texture. The jam ripple can be changed to suit your mood (and whatever you have in the pantry) or omitted completely.

Total: 3 hrs 25 mins

25 mins	3 hrs
Make parfait	Build ice cream, swirl jam & freeze

1 Split your vanilla pods, if using, scrape out the seeds, and set aside.

2 To make the parfait, whisk your egg yolks on high speed until they are very fluffy—at least 5–8 minutes. They should be pale and voluminous. You can't overmix.

3 Add the sugar, honey, and water to a saucepan along with the scraped vanilla pods. Stir to make sure all the sugar is dissolved.

4 Heat the sugar syrup until it reaches 244°F. To avoid crystallization, for the first 1–2 minutes as it's heating up, I like to add a lid. This means any random sugar crystals will be dissolved in the steamy environment.

5 Change the mixer speed to low. In a steady, thin stream, pour the sugar syrup down the edge of the bowl, avoiding the whisk so it doesn't splash. Also, be careful the vanilla pods don't fall in. You need to do this step quite slowly so as not to accidentally pool the syrup at the bottom of the bowl.

6 Turn the mixer back to high speed and whisk until cool—the mixture should be thick and fluffy. Around 10 minutes should be plenty.

7 Meanwhile, whip the cream and scraped vanilla seeds or vanilla paste until very soft peaks are reached.

8 Fold together the two mixtures—you should start by adding a third of the pâté à bombe into the cream and ensuring it's fully combined before adding the rest.

9 Now it's time to build your ice cream! Start by putting around 100g/3½ oz of parfait into the loaf pan followed by a drizzle of the jam. Continue layering it up until you reach the top. Finish with a few spoonfuls of jam and stir slightly.

10 Freeze until totally firm, at least 3 hours. Let it stand for 5–10 minutes out of the freezer before scooping with a hot ice cream scoop. Parfait lasts in the freezer for 3 months, covered.

DIY MINT VIENNESE ICE CREAM CAKE

·

SERVES 6

Techniques

Making meringues	pg.46
Whipping cream	pg.60
Working with chocolate	pg.63
Piping	pg.113

Equipment
8½ x 4½ x 2½-inch/22 x 11 x 6cm loaf pan
Ribbon piping tip

Chocolate shards
170g/6 oz	dark chocolate

Flaky sea salt (optional)

Semifreddo
280g/1 cup plus 3 Tbsp	heavy cream
110g/3–4	egg whites
60g/¼ cup plus 1 Tbsp	granulated sugar

Pinch of flaky sea salt
4–12g/1–3 tsp	peppermint extract, depending on your tolerance
1–2 drops	green food coloring (optional)

Plus
180g/¾ cup	heavy cream
40g/3 Tbsp	granulated sugar
1–2 drops	green food coloring (optional)

Cocoa powder, to dust

Note

You can also make the semifreddo with a Swiss meringue (see page 118) if you are concerned about raw eggs.

Nothing says PARTY like making your own ice cream cake. There are a few steps but they're all simple and this can be made well in advance. You can make this really eighties by adding food coloring for that lovable, mass-produced mint look.

Total: 4 hrs 30 mins

20 mins	20 mins	3 hrs	50 mins
Make chocolate sheets	Make semifreddo & build	Freeze	Decorate & set

1   Line the loaf pan with parchment paper.

2   To make the chocolate shards, melt the chocolate over a bain-marie. Start with the top piece, thinly spreading 20g/2 tablespoons chocolate on a flat baking sheet lined with parchment paper—weigh the paper down with a weight, like dinner knives, so the chocolate doesn't curl as it cools. Try to make it super neat and even. Divide the remaining chocolate in half and spread onto two lined, flat baking sheets. When spreading, make them approximately the length of your loaf pan so you can divide them easily later. Sprinkle with salt, if desired. Place in the freezer until ready to use.

3   For the semifreddo, whisk the cream until semi-whipped with very soft peaks. There should be just a slight resistance when you move it and it should just about support itself and hold trails from the whisk.

4   Whisk the egg whites with the sugar, salt, and peppermint extract to a French meringue (see page 118). It won't be super stiff—it will be tender and just hold peaks. Add the green food coloring until a light mint color is achieved. Whisk a large spoonful of meringue into the semi-whipped cream. Now swap to a spatula and fold in the meringue in thirds until you get a puffy aerated mixture.

5   Start building by placing about 50g/1¾ oz of the mixture in the prepared loaf pan. Spread evenly, then alternate chocolate shards (15–20g/½–¾ oz each) with the semifreddo mixture (30–40g/1–1½ oz), alternating the layers. Continue until the loaf pan is full, finishing with semifreddo and reserving the top piece of chocolate shard to finish later.

6   Allow to freeze for at least 3 hours, but it may take longer. Once solid, remove it from the pan—you may need to briefly dip the pan in warm water to help remove it. Place onto a baking sheet with clean parchment paper or onto your serving plate.

7   To decorate, divide the cream and sugar in half. Add green food coloring to one batch until a mint color is achieved. Whip both mixtures separately until thickened and just able to hold their shape—try not to over-whip, as the cream will continue to get thicker as you pipe.

8   Cut the piping bag tip at a slight angle, around ¼ inch wide, or use a ribbon tip, and start piping. Do a wiggle, then a straight line, then a wiggle, then a straight line. Alternate the colors. If you mess up, just scrape it off and start again! Place the (final) reserved chocolate shard on top, then pipe wiggles on top of the chocolate and along each side using the ribbon tip or continuing with the same piping bag. Dust with cocoa powder.

9   Let set in the freezer for at least 30 minutes or until frozen. ENJOY! It lasts in the freezer for at least 1 month—you may need to wrap it to prevent freezer burn.

RECIPES

A DAY

III

Cakes

Rhubarb and custard crumb cake	232
Horchata tres leches	234
Mango shortcake with candied lime	237
Ultimate chocolate cake	238
Citrus, olive oil, and cream cheese dome	241
Salted vanilla and pistachio layer cake with lemon syrup	243

Tarts & pies

Fancy rhubarb tart	246
Banana pudding pie	248
Parmesan and tomato linzer	250

Breads

Seasonal maritozzo	252
French toast cinnamon buns	254
Milk bread green onion babka	258
Olive oil brie-oche with roasted grapes, honey, and thyme	261

Desserts

Brown sugar canelé	262
Feta whipped cheesecake	265
Secret chocolate cake	266
Apple and vanilla charlotte	268
Apricot custard mille-feuille	270
Choux ice cream sandwich with roasted strawberries	273
Sorbets	275
Chocolate peanut ice cream bars	276

RHUBARB AND CUSTARD CRUMB CAKE

·

SERVES 9

Techniques

Creaming	pg.59
Starch-bound custard	pg.44
Sugar syrup	pg.33
Rubbing in	pg.99

Equipment

8-inch/20cm square pan

Crumb

90g/¾ cup	all-purpose flour
1–2g/¼–½ tsp	flaky sea salt
20g/2 Tbsp	light brown sugar
45g/3 Tbsp	butter

Filling

½ x recipe	pastry cream (see page 338)

Rhubarb

25g/7 oz	pink rhubarb
Zest of ½	orange
25g/2 Tbsp	granulated sugar
30g/2 Tbsp	water or orange juice

Cake

120g/½ cup	butter, softened
60g/¼ cup plus 1 Tbsp	granulated sugar
60g/¼ cup plus 1 Tbsp	light brown sugar
110g/2	whole eggs
160g/1⅓ cups	all-purpose flour
1–2g/¼ tsp	fine salt
2g/⅓ tsp	baking soda
4g/1 tsp	baking powder
120g/½ cup	sour cream

I made this cake for my mum right at the beginning of my pastry chef journey and it's still her favorite to date. Over the years, I've played around with the fruit, but I think there's not much that can beat rhubarb and custard. You can speed this recipe up by not pre-cooking the rhubarb, but you won't be as in control of the texture and color.

Day 1 — **Total:** 1–13 hrs

30 mins	30 mins	12 hrs
Make pastry cream & crumb	Prep & cook rhubarb	Allow rhubarb to chill overnight (optional)

Day 2 — **Total:** 2 hrs 30 mins

30 mins	1 hr	1 hr
Make cake & assemble	Bake	Let cool

1   To make the crumb, stir together the flour, salt, and sugar. Melt the butter and then pour over the top. Using a fork, agitate the mixture until it forms uneven crumbs. Taste and adjust the seasoning. Set aside.

2   Make the pastry cream according to the instructions on page 338.

3   For the rhubarb, preheat the oven to 375°F. Cut the rhubarb into 3¼ x ¾-inch batons, then mix with the orange zest, sugar, and water or orange juice in a small roasting dish. Roast for 15–17 minutes or until the rhubarb is slightly tender. Let cool overnight in the fridge for the best pink color. If you don't mind about that too much, then you can use it right away.

4   To make the cake, cream the butter and sugars together for 2–3 minutes, until light. You don't need to go ultra-white and fluffy here. Next, emulsify in the eggs. Due to the ratio between butter and eggs, it WILL probably look (and be) split. Don't worry. Continue anyway. Stir in the flour, salt, and rising agents.

5   Finally, stir in the sour cream—you're now ready to assemble your cake.

6   Preheat the oven to 375°F. Line the square pan with parchment paper that extends above the lip of the pan by 2 inches to help you remove it later.

7   Spread the batter evenly on the bottom. Loosen the pastry cream, as it will have gelled, by stirring. Dot the cake with generous blobs of cream. Place rhubarb all over the top.

8   Finally, scatter generously with the crumb, making sure there is still space for the cake and custard to peek out.

9   Bake for 45–55 minutes. It's ready when there's only the slightest hint of a wobble in the middle. Check the internal temp is 205°F. A skewer may not come out clean because of the fruit and custard.

10 Let cool for about 30 minutes in the pan before carefully removing it and allowing to cool completely on a rack. Leftovers can be stored in the fridge for 2–3 days.

HORCHATA TRES LECHES

·

SERVES 8

Techniques

Making meringue	pg.46
Folding	pg.113

Equipment

8-inch/20cm square pan

Horchata (from scratch)

75g/6 Tbsp	long-grain white rice
1	cinnamon stick
400g/1⅔ cups	water
2–3g/½–1 tsp	flaky sea salt
4g/1 tsp	good quality vanilla extract
150g/½ cup plus 1 Tbsp	evaporated milk
150g/½ cup	condensed milk

Horchata (speedy version)

600g/2½ cups	rice milk
6g/1 Tbsp	ground cinnamon
30–50g/ 2–4 Tbsp	granulated sugar
2–3g/½–1 tsp	flaky sea salt

Cake

220g/about 4	whole eggs
100g/½ cup	granulated sugar
50g/¼ cup	vegetable oil
50g/3 Tbsp	whole milk
Pinch of cream of tartar (optional)	
80g/⅔ cup	all-purpose flour
30g/¼ cup	cornstarch
2–3g/½–1 tsp	flaky sea salt

Tangy cream topping

60g/¼ cup	sour cream or thick Greek yogurt
140g/½ cup plus 2 Tbsp	heavy cream
30g/2 Tbsp	granulated sugar
1–2g/¼–½ tsp	flaky sea salt

Plus

Roasted corn nuts, crushed

It took me almost 28 years of living on this earth before I tried a tres leches cake. And let me tell you, I won't ever be wasting time like that again. I love bringing airy chiffon back down to earth with the generous amount of soaking liquid. I fell head-over-heels with horchata during a trip to LA and this cake is a perfect vehicle to enjoy it. Once you're confident with the method, try adapting this to suit your own tastes—the soak really can be anything!

Day 1 (optional)   Total: 5 hrs

5 hrs (or overnight)
Soak rice

Day 2   Total: 6 hrs 15 mins

20 mins	35 mins	1 hr	4 hrs 10 mins	10 mins
Make horchata & cake batter	Bake cake	Let cool	Trim cake & soak	Decorate & serve

1   If making the horchata from scratch, soak the rice with the cinnamon stick in the water for at least 5 hours or overnight. Blend until as smooth as possible, then strain through a very fine sieve four to five times until the liquid passes through easily; discard any of the sludge. You could also use a muslin cloth. You should get at least 400g/1⅔ cups. Whisk in the salt, vanilla extract, and evaporated and condensed milks. Horchata will separate over time, so make sure to stir before using. This can be made 3 days in advance and kept in the fridge.

OR

For the speedy version, whisk together the rice milk with the cinnamon, sugar, and salt.

2   Preheat the oven to 375°F. Line the square pan with parchment paper.

3   To make the cake, separate the eggs. Whisk the egg yolks with 30g/2 tablespoons of the sugar until thick, pale, and creamy, about 3 minutes. Whisk in the oil, followed by the milk, and set aside.

4   In the bowl of a stand mixer or using electric beaters, whisk the egg whites and cream of tartar, if using, until frothy, then add the remaining 70g/6 tablespoons of sugar slowly, whisking on medium speed until all the sugar is in. Then whisk on high speed until a fluffy French meringue forms.

5   Whisk 2–3 tablespoons of meringue into the yolk batter to lighten, then fold in the rest of the meringue in three or four additions. Finally, sift in the flour, cornstarch and salt, then fold into a thick batter. Pour into the lined pan and bake for 35 minutes, until the cake springs back when poked.

6   Let cool completely, then remove from the pan. The cake can be made in advance and wrapped for 3 days at room temperature.

Note

You can sub the condensed
and evaporated milks with
300g/1¼ cups whole milk, plus
30g/2½ tablespoons granulated sugar.

7 To help the cake absorb as much as possible, cut the crust off the edges of the cooled cake (this is your snack!). Place the cake back into the cleaned pan and stab with a skewer 20–30 times, or till it is visibly marked. Pour in the horchata mixture until it does not absorb any more. Walk away for 5 minutes, then pour in more. You want it to be completely soaked. Any horchata you do not use, keep on the side to serve with it or dilute with milk/water to enjoy. Chill the cake for 4 hours or overnight in the fridge.

8 To prepare the tangy cream topping, whip everything together until soft peaks form. Spread over the cake and top with crushed roasted corn nuts. Cut and serve.

9 The cake lasts in the fridge, well-covered, for 3 days.

MANGO SHORTCAKE WITH CANDIED LIME

·

SERVES 8

Techniques

Egg foam	pg.45
Whipping cream	pg.60
Sugar syrup	pg.33

Equipment
1 x 8-inch/20cm or
2 x 6-inch/15cm cake pan(s)

Cake

2 x 6-inch	genoise sponges (see page 131) to make a 4-layer cake or 1 x 8-inch sponge to make a 2-layer cake
300–350g/ 10½–12¼ oz	ripe mangoes (about 2 small or 1 large, whole weight), peeled and stoned

Sugared lime zest strips

3	limes, plus 20g/4 tsp lime juice
150g/½ cup plus 2 Tbsp	water
150g/¾ cup	granulated sugar
Coarse sanding sugar, to toss	

Whipped cream

450g/1¾ cups	heavy cream
50g/¼ cup	granulated sugar

Soft, fluffy cake spiked with lime, piles of whipped cream, and the very best mangoes all in one beautiful package, what's not to love? You can adapt this recipe to suit whatever is in season, just make sure you always leave a little bit of time for the flavors to marry and get to know each other. I promise it's worth it.

Total: 5 hrs 40 mins

1 hr 20 mins	20 mins	1 hr 30 mins	30 mins	2 hrs
Candy lime peels	Make genoise	Bake and cool genoise	Assemble	Chill

1   To make the sugared lime zest strips, remove the peel from the limes and cut into thin strips. Bring a small pot of water to a boil. Dunk the peels in boiling water and simmer for 20–30 seconds. Drain, then repeat twice more. This is to ensure that the membrane of the fruit is softened so it is more accepting of your sugar, as well as removing some of the more unpleasant bitterness.

2   Bring your water and sugar to a boil in a small saucepan. Add your peels and turn the heat down to a very gentle simmer. Simmer for 50 minutes–1 hour. Your peels should be very glassy and gem-like. Remove the peels from the syrup and rinse briefly with water to remove any excess syrup. Let dry on a tray for a few hours. Toss in the sanding sugar. The lime zests will keep for 1–2 months in an airtight container at room temperature.

3   After removing the peels, add 20g/4 teaspoons lime juice to the lime candying syrup. You will use this to brush onto your cakes.

4   For the whipped cream, whip the cream and sugar together until soft peaks are reached. You want it to be spreadable and not at all close to splitting or over-whipping. It's better to under-whip as you can always do more. It should only just hold its weight when you lift up the whisk.

5   To assemble, cut the cake(s) in half equally, to make two layers per cake. Cut the mango into ½–¾-inch cubes and set aside—you can keep a few larger pieces to decorate the top. To build the cake, brush the bottom cake with the lime syrup and spread a thin layer of whipped cream, followed by a quarter of the mango chunks (for a four layer cake), then some more cream on top. Continue layering up in this way.

6   When all the layers are in place, cover the cake roughly but elegantly with the remaining cream using an offset spatula. Finish by decorating the sides of the cake with wiggles of lime zest and chunks of mango on top.

7   For best results, rest the cake in the fridge for at least 2 hours, but it will improve over time. Keeps well in the fridge for 3 days.

ULTIMATE CHOCOLATE CAKE

·

SERVES 8

Techniques

Ganache	pg.63

Equipment
3 x 6-inch/15cm cake pans

Cake

90g/6 Tbsp	butter, melted
90g/6 Tbsp	vegetable oil
105g/½ cup	light brown sugar, packed
165g/¾ cup plus 1 Tbsp	granulated sugar
90g/about 2	whole eggs
75g/5 Tbsp	strong brewed coffee (can be warm or room temperature)
3g/1 tsp	flaky sea salt
210g/1⅔ cups	all-purpose flour
50g/⅔ cup	cocoa powder
3g/½ tsp	baking soda
6g/1½ tsp	baking powder
210g/¾ cup plus 3 Tbsp	sour cream, yogurt, or crème fraîche

Chocolate buttercream

90g/7 Tbsp	light brown sugar
300g/1¼ cups	heavy cream
300g/10½ oz	dark chocolate
350g/1½ cups	butter, softened
60g/¾ cup	cocoa powder
6g/1¾ tsp	flaky sea salt, (optional)

Plus

180g/6⅓ oz	dark chocolate bar, for shavings or curls

A really good chocolate cake should be able to be dressed up or down as you wish. It should have a good balance of roasty cocoa and rich chocolate notes. It should also be able to play ball in a multi-layered affair, hold its own as a hefty doorstop-style layer cake, or be happily nestled in an entremet surrounded by mousse. This version is not modest: we take it to the max with 18 alternating layers of cake and buttercream.

Total: 4 hrs 20 mins

20 mins	30 mins	1 hr 30 mins	30 mins	30 mins	30 mins	30 mins
Mix cake	Divide mix & bake	Let cool	Prepare buttercream. Divide cakes	Build cake. Frost	Chill	Decorate cake

1   Preheat the oven to 375°F and line the three pans with parchment paper.

2   For the cake, whisk together the melted butter and oil. Whisk in the sugars followed by the eggs, coffee, and salt. Sift in the flour, cocoa powder, and rising agents and finally whisk in the sour cream (or whatever you are using) until combined and no streaks remain.

3   Divide among the cake pans, about 350g/12¼ oz per pan, and smooth out slightly. Bake for 20–25 minutes. Check to see if the cakes are baked—they should be risen and firm with no wobble, but still tender. You can prod with a toothpick—there shouldn't be liquid but a few crumbs are fine, good, even! If not, bake for another 5 minutes and check. Overbaked chocolate cake is a tragedy so be careful to check this and err on the side of just baked.

4   Let cool for 10 minutes in the pans, then turn out and cool completely on a cooling rack. Wrap and transfer to either the fridge overnight or the freezer. It is essential the cake layers are very cold or they won't cut well.

5   Make the chocolate buttercream according to the instructions on page 144.

6   To assemble, slice each cake into three layers. Remember, they must be chilled! Semi-frozen, even. A large serrated knife is your friend here.

7   Start by placing one layer on a cake stand or serving platter. Spread a layer of chocolate buttercream on top of the sponge cake. Repeat this process, alternating between layers of sponge cake and buttercream, until you have used all nine layers.

8   Wrap the assembled cake with acetate or parchment paper and chill it in the freezer for about 30 minutes. This will help to firm up the cake and make it easier to handle.

9   Remove the cake from the freezer and carefully remove the acetate or parchment paper. Using a spatula or offset knife, coat the outside of the cake with a layer of chocolate buttercream. Because the cake is cold, it may set quickly.

10 Make chocolate curls or shavings by dragging a knife along a thick chocolate bar. Be careful! And go slow!

11 Once the cake is coated in buttercream, finish with the additional chocolate shavings. The cake can be made 1–2 days in advance and leftovers keep well for 5 days in the fridge.

Notes

You can also build this in a cake pan. See the instructions in the salted vanilla and pistachio layer cake (see page 243) for guidance.

If you have limited access to cake pans, this batter holds for 1–2 hours.

CITRUS, OLIVE OIL, AND CREAM CHEESE DOME

·

SERVES 10–12

Techniques

Swapping fats	pg.56

Equipment

15½ x 10½-inch/39 x 27cm baking dish
Mixing bowl, at least 8 inches/
20cm wide at the top with a base of
around 3½ inches/9cm

Olive oil cake

Zest of 2	oranges (about 7g/¼ oz)
200g/1 cup	granulated sugar
160g/¾ cup	extra-virgin olive oil
110g/6 Tbsp	Greek yogurt
160g/3	whole eggs
110g/⅔ cup	fine semolina or all-purpose flour
110g/¾ cup plus 2 Tbsp	almond flour
4g/1 tsp	baking powder
1g/⅛ tsp	baking soda
1–2g/¼–½ tsp	flaky sea salt

Orange syrup

50g/3 Tbsp	orange juice
50g/¼ cup	granulated sugar

Whipped cream cheese

240g/8½ oz	full-fat cream cheese
35g/3 Tbsp	granulated sugar
180g/¾ cup	heavy cream
60g/¼ cup	olive oil
3–4g/½–¾ tsp	fine salt

Honey, rosemary, and orange Swiss meringue buttercream

250g/1 cup plus 2 Tbsp	butter, softened
2	sprigs of rosemary
90g/3	egg whites
40g/2 Tbsp	honey
80g/6 Tbsp	granulated sugar
Zest of 1	orange
1–2g/¼ tsp	flaky sea salt

In case you needed it, this is your permission to go absolutely bananas on decorating your cake. The dome shape is incredibly sturdy and can handle a lot of ornamentation. I love seeing citrus and olive oil come together in this celebratory recipe that will NEVER fall over while you're transporting it to your friend's house. Promise.

Total: 7 hrs 10 mins

1 hr	40 mins	30 mins	4 hrs (or overnight)	1 hr
Mix cake & bake	Make fillings & syrup	Assemble cake	Chill	Make buttercream & finish

1   For the cake, preheat the oven to 375°F.

2   Add the orange zest to the granulated sugar and rub in between your fingers to release the oils. Next, whisk in the olive oil, yogurt, and eggs. In another bowl, whisk together the dry ingredients. Whisk into the wet ingredients until smooth. Pour into the lined baking dish and bake for 22–25 minutes or until firm and springy to the touch and a skewer inserted into the middle comes out clean. Move to a cooling rack, remove the cake from the dish, and let cool completely. This can be made 1–2 days in advance and kept well-wrapped at room temperature.

3   For the syrup, heat everything together and bring to a simmer. Allow to cool. This can be made 1 week in advance and kept in the fridge. This makes more than you need.

4   For the whipped cream cheese, put the cream cheese and sugar in a bowl. Whisk until it is smooth. Add the heavy cream, olive oil, and salt then whisk until stiff and thick. Make this when you are ready to assemble.

5   To prepare the dome, cut 1 x 8-inch circle, 1 x 6-inch circle, and 1 x 3½–4-inch circle from the cake sheet. The leftovers are your snacks. Line the mixing bowl with plastic wrap—make sure it is at least 8 inches wide at the top with a base of around 3½ inches.

6   To build, place the 3½-inch cake circle in the bottom. Douse with orange syrup, then spread 30–40g/1–1½ oz marmalade on top, followed by 150g/5¼ oz of whipped cream cheese. Nestle half the mandarin segments into the cream. Place the 6-inch cake layer on top. Douse with syrup, then spread 50g/1¾ oz marmalade, followed by 300g/10½ oz of whipped cream cheese. Nestle the remaining mandarin segments into the cream cheese. Spread 70g/2½ oz marmalade on the final cake, then place on top, marmalade-side down. Chill the entire cake in the fridge for at least 4 hours or overnight.

7   For the buttercream, first make the rosemary infused butter. Heat 50g/¼ cup of the butter with the rosemary until foaming and slightly browned. Let cool slightly.

8   In a heatproof bowl, whisk the egg whites, honey, and sugar over a bain-marie until you can no longer feel the grittiness from the sugar and it has reached around 158°F.

Continued →

CITRUS, OLIVE OIL, AND CREAM CHEESE DOME
Continued

To assemble

1 x recipe	tangerine marmalade (see page 335)
2	mandarins, segments only (pith removed)
1	blood orange

Honey
Small rosemary sprigs, mixed tulip petals, and other edible flowers

9   Remove from the heat, then whisk in a stand mixer on high speed until the mixture has made a thick, fluffy meringue and is cool to the touch, about 10 minutes. Add the orange zest, followed by the remaining softened butter, bit by bit, 2–3 minutes.

10 Strain the still-melted rosemary-infused butter through a sieve to remove the herbs, then add this in. Whip until fluffy and smooth, about 5 minutes.

11 Finally, add salt to taste. I add the salt at the end because I want there to be crunchy salt crystals in the buttercream. BE BRAVE, people will absolutely LOVE it. For extra-smooth buttercream, change to the paddle attachment and beat on the lowest speed for 10 minutes.

12 The buttercream can be made in advance and kept at room temperature for 24 hours or for 1 week, well-wrapped, in the fridge. It needs to be rewhipped for 5–10 minutes before using and may need to be heated over a bain-marie or in a bowl warmed with a blowtorch as you whip.

13 To segment the blood orange, first zest the orange and save for future recipes. Cut off the top and bottom so you have a flat bottom to work from. Carefully slice the pith and skin away, following the curve of the orange. Once it is all removed, cut segments from between the membranes of the fruit, using your knife at an angle to get clean cuts. Use the white lines of the membranes to guide you and try to cut as close to these as possible. You'll be left with perfect segments and a flappy orange husk, which you can eat/juice/enjoy however you like.

14 To decorate, put a plate/cake board underneath the mixing bowl and flip it over to release the cake so it is the right way up. Spread the buttercream over the cake dome, using an offset spatula to help smooth it out. Cover the cake with the blood orange segments, dabs of honey, rosemary sprigs, tulip petals, and other flowers. The cake will last 3 days in the fridge. Bring to room temperature before enjoying.

Notes

Feel free to use any good quality citrus preserve if you don't feel like making your own!

SALTED VANILLA AND PISTACHIO LAYER CAKE WITH LEMON SYRUP

•

SERVES 12

Techniques

Sugar syrup	pg.33
Crystallization	pg.32
Egg foam	pg.45
Starch-bound custard	pg.44

Equipment

8-inch/20cm cake pan

1 x 8-inch/20cm genoise sponge cake (see page 131)

Vanilla custard

260g/1 cup plus 1 Tbsp	whole milk
1	vanilla pod, scraped or 10g/2 tsp good quality vanilla bean paste
50g/¼ cup	granulated sugar
60g/3	egg yolks (or 1 whole egg)
20g/3 Tbsp	cornstarch
20g/1½ Tbsp	butter, cold
150g/½ cup plus 2 Tbsp	heavy cream

Pistachio mousseline cream

100g/7 Tbsp	whole milk
30g/2 Tbsp	granulated sugar
50g/1	whole egg
75g/¼ cup	pistachio butter
15g/2 Tbsp	cornstarch
140g/½ cup plus 2 Tbsp	butter, softened

Crystallized pistachios (this makes more than you need)

20g/4 tsp	water
75g/6 Tbsp	granulated sugar
100g/¾ cup	shelled pistachios

Vanilla and lemon syrup

zest of 2	lemon, in strips
	spent vanilla pods
75g/5 Tbsp	water
75g/6 Tbsp	granulated sugar

This cake is a total supermodel. Because genoise is a drier sponge, this cake really benefits from a long rest in the fridge to let the flavors meld. This is definitely an elegant "did you make this?!" sort of cake. The color palette with the crystallized pistachios, like little diamonds, will make any recipient of this cake feel special.

Total: 12 hrs

1 hr	1 hr 30 mins	30 mins	8 hrs (or overnight)	1 hr
Make sponge	Make fillings & syrup	Assemble cake	Chill	Make buttercream & decorate

1   For the vanilla custard, make according to the instructions for the pastry cream on page 338. Once cool, whisk on medium speed for 1–2 minutes to loosen until smooth. In a separate bowl, whip the cream till it's thick and can hold a peak (but not stiff!), then fold the mixtures together in two or three additions.

2   For the pistachio mousseline cream, heat the milk and half the sugar on the stovetop until simmering. Whisk the egg with the pistachio paste, cornstarch, and the rest of the sugar. Once the milk mixture is bubbling, pour a little over the paste mix to temper, then add in the rest and return the whole mixture to the stovetop. Cook—whisking all the time—until the mixture is very thick. Pour into a clean container, cover, and chill completely.

3   Once cool, whisk on medium speed for 1–2 minutes to loosen. Once it is smooth, start adding the softened butter. Whisk on medium-low speed until ultra-lush and smooth, 1–2 minutes. If it splits, warm using a blowtorch or warm briefly over a bain-marie and whisk.

4   For the crystallized pistachios, mix together the water and sugar in a small saucepan. Cover with a lid and heat until boiling (this helps prevent early crystallization), then remove the lid and cook until 293°F—the syrup will be very thick and viscous. Turn off the heat and add the pistachios. Stir vigorously. At first, it will just look sticky, but eventually, as you keep stirring, the sugar crystals will form on the nuts. Keep stirring until all the sugar has crystallized. Pour into a clean, heatproof container and cool. Store for 1 month in an airtight container.

5   For the syrup, heat all the ingredients together until boiling, then let cool.

6   To assemble, line the cake pan with acetate and parchment paper at the bottom. Cut the genoise sponge cake into three equal layers. Place one layer into the bottom of the pan and douse with syrup, 2–3 tablespoons, using a pastry brush. Spread half the pistachio mousseline on top, going all the way to the edges. Follow with half of the custard. Repeat with the next sponge layer.

7   To finish, soak the final sponge with syrup, then flip over and place on top. Let the cake chill overnight and allow the flavors to meld together.

Continued →

SALTED VANILLA AND PISTACHIO LAYER CAKE WITH LEMON SYRUP
Continued

Salted vanilla buttercream

90g/3	egg whites
12g/1 Tbsp	good quality vanilla extract
120g/½ cup plus 2 Tbsp	granulated sugar
250g/1 cup plus 2 Tbsp	butter, softened
4g/1¼ tsp	flaky sea salt, start with less if you're nervous

8 To make the buttercream, whisk the egg whites, vanilla, and sugar together in the bowl of your stand mixer. Heat over a bain-marie until you can no longer feel the grittiness from the sugar and it has reached around 158°F. Whisk on high speed until the mixture has made a thick, fluffy meringue and is cool to the touch, about 10 minutes. Add the butter in, bit by bit, until smooth, 2–3 minutes. It will split. Don't panic. Keep going. If the mixture still looks split, see All About Fat on page 64.

9 When it's smooth, finally add salt to taste. I add the salt at the end because I want there to be crunchy salt crystals in the buttercream. BE BRAVE, people will LOVE it. For extra-smooth buttercream, change to the paddle attachment and beat on low speed for 10 minutes. Buttercream can be made in advance and kept at room temperature for 24 hours or for 1 week, well-wrapped, in the fridge. It needs to be rewhipped for 5–10 minutes before using and may need to be heated over a bain-marie or in a bowl warmed with a blowtorch as you whip.

10 Remove the pan, parchment paper, and acetate from the cake. Flip it upside down (the bottom is always flatter!), then coat the cake with a thin layer of buttercream, using an offset spatula to smooth it out. As the cake is cold, it might set slightly. Apply a second, thicker layer to get a smooth finish. You can also use a flat dough scraper to smooth out the sides. Finish with crystallized pistachios.

11 The cake can be made 1–2 days in advance and lasts well for 3–4 days in the fridge.

Note

Look for a good quality 100% pistachio nut butter. You can use other nut praline pastes (or make your own, see page 334) but it will have a different flavor and color.

FANCY RHUBARB TART

•

SERVES 6–8

When forced rhubarb is in season, I love to take advantage of its extraordinary hot pink hue—there is nothing else quite like it. This is actually quite an easy recipe but does take a bit of time for the best results; the key to unlocking the pink rhubarb color is letting it sit in its poaching liquid overnight. Although this is time-consuming, you'll be rewarded with the most beautiful hue.

Techniques

Poaching fruit	pg.107
Lining a tart	pg.108

Equipment
8-inch/20cm tart ring

Tart
1 x recipe	tart pastry or rich tart pastry (see page 119)

Fancy rhubarb strips
200g/7 oz	pink rhubarb, cleaned but left whole (cut the ends off)
30g/2 Tbsp	granulated sugar

Enough water to cover, depending on what baking dish you use

Rhubarb compote
200g/7 oz	pink rhubarb, cut into chunks
50g/¼ cup	granulated sugar
30g/2 Tbsp	water

Frangipane
90g/6 Tbsp	butter
90g/½ cup	granulated sugar
100g/2	whole eggs
55g/½ cup	ground pistachios
20g/3 Tbsp	all-purpose flour
3g/½ tsp	fine salt

Plus
Melted apricot jam or a little simple syrup, to glaze (optional)

Note

This recipe makes more compote than you need, but you can freeze it or add it to yogurt for brekkie. You could just use chopped-up poached rhubarb inside the tart, but I really like the texture/flavor of a compote.

Day 1	Total: 12 hrs	**Day 2**				Total: 3 hrs 35 mins
12 hrs	20 mins	1 hr 40 mins	15 mins	1 hr	20 mins
Poach rhubarb overnight	Make compote	Make & bake pastry case	Mix frangipane	Make & bake	Decorate & serve

1   To make the fancy rhubarb strips, preheat the oven to 350°F.

2   Place the rhubarb and sugar in a long baking dish. You want to keep the rhubarb in long pieces so you can cut long, elegant strips later. Pour in just enough water to submerge the rhubarb. Cover with foil to avoid coloring in the oven.

3   Bake the rhubarb for 15 minutes, then check every 2–3 minutes until you can just pierce it with a sharp knife. We need to be able to cut this into strips later, so it is imperative that you don't overcook it.

4   Remove from the oven and chill overnight in the fridge. The pinker the rhubarb, the pinker it will be after a night in the fridge as the colors are dispersed.

5   To make the rhubarb compote, heat all the ingredients in a pan over low heat until the rhubarb is totally broken down. Check for sweetness—if it's too sweet for you, add some lemon juice! If it isn't sweet enough, add a little more sugar and ensure it's dissolved. No exact science here, I'm afraid.

6   To make the frangipane, follow the instructions on page 339.

7   Preheat the oven to 375°F.

8   To line the tart, roll out the soft tart pastry in between two sheets of parchment paper until it's around ⅛ inch thick. Line and blind bake according to the instructions on page 121 until dry and light golden, about 25 minutes. Let cool.

9   Lower the oven temperature to 350°F. Once cool, spread half the frangipane in the tart case, then spoon the rhubarb compote over the top, followed by the rest of the frangipane. Smooth the top. Bake for 40–50 minutes, until golden. Let cool.

10 To finish, take your fancy rhubarb and cut lengthwise into thin strips. You can follow the natural ridges of the rhubarb. Use a sharp knife! I think a small knife works better than a big one. Lay the strips out on a chopping board and, using a pastry cutter (measure against your tart), cut to the perfect size.

11 Carefully lay the strips over your finished tart. If desired, glaze with melted apricot jam or a little simple syrup.

12 Store leftovers well-wrapped in the fridge for 2–3 days. Bring to room temperature before enjoying.

BANANA
PUDDING PIE

·

SERVES 10

Techniques

Egg foam	pg.45
Whipping cream	pg.60
Making caramel	pg.86

Equipment

8 x 1¼-inch/20 x 3.5cm fluted tart pan
Piping bag

Cocoa case

40g/3 Tbsp	granulated sugar
130g/1 cup	all-purpose flour
20g/¼ cup	cocoa powder
1g/¼ tsp	flaky sea salt
75g/5 Tbsp	butter
15g/½	egg white

Cookie layer

| 1 x recipe | Savoiardi cookie (see page 340) |

Caramel sauce

100g/½ cup	granulated sugar
50g/¼ cup	butter
70g/5 Tbsp	heavy cream
1–2g/¼–½ tsp	flaky sea salt

Crème légère

200g/¾ cup plus 2 Tbsp	whole milk
35g/3 Tbsp	granulated sugar
40g/2	egg yolks
15g/2 Tbsp	cornstarch
10g/2 tsp	butter
160g/⅔ cup	heavy cream, whipped

Sweet whipped cream

150g/½ cup plus 2 Tbsp	heavy cream
15g/1 Tbsp	granulated sugar
350g/3	bananas, peeled and sliced into ¼-inch rounds

Plus

Dark chocolate, to make shavings

Banana pudding is pure pleasure: a heavenly combination of bananas, light cookies, custard, and whipped cream. I love banana pudding in every possible way—straight from the bowl or eaten in a bun, maritozzo-style—but here's my new favorite way: build it up in a tart case, with caramel sauce, add whipped cream on top, and finish with chocolate curls and you really have a winner.

Total: 7 hrs

40 mins	30 mins	20 mins	15 mins	15 mins	1 hr	4 hrs
Make & bake base	Make savoiardi cookie	Make caramel sauce	Make crème légère	Finish crème légère	Assemble pie and chill	Whip cream & chill

1   To make the cocoa case, preheat the oven to 375°F. Mix the dry ingredients together. Melt the butter, then stir it in to form wet, clumpy crumbs. Add the egg white and mix well. Press the crumb into the tart pan to make a ⅛–¼-inch-thick crust. Bake for 25 minutes, until it smells like cookies and the crumb looks set; it will firm up more as it cools. Let cool completely in the pan. This can be made up to 3 days in advance. Wrap well and store at room temperature.

2   For the savoiardi cookie layers, preheat the oven to 375°F. Make the batter for the savoiardi cookies according to the instructions on page 340. Trace 2 x 6-inch circles on parchment paper, flip over, and place on a baking sheet, then spread the batter evenly to make two discs, about 50g/1¾ oz per disc and ½ inch thick. Bake for 12–14 minutes, until golden then transfer to a cool rack. This can be made up to 3 days in advance; wrap well and store at room temperature.

3   To make the caramel sauce, heat the sugar in a saucepan, stirring over medium heat for approximately 7 minutes, until it turns a dark amber. Whisk in the butter, followed by the cream and salt. Careful, it might splutter! Pour into a heatproof container and let cool before storing in the fridge to cool completely—it will be firm. This can be made up to 7 days in advance. Store in the fridge.

4   For the crème légère, make according to the instructions on page 338. This pastry cream can be made up to 5 days in advance and kept in the fridge. The whipped cream should be added when you are ready to build.

5   To assemble, warm the caramel and pipe a layer into the bottom of the tart case (around 50g/1¾ oz), followed by a quarter of the banana slices. Top with a third of the crème légère (around 110g/4 oz), and another quarter of the banana slices, followed by a disc of the cookie layer. Top this with a third of the remaining caramel sauce, another quarter of the banana slices, and another third of the crème légère. Place the next cookie layer on top, followed by the rest of the caramel sauce, bananas, and the rest of the crème légère, building it into a mound shape. Chill for at least 30 minutes.

Note

Instead of making the savoiardi cookie layers, you can use store-bought Nilla wafers or ladyfingers.

6 Whip the cream with the sugar to soft peaks, then pile onto the crème légère. Chill for at least 4 hours before serving or, if you can, overnight. The pudding filling melds and gets better with time!

7 Finish with chocolate shavings, made by dragging a sharp knife along a thick chocolate bar. Be careful! And go slow! The pie lasts well in the fridge for 3–5 days.

PARMESAN AND TOMATO LINZER

·

SERVES 6

Techniques

Making Jam	pg.95
Egg coagulation	pg.40

Equipment
8-inch/20cm tart ring

Tomato jam (makes approx. 500g/1½ cups, enough for two Linzers and leftovers)

850g/1 lb 14 oz	ripe tomatoes
13g/1 Tbsp	olive oil
280g/9¾ oz	white onions, thinly sliced
110g/½ cup plus 1 Tbsp	granulated sugar
55g/¼ cup	dark brown sugar, packed
55g/¼ cup	cider or white wine vinegar
2	bay leaves
75g/5 Tbsp	butter
6g/1¾ tsp	flaky sea salt

Parmesan Linzer dough

60g/3	egg yolks
175g/¾ cup	butter, softened
35g/⅓ cup	Parmesan cheese, grated
190g/1½ cups	all-purpose flour
1–2g/¼–½ tsp	flaky sea salt
50g/⅓ cup	black olives, finely diced
Pinch of black pepper	

To finish
Egg wash (see page 343)
Caraway seeds

Not your average torte! The classic Linzer gets a savory update with a Parmesan-enriched crust that is outrageously crumbly. The egg yolk dough is a curious one but well worth exploring —there's nothing quite like it. And the speckles of black olive tie in beautifully with the sweet tomato jam.

Total: 4 hrs 30 mins

3 hrs	30 mins	10 mins	10 mins	40 mins
Make tomato jam	Mix pastry & shape	Rest	Fill	Bake

1   To make the tomato jam, first peel the tomatoes. Boil a large pot of water for blanching. Turn the tomatoes over and make a little "x" incision on the bottom. Add to the boiling water and cook on high for 1–2 minutes. Drain, then once cool, simply peel the skin off. Depending on the tomatoes, you may want to remove the very thick core pieces as well as the stem.

2   Heat the olive oil in a pan and throw in the onion slices over medium heat. Cover with a lid and cook (you don't need them to color) until they have collapsed slightly, about 10 minutes.

3   Add the tomatoes, sugars, vinegar, and bay leaves and bring to a boil. Once boiling, turn the heat down and simmer until it has reduced significantly, 2–3 hours, stirring regularly to prevent it from sticking.

4   When the jam is ready it'll be much darker in color and when you drag a spoon through it, it won't fill in with liquid: the red tomato seas will simply part. At this point, stir in the butter and salt, then you can take it off the heat. Transfer to a clean container. Keeps in an airtight container for 2 weeks in the fridge.

5   For the yolks for the Linzer dough, either boil the eggs whole in their shells for 10 minutes, remove, peel, and then separate the yolks, or separate your eggs and poach the yolks directly in simmering water for 7–8 minutes before removing and drying off. Push the yolks through a fine sieve.

6   For the dough, beat the butter until smooth, then add the sieved egg yolks and Parmesan cheese and mix until well combined. Finally, stir in the flour, salt, olives, and some black pepper until a dough forms.

7   Divide the dough in half. Roll one half between two sheets of parchment paper to be ⅛–¼ inch thick and around 9 inches wide, then cut into ¾-inch strips. Put into the freezer to chill while you prepare the tart.

8   To create the tart, press the remaining dough into the greased tart ring on a lined baking sheet. Spoon 200g/⅔ cup of the jam onto the dough, spread to the edges, and set aside.

9   Get the pastry strips out carefully and lay as an angled criss-cross on top of the tart. Squish the edges of the pastry case with the lattice top to finish the tart. Put into the fridge to chill while the oven preheats to 375°F.

10 Before baking, brush with egg wash and sprinkle with some caraway seeds. Bake for 20 minutes, turn, then bake for another 20 minutes, until perfectly golden.

SEASONAL MARITOZZO

•

MAKES 8 BUNS

Techniques

Preferments	pg.80
Fermentation	pg.76
Gluten development	pg.14

Preferment

75g/5 Tbsp	whole milk
1	vanilla pod, scraped
4g/1¼ tsp	granulated sugar
Zest of 1	orange
Zest of 1	lemon
3g/1 tsp	dry yeast
120g/1 cup	bread flour

Second dough

50g/1	whole egg
60g/¼ cup	whole milk
120g/1 cup	bread flour
4g/¾ tsp	fine salt
35g/3 Tbsp	granulated sugar
45g/3 Tbsp	butter, softened
Egg wash (see page 343)	

Honey cream

300g/1¼ cups	heavy cream
35g/1½ Tbsp	honey

Plus

Seasonal jam or compote, e.g., rhubarb compote (see page 246)
OR

200g/7 oz	seasonal fruit, e.g., raspberries, strawberries, poached fruit

Powdered sugar, to dust (optional)

The prefermented dough creates the airiest and most fragrant buns of all, but add the smile of cream and they become completely irresistible. Maritozzo are the elegant Roman cousin of the Devonshire splits. Enjoy these at any time of the year by adding seasonal fruit. Compotes work well here, hidden under the blanket of cream, though jam would be just as good.

Total: 7 hrs 15 mins

2 hrs	20 mins	2 hrs	1 hr 40 mins	15 mins	30 mins	30 mins
Make preferment	Mix dough	Bulk ferment	Shape dough & proof	Bake	Cool	Make honey cream, fill & serve

1   For the preferment, heat the milk, vanilla seeds, sugar, and citrus zests until simmering. Cool to 95–104°F, then add the dry yeast and let it sit for 10 minutes, until bubbly.

2   Stir in the bread flour to form a stiff dough, and let it rest for 2 hours, covered, in a warm place. The dough should be risen, very fragrant, and airy. You can keep your preferment in the fridge for up to 3 days and use it anytime. If you are using it from cold, it will take longer to reactivate and the other ingredients must be warm to help it along.

3   To mix the second dough, combine the egg and milk in a mixer bowl. Tear up the preferment and add to the bowl, along with the flour, salt, and sugar. Mix on medium speed for 8–10 minutes, until medium gluten development is reached—this is when you can pull on the dough and it stays together but it is still quite fragile. You can take it further than this, but this is the minimum requirement before adding the butter.

4   Add the soft butter, then mix for 5–8 minutes on medium speed, until full gluten development is reached.

5   Cover the dough and allow to proof for 2 hours or until puffy and somewhat doubled in size.

6   Divide the dough into 55–60g/2–2¼ oz portions, then shape them into balls and let them rest. Finish the buns by shaping them into elongated oval shapes using your hands, then transfer to a lined baking sheet and allow to proof, covered, for 1½ hours, until puffy.

7   Preheat the oven to 375°F.

8   Egg wash the buns carefully and bake for 12 minutes, until deep golden.

9   Let cool on a cooling rack completely before filling. You can wrap the buns for 24 hours and keep them at room temperature before filling.

10 For the honey cream, whip the cream until it is as thick as the honey, then add the honey and whisk until thickened and smooth—don't over-whip it! It should just be soft and flump over on itself.

Note

You can use any of the enriched doughs for this recipe. The tangzhong bun dough (see page 123) would work well.

11 To finish the buns, split the buns horizontally at an angle. Open the buns up a bit, then spoon seasonal jam or compote generously inside, around 20g/1 tablespoon, or a few pieces of seasonal fruit, chopped small. Follow this with a big spoonful of honey cream.

12 Close the buns slightly and use an offset spatula to smooth the cream. You can wipe off any messy cream later. Add a piece of fresh fruit to finish. Dust with powdered sugar, if desired.

13 Eat within 3–4 hours for the best experience. Leftovers can be stored in the fridge for 2 days.

FRENCH TOAST CINNAMON BUNS

·

MAKES 10-12 BUNS

Techniques

Lamination	pg.69
Gluten development	pg.14
Fermentation	pg.76

Equipment
Cupcake pan

1 x recipe	Tangzhong bun dough (see page 123)
Egg wash (see page 343)	

Spiced butter

120g/½ cup	butter, softened
60g/¼ cup	demerara sugar
60g/¼ cup	light brown sugar, packed
1–2g/¼–½ tsp	flaky sea salt
2g/1 tsp	ground cardamom
3g/2 tsp	ground cinnamon

Cinnamon bun soak

200g/¾ cup plus 2 Tbsp	whole milk
100g/2	whole eggs
20g/2 Tbsp	granulated sugar
20g/4 tsp	dark spiced rum
1	vanilla pod, scraped

Tangy butterscotch icing

100g/½ cup	light brown sugar, packed
20g/4 tsp	water
1 tsp	apple cider vinegar
40g/3 Tbsp	butter
1 tsp	dark spiced rum
Pinch of flaky sea salt	

These are the softest and most tender cinnamon buns you'll ever have. Giving your buns the French toast treatment is probably the most luxurious thing you can do. I mean, who doesn't want to have a custard bath? You can (and should) try applying this technique to any and all buns for extra squidginess.

Day 1 — Total: 2 hrs 55 mins

25 mins	1 hr	1 hr 30 mins (or overnight)
Make dough	Proof	Flatten & chill

Day 2 — Total: 3 hrs 50 mins

45 mins	1 hr 30 mins	25 mins	20 mins	30 mins	20 mins
Fill & shape buns	Proof buns	Bake buns. Make soak	Soak buns & bake	Cool	Ice & finish

1 Make the dough according to the tangzhong bun dough method on page 123. Press down the dough onto a tray, wrap well, and chill in the fridge overnight to proof. You can also place it in the freezer for 30 minutes to stop fermentation, followed by 1 hour in the fridge to chill until it is completely solid to forgo the overnight chill.

2 For the spiced butter, mix the soft butter with the demerara sugar, light brown sugar, salt, cardamom, and cinnamon until well combined. You don't want it to be aerated. Set aside until ready to use. You can do this in advance as long as it is soft and spreadable when you use it.

3 To assemble, roll out the dough to about 16 x 10 inches. Spread 100g/7 tablespoons of the spiced butter onto the dough and perform a letter fold/single fold. Fold the dough into thirds, crossing over in the middle. Wrap and put into the freezer for 10 minutes, or the fridge for 30 minutes, to firm up.

4 Turn the dough 90 degrees, then roll out the dough to about 16 x 10 inches again and spread with the rest of the spiced butter. Perform another letter fold/single fold. The dough will be 10 x 6 inches. Lengthen the dough so it is 12 x 6 inches.

5 Turn it 90 degrees, then cut it into 1¼-inch wide pieces, 75–85g/2½–3 oz. To shape, cut three strips into each piece, leaving them attached at one end with 1 inch uncut so they are still connected. Braid the strips, then roll up the dough into a bun. Place into a cupcake pan, lightly cover, and proof for 1 hour or until puffy.

6 Preheat the oven to 400°F.

Continued ⟶

FRENCH TOAST
CINNAMON BUNS
Continued

7 Gently brush the buns with egg wash and bake for 18–22 minutes, until golden. Let cool in the pan for 5–10 minutes.

8 For the soak, whisk together all the ingredients. This can be made 3 days in advance and kept in the fridge.

9 Remove the buns from the pan and place into your soaking custard—try to get them to absorb as much as possible, then place back into the pan.

10 Bake at 375°F for 10 minutes. Remove the buns from the pan carefully using an offset spatula (sometimes they can stick) and let cool completely on a cooling rack.

11 For the icing, heat the sugar, water, and vinegar on the stovetop for 1–2 minutes, until it is viciously bubbling. Take off the heat and whisk in the butter, rum, and salt. Let cool and thicken slightly, about 10 minutes, then drizzle the buns with the icing. Allow to set for 5 minutes before serving.

12 The buns can be kept in the fridge for up to 3 days, then reheated at 350°F for 10 minutes.

MILK BREAD
GREEN ONION BABKA

·

SERVES 6–8

Techniques

Starch gelatinization	pg.20
Gluten development	pg.14
Fermentation	pg.76

Equipment

9 x 5 x 2½-inch/24.5 x 14.5 x 6cm
loaf pan

1 x recipe	milk bread dough (see page 122)

Burnt green onion oil

Vegetable oil

250g/9 oz	thoroughly washed green onions (2–3 bunches), cut into ½-inch pieces
60g/¼ cup	light soy sauce
40g/3 Tbsp	granulated sugar
10g/2 tsp	sesame oil

Plus

20g/2½ Tbsp	sesame seeds (doesn't sound like a lot, but they're so light!)

Egg wash (see page 343)

This classic milk bread makes the perfect base for savory swirls of green onion and soy. It really does have it all: sweet-salty, chewy edges with a soft center. The filling is based on something my dad likes to serve with cold noodles—this bread is an homage to him and his upbringing in both Shanghai and Hong Kong.

Total: 4 hrs 50 mins

30 mins	1 hr 30 mins	1 hr 30 mins	35 mins	45 mins
Mix milk bread	Proof. Make filling	Shape & proof	Bake	Cool & serve

1   To make the burnt green onion oil, heat a little vegetable oil in a low, wide frying pan. Add the green onions and cook until they are completely charred and dark, 10–15 minutes. Keep an eye on them and keep them moving.

2   Once the desired color has been achieved, take off the heat and add the light soy sauce. The pan should bubble.

3   Stir in the granulated sugar and sesame oil. Check the taste! Depending on your green onions, you might want to add a little more sweet or saltiness to suit your preference.

4   Set aside to cool. Keeps in an airtight container in the fridge for up to 2 weeks.

5   Line the loaf pan with parchment paper.

6   Dust the work surface with flour. Roll out the dough to a very thin rectangle, approximately 20 x 16 inches. It really does go super-thin—⅛ inch or just a few millimeters. If it springs back, just keep on it! You might want to check that it isn't sticking, so occasionally lift it up and sprinkle more flour if needed.

7   Spread 150g/5¼ oz burnt green onion oil all over the dough, followed by the sesame seeds.

8   Roll up the dough tightly from the longer side. If it's sticking, use a dough scraper to help lift it and encourage it into shape.

9   Using a sharp or serrated knife (I like serrated), cut the dough log down the center, revealing the layers. I usually leave a bit at the end to hold it all together, then cut that at the end to finish it off.

10 Twist the dough strands over each other to create the babka shape—it's almost like a braid. Shimmy the dough to the length of the loaf pan and place it in. Loosely cover and proof for 1 hour, until puffy. It might be ready sooner than this.

11 Preheat the oven to 375°F.

12 Gently brush the proofed babka with egg wash.

13 Bake for 30–35 minutes. Check the internal temperature is 194°F. If the babka is getting quite dark when you bake it, tent the pan with foil to prevent over-browning. Let cool for 10 minutes in the pan, then remove to cool completely on a cooling rack.

14 Store the bread in an airtight container for 3 days at room temperature.

Notes

The spring onions reduce by approximately half in weight, so just be aware of that if you are making bigger batches in the future.

Also, don't forget to thoroughly wash them before you begin—grit often gets trapped in the green part.

OLIVE OIL BRIE-OCHE WITH ROASTED GRAPES, HONEY, AND THYME

·

MAKES 9–10 BUNS

Techniques

Gluten development	pg.14
Fermentation	pg.76
Sugar swaps	pg.31

Roasted grapes

150g/5¼ oz	seedless red grapes
13g/1 Tbsp	olive oil
1g/¼ tsp	flaky sea salt
5g/1 tsp	balsamic, red wine, or white wine vinegar
2–3	sprigs of thyme
4g/2 tsp	fennel seeds (optional)

Brioche dough

50g/1	whole egg
110g/7 Tbsp	whole milk
230g/1¾ cups plus 1 Tbsp	bread flour
4g/1⅓ tsp	dry yeast
5g/1 tsp	fine salt
20g/1½ Tbsp	butter, softened
50g/¼ cup	olive oil, plus more for finishing
30g/1½ Tbsp	honey

Plus

Egg wash (see page 343)

150g/5¼ oz	brie, sliced
Extra-virgin olive oil, to drizzle	
5–10	sprigs of thyme, stemmed

Honey, to drizzle

Flaky sea salt

For this brie-oche, I've cut down on the sugar and swapped in honey. It also has a slightly higher proportion of fat, split between rich butter and olive oil. Although the oil doesn't hydrate the dough, it can make it feel looser and extra squishy to work with.

Total: 3 hrs 40 mins

30 mins	1 hr	1 hr 30 mins	30 mins	10 mins
Mix brioche	Proof brioche & roast grapes	Shape & proof	Add toppings & bake	Cool & serve

1   To make the roasted grapes, preheat the oven to 425°F.

2   Toss the grapes with the olive oil, salt, vinegar, thyme sprigs, and fennel seeds, if using, on a small baking sheet.

3   Roast for 15–20 minutes—the grapes will burst and have blistered skin. Let cool.

4   To make the brioche dough, in the bowl of a stand mixer, first add the egg and milk, followed by the dry ingredients (put the yeast on the opposite side of the bowl from the salt!). Mix, using the dough hook, on medium speed for 6–8 minutes, until medium gluten development is reached—this is when you can pull on the dough and it stays together, but it is still quite fragile. You can take it further than this, but this is the minimum requirement before adding the fat.

5   Add the soft butter, a small spoonful at a time, with the mixer running, followed by the olive oil and honey. Mix on medium-high speed until very smooth—10–12 minutes—and full gluten development is reached. This is when you can pull a thin, almost translucent layer with the dough. If you haven't reached it in the time frame, rest for 5 minutes, then mix for 5 minutes. Continue this until it is developed. Remove the dough from the bowl and use your hands or a bench scraper to form it into a round shape. Use the work surface to help create some surface tension, so it has a smooth surface.

6   Let rest/rise in a bowl, covered, for 1 hour. It should noticeably puff and almost double in size. This may take less/more time, depending on your environment.

7   Divide the dough into 55–60g/2–2¼ oz portions. Shape into balls using a cupped hand. Place on a parchment paper–lined baking sheet, leaving some space between. Cover lightly with plastic wrap and let proof until very puffy for 1–2 hours.

8   Preheat the oven to 375°F.

9   Brush the buns carefully with egg wash. They rise quite a lot in the oven, so try to get all the way around the edges. Top each bun with 15g/½ oz brie and 15g/½ oz roasted grapes. Drizzle with extra-virgin olive oil and finish with 5–10 thyme leaves (¼–½ teaspoon per bun).

10   Bake for 12–14 minutes or until golden. The cheese should be golden and crispy. Finish with a drizzle of honey, extra-virgin olive oil, and some flaky salt.

11   These buns are best enjoyed on the same day, slightly warm. Leftovers can be stored in the fridge and reheated at 350°F for 10 minutes.

BROWN SUGAR CANELÉ

·

MAKES ABOUT 10 CANELÉ

Techniques

Rubbing in	pg.99
Maillard reaction	pg.84

Equipment

Canelé molds (I use stainless steel)
Grease spray

400g/1⅔ cups	whole milk
1	vanilla pod, scraped, or 12g/1 Tbsp good quality vanilla extract
110g/½ cup	light brown sugar, packed
80g/6 Tbsp	granulated sugar
2g/⅓ tsp	fine salt
100g/¾ cup	all-purpose flour
50g/¼ cup	butter, melted
75g/4	egg yolks (or 1 whole egg and 1 yolk)
50g/3 Tbsp	dark rum (optional if you don't drink alcohol)

Welcome to planet CANELÉ, the crispy, crunchy, custardy pastry of your dreams. Looking at it, you might not think much of it—its unassuming dark shell in that unique fluted shape gives no real clue of what lies ahead when you eat it. But that's part of its charm. Get closer and you will smell the complex aroma—rich notes of rum, vanilla, burnt milk, and sugar. Take a bite and you'll be greeted with a custardy, tender center with no hint of bitterness. The result is a perfectly balanced dessert with a textural interplay that crème brûlée would envy, if it knew how.

Total: 7 hrs 20 mins

1 hr	20 mins	4 hrs	1 hr	1 hr
Infuse milk	Make batter	Rest	Bake	Cool

1   Heat the milk with the scraped vanilla until simmering, then remove from the heat and let it infuse for 30 minutes–1 hour.

2   Whisk the sugars, salt, and flour together, then add the melted butter and agitate with a whisk to create a breadcrumb-like consistency.

3   Reheat the milk to 140–158°F and pour a third into the breadcrumb mixture—whisk until incorporated. Then add the rest of the milk and whisk until smooth. Finally, add the egg yolks and rum. Pour the mixture into a container, cover with plastic wrap, and rest in the fridge for 4–48 hours.

4   Remove the canelé batter from the fridge and stir to reincorporate the batter as it will have separated.

5   Preheat the oven, along with the empty molds set on a baking sheet, to 475°F, for 30–40 minutes.

6   Spray the molds with oil spray, then pour the batter in so the molds are four-fifths full, about 85g/3 oz. It might sizzle!

7   Place into the oven and bake at 475°F for 15 minutes. Turn the oven down to 400°F, turn the baking sheet around (this also helps lower the oven temperature) and bake for 45 minutes.

8   After this time, start checking your canelé. You can remove one from the mold. Do this carefully with oven mitts or a kitchen towel. If it is colored to your liking, remove all the others. If not, return to the oven and bake for 10 minutes—keep going until you're satisfied. Because all our ovens are different, what works for me may be different for you!

9   Remove the canelé from the molds and transfer to a cooling rack to cool for 1 hour, allowing the crust to form. Enjoy within a few hours or the crust will become soft. Leftovers can be kept for 1 day well-wrapped at room temperature. You can reheat and re-crisp in a hot oven for 5 minutes.

Notes

Purists may fight me on this, but I have always had great results simply using a high quality baking release spray for my canelé molds.

If you want to make traditional canelé using copper molds, you can season them by heating them to 248°F in the oven and filling with melted beeswax. Pour out the excess and repeat three times. Do not preheat the molds—just fill them cold and then bake as directed.

FETA WHIPPED CHEESECAKE

·

SERVES 8–10

Techniques

Egg foam	pg.45
Folding	pg.113
Whipping cream	pg.60
Making caramel	pg.86
Sugar syrup	pg.33

Equipment
8-inch/20cm springform pan

Cookie base

40–60g/ 2½–4 Tbsp	butter
1 x recipe	3pm oat cookies (see page 194), blitzed into crumbs (you can sub with 400g/14 oz graham crackers but will need triple the amount of butter)

Feta cheesecake mix

160g/5¾ oz	feta cheese
160g/5¾ oz	full-fat cream cheese
120g/½ cup plus 2 Tbsp	granulated sugar
40g/2 Tbsp	water
60g/2	egg whites
210g/¾ cup plus 2 Tbsp	heavy cream

Caramelized walnuts

20g/4 tsp	water
75g/6 Tbsp	granulated sugar
100g/¾ cup	roasted walnuts, mounded

Plus

4	figs
1	sprig of thyme, stemmed

Honey, to taste

This cheesecake is as light as air but has an unexpectedly punchy flavor with the salty feta. I love serving it with figs and walnuts but this would go beautifully with any fruit—just think of it as an alternative cheese board.

Total: 5 hr 10 mins

10 mins	30 mins	4 hrs	20 mins	10 mins
Make & set cookie base	Make cheesecake mousse	Chill	Make caramelized nuts	Finish

1 For the cookie base, melt the butter and mix the crumbs with the butter, bit by bit, until they look moist and you can get a clump of the crumbs to just hold together in your hands. Cut a 9-inch round of parchment paper and place onto your serving plate. Place the springform pan (without the bottom) on the paper. Press the crumb into the pan—the sides should be around 2 inches tall. Set aside in the freezer or fridge until firm while you prep the filling.

2 For the feta cheesecake mix, using a food processor, blitz the feta to crumbs and keep processing until it's smooth, around 3 minutes. Make sure you scrape the cheese lumps into the mixture so it is evenly combined. Add the cream cheese and process for about 30 seconds, until it's all combined. Set aside.

3 Using the sugar, water, and egg whites, make an Italian meringue according to the instructions on page 118. Meanwhile, whip the heavy cream to soft peaks.

4 Now it's time to combine them all—stir a little of the Italian meringue into the feta/cream cheese mix to lighten it, then fold it all together. Now gently fold the feta/meringue mixture into the whipped cream—it will be ultra-voluminous! I fold a small amount of cream into the feta/meringue mixture, then slowly add more as I go. I don't like adding all the cream at once as there's a risk you can overmix it. Just go bit by bit until you can see very few streaks.

5 Pour the cheesecake mixture into the cookie base and smooth with an offset spatula. Allow to set in the fridge for at least 4 hours.

6 For the caramelized walnuts, make according to the caramelized nuts instructions on page 334.

7 To finish the cheesecake, remove the springform pan and slide the paper out from underneath. Cut the fresh figs into different sizes (approximately sixths), then place around the edge of the cheesecake. Finish with some thyme leaves, the caramelized walnuts, and a drizzle of honey. A little sprinkle of salt works wonders, too!

8 Keeps well in the fridge for 2–3 days. Always serve cold.

 Notes To further stabilize this cheesecake, you can use 1 gelatin leaf (see page 100; I use Dr. Oetker Platinum). Heat 50g/3 tablespoons of the cream until simmering, then pour it over the bloomed gelatin. Let cool to about 86°F, then whisk into the remaining cream before whipping.

SECRET CHOCOLATE CAKE

.

SERVES 8–10

Techniques

Whipping cream	pg.60
Folding	pg.113
Making meringue	pg.46
Whipping egg yolks	pg.47

Equipment

8-inch/20cm loose-bottomed cake pan

75g/½ cup	raisins (golden or black)
100g/7 Tbsp	Sauternes sweet wine
300g/6	whole eggs, separated
225g/1 cup plus 2 Tbsp	granulated sugar
225g/8 oz	dark chocolate, chopped
225g/1 cup	butter
1–2g/¼–½ tsp	flaky sea salt

Plus

Cocoa powder, to dust

This ultra-rich, two-textured cake has a secret. What is it? Well, let me tell you: the fudgy cake and mousse layer is made out of the same mix. One half of the mixture is baked, while the other is simply poured on top and left to set into a mousse. This recipe is based on a Gateau Marcel and is a bit of 2-for-1 magic. Nestled in between the layers are Sauternes-soaked raisins, though you could swap these for brandied cherries or whatever might take your fancy. Finish it off with a thick dusting of bitter cocoa powder and you have, in my opinion, the ultimate chocolate dessert.

Day 1				Total: 11 hrs	Day 2	Total: 40 mins
2 hrs	20 mins	20 mins	20 mins	8 hrs	40 mins	
Soak raisins	Make mixture	Halve & bake	Remove from oven & cool	Scatter raisins on top & pour mixture on top. Chill overnight	Demold & decorate	

1 To soak the raisins, place them in a bowl, pour in the Sauternes, and cover. Soak for at least 2 hours or overnight, but they will keep (covered) for up to 1 month in the fridge.

2 Preheat the oven to 375°F. Line the pan with parchment paper.

3 Whisk your egg yolks with a quarter of the sugar until pale, thick, and custardy-looking—this takes 5–6 minutes on high speed. Set aside.

4 Melt your chocolate and butter over a bain-marie. Once melted, take off the heat and stir in the salt. Fold it into your whisked egg yolks in three additions.

5 Meanwhile, whisk your egg whites and the rest of the sugar to a French meringue (see page 118).

6 Mix a little of the meringue in with your whisk to loosen the egg yolk/chocolate batter and then change to a spatula, folding the meringue into the chocolate mix in thirds, trying to keep as much air in as possible.

7 Pour half of the mix into the lined cake pan and smooth the top. Bake for 20–22 minutes. The cake will rise up and be dry on top. Set aside the other half of the batter and cover with a kitchen towel or plastic wrap to prevent it from drying out. If possible, keep it near the oven so it stays warmish.

8 Remove the cake from the oven and leave it to fall and cool in the pan for about 20 minutes. It can still be warm, but you want to be able to handle the pan.

9 Sprinkle on the Sauternes-soaked raisins. Pour the second half of the batter on top and smooth with a warmed offset spatula. Let cool to room temperature, then move into the fridge and chill overnight or up to 3 days.

10 To remove cleanly from the pan, freeze the cake for 30 minutes before demolding. To finish, carefully remove from the pan and dust thickly with cocoa powder. If you froze the cake, let it defrost for 20–30 minutes before enjoying it. This keeps in the fridge for up to 3 days. You can also store it in the freezer, wrapped, for 30 days.

Note

If you only have a hand mixer, I recommend splitting the mixture in two and making it twice—as it's a large amount of meringue.

APPLE AND VANILLA CHARLOTTE

·

SERVES 6–8

Techniques

Aerating egg whites	pg.46
Making custard	pg.42
Caramelization	pg.84
Using gelatin	pg.100
Whipping cream	pg.60
Preventing oxidation	pg.88

Equipment
8-inch/20cm loose-bottomed cake pan

Apple compote

300g/10½ oz	tart-sweet apples such as Fuji, peeled, cored, and diced into ½-inch chunks
30g/2 Tbsp	granulated sugar
45g/3 Tbsp	light brown sugar
35g/2½ Tbsp	water
30g/2 Tbsp	white wine or apple cider vinegar

Caramel sauce

100g/½ cup	granulated sugar
50g/¼ cup	butter
70g/5 Tbsp	heavy cream
1g/¼ tsp	flaky sea salt
4 x recipe	savoiardi cookies (see page 340)

Vanilla custard mousse

2	gelatin leaves (see page 100; I use Dr. Oetker Platinum)
250g/1 cup	heavy cream
150g/½ cup plus 2 Tbsp	whole milk
4g/1 tsp	good quality vanilla extract or 1 vanilla pod, scraped
70g/6 Tbsp	granulated sugar
160g/3	whole eggs, separated

Plus
Powdered sugar, to dust

1	tart-sweet apple such as Fuji, cored and thinly sliced

A perfect autumnal showpiece, this marries together tender sponge cake, rich apple compote, and caramel. Making your own ladyfingers for the decoration means you can adapt this recipe to many shapes and sizes and the little scalloped edges look adorable.

Total: 7 hrs

1 hr	20 mins	40 mins	30 mins	30 mins	4 hrs
Make apple compote	Make caramel	Make savoiardi cookies	Make custard mousse	Assemble	Chill & decorate

1   To make the compote, put the apples in a saucepan with the other ingredients. Turn the heat to its lowest and allow the mixture to reduce, stirring occasionally, until the apples are shiny and translucent. Add more water, a large spoonful at a time, if things become too dry and keep it moving so it doesn't burn. The compote will take 40 minutes–1 hour to become very translucent.

2   To make the caramel sauce, heat the sugar in a saucepan, stirring over medium heat for approximately 7 minutes, until it turns a dark amber. Whisk in the butter, followed by the cream and salt. Careful, it might splutter! Pour into a heatproof container and let cool before storing in the fridge to cool completely—it will be firm.

3   For the savoiardi cookies, make the batter according to the instructions on page 340.

4   First make the decoration: pipe 2 rows of ½ x 2½-inch fingers—the rows will be around 12 inches long. Draw 2 x 8-inch circles on a baking sheet lined with parchment paper, flip the paper over, and pipe the remaining mixture to create two cake layers. Dust the fingers and circles with powdered sugar. You can see photos of this in action on page 284 for my Tiramichoux recipe.

5   Bake for 10–12 minutes, until golden, and let cool on a cooling rack.

6   To make the vanilla custard mousse, bloom the gelatin in cold water for 10 minutes then squeeze out. Heat 100g/7 tablespoons of the cream, the milk, vanilla extract or scraped vanilla seeds, and 50g/¼ cup of granulated sugar until steaming. Pour a quarter of the mixture over the egg yolks, whisking well to temper, before adding the rest and returning to the stovetop. Cook over low heat, stirring constantly, until the mixture reaches 180°F and is thick. Stir in the bloomed gelatin.

7   Pour through a sieve into a clean bowl and chill over an ice bath until around 54°F—it will be very viscous.

8   Whip the remaining cream to soft peaks and fold into the thickened custard. Set aside and whisk the egg whites with the remaining sugar until stiff peaks form. Fold this into the custard/cream mixture. The mousse is now ready to use and must be used immediately.

Note

You can assemble this cake 24 hours in advance but add the apple slices when you are ready to serve! The salting will prevent browning for 2–3 hours.

9 Place the cake pan (without the bottom) on your intended serving plate. Line the sides with the strips of ladyfingers, trimming so they neatly match up. Trim the circles so they will fit inside the lady finger-lined pan. Place one cake circle in the bottom.

10 Add half the apple compote, spreading it into the edges to prevent the mousse from seeping out of the bottom. Drizzle half of the caramel sauce, followed by half of the mousse.

11 Add the second cake layer and spread with the remaining apple compote and caramel sauce, followed by the final layer of mousse. Allow to chill in the fridge for 3–4 hours to ensure it has set.

12 To finish, soak the apple slices in salt water for 10 minutes. Rinse well then pat dry and use to decorate. Remove the pan to serve. Any leftovers keep well in the fridge for up to 3 days.

APRICOT CUSTARD MILLE-FEUILLE

•

MAKES 6 MILLE-FEUILLE

Techniques

Lamination	pg.69
Caramelization	pg.84
Egg coagulation	pg.40
Starch-bound custard	pg.44

Equipment

Piping bag
15½ x 10½-inch/39 x 27cm baking sheet

½ x recipe	rough puff pastry (see page 128) or pie dough (see page 129)

Poached apricots

10	apricots
500g/2 cups plus 2 Tbsp	water
250g/1¼ cups	granulated sugar
25g/2 Tbsp	lemon juice
½	vanilla pod, scraped
1	chamomile teabag

Noyaux cream

All pits from apricots above	
180g/¾ cup	heavy cream

Noyaux crème légère

160g/⅔ cup	whole milk
40g/3 Tbsp	granulated sugar
30g/about 2	egg yolks
11g/1½ Tbsp	cornstarch
10g/2 tsp	butter
Infused noyaux cream (from above)	

Plus (optional)

Drizzle of honey
Edible flowers and fresh herbs

Note

You can, of course, also use puff pastry or inverted puff pastry for this recipe.

You could make this mille-feuille with any fruit but there's something about apricots and custard that is so comforting. This recipe also makes use of the noyaux (aka "the forbidden almond"), the flavor gem hidden inside your stone fruits. It's worth mentioning that the noyaux hidden within the kernel contains amygdalin, which converts to cyanide after eating. There's little to no risk of this if you're just using the kernels for infusing though as the toxins are very diluted throughout the entire recipe.

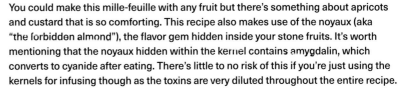

Day 1	Total: 3 hrs	Day 2		Total: 2 hrs 30 mins
20 mins	2 hrs 40 mins	1 hr 30 mins	30 mins	30 mins
Make pastry	Chill pastry, poach fruit & make cream	Roll out pastry & bake	Let cool	Cut & assemble

1   For the poached apricots, halve the apricots, keeping the pits aside. Poach the apricots according to the instructions on page 336.

2   Preheat the oven to 350°F.

3   For the noyaux cream, place the pits on a baking sheet. Bake for 10 minutes to help the pits become more brittle. Let them cool. To crack them open, place inside a kitchen towel and use a hammer, or rolling pin, to decisively hit the pits to release the kernels. Heat the cream until simmering, then add your kernels. Simmer for 1–2 minutes, then let cool and infuse for at least 2 hours but overnight if possible.

4   For the noyaux crème légère, make according to the instructions on page 338.

5   Roll your pastry out to ⅟₁₆–⅛ inch, taking plenty of rest breaks to get the best shape. Continuously lift your pastry up and off the table to see if it shrinks back. If it shrinks back, the gluten is too fired up. Just put it into the fridge to rest and return to it 20 minutes later. Roll it out to the exact size of your lined baking sheet. Measure the pastry against the sheet to check it will fit. Bake and caramelize the puff pastry according to the instructions on pages 126 and 127. Allow to cool on the baking sheet.

6   To assemble, trim your puff pastry sheet of irregular edges, then cut the puff pastry into 12 rectangles, approximately 1¾ x4 inches. Use a serrated knife so as not to crush the layers. Cut the apricots into even strips. For the bottom, alternate apricot strips with the noyaux crème légère onto each puff rectangle. If your cream isn't very firm, try popping this layer into the freezer for 5 minutes to firm up before building the top layer.

7   Place a puff rectangle on top. Snip off the tip of the piping bag at an angle—this creates a faux St Honoré tip. Pipe a bit of noyaux crème légère onto a plate and see if you like the size/angle, then amend. Make sure the skinny bit is at the top when you pipe.

8   Pipe a wiggle of noyaux crème légère on top of the pastry then place some apricot slices on top. Finish with a drizzle of honey or fresh herbs and edible flowers, if using.

9   These are good in the fridge for 4–5 hours but I wouldn't keep them much longer than that. It's better to decorate when you're ready to serve. You can keep them overnight, but the pastry becomes a bit soggy where it's touching the apricot/cream and the cream has a dried-out look to it. They're still pretty good, but definitely not at their best!

CHOUX ICE CREAM SANDWICH WITH ROASTED STRAWBERRIES

•

MAKES 8 LARGE BUNS

Techniques

Egg foam	pg.45
Starch gelatinization	pg.20
Whipping cream	pg.60

Equipment
Piping bag

Choux sandwich

1 x recipe	choux (see page 136)
1 x recipe	craquelin for choux (see page 137)
1 x recipe	jam ripple parfait (see page 227)

Roasted strawberries

200g/7 oz	strawberries
20g/2 Tbsp	granulated sugar

Whipped cream

200g/¾ cup plus 2 Tbsp	heavy cream
20g/2 Tbsp	granulated sugar

Choux and ice cream is an underrated combination—they make the most adorable sandwiches. You can use any ice cream you like, but this is a great way to showcase home-made parfaits and ices. It's a great dinner party dessert because you can make everything in advance and simply build when you're ready.

Total: 5 hrs 30 mins

45 mins	30 mins	30 mins	3 hrs 30 mins	15 mins
Make choux & craquelin	Bake choux	Roast strawberries	Make parfait & freeze	Assemble & serve

1 Transfer the choux paste to a piping bag. Smoosh the paste to try to reduce the pesky air bubbles. Cut a ½-inch hole off the tip then pipe the choux buns onto a baking sheet lined with parchment paper, 25–30g/¾–1 oz in weight and 1¾–2 inches in diameter. Leave a 1½-inch gap between each bun to allow for expansion. You should get around 8 buns.

2 Cut out the craquelin to 1¾–2-inch rounds and place one on top of each bun, about 8g/¼ oz per bun.

3 Preheat the oven to 475°F.

4 Place the choux inside the oven and turn it down to 425°F. Bake for 15 minutes, then turn the oven down to 375°F and bake for 10 minutes. The buns should be well puffed and crisp. If not, bake for 5 more minutes. If you need to turn the sheet, do so only in the last 10 minutes. Remove from the oven and let cool completely on the sheet.

5 Make the roasted strawberries according to the instructions on page 140, then cool.

6 For the whipped cream, whip the cream and sugar together until very soft peaks form—you want it to be a bit floppy and only just hold its weight.

7 To assemble, slice off the top two-thirds of each bun. Allow the parfait to come to room temperature for 10–15 minutes, until it is scoopable, then top the base of each bun with a scoop of parfait. Follow up with a generous spoonful of whipped cream, then finish with some roasted strawberries. Spoon a little strawberry syrup on top, then top with the lids.

SORBETS

•

EACH RECIPE MAKES
1 LB 2 OZ/500G SORBET

Techniques

Freezing	pg.96
Infusions	pg.110
Sugar concentration	pg.98

Equipment
Food processor

Hibiscus and watermelon sorbet

125g/½ cup	water
12g/⅓ oz	dried hibiscus flowers
200g/7 oz	watermelon flesh
120g/½ cup plus 2 Tbsp	granulated sugar
35g/2 Tbsp	lemon or lime juice
1g/¼ tsp	flaky sea salt

Pear, white wine, and ginger sorbet

240g/8½ oz	pears (weight after removing skin and core)
100g/7 Tbsp	dry white wine
100g/½ cup	granulated sugar
20g/¾ oz	fresh ginger, peeled and grated
40g/3 Tbsp	lemon juice
1g/¼ tsp	flaky sea salt

Notes

If you are using a traditional ice cream machine, allow the mix to cool completely before churning according to the manufacturer's instructions.

You can also make this by hand by freezing the mixture in a container for 1 hour. After 1 hour, agitate with a fork. Repeat this every 20–30 minutes until frozen and smooth. It won't be perfect, but it will still be delicious!

Both of these sorbet bases can be churned in an ice cream machine or can be frozen as a block, then blended until smooth in a food processor. This won't be quite as smooth as a professional machine, but it does a pretty good job.

Total: 4 hrs 40 mins

30 mins	4 hrs	10 mins
Make base	Freeze base	Blend until smooth

Hibiscus and watermelon sorbet

1   Boil the water and add the hibiscus flowers. Allow to infuse for 15 minutes. Strain through a sieve, then blend with the watermelon, sugar, citrus juice, and salt until smooth. Strain through a sieve. Pour into a clean container, cover, and freeze for at least 4 hours or overnight. The next day, break up the sorbet base and blend in a food processor until smooth. Serve immediately in scoops. You may need to re-blend after 24–36 hours for the best texture.

2   Keep in a covered container in the freezer for up to 3 months.

Pear, white wine, and ginger sorbet

1   Chop the pears into 1¼–1½-inch chunks, then simmer in the wine and sugar until soft, about 15 minutes. Use a lid to prevent excess evaporation. Add the grated ginger, lemon juice, and salt. Let cool completely, then blend until smooth and strain through a sieve. Pour into a clean container, cover, and freeze for at least 4 hours or overnight. The next day, break up the sorbet base and blend in a food processor until smooth. Serve immediately in scoops. You may need to re-blend after 24–36 hours for the best texture.

2   Keep in a covered container in the freezer for up to 3 months.

CHOCOLATE PEANUT ICE CREAM BARS

·

MAKES AROUND 7 ICE CREAM BARS

Techniques

Whipping cream	pg.60
Making meringues	pg.46
Caramel sauce	pg.86

Equipment

8-inch/20cm square pan
Piping bag

Malt semifreddo

80g/about 3	egg whites
70g/⅓ cup	dark brown sugar, packed
25g/1 Tbsp	barley malt syrup
270g/1 cup plus 2 Tbsp	heavy cream
1g/¼ tsp	flaky sea salt

Freezer soft caramel (makes more than you need)

80g/⅓ cup	water
165g/¾ cup plus 1 Tbsp	granulated sugar
150g/½ cup plus 2 Tbsp	heavy cream
1g/¼ tsp	flaky sea salt

Chocolate dip (better to make more than you need! You can always re-set it and use it for other baking)

300g/10½ oz	chocolate (I use a 70/30 mix of dark and milk, chopped)
75g/2½ oz	cocoa butter or 30g/2 Tbsp vegetable oil, to help fluidity (optional)

Plus

100g/¾ cup	roasted salted peanuts

Cuts

I love the way these DIY ice cream bars look—taking those nostalgic childhood flavors and making them (borderline) gourmet is a joy. It takes a bit of patience to work with these (and I'd avoid making them if your kitchen is hot—the dipping would just be a nightmare) but it's so worth it.

Total: 7 hrs 10 mins

20 mins	4 hrs	2 hrs	50 mins
Make semi-freddo	Freeze & make caramel	Cut, add caramel & nuts. Freeze	Dip & freeze

1   For the malt semifreddo, mix the egg whites with the dark brown sugar and malt syrup in a bowl. Whisk into a French meringue following the instructions on page 118. Meanwhile, whip the cream until it is thick and holding soft peaks. Add a spoonful of meringue to the cream along with the salt and whisk to lighten. Then fold the mixtures together. Pour the mixture into your pan, lined with parchment paper, and smooth over. Freeze until it's VERY hard, at least 4 hours.

2   For the freezer soft caramel, make a wet caramel. In a pan over medium heat, mix the water and sugar together until it reaches a light golden color. Once it turns golden, immediately remove the caramel from the heat and add a splash of the cream. Whisk it well. It will bubble and evaporate like crazy. We want to slowly bring the temperature of the mixture down so we can achieve a freezer-soft caramel. Add the rest of the cream in two or three additions. By the time it gets to the last one, you don't really want it to be spitting too much. If you want to use a thermometer, it should be no more than 221–223°F. Add the salt, then transfer to a clean, heatproof container, and let cool.

3   To assemble, cut the completely frozen-hard semifreddo into your ice cream bars, approximately 1¼ x 4 inches (see guide in bottom right-hand corner of the opposite page). Any offcuts are your chef snacks! Place onto a clean baking sheet and put in the freezer to harden, about 30 minutes.

4   Pipe a line of caramel sauce down the center of each bar, about ¾ inch wide. Sprinkle 10–15g/1–2 tablespoons roasted peanuts on top. Place the bars back into the freezer until the ice cream is very hard, at least 1 hour. The caramel will not harden.

5   To make the dip, melt the chocolate over a bain-marie. Whisk in the cocoa butter or vegetable oil, if using. Let cool until it is no longer warm to the touch but still very fluid.

6   To dip, balance an ice cream bar onto a fork, then lower into the chocolate, using a spoon or something else to coat the top with chocolate. The dip will harden almost immediately when you dip, so be confident and work fast. Return to the lined sheet.

7   Let chill in the freezer until set, about 20 minutes, then enjoy. Once set, I recommend transferring these to a covered container so they don't get freezer burn. They will last for a long time: 1–2 months.

A WEEKEND

Bread

3-day focaccia   280

Desserts

Tiramichoux   284
Mocha passionfruit opera cake   288
Cross laminated galette des rois   291

Viennoiserie

The building blocks   295
Croissant theory   296
Lamination theory   297
Croissant dough   298
Cutting pastries   301
Croissants   306
Pain au chocolat   307
Swirly buns   310
Twisty strips   312
Chocolate squiggles   315
Classic fruit custard danish   316
St. Honoré cherry danish   317
Peach panzanella deep-dish danish   320
Chocolate-chip pain suisse   321
Kouign amann scraps   322
Pan con tomate danish   325
Cheesy potato danish   326
Almond croissants 2.0   329

3-DAY FOCACCIA

·

MAKES 1 LARGE OR 2 SMALL LOAVES
(I BAKE MINE IN A 10 X 14-INCH/25 X 35CM BAKING SHEET)

Techniques

Preferments	pg.80
Gluten development	pg.14
Cold fermentation	pg.80
Autolyse	pg.16

Poolish

110g/¾ cup plus 2 Tbsp	bread flour
Pinch of dry yeast	
110g/7 Tbsp	water

Dough part I

550g/4⅓ cups	bread flour
385g/1½ cups plus 2 Tbsp	water
2g/⅔ tsp	dry yeast

Dough part II

13g/2½ tsp	fine salt
50g/3 Tbsp	water
100–150g/ ½–⅔ cup	olive oil

Slow-roast tomatoes

350g/12¼ oz	cherry tomatoes
13–27g/ 1–2 Tbsp	olive oil

Plus

Olive oil
Few sprigs of rosemary
Flaky sea salt

Note

Once your focaccia is formed, make sure your hands are oiled when you touch it! Though the dough is strong, a good structure can be wrecked with sticky hands.

I strongly believe that the best airy focaccia needs to be made over three days. I've tried to shorten this process, but this is truly the best I've ever had. You can easily turn a focaccia into an entire meal with the right toppings and serve with a simple acidic green salad on the side.

Day 1	Total: 5 mins	Day 2			Total: 13 hrs
5 mins		4 hrs		8 hrs	1 hr
Mix poolish		Mix, fold & stretch dough. Transfer to fridge		Chill	Roast tomatoes

Day 3			Total: 3 hrs
1 hr 30 mins		1 hr	30 mins
Stretch dough onto sheet & proof		Oil & dimple. Proof	Add toppings & bake

Day 1

1   Mix the flour, yeast, and water together to make a poolish. Cover and let the poolish rest for 12 hours.

2   After 12 hours, it should be bubbly and ripe, aka ready to use. You can check it's well aerated by seeing if it floats in water.

Day 2

1   Mix the poolish, flour, water, and yeast together until it forms a rough dough. It will look shaggy and ugly. Cover and allow to autolyse for 30 minutes.

2   Dissolve the salt in the water and then mix this into the dough—squeeze it in with your hands until combined. Rest for 30 minutes, keeping it covered. Now add 1–2 tablespoons of the olive oil, coat your hands and stretch and fold the dough—pick the dough up from the middle, stretching it, then folding it over itself gently. Repeat this four or five times, until smooth. Cover and let rest for 1 hour.

3   Add 1–2 tablespoons of olive oil and stretch and fold the dough—it should be quite puffy at this stage. I call it a puppy's belly!

4   Cover and let rest for 1 hour—it should be getting puffy and big each time you leave it.

5   Check the gluten development. It should be stronger but may not be fully developed (e.g., the dough tears). If needed, add more olive oil and stretch the dough.

6   After 30 minutes, check the gluten development again—you should be able to make a thin stretchy windowpane. If it is well developed, you can move it into an oiled bowl and put into the fridge. Keep it covered so it doesn't dry out.

7   After 1 hour, check and de-gas the dough by pressing it down. If it is bubbling up too much in the fridge (it probably will), check later to see it's in check.

8   Cover and chill for at least 8 hours, ideally overnight.

9   Make the slow-roast tomatoes: Preheat the oven to 325°F. Cut the cherry tomatoes in half, toss with the olive oil, and lay on a baking sheet. Season with salt and black pepper. Bake for 1 hour or until wrinkled but not colored. Cool, then move into a container and keep in the fridge.

Day 3

1   With oiled hands, move the dough onto an oiled baking sheet, balling it in your hands slightly to help give it a smooth surface. Spread the dough out slightly, then cover with olive oil so it doesn't form a crust. Let rest for 1–1½ hours, until it relaxes.

2   Oil your hands, then dimple the top of the dough and redistribute the air bubbles. You can also lift up the edges and sides of the focaccia, which can help reveal hidden side bubbles! Let rest for 30 minutes.

3   Preheat the oven to 475°F.

4   Dimple the dough again and press the roasted cherry tomatoes into the dough. Remember to poke them quite deep into the dough. Toss sprigs of rosemary with a little olive oil so they are lightly covered then press into the dough, followed by a little flaky salt.

5   Bake for 10 minutes, then turn the oven down to 425°F and bake for 10–15 minutes, until golden. Remove from the sheet and cool on a rack.

6   Focaccia is best enjoyed the day it is made, but you can store it in the fridge for 3 days and reheat in the oven.

OTHER TOPPINGS

Classic salt and rosemary

Toss 3–4 sprigs of rosemary with olive oil, then press deeply into the dough. Sprinkle flaky salt on top.

Fig and chocolate

This is a flavor championed by the ever so talented Milli Taylor. Chop 75g/2½ oz dark chocolate into ½–¾ inch pieces. Slice 3 fresh figs into 5–6 pieces each. Toss the figs in olive oil. Press the chocolate and figs deeply into the focaccia dough along with small sprigs of rosemary. Salt generously.

Crispy potato and olive

Thinly slice potatoes on a mandolin (paper thin—⅟₁₆ inch thick) and toss in olive oil and flaky salt. Press black olives into the dough and scatter the potatoes on top. Rosemary would go nicely here, too!

Plum and arugula

My friend Olaire loves the spicy/bitter/sweet combination here; pit and halve ripe plums and press deeply into the dough. Drizzle with olive oil and sprinkle with flaky salt, along with rosemary sprigs or sage leaves if you want some herbiness. Once cool, serve with arugula on top.

Note

Everyone's environments are different and focaccia may be faster/slower where you are depending on temperature. So, as long as you have a good gluten development shown by the windowpane and the dough is puffy and bubbling, you're on the right track! Don't be scared to get it in the fridge to chill out if it's going crazy and is very active.

TIRAMICHOUX

·

SERVES 10-12

Techniques

Piping	pg 113
Making custard	pg.42
Maillard reaction	pg.84
Aerating egg whites	pg.46
Starch gelatinization	pg.20

Equipment
Piping bag with star nozzle

| 2 x recipe | savoiardi cookies (see page 340) |
| Powdered sugar, for dusting (optional) | |

Coffee syrup

35g/2½ Tbsp	espresso shot
100g/7 Tbsp	water
2g/1 tsp	espresso powder
30g/2½ Tbsp	granulated sugar

Salted brown butter coffee sauce

100g/7 Tbsp	salted butter
100g/7 Tbsp	heavy cream
30g/2 Tbsp	dark brown sugar
4g/2 tsp	espresso powder
100g/3½ oz	white chocolate, chopped
2g/½ tsp or to taste	flaky sea salt

Cocoa craquelin

90g/7 Tbsp	light brown sugar
70g/½ cup plus 1 Tbsp	all-purpose flour
20g/¼ cup	cocoa powder
90g/6 Tbsp	butter, softened

Mascarpone custard

400g/1⅔ cups	whole milk
80g/6 Tbsp	granulated sugar
100g/2	whole eggs
40g/⅓ cup	cornstarch
40–50g/ 2½–3 Tbsp	liqueur of choice, e.g., Amaretto, Marsala (optional)
350g/1½ cups	mascarpone, at room temp

This dessert is an embarrassment of riches. Combining the universally loved tiramisu with a choux bun tower, this is the sort of dessert that wins over the heads and hearts of your guests. You can break up the work over several days to make it easier, though choux has diminishing returns once filled, so it's best to build this when you're ready.

Day 1
Total: 2 hrs 25 mins

40 mins	15 mins	15 mins	45 mins	30 mins
Make savoiardi cookies	Make coffee syrup	Make coffee sauce	Make craquelin	Make custard

Day 2
Total: 3 hrs 30 mins

1 hr 30 mins	2 hrs
Make choux	Fill & assemble tower

Day 1

1   For the savoiardi cookies, preheat the oven to 375°F.

2   Make the savoiardi cookie batter according to the instructions on page 340.

3   Pipe 18–20 ladyfingers, 4 inches in length onto a lined baking sheet then dust with powdered sugar, if you want a more crusty finish. Bake for 12 minutes, until golden. Let cool.

4   To make the coffee syrup, heat all the ingredients together. Set aside to cool completely. This can be kept in the fridge for 1 week.

5   To make the salted brown butter coffee sauce, in a saucepan, heat the butter until foaming, then continue cooking, stirring regularly, until all the milk solids brown. Add the cream to the hot butter and whisk until evenly combined, followed by the dark brown sugar and espresso powder, whisking well. Turn off the heat, then whisk in the chopped white chocolate and salt until completely melted and combined and a lush sauce forms. Let cool completely. The sauce will keep well in the fridge for 3 days.

6   To make the cocoa craquelin, mix together all the ingredients. Roll out between two sheets of parchment paper to about ⅛ inch thick. Chill for at least 30 minutes in the fridge or 10 minutes in the freezer. This will last for 3 months in the freezer until needed.

7   To make the mascarpone custard, heat the milk until simmering. Whisk together the sugar, eggs, and cornstarch. Pour a little hot milk over the mixture to temper and then add the rest and return to the stovetop. Cook for 3–4 minutes over medium heat until boiling, whisking the whole time. Once thick, take off the heat and whisk in the alcohol, if using. Pour into a clean, heatproof container and let cool for 20 minutes, then transfer to the fridge to cool completely, with plastic wrap or parchment paper touching the surface to prevent a skin from forming. This keeps well in the fridge for 3 days.

Continued ⟶

TIRAMICHOUX
Continued

Coffee choux

80g/⅓ cup	whole milk
80g/⅓ cup	water
80g/6 Tbsp	butter
3g/½ tsp	salt
6g/1½ tsp	granulated sugar
1g/¾ tsp	espresso powder, sifted
105g/¾ cup plus 1 Tbsp	all-purpose flour
180–200g/4–5	whole eggs, beaten

Day 2

1   To make the choux, preheat the oven to 415°F. Heat the milk, water, butter, salt, and sugar. Once simmering, add the sifted espresso powder and flour all at once, then stir to form a thick dough ball that will leave a film on the pan.

2   Move to a bowl and let cool slightly before adding the beaten eggs bit by bit—a smooth shiny paste should form.

3   Pipe the choux buns onto a baking sheet lined with parchment paper, each around 10g/⅓ oz in weight and 1¼ inches in diameter. Leave a 1½-inch gap between each bun to allow for expansion. You should get around 35 buns.

4   Cut the cocoa craquelin into 1-inch rounds and place on top.

5   Put into the oven, decrease the heat to 400°F, and bake for 10 minutes. After 10 minutes, decrease the temperature to 350°F and bake for 15 minutes. The shells should be well baked and crisp. Remove from the oven and let cool completely on a cooling rack.

6   To finish the mascarpone custard, beat the custard until smooth and no longer jelly-like, then fold in the mascarpone—it should make a very thick cream. You can do this by hand or in a stand mixer with the paddle attachment. Chill in the fridge until ready to use.

7   To assemble, transfer the mascarpone custard to a piping bag with a star nozzle. Set aside. Cut each lady finger into four small pieces, around ½ x ¾ inch.

8   Cut the top third off each bun. Pipe a little mascarpone in the bottom, then around the edge of the bun creating a border. Dip the lady fingers into the coffee syrup for 5–10 seconds, until completely saturated, then place in the choux bun. Pipe more cream on top, then place the choux lid back on. Repeat for all buns.

9   Chill in the fridge for 1 hour or freezer for 20 minutes to allow the cream to harden, ready to build the tower.

10 Pipe the coffee sauce in a circle on the serving plate to help support the buns. Build each layer, then pipe a spiral of sauce to help the next layer stick. As a guide, the bottom layer will be 12–14 buns, the second layer is 10–12 buns, the third layer is 6–8 buns, the fourth layer is 3–4 buns, and the top layer is 1–2 buns. If desired, warm the leftover sauce slightly, then drizzle over the whole tower just before serving.

Notes

The built tower can be made 2–4 hours in advance. The choux buns will lose their crispness in the fridge over time. The choux buns can be made 3 days in advance and kept at room temperature but can be refreshed at 350°F for 10 minutes before building.

Choux dough can also be kept in the freezer for 1 month, well-wrapped, before using.

MOCHA PASSIONFRUIT
OPERA CAKE

·

SERVES 10

Techniques

Ganache	pg.63
Egg foam	pg.45
Making meringues	pg.46
Making caramel	pg.86

Equipment
15½ x 10½-inch/39 x 27cm baking pan

Mocha sponge

20g/4 tsp	boiling water
1g/¼ tsp	flaky sea salt
4g/2 tsp	instant coffee
15g/3 Tbsp	cocoa powder
50–60g/about 3	egg yolks
100g/½ cup	granulated sugar
90g/3	egg whites

Dacquoise

120g/4	egg whites
60g/¼ cup plus 1 Tbsp	granulated sugar
20g/3 Tbsp	cornstarch
100g/¾ cup plus 2 Tbsp	ground hazelnuts
5g/⅔ cup	powdered sugar

Passionfruit caramel

85g/7 Tbsp	granulated sugar
100g/7 Tbsp	passionfruit juice
50g/¼ cup	butter
25g/2 Tbsp	heavy cream
5g/1 tsp	good quality vanilla bean paste or 1 vanilla pod, scraped
1g/¼ tsp	flaky sea salt

Note

If you are new to making caramel, I suggest warming the passionfruit juice before adding it to the sugar to help prevent it from seizing.

The opera cake is undeniably a classic with its impressive layers and elegant finish. It takes a bit of patience to cut neatly, but you'll be rewarded with an outrageous cut through that belongs in any fancy patisserie—and whatever you do, please, please wipe your knife between cuts!

Day 1			Total: 6 hrs 20 mins		Day 2	Total: 1 hr 10 mins
20 mins	20 mins	1 hr	40 mins	4 hrs	1 hr	10 mins
Mix sponge & dacquoise	Bake	Make fillings	Assemble	Chill	Glaze & chill	Cut

Day 1

1   Preheat the oven to 350°F.

2   To make the mocha sponge, whisk the boiling water with the salt, coffee, and cocoa powder and allow to cool slightly.

3   In a separate bowl, whisk the egg yolks with 50g/¼ cup of the granulated sugar over a bain-marie until ribbon stage, thick, and voluminous. Remove from heat and fold in the coffee/cocoa mixture gently, in three stages.

4   In another bowl, whisk the egg whites and the remaining granulated sugar to a French meringue (see page 118) with medium peaks.

5   Fold the meringue into the egg yolk mixture in three stages. Work carefully so as not to deflate—there should be no streaks left by the end of the folding process. Spread the mixture evenly into a baking pan lined with parchment paper sprayed with oil and smooth with an offset spatula. Bake for 12–15 minutes or until dry to the touch. It will rise, then fall as it cools. Let cool completely in the baking pan. The mocha sponge cake will keep for 1–2 days, well-wrapped at room temperature or frozen for 30 days. For clean removal, place the sponge in the freezer before removing the paper.

6   To make the dacquoise, preheat the oven to 375°F. Whisk the egg whites and granulated sugar to a French meringue (page 118) with stiff peaks. In a separate bowl, mix the cornstarch, hazelnuts, and powdered sugar together. Fold this into the stiff meringue, then spread evenly into a baking pan lined with a silicone mat or greased parchment paper smoothing with an offset spatula.

7   Bake the dacquoise for 20–25 minutes, until light golden and crisp. Let cool completely in the baking pan, then remove and peel off the paper. The dacquoise will keep, well-wrapped, for 3 days at room temperature and will soften over time.

8   For the passionfruit caramel, in a saucepan, melt the sugar over medium heat, until it is light golden. Remove from the heat and whisk in the passionfruit juice. Be careful, as the mixture will bubble and steam. Return the pan to medium heat and whisk until smooth. Add the butter and heavy cream, whisking until incorporated. Bring to a bubble, then take off the heat. Stir in the scraped vanilla seeds or vanilla bean paste and salt, then cool for a few minutes before transferring the caramel to a clean jar or container. Once cooled to room temperature, store the passionfruit caramel in the fridge until ready to use. This will make more than you need and will last in the fridge for 1 week.

Continued →

MOCHA PASSIONFRUIT OPERA CAKE
Continued

Whipped coffee ganache

200g/¾ cup plus 2 Tbsp	heavy cream
2g/1¼ tsp	instant coffee
25g/2 Tbsp	light brown sugar
80g/3 oz	white chocolate, chopped
1–2g/¼–½ tsp	flaky sea salt

Chocolate ganache

100g/7 Tbsp	heavy cream
100g/3½ oz	dark chocolate, cut into small pieces
1g/⅛ tsp	fine salt
30g/2 Tbsp	butter, softened

Chocolate glaze

65g/2⅓ oz	dark chocolate
80g/⅓ cup	heavy cream
20g/1½ Tbsp	vegetable oil
15g/1 Tbsp	hot water
15g/1 Tbsp	golden syrup or light corn syrup

Plus

Gold leaf, to decorate (optional)

9 For the whipped coffee ganache, in a medium saucepan, heat the heavy cream, instant coffee, and light brown sugar over medium heat until the sugar has dissolved, stirring occasionally. Pour the hot cream/sugar over the chopped white chocolate and salt. Let stand for 1 minute, then whisk gently until the chocolate has melted and the mixture is smooth. Transfer the mixture to a clean container and refrigerate until cold, 1–2 hours. When you are ready to assemble the cake, whip the ganache on medium speed until light and airy, 1–2 minutes.

10 For the chocolate ganache, heat the cream in a saucepan until steaming. Pour over the chocolate and salt. Let melt for 1 minute without touching. Gently whisk to emulsify together, starting in the center and working slowly to the outside. Whisk in the butter. Chocolate ganache can be kept in an airtight container at room temperature for 1 day or in the fridge for 1–2 weeks.

11 To assemble, measure and cut the mocha sponge and dacquoise in half. Divide the whipped ganache into three (each approximately 100g/3½ oz). Build your opera cake in the order below, making sure to spread each layer as evenly as possible and going right to the edges. Allow to chill completely in the fridge for 4 hours or overnight.

1. Mocha sponge	6. Mocha sponge
2. Whipped coffee ganache	7. Whipped coffee ganache
3. Passionfruit caramel (75g/2½ oz)	8. Passionfruit caramel (75g/2½ oz)
4. Hazelnut dacquoise	9. Hazelnut dacquoise
5. Chocolate ganache (single layer)	10. Whipped coffee ganache

Day 2

1 To make the glaze, heat all the ingredients over a bain-marie and whisk together until smooth. Set aside until cool to the touch. Pour the chocolate glaze over the cake and spread to coat evenly. It may go over the sides—this is fine as we will trim it. Allow to chill in the fridge for 45 minutes–1 hour.

2 Trim ¼ inch from the edges of the cake to reveal the layers. A hot serrated knife (pour boiling water over it, then wipe dry) is my favorite way to do this cleanly.

3 Mark the opera cake into ten 2 x 3¼-inch (approximate) portions. Use a sawing action to cut through the top third of the cake, then press down. Wipe the knife between each cut.

4 Decorate with gold leaf, if desired. This cake keeps well in an airtight container in the fridge, although it will not stay shiny and the dacquoise will soften. You can make the top shiny again by melting it slightly—pass over it gently a few times with a blowtorch. You can keep the opera cake well-wrapped and unglazed in the freezer for up to 2 weeks, before defrosting and glazing.

CROSS LAMINATED GALETTE DES ROIS

·

SERVES 10

Techniques

Lamination	pg.69

| 1 x recipe | classic puff pastry (see page 124) or inverted puff pastry (see page 125) |
| ½ x recipe | frangipane (see page 339) |

Poached pears

150g/¾ cup	granulated sugar
300g/1¼ cup	dry white wine
Aromatics, like loose-leaf tea, whole spices, vanilla pod	
25g/2 Tbsp	lemon juice
300g/2	pears

Cross lamination dough

300g/2⅓ cups	bread flour or all-purpose flour
10g/1 Tbsp	granulated sugar
6g/1 tsp	fine sea salt
2g/½ tsp	wine white vinegar
130g/½ cup plus 1 Tbsp	water
40g/3 Tbsp	butter, softened

Butter block

| 125g/½ cup plus 1 Tbsp | butter, cold |

Cross laminated puff pastry is an intriguing technique where you affix a layer of laminated dough that faces upward to the top of your dough. When it bakes, the layers separate and you get to marvel at all the layers of pastry and dough—it's quite a sight to see. Achieving this effect in a home kitchen is not the simplest, but it does look amazing. Because puff pastry has so many layers, the dough is not thick enough to make a defined strand when baked in the cross lamination-style. This means we have to make a special laminated dough with less butter and less turns. Once this is ready, we cut very thin strips (paper thin—1⁄16 inch) and affix them to our classic puff pastry.

Although you could use this technique for any dough, I think it looks particularly stunning in a galette des rois, aka the King's cake, which is eaten on Epiphany in France. Traditional galette des rois are round in shape, but the cross lamination suits a more geometric shape. A fève, the prize traditionally nestled inside the galette to determine who will be the king for the day, is optional but always a fun edition.

Day 1	Total: 5 hrs 55 mins	Day 2				Total: 3 hrs 50 mins	
55 mins	5 hrs	30 mins	1 hr	20 mins	1 hr	50 mins	10 mins
Make fillings. Chill	Make & laminate doughs. Rest	Roll out & form galette	Rest	Fill	Rest	Bake	Glaze

Day 1

1   Poach the pears according to the basic poached fruit instructions on page 336. Let cool completely.

2   Make the frangipane according to instructions on page 339.

3   For the cross lamination dough, mix the détrempe and prepare the butter block according to the instructions on page 124 or 125.

4   Lock the butter into the dough. Turn the dough about 90 degrees, roll out until it is about 20 x 6½ inches and perform 1 double fold according to the instructions on page 126. Rest the dough, well-wrapped, for 1–2 hours in the fridge.

5   Roll out the dough to approximately 20 x 6½ inches, then perform one single fold Lengthen the dough so it is about 6½ x 9 inches and about ½ inch thick. Rest the dough, well-wrapped, for at least 4 hours in the fridge. Overnight is best.

Day 2

1   To make the cross lamination dough, cut very thin slices of dough, about 1⁄16 inch thick, from the block using a very sharp knife so as not to crush the layers. Lay these strips, cut-side upward, on a baking sheet. Line them up so they are touching. Continue until you have a full baking sheet. You might have leftover dough—this can be rolled out and used in any recipe requiring pie dough/rough puff/puff pastry. Place a piece of parchment paper on top and gently roll over the cross lamination strips with a rolling pin lightly to seal together—it should be about ⅛ inch thick. Place into the fridge, covered, for at least 30 minutes or until needed.

Continued →

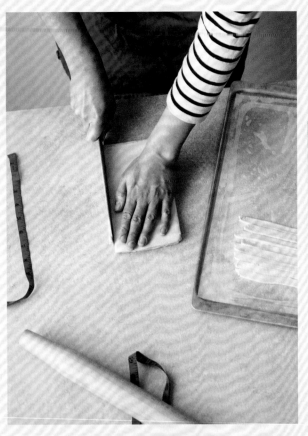

2 To finish, roll out the puff pastry until it is about 16 x 10 inches and ¹⁄₁₆–⅛ inch thick. Cut the pastry in half and reserve half on a baking sheet in the fridge, well-covered. Take the cross lamination sheet out of the fridge and place the other puff pastry rectangle on top. Press down, then roll lightly with a rolling pin to adhere. Move into the fridge with the other puff pastry sheet. Rest for 30 minutes–1 hour.

3 To assemble the galette, on the bottom piece of puff pastry (without the cross lamination), mark a 7-inch square. Pipe 250–300g/9–10½ oz frangipane in the square. Drain the poached pears and slice into thin ½-inch strips—you need about 200g/7 oz pears in total. Lay the pears on top of the frangipane. Tuck in a fève, if desired.

4 Brush water around the edge of the frangipane square. Get the reserved cross lamination puff sheet from the fridge. Lay it over the top of the frangipane, then press around the edge of the square to seal. Transfer the galette to a baking sheet and rest in the fridge for 30 minutes. Trim the pastry so you have an 8–8½-inch square. Rest in the fridge for another 30 minutes.

5 Preheat the oven to 425°F. Bake the galette for 25 minutes, then lower the oven to 400°F. Bake for another 20–25 minutes, until golden.

6 While the galette is baking, reduce the pear poaching liquid by half to two-thirds, until syrupy. Remove the galette from the oven and let cool for 2–3 minutes, then brush with the thickened syrup. Store at room temperature in an airtight container for 3 days. Refresh in a 350°F oven for 5–10 minutes.

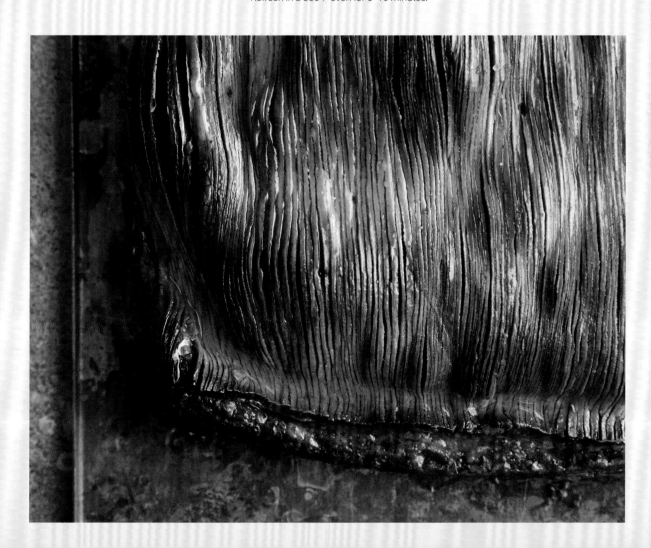

VIENNOISERIE

**Whenever someone asks me what my favorite thing
to make is, I always have the same answer: croissants.**

**Croissants and viennoiserie, the category of morning goods that encompasses
all things buttery and flaky, are universally beloved. And I think that's only fair—it
is a labor of love to make them after all. With love, technique, and lots of butter,
the croissant's transformation from beige blocks to a feat of honeycombed dough
engineering, lighter than air but laden with butter in that golden fluffy-crispy
intersection, is the greatest. Above meringues, layer cakes, and choux towers,
the croissant glow-up is by far my favorite.**

But let me be real with you: making croissants by hand is hard work and is
not always rewarding. Even though I had made hundreds of thousands (this is
not an exaggeration!) of croissants in professional bakeries, the first time I tried
to hand laminate at home it fell completely flat. Was it the recipe? Was it my lack
of equipment? Or was it me? I went into meltdown.

Turns out it was a mixture of all three. But don't worry, this story has a happy ending.
Over six months, I played around with the hydration, butter, and yeast percentages
and got to understand the environment, limitations, and processes. I tweaked and
tweaked and tweaked (and tweaked) until it was just right. While the hand-laminated
croissants I have ended up with have less dramatic definition on the outside than
what I was used to, everything else slipped into place.

Developing this croissant recipe and method is what made me fall in love with
the why of baking. Knowing the theory behind all the pastries and desserts we
make gives you the agency to take control of your recipes.

I don't want you to be discouraged, but I want you to know that nailing croissants
at home is by far the hardest thing I've ever done. Fortunately, it is also incredibly
rewarding and I've every confidence that you will do it! And it should be known
that every batch I've made, even the butter-leaking-under-yet-over-proofed "failures,"
has always been delicious.

So, let's dive in. To give you the best opportunity for success in making
these at home, I've broken down the process into stages.

ONTO THE VIENNOISERIE ⟶

THE BUILDING BLOCKS

The dough

To begin our croissant journey, we make a simple dough of bread flour, milk, yeast, salt, sugar, a little butter, and water. A high-protein flour is essential for the structure of the final croissant— just think of that intricate honeycombed center. To achieve this structure, we need gluten, but we don't develop this too early in the process.

If the dough is too strong, then the lamination process will be harder than it has to be. Gluten is like an elastic band—you don't want the dough constantly trying to spring back on you (see All About Flour on page 14). So, take it easy during the mixing stage. Don't worry, plenty of gluten is developed during the lamination process.

Once the dough is mixed, it has a short rest at room temperature to activate the yeast. It then has a long, cold overnight rest in the fridge to be ready for lamination. In the recipe that follows, the base croissant dough will be divided into three smaller individual doughs, which we will laminate one by one. This will help give us the best chance of success.

Let's talk butter

As you make your pastries, the needs of the butter change. When you start laminating, the butter layer is comparatively thick. When the butter is thick, it is much more susceptible to breaking/splitting apart than when it's cold.

As you roll out your dough and start putting folds into it, your butter (and dough!) will get thinner and thinner. When the butter layer is thinner, it isn't as much at risk of splitting but is more at risk of warming up and smearing. Smearing/warmed butter results in bready croissants.

This means that your main focus on the management of the butter temperature changes throughout the croissant-making process. At the beginning, you want to make sure the butter doesn't break up from being too cold. Toward the end, you want to be thinking about it warming up too much and smearing.

The yeast

Compared to puff pastry, the addition of yeast to the dough makes the lamination a bit harder to manage. As you know, microbial activity is minimal between 39–43°F (aka in the fridge) and every time you take it out, whether it's to laminate or to cut it into shapes, it will warm up and microbial activity will begin to pick up. So, when we put the dough back in the fridge between turns, it has two purposes:

1. Firstly, to rest so the gluten relaxes and you can roll it out again later.

2. Secondly, to keep the dough at a lower temperature to minimize microbial activity.

CROISSANT THEORY

Laminating croissants by hand is no joke (but you can do it!)—it is much harder than making puff pastry because your dough is ALIVE! To get the best results, I've radically reduced the batch size to make it manageable. As you get more confident working with doughs, you can increase the size. It might feel like laminating multiple doughs is more work. But it's much faster to roll out a smaller dough, so I think you make the time back quickly.

We will start off by making a larger dough and then split it into three smaller doughs of approximately 350g/12¼ oz. Each of these 350g/12¼ oz doughs will be laminated with 125g/4½ oz butter. It's important for you to use a good quality butter that is at least 80% butterfat to get the best end product. Each of these doughs will be laminated with 3 x single folds. Each of these doughs can be turned into a range of pastries (see the recipes that follow). The scraps or offcuts from these will be kept and—with a little magic trick—we will turn these into our kouign amann (see page 322).

As you get more confident with laminating doughs, you can play around with the number of folds and turns in your pastries. 3 x single folds will give you an airy croissant with a detailed honeycomb structure. A single fold with 1 double fold will give you less layers but a more open structure inside.

LAMINATION THEORY

- When you are laminating, there are many factors at play. You must pay particular attention to the temperature and plasticity of both the butter and the dough itself—although we give you resting times, everybody's fridge and environment are different, so you have to learn to feel the dough. Have a feel of the dough after the overnight rest in the fridge. This is the ideal texture/consistency and you want to maintain this at all times. The butter, although it will be at a warmer temperature, must feel the same.

- It is not advisable to make croissants on a hot day. If you do, then you must work very quickly and extend the fridge resting times. You know your environment and how best to approach this.

- Making pastries by hand is a very tactile process and must be done both lightly and firmly. It's important that you apply the right kind of pressure on the croissants—you can start by pressing gently but decisively with the rolling pin to improve plasticity and then continue by rolling with intention and even pressure. If you go at it too hard, then you can smear the layers, leading to uneven lamination.

- The ideal dough temperature for laminating is 39–43°F, straight from the fridge, BUT the ideal butter temperature for laminating is 52–57°F. This is the point at which the butter has good plasticity but is not greasy—it does not smudge but you can bend it. This is key for getting beautiful layers in your pastry! Too warm and the butter smears/melts into dough, creating a heavier end product. Too cold and the butter may split and shatter as it is rolled, creating uneven lamination and indistinct layers. As your butter layers get thinner (as in the more turns that you do), the less likely it is to shatter/split as you are rolling.

- You can use flour to dust your work surface as you roll out the dough but be sure to brush any excess off with a clean pastry brush. Too much flour can prevent the layers from properly adhering together.

- It is essential to rest your pastry long enough for the gluten to relax before attempting to perform another fold. This must be done in the fridge because otherwise the yeast will begin to ferment and the butter will get too warm.

- To manage the butter temperature, I rest the dough for about 45 minutes between the first and second fold. You don't want to go longer than this as this is the point when the butter is still quite thick and can split during the roll out. You can chill it slightly longer between the second/third fold to work with your schedule.

- Unless you are very confident working with lamination, do not put your croissant in the freezer at any point between folds. This is just asking for trouble with your butter. As you know, butter that is too cold will crack and split and you will lose the integrity of the layers.

- Aim for around ¼-inch-thick dough when performing folds. This will ensure the butter is not stretched too thin/smears too much.

- Rolling out dough by hand works the dough a LOT—it puts lots of pressure/stress onto your dough, which means that it does need proper time to relax so you can continue working on it. You will notice it tends to spring back a lot. If your dough is difficult to roll out, it is best to put it back into the fridge and let it rest. Fighting the dough to roll it out will only lead to damage of the layers. Do not pick a fight with your dough.

- If you want to tidy up your dough as you go by trimming the edges, you can. But with such small doughs, I find you lose too much.

- For the absolute best final product, I recommend freezing your laminated dough for at least 4 hours, then thawing it in the fridge. This stage is to completely stop the yeast in its tracks for the final shaping. PLEASE do not try to roll it out while the center is still frozen. This is going to end in major tears (both kinds). Don't do it to yourself!

- Unlaminated and laminated croissant dough are happy wrapped well in the freezer for 2 weeks. Any more than this and the yeast will begin to degrade.

- You can also freeze shaped pastries and then proof from frozen. Notes on proofing times from frozen are on the following pages.

CROISSANT DOUGH

·

MAKES 3 X 12¼ OZ/350G PASTRY BLOCKS

Techniques

Lamination	pg.69
Fermentation	pg.76
Gluten development	pg.14

165g/⅔ cup	water, hot (158–176°F)
165g/⅔ cup	whole milk, fridge-cold
605g/4¾ cups	bread flour
12g/2½ tsp	fine salt
75g/6 Tbsp	granulated sugar
13g/4½ tsp	dry yeast
30g/2 Tbsp	butter, softened

Butter block

125g/½ cup plus 1 Tbsp	butter, very cold (per 350g/12¼ oz dough)

In this recipe, we will make a base batch of dough, then divide it into three. These three smaller doughs will be laminated separately. Once complete, each of these doughs can be rolled out and cut into whatever shapes you desire—each one will make 4–8 pastries, depending on what you are making.

Day 1		Total: 10 hrs 40 mins
10 mins	30 mins	10 hrs
Mix dough	Round & rest	Rest overnight

Day 2				Total: 14 hrs 30 mins
10 mins	1 hr	1 hr 10 mins	10 mins	12 hrs
Make butter block	Lock in butter. Single fold & rest	Single fold & rest	Singlefold	Wrap & rest in the freezer overnight. Thaw for 2 hours

Day 1

1   Mix the water and milk together and check the temperature—it should be 95–104°F. Pour the liquid into the bowl of a stand mixer and add the dry ingredients. Mix slowly using the paddle attachment. When combined, change to the hook attachment. Mix for 1 minute on low speed until well combined.

2   Add the soft butter. Mix for 3–4 minutes on medium speed until smooth. It's a large, stiff dough, so you may need to adjust the dough in the bowl a few times.

3   Remove the dough from the mixer and smooth into a ball. Rest, covered, for 30 minutes at room temperature. It will be somewhat puffed (though not dramatically) and active.

4   Split the dough into 3 portions, each about 350g/12¼ oz. Shape into rectangles and wrap in reusable plastic bags/something very well sealed.

5   Put the dough in the fridge for 8–10 hours or overnight.

6   The dough will expand overnight. This is good. It means your yeast is alive. If it is totally flat, I highly recommend testing your yeast before moving on with the laminating to avoid disappointment later down the line.

7   At this stage, the dough can be tightly wrapped and frozen for 1 week; thaw before use. It will keep wrapped for 1–2 days in a very cold fridge, pre-lamination.

Note

The butter must be very cold before working into a block.

Continued →

Note

While you are getting used to working with lamination, the butter block must be made JUST before laminating. This way you will be able to get the best plasticity for your butter and it will give you the best results.

Day 2

1   For the butter block, working quickly, cut the butter into strips and lay them into an approximate rectangle shape on some parchment paper.

2   Fold the paper around the butter in an approximate 5 x 6½-inch shape.

3   Using a rolling pin, tap/squash the butter into shape, rolling over it several times to ensure it is even.

4   Neaten, shape, and smooth the butter block.

5   Depending on its plasticity and your room temperature (on a cool day, it's probably OK staying out), pop it in the freezer/fridge to rest while you roll out your dough, but do not prepare your butter block until you are ready to laminate. Check it is still bendy/doesn't snap or break, but is not greasy, before you laminate with it.

Continued →

Note

When you roll out the dough, you can dust your work surface to help prevent it from sticking. But make sure to always brush off excess flour with a clean pastry brush before folding.

Day 2 (continued)

6   Straight from the fridge, roll your dough out to about 6½ x 12 inches, about double the size of your butter block and about ¼ inch thick (note: this is the approximate thickness you will always be looking for during the lamination).

7   Place your butter block into the middle of the dough. Make sure that it is still pliable yet cold and not greasy.

8   Bring the top and bottom parts of the dough over the butter block to meet in the middle, pinching the dough together to close the butter in—the seam will be horizontal and the dough size is about 6½ x 6 inches.

9   Turn the dough 90 degrees so the seam is now vertical.

10 Press down on the dough with the rolling pin, leaving indentations along the length of the dough—this helps fuse together the butter and dough. It also lengthens the dough without heating it up. Now roll the dough out to nearly three times its length, approximately 6½ x 16 inches.

11 Perform a single fold. Make a cut on the right edge of the dough where it is folded to release tension.

12 Wrap the dough and rest in the fridge for 45 minutes.

13 Make sure the dough is rotated 90 degrees, so the cut folded edge is on either the right or left. Press down on the dough to leave indentations with the rolling pin to plasticize the butter and to lengthen the dough without heating it too much. Roll out the dough to about 6½ x 16 inches.

14 Perform a single fold. Make a cut on the right edge of the dough where it is folded to release tension.

15 Wrap the dough and rest in the fridge for 1–1½ hours.

16 Make sure the dough is rotated 90 degrees, so the cut folded edge is on either the right or left. Press down on the dough to leave indentations with the rolling pin to plasticize the butter and lengthen the dough. Roll out the dough to about 6½ x 16 inches. Perform a single fold.

17 Your lamination is now complete! Rest your dough in the freezer overnight (and thaw for at least 2 hours in the fridge). You can also chill the dough in the freezer for 1 hour, then fridge for 2 hours before rolling out.

18 At this stage, your dough can be tightly wrapped and frozen for 1 week; thaw before use.

Note

Remember, when you feel more confident, you can start changing up the amount of turns in your croissants dough (see page 70).

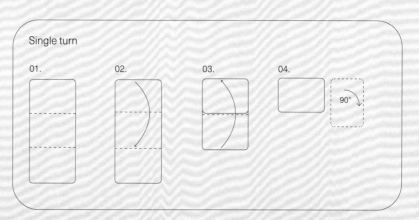

Single turn

01.   02.   03.   04.

90°

CUTTING PASTRIES

Always cut your dough with a very sharp knife or a serrated knife
so as not to destroy the layers.

Name	Roll out size	Thickness	Action	Cut shape	Size	Quantity	Weight	Action	Final shape	Proofing time
Croissant	8 x 14 inches	⅛–¼ inch	Cut	Triangle	3¼ x 9½ inches	4	80–95g/ 3–3½ oz	Rest fridge 20 minutes	Roll up	2–4½ hours
Pain au chocolat	10¼ x 14 inches	¼ inch	Cut	Rectangle	6½ x 3 inches	4	90–100g/ 3¼–3½ oz	Rest fridge 20 minutes	Add chocolate and roll	1½–3½ hours
Danish/ kouign amann	7 x 14 inches	⅛–¼ inch	Cut	Squares/ circle	3½–4-inch square or 4-inch round	6	50–60g/ 1¾–2¼ oz	Go to final shape	Leave flat or press into cupcake pans	1½– 2 hours
Squiggle buns	8 x 14 inches	⅛–¼ inch	Cut	Strips	8 x 2 inches	7	60g/2¼ oz	Go to final shape	Zig-zag into pan	1½– 3 hours
Buns	8 x 14 inches	⅛–¼ inch	Cut	Strips	6 x ¾ inches	5–6	20g/¾ oz per strip, 60g/ 2¼ oz per bun	Go to final shape	Lay 3 pieces on top and spiral into a bun	1½–2½ hours
Twisty strips	8 x 14 inches	⅛–¼ inch	Cut	Strips	6½ x 1¼ inches	10	30–40g/ 1–1½ oz per strip	Go to final shape	Cut strip down the middle and twist over itself	1½– 2 hours
Pain suisse	11 x 12½ inches	⅛ inch	Add fillings. Close dough. Rest in freezer. Roll slightly when firm to lengthen	Strips	2 x 5½ inches	6	70–80g/ 2½–3 oz	n/a	n/a	2–3½ hours

Notes on final roll out

One of the biggest challenges is keeping the dough sufficiently rested. Rolling out by hand puts a lot of pressure on the dough and gets the gluten really revved up—just take your time and be willing to put things back into the fridge to rest if they are fighting you, especially during the final roll out. Do not force the dough—not only are the layers at risk, it may force your dough to spring back when you cut it, giving you uneven shapes. For more complex shapes, like the long triangles needed for croissants, I advise letting them rest for 30 minutes, well-wrapped, in the fridge before shaping. This will help prevent warping and get you the best final product.

Notes on freezing

Once your pastries have been shaped, you can freeze them. The best way to do this is:

- Put the pastries onto a lined baking sheet and make sure they are covered, using either plastic wrap or a reusable plastic bag.
- Put them into the freezer, the coldest part you can, and chill until totally frozen.
- At this point, they can be moved into a freezer bag or something that takes up less space, but you must make sure they are always well-wrapped. After this, you can keep your pastries frozen for up to 2 weeks. After this, your yeast will begin to degrade. It may even degrade faster depending on how fresh your yeast was to begin with. To defrost and proof the pastries, simply follow the proofing steps outlined on the next pages. You can expect to add 1–1½ hours onto the proofing times.

Proofing—how long will it take?

Proofing your pastries correctly is one of the most essential steps to success and, like every other part of the croissant-making process, can be a bit of a challenge. Without making a makeshift proofing chamber and managing the temperature and humidity of your home environment (see page 80), your pastries will move incredibly slowly and proof poorly. If exposed to dry air, the pastries will crack as they proof. At the very least, cover your pastries with a large overturned container to help prevent crusting.

So how long does it take? First things first, every single person's experience will be different. Proofing time is directly related to tension. So, the more tightly you roll/the more rotations in your croissant or pain au chocolat, the longer it will take to proof. This is because it takes longer for the temperature to penetrate the center of the pastry and become fully expanded! Using the same logic, a flatter Danish pastry and kouign amann will proof much more quickly.

Here are some approximate proofing times. Please note that these are just a range and you must watch your pastries in your environment:

- Croissant: 2–4½ hours
- Pain au chocolat: 1½–3½ hours
- Danish pastry: 1½–2 hours
- Kouign amann: 1½–2 hours

I think it's better for you to bake your pastries slightly under-proofed, rather than the other way around! So, if you are using the proofing chamber method, it is advisable to remove your pastries from this 30–45 minutes before you think they are ready. This means you can preheat your oven so you can immediately bake your pastries when they reach optimal proof. A good way to keep track of the proofing time is to jot down the time on the baking sheet—that way, you'll always have a reference point.

Calling proof

Calling proof is HARD! This is an image of a well-proofed croissant. The more you make them, the more you'll be able to see it, but these are the things to look out for:

- Pastries that have expanded to at least double in size.
- Pastries that jiggle when you move the baking sheet back and forth.
- The yeasted dough will have physically pushed the layers apart and you can see separation in the lamination.
- If you gently touch the pastries, they feel filled with air.
- The pastries look inflated and yet strong (if they look like they're about to deflate, then they have gone too far).

Baking

Individual baking instructions are on each recipe.

Diagnosing

Even though all pastries are beautiful, it can sometimes be helpful to know what has happened. The easiest way to know if your pastries have been successful (in the traditional sense) is by picking them up—they should feel light, incredibly light. If your croissants feel heavier than you expect, it's probably one of these issues:

• The croissant has not expanded to its full potential	**DIAGNOSIS**
• The crumb is very tight and close in the center	Underproofed!
• It is a bit bready and heavy	*(pictured opposite on left)*
• It has a dry texture rather than buttery and flaky	
• It has leaked lots of butter in the oven	

• The croissant has a sagging profile	**DIAGNOSIS**
• The crumb is tight but buttery	Overproofed OR butter too warm during lamination, i.e., butter has smeared throughout or proofing chamber was too warm
• Honeycomb structure is not very clear	
• The croissant grows, then deflates in the oven	
	(pictured opposite on right)

Scraps

At the bakery where we used to make ten thousand pastries a week, we used to have a lot of croissant trim and none of it would ever go to waste. There are lots of ways you can use this up. For example, you can add a handful to a bread/bun recipe to improve flavor (it's kind of like using a preferment, too, so your dough will be very active!) or squash them all together, work into a dough, and bake as buttery buns.

However, there is a technique for you to make the most of your scraps. When you trim your dough, keep all of your scraps and lay them onto a baking sheet in a single layer, lining up the laminations as much as possible. Keep this in the fridge while you are working.

Once you've trimmed all of your pastries and you have all of the scraps lined up, use a rolling pin to press all of the pieces together and roll out until it is big enough for you to perform a single fold.

It won't be beautiful, but after you've rested this for 2 hours, you will be able to roll out the dough and cut shapes out of it. This won't make good croissants or pain au chocolat but it will make great kouign amann or buns.

CROISSANTS

·

MAKES 4 CROISSANTS

Techniques

Lamination	pg.69
Gluten development	pg.14
Fermentation	pg.76
Proofing	pg.79

350g/12¼ oz   unlaminated croissant
dough (see page 298)
125g/½ cup   butter, very cold
plus 1 Tbsp   (for lamination)
Egg wash (see page 343)

Watching a batch of croissants rise to the occasion is a unique joy, as is eating one warm from the oven. It is a fairly unforgiving shape—the quality of lamination in the croissant is the most apparent of all the shapes, so take your time and don't rush the proofing!

Day 1	**Total:** 12 hrs 40 mins		Day 2	**Total:** 16 hrs	Day 3			**Total:** 5 hrs
40 mins	12 hrs	4 hrs	12 hrs	30 mins	4 hrs	20 mins	10 mins
Make dough	Let rest overnight	Laminate dough	Chill	Roll out dough & shape pastries	Proof pastries	Bake	Cool

1   Laminate the croissant dough with 3 single turns following the instructions on page 300.

2   Make sure the dough is rotated 90 degrees, so the folded edge is on either the right or left. Roll out the dough to be about 10¼ inches in length. Do not fight the dough— you can always put it in the fridge to rest, well-wrapped, for 20 minutes before continuing.

3   Then work the dough crosswise until it is ⅛ x ¼ inch thick. Trim the edges of the dough to reveal the lamination. Reserve the scrap dough.

4   For croissants, cut out long triangles, each approximately 3¼ x 9½ inches and weighing 80–95g/3–3⅓ oz.

5   Rest the shapes for 20 minutes in the fridge, well-wrapped.

6   Stretch each triangle slightly and roll up the triangle on itself without crushing the layers, aiming for as many rotations as possible. Place on a baking sheet lined with parchment paper, with the tails tucked underneath, and lightly cover.

7   Proof until jiggly, 2–4½ hours (see proofing instructions on page 302).

8   Preheat the oven to 425°F.

9   Gently brush the croissants with egg wash. Turn down the oven to 400°F and bake the pastries for about 18 minutes, turning after 12 minutes if needed.

10   Let cool completely on the baking sheet. These pastries are best enjoyed within 2–3 hours of baking. Leftovers should be kept in an airtight container at room temperature and reheated at 350°F for 10 minutes.

PAIN AU CHOCOLAT

·

MAKES 4 PAIN AU CHOCOLAT

Techniques

Lamination	pg.69
Gluten development	pg.14
Fermentation	pg.76
Proofing	pg.79

350g/12¼ oz	croissant dough (see page 298)
8	dark chocolate batons (10g/⅓ oz per baton) or 80g/3 oz dark chocolate, broken into smaller pieces
Egg wash (see page 343)	

This classic needs no introduction—a perfect swirl of dough. Use the best chocolate you can find—it'll make all the difference when you eat it fresh and still warm.

Day 1	Total: 12 hrs 40 mins	Day 2	Total: 16 hrs	Day 3			Total: 4 hrs
40 mins	12 hrs	4 hrs	12 hrs	30 mins	3 hrs	20 mins	10 mins
Make dough	Let rest overnight	Laminate dough	Chill	Roll out dough & shape pastries	Proof pastries	Bake	Cool

1 Laminate the croissant dough with 3 x single turns following the instructions on page 300.

2 Make sure the dough is rotated 90 degrees, so the folded edge is on either the right or left.

3 To cut, roll out the dough until it is about 7 inches in length. Then roll it crosswise until it is about ¼ inch thick. Do not fight the dough—you can always put it in the fridge to rest, well-wrapped, for 20 minutes before continuing.

4 Trim the edges of the dough to reveal the lamination. Reserve the scrap dough.

5 Cut out the pastries, each about 6½ x 3 inches and weighing between 90–100g/3¼–3½ oz.

6 Shape with the chocolate batons or chopped chocolate inside, place onto a lined baking sheet, and lightly cover.

7 Proof until jiggly, 1½–3 ½ hours (see proofing instructions on page 302).

8 Preheat the oven to 425°F.

9 Gently brush the pain au chocolat with egg wash. Turn down the oven to 400°F and bake the pastries for about 18 minutes, turning after 12 minutes if needed.

10 Let cool completely on the baking sheet. The pastries are best enjoyed within 2–3 hours of baking. Leftovers should be kept in an airtight container at room temperature and reheated at 350°F for 10 minutes.

SWIRLY BUNS

·

MAKES 5–6 BUNS

Techniques

Lamination	pg.60
Gluten development	pg.14
Fermentation	pg.76
Proofing	pg.79

Equipment
Cupcake pan
Piping bag with a long Bismarck tip

350g/12¼ oz	unlaminated croissant dough (see page 298)
125g/½ cup plus 1 Tbsp	butter, very cold (for lamination)

Egg wash (see page 343)

Crème légère

½ x recipe	pastry cream (see page 338)
100g/7 Tbsp	heavy cream, whipped

Plus
Coarse sanding sugar, to finish

This useful shape lends itself well to plain buns as well as being the perfect shape to be stuffed with custard. This is a pretty forgiving shape, so a great format to give compound butters (see page 332) a whirl.

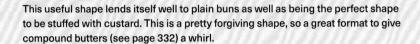

Day 1 Total: 12 hrs 40 mins		**Day 2** Total: 16 hrs		**Day 3**		Total: 3 hrs 20 mins	
40 mins	12 hrs	4 hrs	12 hrs	30 mins	2hrs	20 mins	30 mins
Make dough	Let rest overnight	Laminate dough	Chill	Roll out dough & shape pastries	Proof pastries	Bake	Cool & finish

1   Laminate the croissant dough with 3 single turns following the instructions on page 300.

2   For the final roll out, make sure the dough is rotated 90 degrees, so the folded edge is on either the right or left.

3   To cut, roll out the dough to be about 8 inches in length, then roll it crosswise until it is ⅛–¼ inch thick, and about 14 inches wide. Do not fight the dough—you can always put it in the fridge to rest, well-wrapped, for 20 minutes before continuing.

4   Trim the edges to reveal the lamination and reserve the scraps.

5   Cut the dough into 6 x ¾-inch strips, about 20g/¾ oz per strip.

6   Stack three strips on top of each other with a ¾-inch gap between the beginning of each strip so there is space to roll it. Then spiral up into a swirl. Nestle into a cupcake pan.

7   Cover lightly and proof until the layers are pushing apart (see proofing instructions on page 302), 1½–2½ hours.

8   Preheat the oven to 425°F.

9   Brush the buns lightly with egg wash—too much and the layers will stick together.

10 Turn down the oven to 400°F and bake the pastries for about 18 minutes, turning them after 12 minutes if needed. Cool completely.

11 To fill the buns, make the crème légère according to the instructions on page 338. Move into a piping bag fitted with a long Bismarck tip. Poke halfway into a bun, then squeeze the bag. Wiggle the tip to move the cream around evenly. About 25g/¾ oz is perfect here. Once filled, you can roll in sanding sugar to finish. If you can see the hole where the cream went in, you can cover it with the decoration of your choice. Repeat for all the buns.

12 Serve immediately. The pastries are best enjoyed within 2–3 hours of baking. Leftovers can be kept in the fridge for 1–2 days.

Note

This shape works well with compound butters. The nduja butter (see page 332), laminated into the dough in place of regular butter, then finished with a drizzle of honey, is a wonder.

TWISTY STRIPS

·

MAKES 10 STRIPS

Techniques

Lamination	pg.69
Gluten development	pg.14
Fermentation	pg.76
Proofing	pg.79

350g/12¼ oz	unlaminated croissant dough (see page 298)
1 x recipe	chile crisp soy butter (see page 332)
Egg wash (see page 343)	

Plus

A drizzle of chile oil	
2	sprigs of rosemary, stemmed (optional)

This long, flat shape makes super-crispy pastries that are fun to shape (and eat!).

Day 1	Total: 12 hrs 40 mins		Day 2	Total: 16 hrs		Day 3		Total: 3 hrs 20 mins	
40 mins	12 hrs		4 hrs	12 hrs		30 mins	2 hrs	20 mins	30 mins
Make dough	Let rest overnight		Laminate dough	Chill		Roll out dough & shape pastries	Proof pastries	Bake	Cool & finish

1   Laminate the croissant dough with the chile crisp soy butter. Perform 3 x single turns following the instructions on page 300.

2   For the final roll out, make sure the dough is rotated 90 degrees, so the folded edge is on either the right or left.

3   Roll out the dough until it is about 8 inches in length. Then roll it crosswise until it is ⅛–¼ inch thick, about 14 inches wide. Cut the dough into 6½ x 1¼ inch strips, 30–40g/ 1–1½ oz per strip. Do not fight the dough—you can always put it in the fridge to rest, well-wrapped, for 20 minutes before continuing.

4   To shape, cut a line down the center of each strip, leaving a 1-inch gap on either end. Open the slit and start looping one edge over itself to create a twisty shape. Place on a lined baking sheet.

5   Cover lightly and proof until the layers are pushing apart (see proofing instructions on page 302), 1½–2 hours.

6   Preheat the oven to 425°F.

7   Brush the strips lightly with egg wash—too much and the layers will stick together.

8   Turn down the oven to 400°F and bake the pastries for 16–18 minutes, turning after 12 minutes if needed.

9   Let cool completely on the baking sheet, then top with a drizzle of chile oil and the rosemary leaves, if using. The pastries are best enjoyed within 2–3 hours of baking. Leftovers should be kept in an airtight container at room temperature and reheated at 350°F for 10 minutes.

Note

This shape works well with other compound butters—see page 332 for other ideas.

CHOCOLATE SQUIGGLES

·

MAKES ABOUT 6 SQUIGGLES

Techniques

Lamination	pg.69
Gluten development	pg.14
Fermentation	pg.76
Proofing	pg.79

Equipment

6 mini loaf pans, each
4 x 3 x 2 inches/10 x 7 x 5cm

350g/12¼ oz	unlaminated croissant dough (see page 298)
125g/½ cup plus 1 Tbsp	butter, very cold (for lamination)
24	dark chocolate batons (5–10g/¼–⅓ oz per baton), each 1½–2 inches long

Egg wash (see page 343)

A lateral take on the pain au chocolat. Who doesn't want their own individual breakfast pastry loaf?!

Day 1	Total: 12 hrs 40 mins		Day 2	Total: 16 hrs		Day 3			Total: 3 hrs 10 mins	
40 mins	12 hrs		4 hrs	12 hrs		30 mins	2 hrs	20 mins	20 mins	
Make dough	Let rest overnight		Laminate dough	Chill		Roll out dough & shape pastries	Proof pastries	Bake	Cool	

1   Laminate the croissant dough with 3 single turns following the instructions on page 300.

2   For the final roll out, make sure the dough is rotated 90 degrees, so the folded edge is on either the right or left.

3   To cut, roll out the dough to be about 8 inches in length, then roll it crosswise until it is ⅛–¼ inch thick, about 14 inches wide. Do not fight the dough—you can always put it in the fridge to rest, well-wrapped, for 20 minutes before continuing.

4   Trim the edges to reveal the lamination and reserve the scraps.

5   Cut the dough into 8 x 2-inch strips, 50–60g/1¾–2¼ oz per strip. Zig-zag each strip of dough on itself and place into a mini loaf pan. Nestle some chocolate batons into the curves.

6   Cover lightly and proof until the layers are pushing apart (see proofing instructions on page 302), between 1½–3 hours.

7   Preheat the oven to 425°F.

8   Brush the squiggles lightly with egg wash—too much and the layers will stick together.

9   Turn down the oven to 400°F and bake the pastries for about 18 minutes, turning after 12 minutes if needed.

10   Let cool for 10 minutes in the pans then move to a rack to cool completely. The pastries are best enjoyed within 2–3 hours of baking. Leftovers should be kept in an airtight container at room temperature and reheated at 350°F for 10 minutes.

CLASSIC FRUIT CUSTARD DANISH

·

MAKES 8 DANISHES

Techniques

Lamination	pg.69
Gluten development	pg.14
Fermentation	pg.76
Proofing	pg.79

Equipment
3½ or 4-inch round cutter

350g/12¼ oz	unlaminated croissant dough (see page 298)
125g/½ cup plus 1 Tbsp	butter, very cold (for lamination)
¼ x recipe	pastry cream (see page 338), beaten until smooth

Prepared seasonal fruit (fresh, roasted, or poached, see page 336)
Egg wash (see page 343)

Crumb
Apricot jam

½ x recipe	basic crumb (see page 343)

Crème légère (good for berry Danishes)

100g/7 Tbsp	heavy cream, whipped
½ x recipe	pastry cream (see page 338)

The square is the most efficient shape for this dough, and makes the perfect bed for any kind of seasonal fruit. Custard can be added before, or after—or both!

Day 1	**Total:** 12 hrs 40 mins		Day 2	**Total:** 16 hrs		Day 3		**Total:** 3 hrs 20 mins	
40 mins	12 hrs		4 hrs	12 hrs		30 mins	2 hrs	20 mins	30 mins
Make dough	Let rest overnight		Laminate dough	Chill		Roll out dough & shape pastries	Proof pastries	Bake	Finish

1 Laminate the croissant dough with 3 single turns following the instructions on page 300.

2 For the final roll out, make sure the dough is rotated 90 degrees, so the folded edge is on either the right or left.

3 To cut, roll out the dough until it is about 8 inches in length. Then roll it crosswise until it is ⅛–¼ inch thick, about 14 inches. Do not fight the dough—you can always put it in the fridge to rest, well-wrapped, for 20 minutes before continuing.

4 Trim the edges of the dough to reveal the lamination and reserve the scraps.

5 Cut out the pastries using a 3½ or 4-inch round cutter for the circular shapes and cut the squares about 3½ inches square and weighing 50–60g/1¾–2¼ oz. Lightly score the dough where you will put the fillings, leaving a ½–¾-inch border. Place on a lined baking sheet.

6 Cover lightly and proof until the layers are pushing apart (see proofing instructions on page 302), between 1½–2 hours.

7 Preheat the oven to 425°F.

8 Pipe a 15g/½ oz splodge of pastry cream in the center of each round/square of dough.

9 If you are using fruit that can withstand an oven bake, like poached pears or fresh plums, tuck about 30g/1 oz of fruit per Danish into the custard. For fragile fruits like berries, bake the Danishes with custard alone, then add the fruit after.

10 Gently brush the edges of the pastries with egg wash.

11 Turn down the oven to 400°F and bake the pastries for 16–18 minutes, turning after 12 minutes if needed. Cool completely if finishing with crème légère.

12 For crumb Danishes, melt some apricot jam until liquid, then spread onto the pastries with a brush. Sprinkle some crumb on to stick and set aside to cool.

13 For fresh berry Danishes, once cool, fold the whipped cream into the pastry cream to make a crème légère (see page 338), then add a spoonful of this cream on top of the baked custard and top with the berries.

14 The pastries are best served fresh. Store in an airtight container in the fridge for 2–3 days. Refresh in a 350°F oven for 5–10 minutes, removing any fresh fruit and putting back on top before eating.

Note

You can also bake the custard without fruit and add fresh fruit, like berries, on top afterward.

ST. HONORÉ CHERRY DANISH

·

MAKES 8 DANISHES

Techniques

Lamination	pg.69
Gluten development	pg.14
Fermentation	pg.76
Proofing	pg.79

Equipment
4-inch round cutter
2 x piping bags, one with a St Honoré tip

350g/12¼ oz	unlaminated croissant dough (see page 298)
125g/½ cup plus 1 Tbsp	butter, very cold (for lamination)
150g/5¼ oz	fresh cherries
¼ x recipe	pastry cream (see page 338), beaten until smooth
Egg wash (see page 343)	

Cream decoration

150g/½ cup plus 2 Tbsp	heavy cream
150g/5¼ oz	pastry cream (leftover from above), beaten until smooth (you can also use ½ x recipe whipped vanilla ganache (see page 160)

Choux pastry decoration

¼ x recipe	choux pastry (see page 136)
50g/¼ cup	granulated sugar

Taking inspiration from the classic St. Honoré gateau, which combines puff pastry, cream, and choux, this is a spectacular-looking Danish. All the elements can be made separately and assembled at the last minute.

Day 1	Total: 12 hrs 40 mins	Day 2	Total: 16 hrs	Day 3		Total: 3 hrs 52 mins	
40 mins	12 hrs	4 hrs	12 hrs	30 mins	2 hrs	22 mins	1 hr
Make dough	Let rest overnight	Laminate dough	Chill	Roll out dough & shape pastries	Proof pastries	Bake pastries	Chill & make decorations

1   Laminate the croissant dough with 3 single turns following the instructions on page 300.

2   For the final roll out, make sure the dough is rotated 90 degrees, so the folded edge is on either the right or left.

3   To cut, roll the dough until it is about 8 inches in length. Then roll it crosswise until it is ⅛–¼ inch thick, about 14 inches wide. Do not fight the dough—you can always put it in the fridge to rest, well-wrapped, for 20 minutes before continuing.

4   Trim the edges of the dough to reveal the lamination and reserve the scraps.

5   Cut out the pastries using a 4-inch round cutter for the circular shapes. They should weigh 50–60g/1¾–2¼ oz. Place on a lined baking sheet.

6   Cover lightly and proof until the layers are pushing apart (see proofing instructions on page 302), between 1½–2 hours.

7   Preheat the oven to 425°F.

8   Halve and pit the cherries, then pipe a 10–15g/⅓–½ oz splodge of the pastry cream in the center of the dough shapes, followed by 3–4 cherry halves in each. Gently brush the edges of the pastries with egg wash.

9   Turn down the oven to 400°F and bake the pastries for 16–18 minutes, turning after 12 minutes if needed. Cool completely.

10   Make choux pastry according to the instructions on page 136, then pipe 5g/¼ oz buns onto a lined baking sheet. Bake at 400°F for 22 minutes, until puffed and golden. Let cool completely, then poke a hole in the bottom of the buns and fill with some of the reserved cream when ready to use.

11   For the cream decoration, whip the cream until medium peaks form, then fold in the remaining pastry cream. Set aside in a piping bag fitted with a St. Honoré tip (or cut the tip off the piping bag at a sharp angle).

12   Make a dry caramel by melting the sugar in a low wide pan, stirring constantly until it becomes an amber caramel. Take off the heat, then dip the top of each bun into the caramel to coat. Move onto lightly greased paper to set completely, caramel-side down.

13   To finish, fill the center of each Danish with the remaining cream, then pipe blobs around the top of each Danish. Finish with a few cherry halves and a choux bun on top. Serve immediately. These do not keep well.

PEACH PANZANELLA DEEP-DISH DANISH

·

MAKES 8 DANISHES

Techniques

Lamination	pg.69
Gluten development	pg.14
Fermentation	pg.76
Proofing	pg.79

Equipment
Cupcake or muffin pan

350g/12¼ oz	unlaminated croissant dough (see page 298)
125g/½ cup plus 1 Tbsp	butter, very cold (for lamination)
Egg wash (see page 343)	

Peach, tomato, and mozzarella mix

120g/4¼ oz	ripe peaches, pitted (pitted weight)
160g/5¾ oz	cherry tomatoes
18g/4 tsp	extra-virgin olive oil
10g/2 tsp	white wine vinegar
1–2g/¼–½ tsp	flaky sea salt
12	basil leaves, thinly sliced
80g/3 oz	buffalo mozzarella, drained

Plus
Small basil leaves, to finish

Baking croissant dough in molds provides a perfect shell for you to fill with anything your heart desires. You can fill before baking—think frangipane, custard, etc.—or let your imagination go wild with post-bake toppings. This sweet, salty, acidic panzanella-inspired filling is a real treat.

Day 1	Total: 12 hrs 40 mins		Day 2	Total: 16 hrs	Day 3		Total: 3 hrs 20 mins	
40 mins	12 hrs		4 hrs	12 hrs	30 mins	2 hrs	20 mins	30 mins
Make dough	Let rest overnight		Laminate dough	Chill	Roll out dough & shape pastries	Proof pastries	Bake	Finish

1   Laminate the croissant dough with 3 single turns following the instructions on page 300.

2   For the final roll out, make sure the dough is rotated 90 degrees, so the folded edge is on either the right or left. Do not fight the dough—you can always put it in the fridge to rest, well-wrapped, for 20 minutes before continuing.

3   To cut, roll out the dough until it is about 8 inches in length. Then roll it crosswise until it is ⅛–¼ inch thick, and about 14 inches wide. Trim the edges of the dough to reveal the lamination and reserve the scraps.

4   Cut the dough into 3½–4-inch squares, each weighing 50–60g/1¾–2¼ oz. Press into the cupcake or muffin pan.

5   Cover lightly and proof until the layers are pushing apart (see proofing instructions on page 302), between 1½–2 hours.

6   Preheat the oven to 425°F.

7   Cut out 3½–4 inches squares of parchment paper and press into the proofed pastries. Fill carefully with baking beans or raw rice. Brush the edges of the pastries gently with egg wash.

8   Turn down the oven to 400°F and bake the pastries for 16–18 minutes, turning after 12 minutes if needed. Remove the baking beans and paper and press the center of the cups to the edges, if needed, to create space. Return to the oven for 2 minutes to brown the middles. Cool completely.

9   For the panzanella mix, dice the peaches and tomatoes. Toss with the olive oil, vinegar, and salt. This can be made 24 hours in advance and kept refrigerated. When you are ready to assemble, stir in the thinly sliced basil and tear up the mozzarella into chunks, stirring it in.

10 Pile the filling into the pastry cups, 50–60g/1¾–2¼ oz per cup. Serve immediately. These do not keep well. Top each with a few fresh basil leaves.

CHOCOLATE-CHIP PAIN SUISSE

·

MAKES 6 PASTRIES

Techniques

Lamination	pg.69
Gluten development	pg.14
Fermentation	pg.76
Proofing	pg.79

350g/12¼ oz — unlaminated croissant dough (see page 298)

125g/½ cup plus 1 Tbsp — butter, very cold (for lamination)

½ x recipe — pastry cream (see page 338), beaten until smooth

40g/¼ cup — dark chocolate chips, about ¼ inch

Egg wash (see page 343)

The pain suisse is a shape that doesn't get enough love! Traditionally made with brioche, this version using croissant dough has the most spectacular layers. And who doesn't love custard and chocolate chips?

Day 1	Total: 12 hrs 40 mins	Day 2	Total: 16 hrs	Day 3			Total: 3 hrs 20 mins	
40 mins	12 hrs	4 hrs	12 hrs	50 mins	2 hrs	20 mins	10 mins	
Make dough	Let rest overnight	Laminate dough	Chill	Roll out dough & shape pastries	Proof pastries	Bake	Cool & serve	

1   Laminate the croissant dough with 3 single turns following the instructions on page 300.

2   For the final roll out, make sure the dough is rotated 90 degrees, so the folded edge is on either the right or left.

3   To cut, roll out the dough until it is about 11 inches in length, then roll it crosswise until it is about 12½ inches wide. It should be about ⅛ inch thick. Do not fight the dough—you can always put it in the fridge to rest, well-wrapped, for 20 minutes before continuing. Trim the edges of the dough to reveal the lamination. Reserve the scraps.

4   Spread the pastry cream over the middle third of the pastry. Sprinkle on the chocolate chips. Bring the top and bottom edges together to meet, sandwiching the pastry cream inside. Transfer the dough to the freezer for 20 minutes to chill.

5   Lightly flatten the chilled dough (be careful the custard doesn't splurge out), so it is 5½ inches long, then cut into 2-inch wide strips, weighing 70–80g/2½–3 oz per strip. Place them on a lined baking sheet so where the dough meets is facedown, leaving 1–2 inches of space in between for air flow. You may need to use more than one baking sheet.

6   Cover lightly and proof until jiggly (see proofing instructions on page 302), between 2–3½ hours.

7   Preheat the oven to 425°F.

8   Gently brush the pastries with egg wash. Turn down the oven to 400°F and bake the pastries for about 18 minutes, turning after 12 minutes if needed. Cool slightly and serve warm or cool completely on the tray.

9   The pastries are best served fresh. Store in an airtight container in the fridge for 2–3 days. Refresh in a 350°F oven for 5–10 minutes before eating.

Notes

Use extra cornstarch to make this pastry cream more stable (see note on page 338).

You can also make a savory version—use the extra thick bechamel recipe on page 342 and stuff with your favorite ingredients. I personally love a pickled jalapeño and nduja paste to give me some "American Hot" energy!

KOUIGN-AMANN SCRAPS

·

MAKES ABOUT 8 PASTRIES

Techniques

Lamination	pg.09
Gluten development	pg.14
Fermentation	pg.76
Proofing	pg.79

Equipment

Cupcake or muffin pan

350g/12¼oz	scraps from lamination (see Note)
100g/½ cup	granulated sugar, plus extra for the pan
10g/2 tsp	fine salt, decrease to taste
50g/¼ cup	butter, melted

The kouign-amann (pronounced koon-ya-mahn, merci to Claire for that translation!) is a pastry from Britanny that toes the line between salty and sweet—buttery laminated dough laced with sugar and salt and baked until crisp and caramelized. You can use regular croissant dough for this, but I personally think scrap dough makes fantastic kouign-amann.

Day 1	Total: 3 hrs 20 mins	Day 2		Total: 2 hrs 15 mins
20 mins	3 hrs	10 mins	1 hr 30 mins	35 mins
Re-roll dough scraps	Rest	Cut & dip in sugar	Proof	Bake & cool

1 Line up the lamination, as best you can, for all of your (cold!) scraps.

2 Roll out between two pieces of parchment paper and perform a single fold.

3 Rest in the fridge for 1–3 hours.

4 Roll out to ⅛ inch thick and cut into 4-inch squares. You will get about 8 squares.

5 Mix your sugar and salt together and check the flavor—start with half the amount of salt and add until it suits you. You want it to be salty and sweet at the same time. It will be quite intense. Make sure it is in a low, wide vessel for dipping.

6 Prepare your pan by adding a small spoonful of the sugar/salt mixture to the bottom of each hole. This will make the super-caramelized bottom.

7 To shape, brush one side of each pastry square with a very thin layer of melted butter and place, butter-side down, into the sugar/salt mixture. Brush the other side with melted butter, then flip the pastry over so it gets well coated.

8 Bring the edges of each square into the center and press together, then squish into the muffin/cupcake pan.

9 Cover lightly and proof until the pastries are splitting apart and puffy, 1½–2 hours.

10 Preheat the oven to 400°F.

11 Bake the pastries for 15–18 minutes, watching for color. While they are still warm, remove the pastries from the pan, otherwise the caramel will harden. Either flip the whole pan upside down onto a cooling rack as soon as they come out of the oven or, if you forget to do this, put the pastries back in the oven for 5 minutes to melt the caramel.

12 These will last for 3 days in a covered container but really are at their best on the first day, served cold.

Notes

Once you've mixed your sugar and salt together, give it a taste! If it's too salty for your taste, add more sugar! I would go for minimum 5% salt to sugar, but it's really up to you!

You can also make this recipe with 350g/12¼ oz croissant dough (see page 298).

PAN CON TOMATE DANISH

·

MAKES 8 DANISHES

Techniques

Lamination	pg.69
Gluten development	pg.14
Fermentation	pg.76
Proofing	pg.79

350g/12¼ oz	unlaminated croissant dough (see page 298)
125g/½ cup plus 1 Tbsp	butter, very cold (for lamination)
Egg wash (see page 343)	

Tomato mix

220g/8 oz	large ripe tomatoes
3g/1 tsp	flaky sea salt
5g/1 tsp	white wine vinegar
13g/1 Tbsp	extra-virgin olive oil

Plus

1	garlic clove, to finish

This is one of my favorite Danishes ever—so simple, but the combination of flaky pastry and the fresh tomato makes this a total winner.

Day 1	Total: 12 hrs 40 mins		Day 2	Total: 16 hrs		Day 3		Total: 3 hrs 20 mins	
40 mins		12 hrs	4 hrs		12 hrs	30 mins	2 hrs	20 mins	30 mins
Make dough		Let rest overnight	Laminate dough		Chill	Roll out dough & shape pastries	Proof pastries	Bake	Finish

1 Laminate the croissant dough with 3 x single turns following the instructions on page 300.

2 For the final roll out, make sure the dough is rotated 90 degrees, so the folded edge is either on the right or left. Roll out the dough until it is about 8 inches in length. Then roll it crosswise until it is ⅛–¼ inch thick, about 14 inches wide. Do not fight the dough—you can always put it in the fridge to rest, well-wrapped, for 20 minutes before continuing.

3 Trim the edges of the dough to reveal the lamination and reserve the scraps.

4 Cut the dough into 3½–4 inch squares that each weigh 50–60g/1¾–2¼ oz. Lightly score the dough where you will put the fillings, leaving a ½–¾ inch border. Place on a lined baking sheet.

5 Cover lightly and proof until the layers are pushing apart (see proofing instructions on page 302), between 1½–2 hours.

6 Preheat the oven to 425°F.

7 Press the Danish down in the center where you have scored to make an indentation. Gently brush the edges of the pastries with egg wash.

8 Turn down the oven to 400°F and bake the pastries for about 18 minutes, turning after 12 minutes if needed. Cool completely on a cooling rack.

9 For the tomato mix, grate the tomatoes coarsely, then combine with the rest of the ingredients. Cut the end off the garlic clove, then rub over the warm Danish pastries. Spoon 30g/1 oz of the tomato mix on top of each pastry, then serve immediately. These do not keep well once assembled.

CHEESY POTATO DANISH

·

MAKES 8 DANISHES

Techniques

Lamination	pg 69
Gluten development	pg.12
Fermentation	pg.76
Proofing	pg.79

350g/12¼ oz	unlaminated croissant dough (see page 298)
125g/½ cup plus 1 Tbsp	butter, very cold (for lamination)
3–4	small waxy potatoes, like fingerlings
Extra-virgin olive oil	
½ x recipe	extra-thick bechamel (see page 342)
Fresh thyme leaves	
Flaky sea salt	
Egg wash (see page 343)	

There are few combinations that give me more pleasure than the combination of crisp potatoes and cheese. Baked atop crisp croissant dough, this is a savory breakfast pastry-lover's dream.

Day 1	**Total:** 12 hrs 40 mins	Day 2	**Total:** 16 hrs	Day 3				**Total:** 3 hrs
40 mins	12 hrs	4 hrs	12 hrs	30 mins	2 hrs	10 mins	20 mins	
Make dough	Let rest overnight	Laminate dough	Chill	Roll out dough & shape pastries	Proof pastries	Fill	Bake	

1   Laminate the croissant dough with 3 single turns following the instructions on page 300.

2   For the final roll out, make sure the dough is rotated 90 degrees, so the folded edge is on either the right or left. Roll out the dough until it is about 8 inches in length. Then roll it crosswise until it is ⅛–¼ inch thick, and about 16 inches wide. Do not fight the dough—you can always put it in the fridge to rest, well-wrapped, for 20 minutes before continuing.

3   Trim the edges of the dough to reveal the lamination and reserve the scraps.

4   Cut the dough into 3½–4 inch squares, each weighing 50–60g/1¾–2¼ oz. Lightly score the dough where you will put the fillings, leaving a ½–¾-inch border. Place on a lined baking sheet.

5   Cover lightly and proof until the layers are pushing apart (see proofing instructions on page 302), between 1½–2 hours.

6   Preheat the oven to 425°F.

7   Slice your potatoes paper thin—¹⁄₁₆ inch thick, then toss in extra-virgin olive oil to prevent burning.

8   Press each Danish down in the center where you have scored to make an indentation. Pipe in a large spoonful-size blob of bechamel, then cover each Danish in sliced potatoes. Sprinkle with thyme leaves and flaky salt.

9   Gently brush the edges of the pastries with egg wash.

10 Turn down the oven to 400°F and bake the pastries for about 18 minutes, turning after 12 minutes if needed.

11 Let cool slightly on the sheet, but these are best served warm. Leftovers should be kept in an airtight container in the fridge and reheated at 350°F for 10 minutes.

ALMOND CROISSANTS 2.0

·

MAKES 7-8 CUBES

Sure, you could make an almond croissant by splitting open a plain croissant, filling it with frangipane, then rebaking it (for about 15 minutes at 350°F, by the way), but let me introduce you to the almond croissant 2.0. This is a dream pastry for me—dense croissant flakes soaked in cinnamon syrup, then interwoven with rich almond paste and baked until crisp.

Techniques

Baking with nuts	pg.55
Sugar syrup	pg.33

Equipment

Piping bag
2-inch/5cm square molds

4–5	leftover croissants
½ x recipe	frangipane (see page 339)

Powdered sugar, to dust

Cinnamon syrup

100g/½ cup	granulated sugar
100g/7 Tbsp	water
1 large	cinnamon stick

Total: 2 hrs 10 mins

15 mins	40 mins	20 mins	30 mins	25 mins
Mix frangipane	Make syrup	Divide pastries & fill molds	Bake	Cool & serve

1   To make the syrup, heat the ingredients together in a pan, then allow to cool and infuse for at least 30 minutes. Can be made up to 30 days in advance and kept in the fridge.

2   Preheat the oven to 400°F.

3   Tear the croissants up into 2–3¼-inch pieces. They can be different sizes and shapes—a mixture of middle bits and crust is good. Put the frangipane into a piping bag.

4   Soak the croissant pieces in the syrup, then alternate into the molds with frangipane until they are about 90% full. You should have 30–45g/1–1½ oz frangipane per mold and 40–55g/1½–2 oz syrup-soaked croissants.

5   Place the molds on a baking sheet, place a piece of parchment paper on top, then weigh down with a baking sheet on top.

6   Bake for 30 minutes. Let cool slightly in the molds, about 10 minutes, then turn out onto a cooling rack to cool completely. If desired, you can return them to the oven to brown the other edges for about 10 minutes at the same temperature. Once you are happy with the color, move to a rack to cool completely.

7   Dust with powdered sugar before serving. The croissants will keep in an airtight container for 2–3 days at room temperature but the powdered sugar will need to be reapplied.

RECIPES

EXTRAS

V

Compound butters   332
Brown butter   333
Caramelized nuts   334
Nut praline paste   334
Raspberry rhubarb jam   335
Tangerine marmalade   335
Basic poached fruit   336
Basic roasted fruit   336
Pastry cream   338
Frangipane   339
Basic ganache   340
Savoiardi cookies   340
Chocolate custard   341
Chocolate glaze   341
Vanilla crème anglaise   342
Extra-thick bechamel   342
Basic crumb   343
Egg wash   343

COMPOUND BUTTERS

·

MAKES ENOUGH TO LAMINATE 12¼ OZ/350G CROISSANT DOUGH

Techniques

Compound butters	pg.58

Roasted garlic butter

1	head of garlic
4–8g/1–2 tsp	olive oil
130g/½ cup plus 1 Tbsp	butter, softened

Speculoos spiced butter

125g/½ cup plus 1 Tbsp	butter, softened
½ tsp	ground ginger
½ tsp	ground cardamom
½ tsp	ground cinnamon
½ tsp	ground nutmeg

Nduja butter

| 135g/½ cup plus 2 Tbsp | butter, softened |
| 40g/1½ oz | nduja |

Chili crisp soy butter

110g/½ cup	butter, softened
25g/2 Tbsp	chili crisp oil
10g/2 tsp	light soy sauce
10g/⅓ oz	green onions, finely sliced

Cocoa butter

| 125g/½ cup plus 1 Tbsp | butter, softened |
| 25g/¼ cup | cocoa powder |

Once you are confident with laminating, you can have a lot of fun laminating with compound butters (see All About Fat on page 63). Because of the structure of the butters, these laminated doughs will work best as buns or flat shapes, rather than more complex shapes like pains au chocolat or croissants. When you laminate with compound butters, you have to make sure the butter is plastic before adding it in—this means you can bend it without it snapping.

Total: 1 hr 45 mins

1 hr 15 mins	10 mins	20 mins
Roast garlic	Mix	Chill

Roasted garlic butter

1 Preheat the oven to 400°F.

2 Remove the outer layers of papery garlic skin but leave the garlic head intact. Slice off the top, revealing the cloves. Place in foil and drizzle with the olive oil, then close the foil. Roast for 45 minutes–1 hour 15 minutes, until the cloves are golden and soft. Let cool completely.

3 For the butter, squeeze 25g/¾ oz of the roasted cloves into a bowl and mash. Add the softened butter and combine completely—try to get it as well combined as possible.

4 Scrape the butter onto parchment paper, then close the paper in a rectangle around it, about 5 x 6½ inches.

5 Chill completely before using.

Speculoos spiced butter

1 Mix all the ingredients together—as fully combined as possible.

2 Scrape the butter onto parchment paper, then close the paper in a rectangle around it, about 5 x 6½ inches.

3 Chill completely before using.

Nduja butter

1 Mix all the ingredients together—as fully combined as possible.

2 Scrape the butter onto parchment paper, then close the paper in a rectangle around it, about 5 x 6½ inches.

3 Chill completely before using.

Chili crisp soy butter

1 Mix all the ingredients together—as fully combined as possible.

2 Scrape the butter onto parchment paper, then close the paper in a rectangle around it, about 5 x 6½ inches.

3 Chill completely before using.

Cocoa butter

1 Mix all the ingredients together—as fully combined as possible.

2 Scrape the butter onto parchment paper, then close the paper in a rectangle around it, about 5 x 6½ inches.

3 Chill completely before using.

Note

All of these butter quantities have been formulated to work with 350g/12¼ oz croissant dough—the different sizes compensate for the varying ingredients, ensuring the fat content is similar across all of them.

BROWN
BUTTER

·

MAKES 1 CUP PLUS 2 TBSP/250G

Techniques

Maillard reaction	pg.84
Browning butter	pg.88

250g/1 cup   butter
plus 2 Tbsp

Browning butter is one of those little kitchen tricks that everyone should have up their sleeve—it's another way of seasoning your baking. No matter what you're making—from cookies to cakes to biscuits—brown butter can elevate your food and make people go "Omg, how did you do that?" or "Give me a second helping, immediately." Butter is made up of 80–84% fat, 1–3% milk proteins, and the rest is water. So, when you brown butter, what you're actually doing is browning the milk solids in butter. This always seemed pretty wild to me—all of that flavor from just a puny 1–2% Maillard reaction really is impressive (see All About Color on page 88).

Total: 1 hr 40 mins

10 mins	1 hr 30 mins
Brown butter	Cool

1   To brown the butter, melt it in a saucepan over medium heat. It will be noisy while all the water evaporates.

2   Once it goes quiet, it will be foamy and the butter will begin browning quickly. Use a spoon or spatula to scrape the milk solids as they will want to stick to the bottom of the pan.

3   Do your best to clear the foam and check the color of your brown butter. I like to go for a deep amber. As soon as it is the right color, take it off the heat and pour it into a heatproof container.

4   Depending on the recipe, you may need to use this in a warm liquid state, or you may need it to cool completely. You can do this at room temperature or speed it up by putting it into the fridge for 1½ hours. You can also pop it into the freezer for 20 minutes until cool and solid, then transfer it to the fridge.

CARAMELIZED NUTS

•

MAKES ABOUT 5¼ OZ/150G BRITTLE

Technique

Caramelization	pg.84

20g/4 tsp	water
75g/6 Tbsp	granulated sugar
100g/¾ cup	toasted nuts

Note

I like to toast nuts on a baking sheet, in a single layer, in the oven. Start with 350°F for 15–20 minutes and check the color.

Use this technique for well-coated caramelized nuts. For knobbly nuts like walnuts, it can be a real test of patience, but just trust the process!

Total: 30 mins

15 mins	15 mins
Make syrup	Stir in nuts and let sugar melt

1   Mix together the water and sugar in a small saucepan. Cover with a lid and heat until boiling (this helps prevent early crystallization), then remove the lid and cook until it is 293°F—the syrup will be very thick and viscous.

2   Turn off the heat and add the nuts. Stir vigorously. At first the mixture will just look sticky, but eventually, as you keep stirring, the sugar crystals will form on the nuts. Keep stirring until all the sugar has crystallized, then continue heating until the crystallized sugar caramelizes.

3   Finally, pour the nuts into a clean, heatproof container. Store in an airtight container at room temperature for 3 months.

NUT PRALINE PASTE

•

MAKES ABOUT 10½ OZ/300G PASTE

Techniques

Caramelization	pg.84

Equipment
Blender

100g/½ cup	granulated sugar
200g/1½ cups	roasted nuts, e.g., almonds, hazelnuts, peanuts, pistachios
10–20g/2–4 tsp	warm water (optional)

This is a basic formula to get you started making nut praline pastes. You need both a decent blender and some patience to get the paste smooth, but it's very satisfying when it happens!

Total: 1hr 15 mins

15 mins	30 mins	30 mins
Make caramel and add nuts	Cool	Blend

1   Melt the sugar in a saucepan, constantly stirring, until an amber caramel forms. Turn off the heat, add the nuts, and stir to coat. Pour onto a greased piece of parchment paper and let cool completely.

2   Once cool, transfer to a blender and blend for 5 minutes, then rest for 5 minutes, then blend for 5 minutes. Continue this until you achieve a smooth paste. In my blender, it takes about 30 minutes including breaks.

3   Some mixtures may benefit from a little warm water to help the oils emulsify. If you are having trouble blending, try adding a little at a time.

4   Store in an airtight container at room temperature for 1 month.

PRESERVES

•

MAKES ABOUT 1½ CUPS/500G (ENOUGH FOR 2 SMALL JARS)

Techniques

Sugar as a preserve	pg.29
Setting with pectin	pg.95
Macerating	pg.30

Raspberry rhubarb jam

350g/12¼ oz	rhubarb
150g/1¼ cups	raspberries
25g/2 Tbsp	lemon juice
275g/1 cup plus 6 Tbsp	granulated sugar

Tangerine marmalade

240g/8½ oz	tangerines
120g/½ cup	water
20g/4 tsp	lemon juice
160g/¾ cup plus 1 Tbsp	granulated sugar

Notes

The signs of readiness include:

- Bubbles slow down and look visibly thicker and glossier. When you lift your spatula out of the jam, it will cling to it.

- To test, put a small spoonful of jam/marmalade onto a cold plate (keep a few in your freezer) and return to the freezer for 2–3 minutes. If it is set/wrinkles when pressed, it's ready!

- Alternatively, you can also swipe your finger through the middle of the spooned jam/marmalade on the chilled plate, and if it's ready, the line won't fill.

The world of preserves is a marvelous one (and I will say now I learned almost everything I know about jamming from the fantastic Camilla Wynne!). I just love how you can taste summer in the middle of winter, and vice versa. These recipes are two jumping off points for you to get started with. You can judge jams by temperature, but it's good to use your other senses, too.

Total: 27 hrs

1 hr	2 hrs	24 hrs
Macerate fruit	Cook preserve	Set

Raspberry rhubarb jam

1   Cut up the rhubarb into 1¼-inch pieces and place into a large saucepan with the raspberries and lemon juice. Add the sugar and gently combine. If you have time, macerate overnight at room temperature, but let rest for at least 1 hour. You can also macerate (covered) in the fridge for up to 1 week.

2   Before cooking the jam, place a plate or ramekin in the freezer so you can test the jam. If you want to store the jam, prepare clean jars by baking them upside down in a preheated 275°F oven for 20 minutes.

3   When you are ready to make the jam, heat the fruit over medium-high heat and bring the mixture to a boil, stirring regularly. As it starts to thicken, I suggest lowering the temperature so you can get the set just right. Check for signs of readiness. When the jam is ready, the thermometer should read 219°F (see Notes).

4   Pour into a heatproof container and allow to set (I keep my jam in the fridge in an airtight container for several months). Alternatively, pour into your sterilized jars, seal with lids, invert for 5 minutes, then place the right way up and allow the jam to set for at least 24 hours at room temperature.

Tangerine marmalade

1   Peel the tangerines and thinly slice the skin into strips with a sharp knife, removing any thick stalk bits/eyes. Roughly chop the tangerines and remove the seeds.

2   Add the peels and water to a large saucepan and simmer uncovered until soft, 10–15 minutes. Next, add the citrus flesh, lemon juice, and sugar

3   Before cooking the marmalade, place a plate or ramekin in the freezer so you can test the set of the marmalade. If you want to store the jam, prepare clean jars by baking them upside down in a preheated 275°F oven for 20 minutes.

4   Now, cook the marmalade over high (!) heat, with lots of stirring, until it reaches 220.1–221°F and looks ready (see Notes).

5   Pour into a clean, heatproof container and allow to set (I keep my marmalade in the fridge in an airtight container for several months). Alternatively, pour into your sterilized jars, seal with lids, invert for 5 minutes, then place the right way up and allow the marmalade to set for at least 24 hours at room temperature.

BASIC POACHED FRUIT

·

MAKES ABOUT 1 LB 2 OZ/500G (DEPENDING ON THE FRUIT)

Technique

Poaching fruit	pg.107

250g/1¼ cups	granulated sugar
500g/2 cups plus 2 Tbsp	liquid (wine or water)
Aromatics, like loose-leaf tea, whole spices, vanilla pod	
25g/2 Tbsp	lemon juice
500g/1 lb 2 oz	your choice of fresh fruit

Note

The liquid you use can change depending on what you are making. For example, red wine poached pears is a classic, while peaches may be better in a lemon verbena tea.

For poaching liquids, I like to start with a basic ratio of 1:2 sugar to liquid, plus a little lemon juice always helps. You can scale this poaching liquid up or down, depending on how much fruit you have to cook. Adjust it to suit your taste!

Total: 1 hr 20 mins

10 mins	40 mins	30 mins
Make poaching liquid	Poach fruit	Cool

1 In a large, wide saucepan (scale up the pan size, depending on how much fruit you are poaching), dissolve the sugar well in the liquid, then add the aromatics and lemon juice. Bring to a boil, then turn the heat right down. Add your fruit, either halved or whole, snugly into the pan in a single layer.

2 Place a piece of parchment paper on top of the liquid (a cartouche) to stop the fruit from bobbing up. Poach the fruit gently until there is no resistance when you pierce it with a sharp knife. Depending on the ripeness, this could take anywhere from 5 to 40 minutes. Soft stone fruits, like plums, peaches, or apricots, will be faster, while firmer fruits, like pears, will take longer.

3 Once ready, transfer the fruit from the hot liquid to a clean, heatproof container. Wait for the poaching liquid to cool down to room temperature, then pour it over the fruit.

4 Store the poached fruit in its liquid in the fridge for 3–5 days.

BASIC ROASTED FRUIT

·

MAKES ABOUT 7 OZ/200G (DEPENDING ON THE FRUIT)

Technique

Sugar syrup	pg.33

250g/9 oz	fresh fruit
25–50g/ 2–4 Tbsp	granulated sugar
25–50g/ 2–3 Tbsp	liquid, like sweet white wine or tea or citrus juice

Note

For soft fruits like strawberries, low and slow tends to work better! See roasted strawberry Victoria sponge on page 140.

This works well for stone fruits and other firm fruits that can take a bit of color—peaches are a firm favorite!

Total: 45 mins

5 mins	40 mins
Mix	Roast fruit

1 Preheat the oven to 400°F. Line a baking sheet with parchment paper.

2 Halve the fruit, mix with the sugar and liquid, and add to the lined baking sheet in a single layer. Roast until slightly collapsed and surrounded by syrup. Depending on the fruit, this could be anywhere from 15 to 40 minutes.

3 Let cool, then move to an airtight container, and store in the fridge for up to 1 week.

PASTRY CREAM

•

MAKES 1 LB 2 OZ/500G

Also known as crème pâtissière, this is a starch-stabilized custard that can be used for fillings. Thanks to the starch, it is oven-stable, making it very useful for viennoiserie. The exact amount of starch used may vary among bakers, but it tends to be 6–10%. You can vary this depending on how thick you want the final cream to be. The recipe below is about 7.5% starch to liquid, giving it a medium set.

Techniques

Starch gelatinization	pg.20
Egg coagulation	pg.40

330g/1⅓ cups	whole milk
5–10g/1–2 tsp	good quality vanilla bean paste or extract or 1 vanilla pod, scraped (optional)
65g/¼ cup plus 1 Tbsp	granulated sugar
80g/4	egg yolks (see Note)
25g/3½ Tbsp	cornstarch
15g/1 Tbsp	butter, cold

Total: 45 mins

10 mins	5 mins	30 mins
Heat mixture	Temper eggs & cook until thick	Strain through sieve & cool

1   Heat the milk, vanilla, and half the sugar in a pan over medium heat until simmering. Adding the sugar at this stage helps to prevent the milk solids from scorching.

2   Whisk the egg yolks with the cornstarch and the remaining sugar.

3   Once the milk is bubbling, pour a little over the egg yolks to temper and then add the rest and return the whole mixture to the stovetop. Cook—whisking all the time—until the mixture is thick and bubbling, about 1 minute. Whisk in the cold butter.

4   Pour into a clean, heatproof container, straining through a sieve, then cover and cool completely. Parchment paper or plastic wrap touching the surface will help prevent a skin from forming.

5   As it cools, it will turn into a jelly-like texture and it will need to be beaten with a whisk before using. Pastry cream lasts for 3 days in an airtight container in the fridge.

Crème légère

Once the pastry cream has cooled, whisk until smooth. Whip up to 100% of the weight in heavy cream to soft peaks, then fold into the pastry cream. The amount of cream you use will depend on the texture you want—the more whipped cream you add, the lighter the resulting cream.

Crème mousseline

Once the pastry cream has cooled, whisk until smooth. Add softened butter, bit by bit, and whip until a rich, luscious cream forms. Although you can play around with this ratio, a good ratio of butter to mousseline cream is about 30% (150g/5¼ oz) of the pastry cream weight. If your mousseline splits, try warming the bowl slightly, then rewhipping.

Crème chiboust

Once the pastry cream has cooled, whisk until smooth. You can play around with the ratio, but make an Italian meringue up to 100% of the pastry cream weight (500g/1 lb 2 oz), then fold together.

Crème diplomat

When making the pastry cream, bloom 3g/1 tsp powdered gelatin or 1 gelatin leaf (see page 100; I use Dr. Oetker Platinum) in cold water (then squeeze out if using a leaf). When the pastry cream is ready, whisk the bloomed gelatin into the hot pastry cream, then strain through a sieve to remove any lumps. Once cooled, whisk until smooth, then whip up to 50% of the weight (250g/9 oz) in heavy cream and fold into the pastry cream.

Crème madame

Once the pastry cream has cooled, whisk until smooth. Add 10–20% of the pastry cream weight in soft butter (50–100g/1¾–3½ oz), piece by piece. If your cream splits, try warming the bowl slightly, then rewhipping. Once smooth, fold in 10–20% of the pastry cream weight in whipped cream (50–100g/1¾–3½ oz).

Note

Use whole eggs for a less pigmented and rich cream. Increase the cornstarch to 30g/¼ cup for a firmer set that may be more suitable for baking (e.g., for Danish pastries). You can also decrease the egg yolks to 60g (3) for a less rich cream.

FRANGIPANE

·

EACH RECIPE MAKES 1 LB 7 OZ/650G FRANGIPANE

Techniques

Creaming	pg.59
Baking with nuts	pg.55

Classic frangipane

165g/¾ cup	butter, softened
165g/¾ cup plus 1 Tbsp	granulated sugar
105g/2	whole eggs
165g/1¾ cups	almond flour (can be subbed for other finely ground nuts)
40g/⅓ cup	all-purpose flour
4g/1¼ tsp	flaky sea salt
2g/¼ tsp	almond extract (optional)
4g/1 tsp	good quality vanilla extract (optional)

Chocolate frangipane

100g/7 Tbsp	butter, softened
100g/½ cup	granulated sugar
50g/1	whole egg
100g/1 cup	almond flour
25g/3 Tbsp	all-purpose flour
10g/2 Tbsp	cocoa powder
1–2g/¼–½ tsp	flaky sea salt
75g/2½ oz	chocolate, chopped

The classic buttery, almondy filling that goes the distance. You can adapt this base recipe by changing the nuts, browning the butter, or adding chocolate or cocoa powder. Straight from the fridge, frangipane is very firm, so it's sometimes best to make it just before you're ready to use it or make sure you have time to allow it to come to room temperature.

Total: 10 mins

5 mins	5 mins
Cream butter & sugar	Mix

Classic frangipane

1 Beat together the butter and granulated sugar until combined. You don't need to aerate it, but make sure there are no lumps of butter.

2 Add the eggs and mix until combined, scraping the bowl as needed, then stir in your dry ingredients and the extracts, if using.

3 The frangipane is now ready to use immediately or it can be stored in an airtight container in the fridge for 5 days.

Chocolate frangipane

1 Beat together the butter and granulated sugar until combined. You don't need to aerate it, but make sure there are no lumps of butter.

2 Add the egg and mix until combined, scraping the bowl as needed, then stir in your almond flour, all-purpose flour, cocoa powder, and salt.

3 Melt the chocolate over a bain-marie, then add it to the mixture in one go, stirring until combined.

4 The frangipane is now ready to use immediately or it can be stored in an airtight container in the fridge for 5 days.

Note

You can use other nuts for frangipane, but be aware of the varying fat content between them (see page 55) and adjust accordingly.

BASIC GANACHE

•

MAKES ABOUT 8 OZ/220G GANACHE

Techniques

Ganache	pg.63
Emulsification	pg.61

100g/7 Tbsp	heavy cream
100g/3½ oz	dark chocolate (see page 63 for ratios)
20g/1½ Tbsp	butter (adds shine and softness, optional)

Note

Milk chocolate will make a less firm ganache than dark chocolate. Lower-quality chocolate with lots of stabilizers may not emulsify well.

The ratio of a ganache changes depending on what you are using it for—a whipped ganache, for example, tends to have a higher ratio of cream to chocolate. A good place to start for standard ganache, which can be scooped and enjoyed as truffles or poured into tart cases, is 1:1 cream to chocolate. See All About Fat on page 63.

Total: 45 mins

10 mins	5 mins	30 mins
Heat cream	Pour over chocolate & whisk	Cool

1   In a medium saucepan, heat the cream until simmering.

2   Chop up the chocolate into pieces—¼–½ inch—and put into a heatproof bowl.

3   Pour the hot cream over the chocolate and let stand for 1 minute before whisking to a smooth ganache. You don't need to incorporate air, you just need the mixture to be fully combined.

4   If using the butter, add with the chocolate into the bowl before adding the cream.

5   If it splits, whisk in 1 teaspoon of hot (140–158°F) water at a time.

6   Let cool, then cover and move to the fridge. Store for 3 days.

SAVOIARDI COOKIES

•

MAKES 2 X 6-INCH CIRCLE LAYERS OR CAN BE PIPED AS
LADYFINGERS AND USED IN TIRAMISU, ETC.

Techniques

Egg foam	pg.45
Folding	pg.113

50g/1	whole egg, separated
25g/2 Tbsp	granulated sugar
20g/3 Tbsp	all-purpose flour

This light cookie mixture is useful for making your own sponge fingers for trifle or tiramisu, or for layering up a banana pudding.

Total: 40 mins

15 mins	10 mins	15 mins
Make batter	Pipe	Bake

1   Preheat the oven to 375°F.

2   Whisk the egg yolk with half of the sugar and set aside.

3   Whisk the egg white and the remaining sugar to a French meringue following the instructions on page 118.

4   Fold the two mixes together, then sift the flour on top and fold in.

5   Use as required. Depending on the size and shape, bake for 10–14 minutes, until golden. Cool on a baking sheet.

6   Can be made 3 days ahead and kept, well-wrapped, at room temperature.

CHOCOLATE CUSTARD

·

MAKES ABOUT 1 LB 2 OZ/500G CUSTARD

Technique

Egg coagulation	pg.40

250g/1 cup	whole milk
60g/¼ cup plus 1 Tbsp	granulated sugar
5g/2 tsp	cocoa powder
15g/2 Tbsp	cornstarch
45g/about 3	egg yolks
60g/2¼ oz	dark chocolate, chopped
1–2g/about ½ tsp	salt
75g/5 Tbsp	heavy cream

A super-lush filling that works with everything—particularly good inside choux, but spread it on cakes or just eat it with a spoon!

Total: 45 mins

5 mins	10 mins	20 mins	10 mins
Heat milk	Temper eggs & cook until thick	Stir in chocolate, strain & cool	Whip & fold in cream

1   Heat the milk and half the sugar together in a pan over medium heat.

2   In a separate bowl, whisk together the remaining sugar, the cocoa powder, cornstarch, and egg yolks. Temper the egg yolks by gradually whisking in some of the hot milk. Pour everything back into the pan and cook over medium heat until thickened, stirring.

3   Stir in the chopped chocolate and salt, then strain the mixture through a sieve and let it cool, placing parchment paper or plastic wrap on top to prevent a skin from forming. This can be made 3 days in advance. Keep in an airtight container in the fridge.

4   Once cool, whisk the custard until smooth. Whip the heavy cream to very soft peaks, then fold into the custard. This can also be made 3 days in advance.

CHOCOLATE GLAZE

·

MAKES ABOUT 9 OZ/250G GLAZE

140g/5 oz	dark chocolate, chopped
100g/7 Tbsp	butter
20g/1 Tbsp	golden syrup

This simple glaze is perfect for dipping profiteroles or eclairs in—it's shiny and has good lasting power.

Total: 15 mins

10 mins	5 mins
Mix	Cool

1   To make the glaze, heat everything together in a bain-marie with a pinch of salt and stir until combined. Allow to cool till about 95°F so it thickens slightly, making it easier to dip.

2   This can be stored in an airtight container at room temperature for 3 days or in the fridge for 1 week.

VANILLA CRÈME ANGLAISE

·

MAKES 1 LB 2 OZ/500G

Techniques

Egg coagulation	pg.40
Infusions	pg.110

200g/¾ cup plus 2 Tbsp	whole milk
200g/¾ cup plus 2 Tbsp	heavy cream
1	vanilla pod, scraped, or 10g/2 tsp good quality vanilla extract
50g/¼ cup	granulated sugar
50g/about 3	egg yolks

This is a classic pouring custard that you can enjoy with pretty much anything. Pay attention to the way it thickens—you want it to coat the back of a spoon. If you're not confident on knowing when it's ready, a thermometer is your best friend here!

Total: 50 mins

10 mins	10 mins	30 mins
Heat mixture	Temper eggs & cook until thick	Strain through sieve & cool

1 Heat the milk, heavy cream, scraped vanilla seeds (or extract), and half the sugar together in a pan over medium heat.

2 Meanwhile, whisk the egg yolks with the rest of the sugar.

3 When the milk/cream is simmering, pour a little over the egg yolks and whisk to temper the egg.

4 Pour the tempered egg mixture back into the pan and set the heat to low. Stir the mixture constantly until it visibly thickens and coats the spoon. You can also check it using a probe thermometer; 176–180°F is good.

5 Strain through a sieve and let cool completely with plastic wrap touching the surface to prevent a skin from forming.

6 Keeps in an airtight container for up to 5 days in the fridge.

EXTRA-THICK BECHAMEL

·

MAKES ABOUT 12¼ OZ/350G

Techniques

Thickening with starch	pg.94
Starch gelatinization	pg.20

40g/3 Tbsp	butter
50g/6 Tbsp	all-purpose flour
210g/¾ cup plus 2 Tbsp	whole milk
3g/1 tsp	flaky sea salt
Pinch of black pepper	
85g/¾ cup	grated cheese, like Cheddar

This bechamel is good for piping inside buns and pastries that will get baked.

Total: 50 mins

5 mins	15 mins	30 mins
Make roux	Add milk, heat & whisk	Chill

1 Melt the butter in a saucepan over medium heat. Add the flour and cook into a paste, i.e., your roux.

2 Slowly add the milk, a few large spoonfuls at a time, whisking a lot to avoid lumps.

3 Once all the milk is added and there are no lumps, lower the heat, and season with the salt and some pepper. Finally, stir in the cheese and stir until it's completely melted.

4 Pour into a shallow dish, cool, cover, and chill in the fridge. Bechamel needs to be totally cold when you use it. This can be made up to 3 days ahead of time, kept covered in the fridge.

BASIC CRUMB

·

MAKES 7 OZ/200G

Technique

Maillard reaction	pg.84

150g/1 cup plus 3 Tbsp	all-purpose flour
1g/¼ tsp	flaky sea salt
50g/¼ cup	granulated sugar
100g/7 Tbsp	butter

Notes

For a clumpy oat crumble, sub 60g/½ cup of the all-purpose flour for rolled oats and the granulated sugar for soft light brown sugar.

This also works well made with brown butter (see page 333).

The simple 1, 2, 3 ratio of sugar, butter, flour never fails! Play around with the sugar and flour or add ground spices or zest.

Total: 40 mins

5 mins	20 mins	15 mins
Mix	Bake	Cool

1 Preheat the oven to 350°F.

2 Stir together the flour, salt, and sugar.

3 Melt the butter and then pour over the top. Using a fork, agitate the mixture until it forms uneven crumbs. Taste and adjust the seasoning with extra salt or sugar, if needed. Spread the crumb mixture evenly on a baking sheet lined with parchment paper.

4 Bake the crumb mixture for 15–20 minutes or until golden. Let cool completely on the baking sheet.

5 This keeps for 5 days in an airtight container at room temperature.

EGG WASH

Technique

Maillard reaction	pg.84

100g/2	whole eggs
1g/⅛ tsp	fine salt

An all-purpose egg wash for pastries and bread alike. The salt helps break down the eggs to make it easier to brush on.

Total: 5 mins

5 mins
Mix

1 Whisk everything together until combined, then leave for at least 20 minutes before using so the eggs break down. This can be made 3 days in advance and kept in an airtight container in the fridge.

MATRIX OF JOY

	Pastry cream pg.388	Jam pg.335	Frangipane pg.339	Lemon curd pg.156	Chocolate ganache pg.340	Apple compote pg.268
Sweet pastry/sablé Breton pg.119	Fruit custard tarts / Flan pâtissiére	Jam tarts / Linzer cookies	Bakewell tart		Chocolate tartlets / Sandwich cookies	
Pie dough pg.129	Custard pie	Flaky jam tarts		Lemon meringue pie	No-bake chocolate cream pie	Mini apple pies
Puff pastry pg.124/128	Mille-feuille/ vanilla slice		Galette des rois			
Brioche/bun dough pg.133	Custard swirl buns	Classic jam doughnuts	Frangipane stuffed buns	Lemon doughnuts		Apple doughnuts—add caramel sauce!
Choux pg.136	Custard choux buns			Lemon meringue choux buns	Filled choux buns	Apple pie choux buns
Chocolate cake pg.238						
Meringue pg.118				Fruit meringue roulade		
Chiffon/ Genoise pp.131/151	Boston cream pie			Light lemon sandwich cake		

The best thing about mastering one recipe is realizing that it has the potential to unlock so many more great bakes. Here are a few ideas to get you started on mixing and matching some of the recipes in this book. I can't wait to see what you come up with!

Whipped cream pg.273	Whipped ganache pg.160	Panna cotta pg.215	Fresh fruit	Vanilla parfait pg.227	Marshmallow pg.198	Banana pudding pg.248
		Vanilla panna cotta tart with fresh fruit			Tea cakes	
					S'mores	
			Fruit pies			
	Mille feuille		Tarte fine aux pommes			
Cream buns Devonshire splits	Filled doughnuts			Ice cream sandwich		Banana pudding maritozzo
Profiteroles	Filled choux buns					
			Black forest Gateau with whipped cream			
Pavlova			Eton mess	Baked Alaska		Banana pudding pavlova
Swiss roll						

00 flour, 18
3-day Focaccia, 280–01
3pm Oat Cookies, 194

A

acetate liners, 9
acids
    and browning, 87–88
    and dairy, 101
    and eggs, 41, 46
    and fat, 56
    and gelatin, 100
    and pectin, 95
    and texture, 92
aeration, 73
    and eggs, 45–47
    fat, 59–60
    rising, 68
    and sugar, 31
agar agar, 93
alcohol
    frozen desserts, 97
    and gluten, 14, 19
all-purpose flour, 18
almonds, 55
    Almond Croissants 2.0, 329
    Amarettis, 188
    Apricot and Rosemary Polenta Cake, 148
    Chocolate Frangipane, 339
    Frangipane, 339
    Lemon Pistachio Amaretti, 188
Amarettis, 188
    Lemon Pistachio Amaretti, 188
amino acids, 39, 100
Any Galette, 168
apples, 344
    air content, 73
    Apple and Vanilla Charlotte, 268–69
    Tart Apple Granita, 224
    Orchard Turnovers, 211
apricots
    Apricot and Rosemary Polenta Cake, 148
    Apricot Custard Mille-Feuille, 270
    Coriander and Panela Cake, 143
autolyse, 16

B

Babka, Milk Bread Spring Onion, 258
bacteria, sugar and, 29
bagels, 21
bain-marie. See water baths
baked custard, 42, 93
baker's percentages, 22
baking, 107
    baking process, 104
    carryover cooking, 105
    knowing when it is ready, 106–7
    rise and fall, 105
    temperatures, 105
baking beans, 109
baking powder, 74–75
baking sheets, 8, 112
bananas
    Banana Pudding Pie, 248–49

Brown Butter Banana Cookies, 184
béchamel, 94, 342
beet sugars, 26
baking soda, 28, 74–75
biga, 81
blackberries
    Black n Glaze, 221
    Lemon Curd Meringue Tarts with
        Blackberries, 156
blind baking, 109, 121
Blonde Rice Pudding, 222–23
bran, 17
Brazil nuts, 55
bread. See also brioche
    Milk Bread Spring Onion Babka, 258
    3-day focaccia, 280–81
bread-and-butter pudding, 212
bread-making
    baker's percentages, 22
    color, 89
    eggs in, 39
    enriched breads, 22
    flours, 12, 14, 17, 18
    kneading dough, 15
    milk bread, 122
    no-knead bread, 16
    rising, 76–77, 81
    starch gelatinization, 21
    sugar content, 29
brioche, 20, 22, 54, 99, 133–35, 344–45
    bread-and-butter pudding, 212
    Olive Oil Brie-oche, 261
brown butter, 56, 88, 333
    Brown Butter Banana Cookies, 184
brown sugar, 46
    Brown Sugar Canelé, 262
    brown sugar custard tart, 163
browning. See color
bubbles, knowing when it is ready, 106
buckwheat flour, 14, 18
building a bake, 114
bun dough, 123
buns, 301
    Festive Buns, 179
    French Toast Cinnamon Buns, 254–56
    Hot Cross Buns, 179
    Seasonal Maritozzo, 252–53
    Spiced Pumpkin Buns, 175–76
    Swirly Buns, 310
butter, 52, 53, 56, 57–58
    brown butter, 88, 333
    Chile Maple Butter, 175
    compound butters, 58, 332
    croissants, 295
    Inverted Puff Pastry, 72
    laminated pastries, 69–72
    plasticizing, 56
    butter caramels, 86
buttercream
    Chocolate Buttercream, 238
    Golden Syrup Buttercream, 189
    Honey, Rosemary, and Orange Swiss
        Meringue Buttercream, 241–42
    Salted Vanilla Buttercream, 245

splitting, 64
buttermilk, 56, 60
    Flaky Cheese and Pickle Scones, 183
    Steamed Plum Buttermilk Sponge Cake, 155
butterscotch icing, 254–56

C

cake flour, 18
cake-making
cake pans, 8, 9
    cooling, 104
    doming, 104
    knowing when it is ready, 106
    oxidation, 88
    rise and fall, 105
    splitting batter, 64
    starch gelatinization, 21
    sugar content, 29
cakes
    Apricot and Rosemary Polenta Cake, 148
    Chamomile and Toasted Flour Chiffon
        Cake, 151
    Citrus, Olive Oil, and Cream Cheese Dome,
        241–42
    Coriander and Panela Cake, 143
    Horchata Tres Leches, 234–35
    Mango Shortcake with Candied Lime, 237
    Marble Cake with Chocolate Frosting, 144
    Mocha Passionfruit Opera Cake, 288–90
    Plum and Mascarpone Karpatka, 204–5
    Rhubarb and Custard Crumb Cake, 232
    Ricotta, Marmalade, and Hazelnut
        Chocolate-Chip Cake, 147
    Roasted Strawberry Victoria Sponge, 140
    Salted Vanilla and Pistachio Layer Cake,
        243–45
    Secret Chocolate Cake, 266
    Steamed Plum Buttermilk Sponge Cake, 155
    Ultimate Chocolate Cake, 238
    Upside-Down Sticky Pear and Walnut
        Cake, 152
cane sugars, 26
canelé, 9, 20
    Brown Sugar Canelé, 262
caramel
    Baked Lemon Custard Brûlée, 216
    Banana Pudding Pie, 248–49
    Caramel Mandarins, 212
    Caramel Poached Oranges, 207
    Caramel Sauce, 88, 268–69
    Caramelized Nuts, 334
    Caramelized Peanuts, 218–19
    Caramelized Walnuts, 265
    Crème Brûlée, 99
    dry, 86
    Freezer Soft Caramel, 276
    Mocha Passionfruit Opera Cake, 288–90
    Nut Praline Paste, 334
    Tomato and Fennel Tarte Tatin, 167
    wet, 96
caramelization, 84–88
    honey, 87
    puff pastry, 127
    stages, 33

sugar, 31
temperatures, 33
carbon dioxide, 68, 74
carrageenan, 93
carryover cooking, 105
cashews, 55
Chamomile and Toasted Flour Chiffon
    Cake, 151
Charlotte, Apple and Vanilla, 268–69
cheese. See also mascarpone; ricotta
    Cheesy Potato Danish, 326
    Extra-Thick Bechamel, 342
    Flaky Cheese and Pickle Scones, 183
    Olive Oil Brie-oche, 261
    Peach Panzanella Deep-Dish Danish, 320
cheesecakes, 44, 93, 94, 112
    Feta Whipped Cheesecake, 265
    Lemon Basque Cheesecake, 208
chemical rising agents, 74–75
Cherry Danish, St. Honoré, 317
Chicken Pie with Rich Pastry, 173
Chiffon Cake, 344–45
    Chamomile and Toasted Flour Chiffon
        Cake, 151
Chile Crisp Soy Butter, 332
Chile Maple Butter, 175
Cucumber-Jalapeño Granita, 224
chocolate
    3pm Oat cookies, 194
    Amarettis, 188
    Banana Pudding Pie, 248–9
    Blonde Rice Pudding, 222–23
    Chocolate Buttercream, 238
    Chocolate Cake, 344–45
    Chocolate-Chip Pain Suisse, 321
    Chocolate Crémeux, 159
    Chocolate Custard, 341
    Chocolate Frangipane, 339
    Chocolate Glaze, 290, 341
    Chocolate, Peanut, and Coconut
        Twice-Baked Cookies, 187
    Chocolate Peanut Ice Cream Bars, 276
    Chocolate Squiggles, 315
    Choconut Tart, 159
    Cocoa Butter, 332
    DIY Mint Viennese Ice Cream Cake, 228
    Festive Buns, 179
    Fig and Chocolate Focaccia, 281
    ganache, 63, 64, 290, 340, 344
    Maple Pretzel Buttercrunch, 201
    Marble Cake with Chocolate Frosting, 144
    melting, 62, 63
    Miso Walnut Double-Thick Chocolate-Chip
        Cookies, 197
    Mocha Granita, 224–25
    Mocha Passionfruit Opera Cake, 288–90
    Pain au Chocolate, 301, 302, 307
    Panna Cotta with Burnt White Chocolate
        and Soy, 215
    Ricotta, Marmalade, and Hazelnut
        Chocolate-Chip Cake, 147
    Salted Double-Chocolate Shortbread, 193
    Secret Chocolate Cake, 266
    tempering, 63

Tiramichoux, 284–86
toasting white chocolate, 88, 215
Ultimate Chocolate Cake, 238
and water, 62
choux pastry, 20, 21, 136, 344–45
    Choux Ice Cream Sandwich, 273
    Craquelin, 137
    Crullers, 221
    PBJ Paris Brest, 218–19
    Plum and Mascarpone Karpatka, 204–5
    Tiramichoux, 284–86
cinnamon
    Cinnamon Syrup, 329
    French Toast Cinnamon Buns, 254–56
    Vanilla Cinnamon Glaze, 221
Citrus, Olive Oil, and Cream Cheese Dome,
    241–42
citrus zest, infusions, 111
clarified butter, 56
coagulation, eggs, 40–42
cocoa butter, 53, 56, 332
coconut
    Chocolate, Peanut, and Coconut Twice-Baked
        Biscuits, 187
    Choconut Tart, 159
coconut oil, 53, 56
coffee
    infusions, 111
    Mocha Granita, 224–25
    Mocha Passionfruit Opera Cake, 288–90
    Tiramichoux, 284–86
    Ultimate Chocolate Cake, 238
    Whipped Coffee Ganache, 290
cold proofing, 80
colloids, 61
color, 82–89
    and fermentation, 89
    knowing when it is ready, 106
    Maillard reaction vs. caramelization, 84–88
    and sound, 87
    and steaming, 88
compotes, 93
compound butters, 58, 332
condensed milk, 56, 97
    Horchata Tres Leches, 234–35
    Panna Cotta with Burnt White Chocolate and
        Soy, 215
contrast, texture, 99
cookies, 104
    3pm Oat Cookies, 194
    Amarettis, 188
    Banana Pudding Pie, 248–49
    Brown Butter Banana Cookies, 184
    Chocolate, Peanut, and Coconut Twice-Baked
        Cookies, 187
    Golden Syrup Crunch Cookies, 189
    Langues de Chat, 207
    Lemon Pistachio Amaretti, 188
    Miso Walnut Double-Thick Chocolate-Chip
        Cookies, 197
    Salted Double-Chocolate Shortbread, 193
    Salted Vanilla Shortbread, 192
    Savoiardi Cookies, 340
    sugar content, 29

cooling bakes, 104
Coriander and Panela Cake, 143
corn syrup, 27
cracking, 105
craquelin, 137
    Tiramichoux, 284–86
cream. See also custard; ice cream
    Banana Pudding Pie, 248–49
    Brown Sugar Custard Tart, 163
    Chocolate Crémeux, 159
    Chocolate Ganache, 63, 64, 290, 340, 344
    Crème Légère, 310, 316
    fat content, 60
    freezing, 96–97
    Honey Cream, 151
    mango shortcake, 237
    Noyaux Cream, 270
    Passionfruit Posset Flower Tarts, 160
    piping, 60
    posset, 101
    splitting, 64
    thickening, 93
    Vanilla Crème Anglaise, 342
    water content, 56
    Whipped Coffee Ganache, 290
    Whipped Cream, 345
    Whipped Vanilla Ganache, 160
    whipping, 60, 64
cream cheese, 56
    Citrus, Olive Oil, and Cream Cheese Dome,
        241–42
    Honey Cream Cheese Frosting, 143
creaming fat and sugar, 59
crème anglaise, 42, 44, 93
    Chocolate Crémeux, 159
    Vanilla Crème Anglaise, 342
Crème Brûlée, 42, 44, 99
Crème Chiboust, 338
Crème Diplomat, 338
Crème Fraîche, 56
Crème Légère, 248–49, 270, 310, 316, 338
Crème Madame, 338
Crème Mousseline, 338
crème pâtissière, 44
croissants, 294–306
    Almond Croissants 2.0, 329
Cross Laminated Galette des Rois, 291–93
Crullers, 221
crumb, basic, 343
crust, texture, 92
crystallization, sugar, 32
Crystallized Pistachios, 243
Cucumber-Jalapeño Granita, 224
curdling, 44, 64
custard, 21, 42, 44
    Baked Lemon Custard Brûlée, 216
    Bread-and-Butter Pudding with Caramel
        Mandarins, 212
    Brown Sugar Custard Tart, 163
    carryover cooking, 105
    Chocolate Custard, 341
    curdling, 44
    custard tart, 44
    Plum and Mascarpone Karpatka, 204–5

custard (continued)
    starch in, 45
    thickening, 93
    Vanilla Crème Anglaise, 342

D

dacquoise, 288
dairy, and acid, 101
dairy ratio, 44
Danish pastries, 301, 302
    Cheesy Potato Danish, 326
    Classic Fruit Custard Danish, 316
    Pan con Tomate Danish, 325
    Peach Panzanella Deep-Dish Danish, 320
    St. Honoré Cherry Danish, 317
dark brown sugar, 27
deep frying, 9, 107
demerara sugar, 26, 27
DIY Mint Viennese Ice Cream Cake, 228
docking, 109
doming, cakes, 104
dough
    kneading, 15
    no-knead bread 16
    proofing, 79–81
    relaxation, 16
    rising, 76–77, 81
    strength vs. stretch, 16–17
dry caramel, 86
Dulce de Leche, 86

E

Earl Gray Scones, 180
egg test, sugar concentration, 98
egg wash, 84, 343
    lining tart cases, 109
egg whites, 39–41
    meringue, 46–47
    over-beaten, 45
    whipping, 45, 47
egg yolks, 39–41
    and sugar, 47
eggs, 36–49
    aeration, 45–47
    coagulation, 40–42
    contents, 38–39
    custard, 42, 44
    dairy ration, 44
    effects of sugar, 28
    egginess, 41
    foams, 48–49
    heating, 42
    meringues, 118
    over-beaten whites, 45
    sabayon, 207
    splitting, 64
    sugar and, 44, 46, 47
    temperature, 47
    tempering, 42
    and texture, 92
einkorn, 12
elasticity, dough, 16–17
elderflower infusions, 111
emulsions, 40, 61–2

enriched doughs, 22, 78, 81. See also brioche
    Bun Dough, 123
enzymes, 88, 100
equipment, 8–9
evaporated milk
    Horchata Tres Leches, 234–5
    Panna Cotta with Burnt White Chocolate and
        Soy, 215

F

Fancy Rhubarb Tart, 246
fat, 50–65. See also butter; cream
    aeration, 59–60
    colloids, 61
    effects of, 53–54
    effects of sugar, 28, 31
    emulsions, 61–62
    frozen desserts, 96
    and gluten, 19
    melting point, 53
    in nuts, 55
    state of, 55
    and texture, 92
    types of, 52
    and water, 56
Fennel Tarte Tatin, Tomato and, 167
fermentation, 76, 78, 89
Festive Buns, 179
Feta Whipped Cheesecake, 265
Fig and Chocolate Focaccia, 281
flaky pastry, 54
Flaky Sweet Shortcrust Pastry, Monique's, 120
flour, 10–23
    autolyse, 16
    bread, 14, 17, 18
    effects of sugar, 28
    gluten, 14–19
    starch, 20–23
    swapping, 17
    T system, 18
    and texture, 92
    thickening, 94
    toasting, 18
foam cakes, 46
foams, 61
    egg, 48–49
focaccia, 20
    3-day Focaccia, 280–81
folding, 113
food processors, 9, 98, 112
frangipane, 339, 344
    Almond Croissants 2.0, 329
    Chocolate Frangipane, 339
    Cross Laminated Galette des Rois, 291–93
    Fancy Rhubarb Tart, 246
freezing pastries, 302
French Meringue, 48, 118
French Toast Cinnamon Buns, 254–56
frosting
    Chocolate Frosting, 144
    Honey Cream Cheese Frosting, 143
frozen desserts, 28, 30, 96–98
fructose, 26, 32

fruit, 345
    Any Galette, 168
    Basic Poached Fruit, 336
    Basic Roasted Fruit, 336
    Classic Fruit Custard Danish, 316
    effects of sugar, 28
    Fruity Marshmallows, 198
    and gelatin, 100
    maceration, 30
    oxidation, 88
    pie fillings, 94
    Sablé Breton Fruit Tarts, 164
    sorbets, 97
fruit pits, infusions, 111
fudge, 86

G

Galette, 168–69
Galette des Rois, Cross Laminated, 291–93
ganache, 63, 340, 344
    Chocolate Ganache, 290
    splitting, 64
    Whipped Coffee Ganache, 290
    Whipped Ganache, 345
    Whipped Vanilla Ganache, 160
Garlic Butter, Roasted, 332
gelatin, 100
gelatinization, starch, 20–21, 44, 95
gels, 61
Genoise Sponge, 131
ghee, 56
ginger, infusions, 111
    Pear, White Wine, and Ginger Sorbet, 275
glaze
    Chocolate Glaze, 290, 341
    Vanilla Cinnamon Glaze, 221
glucose, 26, 32
glucose syrup, 27
gluten, 14–19
    Inverted Puff Pastry, 72
    minimizing or maximizing, 19
    in pastry, 108
    toasting flour, 18
golden syrup, 27, 32
    Golden Syrup Buttercream, 189
    Golden Syrup Crunch Cookies, 189
granitas
    Cucumber-Jalapeño Granita, 224
    Mocha Granita, 224–5
    Pink Lemonade Granita, 224
    Tart Apple, 224
granulated sugar, 27
grilling, 107

H

Half-and-half, 56, 60
hazelnuts, 55
    Amarettis, 188
    Blonde Rice Pudding, 222–23
    Mocha Passionfruit Opera Cake, 288–90
    Ricotta, Marmalade, and Hazelnut
        Chocolate-Chip Cake, 147
heavy cream, 56, 60, 96–97
herbs, infusions, 111

heritage grains, 12
Hibiscus and Watermelon Sorbet 275
Hibiscus Sugar, Spicy, 221
high-fructose corn syrup, 27
honey, 27, 30, 31
    caramelized honey, 87
    Honey Cream, 151
    Honey Cream Cheese Frosting, 143
    Honey, Rosemary, and Orange Swiss
        Meringue Buttercream, 241–42
    Seasonal Maritozzo, 252–3
Horchata Tres Leches, 234–35
Hot Cross Buns, 179
hybrid colloids, 61
hydration, baked goods, 23
hydrocolloids, 93

I

ice cream, 29, 93, 96–98
    Chocolate Peanut Ice Cream Bars, 276
    Choux Ice Cream Sandwich, 273
    DIY Mint Viennese Ice Cream Cake, 228
    Jam Ripple Parfait, 227
ice cream machines, 98
iciness, 96
icing. See also buttercream; frosting
    Tangy Butterscotch Icing, 254–56
infusions, 110–11
Inverted Puff Pastry, 72, 125–27
inverted sugar, 32
Italian meringue, 48, 49, 118

J

jam, 344
    effects of sugar, 28, 29
    Jam Ripple Parfait, 227
    PBJ Paris Brest, 218–19
    pectin, 95
    Raspberry Rhubarb Jam, 335
    testing, 106
    thickening, 93
jelly, 93, 100

K

kneading dough, 15
kouign-amann, 301, 302, 322

L

lactose, 26
lamination
    croissants, 294–300
    pastries, 54, 60–72
Langues de Chat, 207
lard, 53, 56
leavening. See rising
lecithin, 39
leeks
    Chicken Pie with Rich Pastry, 173
    Leek and Mustard Tart 174
lemon
    Baked Lemon Custard Brûlée, 216
    Lemon Basque Cheesecake, 208
    Lemon Curd, 344
    Lemon Curd Meringue Tarts, 156

Lemon Pistachio Amaretti, 188
    lemon tart, 44
    Pink Lemonade Granita, 224
    posset, 101
    Salted Vanilla and Pistachio Layer Cake,
        243–45
    Sticky Lemons, 208
lemongrass, infusions, 111
liaison batter, 113
light brown sugar, 27
Lime, Candied, 237
lining pastry cases, 121
lining tart cases, 108–9
Linzer, Parmesan and Tomato, 250
lock-in, laminated pastries, 69
lye, 75

M

macadamias, 55
maceration, 30
Maillard reaction, 18, 84–88
malt syrup, 27
    Malt Cemifreddo, 276
maltose, 26
Mango Shortcake with Candied Lime, 237
maple syrup
    Chile Maple Butter, 175
    Maple Pretzel Buttercrunch, 201
Marble Cake with Chocolate Frosting, 144
Maritozzo, Seasonal, 252–53
marmalade
    Ricotta, Marmalade, and Hazelnut
        Chocolate-Chip Cake, 147
    Tangerine Marmalade, 335
marshmallow, 93, 345
    Fruity Marshmallows, 198
mascarpone, 56
    Plum and Mascarpone Karpatka, 204–5
    Tiramichoux, 284–86
meringue, 46–47, 93, 118, 344–45
    Lemon Curd Meringue Tarts, 156
meringue buttercream, 64
    Honey, Rosemary, and Orange Swiss
        Meringue Buttercream, 241–42
milk, 56
    Blonde Rice Pudding, 222–23
    Chocolate Custard, 341
    Crème Légère, 248–49
    Pastry Cream, 338
    Vanilla Crème Anglaise, 342
    and yeast, 78
milk bread, 122
    Milk Bread Spring Onion Babka, 258
milk solids, 97
Mille-Feuille, Apricot Custard, 270
Mint Viennese Ice Cream Cake, DIY, 228
Miso Walnut Double-Thick Chocolate-Chip
    Cookies, 197
Mocha Granita, 224–25
Mocha Passionfruit Opera Cake, 288–90
moisture, sugar and, 31
molasses, 26, 27
Monique's Flaky Sweet Shortcrust Pastry, 120
mousseline cream, 45

mouthfeel, 52
muscovado sugar, 27

N

Nduja Butter, 332
Noyaux cream, 270
nuts. See also almonds; Brazil nuts; pecans;
        walnuts
    caramelized, 334
    fat content, 55
    infusions, 111
    Nut Praline Paste, 334
    as thickeners, 94

O

Oat Cookies, 3pm, 194
oils, 52, 54, 56
olive oil
    Citrus, Olive Oil, and Cream Cheese Dome,
        241–42
    Olive Oil Brie-oche, 261
    Olive Oil Lemon Curd, 156
Olive focaccia, Crispy Potato and, 281
oranges
    Caramel Mandarins, 212
    Caramel Poached Oranges, 207
    Citrus, Olive Oil, and Cream Cheese Dome,
        241–42
    Honey, Rosemary, and Orange Swiss
        Meringue Buttercream, 241–42
Orchard Turnovers, 211
oven thermometers, 8, 105
oxidation, 88

P

Pain au Chocolate, 301, 302, 307
Pain Suisse, 301
    Chocolate-Chip Pain Suisse, 321
Pan con Tomate Danish, 325
Panela Cake, Coriander and 143
panna cotta, 93, 345
    Panna Cotta with Burnt White Chocolate and
        Soy, 215
parfait
    Jam Ripple Parfait, 227
    Vanilla Parfait, 345
Paris Brest, PBJ, 218–19
Parmesan and tomato linzer, 250
passionfruit
    Mocha Passionfruit Opera Cake, 288–90
    Passionfruit Posset Flower Tarts, 160
pastries
    Almond Croissants 2.0, 329
    Apricot Custard Mille-Feuille, 270
    Brown Sugar Canelé, 262
    Chocolate-Chip Pain Suisse, 321
    Chocolate Squiggles, 315
    croissants, 294–306
    Cross Laminated Galette des Rois, 291–93
    Crullers, 221
    cutting, 301
    Danish pastries, 301, 302, 316–20, 325–26
    freezing, 302
    Kouign-Amann Scraps, 322

pastries (continued)
  laminating with compound butters, 332
  lamination, 54, 69–72
  Orchard Turnovers, 211
  Pain au Chocolate, 301, 302, 307
  PBJ Paris Brest, 218–19
  proofing, 80, 302–3
  Swirly Buns, 310
  Twisty Strips, 301, 312
pastry
  blind baking, 109, 121
  Choux Pastry, 20, 21, 136
  docking, 109
  fat content, 54
  Inverted Puff Pastry, 125–27
  lining pastry cases, 121
  lining tart cases, 108–9
  Monique's Flaky Sweet Shortcrust Pastry, 120
  pâté sablée, 99
  pâté sucrée, 99
  Pie Dough, 129
  Puff Pastry, 124
  Rich Tart Pastry, 119
  Rough Puff Pastry, 128
  Sablé Breton, 130
  Savory Shortcrust Pastry, 120
  shrinking, 108
  Suet Pie Dough, 130
  Tart Pastry, 119–20
pastry cream, 338, 344
  Chocolate-Chip Pain Suisse, 321
  Classic Fruit Custard Danish, 316
  Crème Légère, 310, 316
  dairy ratio, 44
  Peanut Butter Pastry Cream, 218–19
  Rhubarb and Custard Crumb Cake, 232
  starch, 44, 45, 94
  St. Honoré cherry Danish, 317
  thickeners, 93
pâté à bombe, 48, 49
Pâte de Fruit, Pickled Pineapple, 203
pâté sablée, 99
pâté sucrée, 99
Peach Panzanella Deep-Dish Danish, 320
peanuts, 55
  Caramelized Peanuts, 218–19
  Chocolate, Peanut, and Coconut
    Twice-Baked cookies, 187
  Chocolate Peanut Ice Cream Bars, 276
pearl sugar, 27
pears
  Blonde Rice Pudding, 222–23
  Cross Laminated Galette des Rois, 291–93
  Orchard Turnovers, 211
  Pear, White Wine, and Ginger Sorbet, 275
  Upside-Down Sticky Pear and Walnut
    Cake, 152
pecans, 55
pectin, 95
Pepper Sugar, 203
pH values: and browning, 87–88
  and fat, 56
  gluten, 19
Pickle Scones, Flaky Cheese and, 183

Pickled Pineapple Pâte de Fruit, 203
Pie Dough, 99, 129, 344–45
  Suet Pie Dough, 130
pie fillings, 21, 93, 94
pies. See also tarts
  Banana Pudding Pie
  Chicken Pie with Rich Pastry, 173
pine nuts, 55
Pineapple Pâte de Fruit, Pickled, 203
piping, 60, 113
piping tips, 9, 113
pistachios, 55
  Fancy Rhubarb Tart, 246
  Lemon Pistachio Amaretti, 188
  Salted Vanilla and Pistachio Layer Cake,
    243–45
plasticised butter, 56
plums
  Plum and Mascarpone Karpatka, 204–5
  Plum and Rocket Focaccia, 281
  Steamed Plum Buttermilk Sponge Cake, 155
poaching, 107
Polenta cake, Apricot and Rosemary, 148
poolish, 81
posset, 93, 101
  Passionfruit Posset Flower Tarts, 160
potatoes
  Cheesy Potato Danish, 326
  Crispy Potato and Olive Focaccia, 281
  starch, 20
powdered sugar, 27
Praline Paste, Nut, 334
preferments, proofing, 80–81
preserves, 335
Pretzel Buttercrunch, Maple, 201
proofing
  pastries, 302–3
  yeast, 79–81
protein, 14, 38, 39, 40
Puff Pastry, 124, 344–45
  Cross Laminated Galette des Rois, 291–93
  Inverted Puff Pastry, 72, 125–27
  Rough Puff Pastry, 128
Pumpkin Buns, Spiced, 175–76

Q
quiches, 44

R
rising agents, 114
raisins
  Brown Butter Banana Cookies, 184
  Festive Buns, 179
Secret Chocolate Cake, 266
raspberries
  PBJ Paris Brest, 218–19
  Pink Lemonade Granita, 224
  Raspberry Rhubarb Jam, 335
refined sugar, 26
relaxation, dough, 16
rhubarb
  Fancy Rhubarb Tart, 246
  Raspberry Rhubarb Jam, 335
  Rhubarb and Custard Crumb Cake, 232

rice
  Blonde Rice Pudding, 222–23
  Horchata Tres Leches, 234–35
  rice pudding, 21
Rich Tart Pastry, 119
ricotta, 56
  Ricotta, Marmalade, and Hazelnut
    Chocolate-Chip Cake, 147
  Veg Galette, 169
rising, 66–81
  air, 73
  carbon dioxide, 74
  chemical rising agents, 74–75
  laminated pastries, 69–72
  yeast and forments, 76–81
roasting, 107
Rocket Focaccia, Plum and, 281
rosemary
  Apricot and Rosemary Polenta Cake, 148
  Honey, Rosemary, and Orange Swiss Meringue
    Buttercream, 241–42
  Salt and Rosemary Focaccia, 281
Rough Puff Pastry, 128
rubaud technique, kneading dough, 15
rye flour, 18

S
Sabayon, 48, 207
Sablé Breton, 130, 344–45
  Sablé Breton Fruit Tarts, 164
St. Honoré Cherry Danish, 317
salt, 35
  and color, 89
  and eggs, 41
  and fermentation, 76
  frozen desserts, 97
  and gluten, 19
Salted Double-Chocolate Shortbread, 193
Salted Vanilla and Pistachio Layer Cake, 243–45
Salted Vanilla Shortbread, 192
saturated fatty acids, 52
Savoiardi Cookies, 340
  Apple and Vanilla Charlotte, 268–69
  Banana Pudding Pie, 248–9
  Tiramichoux, 284–86
Savory Shortcrust Pastry, 120
scales, digital, 8
scones
  Earl Grey Scones, 180
  Flaky Cheese and Pickle Scones, 183
Seasonal Maritozzo, 252–53
Secret Chocolate Cake, 266
Semifreddo, 228
semolina, 18
setting agents, 100
shortbread, 20
  Salted Double-Chocolate Shortbread, 193
  Salted Vanilla Shortbread, 192
Shortcrust Pastry, 54, 120
shortening, 53
simple syrup, 33
slap and fold technique, kneading dough, 15
sorbets, 97
  Hibiscus and Watermelon Sorbet, 275

Pear, White Wine, and Ginger Sorbet, 275
sound, and color, 87
sour cream, 56
Speculoos Spiced Butter, 332
spices, infusions, 111
splitting, 64
sponge cake
    Genoise, 131
    Victoria, 140
spread, fat, 54
spring, cakes, 106
Spring Onion Babka, Milk Bread, 258
Squiggle Buns, 301
Squiggles, Chocolate, 315
stale bakes, 95
stand mixers, 9
starch, 20–23
    in custard, 45
    effects of sugar, 28, 31
    and eggs, 44
    gelatinization, 20–21, 44, 95
    texture, 94–95
steam, and rising, 68
Steamed Plum Buttermilk Sponge Cake, 155
steaming, 88, 107
strawberries
    Choux Ice Cream Sandwich, 273
    Roasted Strawberry Victoria Sponge, 140
stretch and fold technique, kneading dough, 15
sucrose, 26, 32
suet, 56
    Suet Pie Dough, 130
sugar, 24–35
    and air, 31
    amounts, 29
    caramelization, 31, 84–86
    crystallization, 32
    egg yolks and, 47
    and eggs, 44, 46, 47
    frozen desserts, 97, 98
    and gluten, 19
    maceration, 30
    meringue, 46
    pepper sugar, 203
    role of, 28
    Spicy Hibiscus Sugar, 221
    swaps, 31
    and texture, 92
    types of, 26–27
    and water, 29–30
sugar syrup, 93
sweet pastry, 54, 344–45
sweetness, sugar swaps, 31
Swirly Buns, 310
Swiss-French Meringue, 48, 118
Swiss Meringue, 48, 118
syrup, 27, 32–33

T
T system, flour, 10
Tangerine Marmalade, 335
tangzhong technique, 20, 122, 123
Tart Apple Granita, 225
Tart Pastry, 119–20

lining tart cases/rings, 108–9, 121
tart pans, 8
tarts. See also pies
    Any Galette, 168
    Brown Sugar Custard Tart, 163
    Choconut Tart, 159
    Fancy Rhubarb Tart, 246
    Leek and Mustard tart, 174
    Lemon curd meringue tarts, 156
    Parmesan and Tomato Linzer, 250
    Passionfruit Posset Flower Tarts, 160
    Sablé Breton Fruit Tarts, 164
    Tomato and Fennel Tarte Tatin, 167
    Veg Galette, 169
tea
    Earl Gray Scones, 180
    infusions, 111
temperatures
    baking, 105
    building a bake, 114
    eggs, 47
    infusions, 110
    knowing when baked goods are ready, 106
    laminated pastries, 72
    melting point of fat, 53
    sugar syrup, 33
tempering, 42, 63
tenderizers, 53, 92, 101
texture, 52, 90–101
    contrast, 99
    frozen desserts, 96–98
    gelatin, 100
    starch, 94–95
    sugar and, 31
    thickeners, 93
    tougheners vs. tenderizers, 92, 101
    via techniques, 99
    thermometers, 8, 9, 105
    thickeners, 93, 94
timers, 9
Tiramichoux, 284–86
toasting flour, 18
tomatoes
    Pan con Tomate Danish, 325
    Parmesan and Tomato Linzer, 250
    Peach Panzanella Deep-dish Danish, 320
    Tomato and Fennel Tarte Tatin, 167
toothpick test, 107
tougheners, 92, 101
treacle, 27
Turnovers, Orchard, 211
Twisty Strips, 301, 312

U
Ultimate Chocolate Cake, 238
unrefined sugar, 26
unsaturated fatty acids, 52
Upside-down Sticky Pear and Walnut Cake, 152

V
vanilla
    Apple and Vanilla Charlotte, 268–69
    infusions, 111
    Jam Ripple Parfait, 227

Pastry Cream, 338
Salted Vanilla and Pistachio Layer Cake,
    243–45
Salted Vanilla Shortbread, 192
Vanilla Cinnamon Glaze, 221
Vanilla Crème Anglaise, 342
Vanilla Parfait, 345
Whipped Vanilla Ganache, 160
Veg Galette, 169
Victoria Sponge, 20, 74
    Roasted Strawberry Victoria Sponge, 140
Viennese Ice Cream Cake, DIY Mint, 228
Viennoiserie, 294–329

W
walnuts, 55
    Caramelized Walnuts, 265
    Miso Walnut Double-Thick Chocolate-Chip
        Cookies, 197
    Upside-down Sticky Pear and Walnut
        Cake, 152
water
    and chocolate, 62
    and fat, 56
    freezing, 96
    and starch, 20
    steam, 68
    sugar and, 29–30
    in syrups, 32
water baths, 42, 47, 112
Watermelon Sorbet, Hibiscus and, 275
wet caramel, 86
wheat, 12–13
wheat flour, 94
whipping cream, 56, 60, 64, 93
whisking meringue, 118
white chocolate, toasting, 88, 215
whole-wheat flour, 17–19
wild yeast, 77
windowpane test, 14–15
wine
    Pear, White Wine, and Ginger Sorbet, 275
    Sabayon, 207
    Secret Chocolate Cake, 266
wobble, knowing when it is ready, 106

X
xanthan gum, 93

Y
yeast, 74, 76–81
    croissants, 295
    effects of sugar on, 28, 29
    enemies of, 78
    enriched breads, 22
    proofing, 79–81
yogurt, 56

A huge thank you goes out to all the people who made this book happen in such a variety of ways. To my agent, Emily Sweet—without your encouragement and belief, this book would not exist! To Nell Warner, my glorious editor, I feel sorry for every author who doesn't get to work with you. To Kay, Anne, and Elise for your impressive levels of patience and attention to detail. To the brilliant US team—thank you for believing in *Sift*. Susan Roxborough, I'm so grateful to work with you. Maria Zizka, thank you for your incredible effort to make this book accessible for US readers. To Josh Harker and Chris Nuelle, two penguins in a sea of peacocks and the designers of my dreams who extraordinarily made this book as beautiful as it is useful.

The beautiful photographs you see in this book are entirely thanks to these brilliant people: to Sam and Matt, seeing you work was an honor. To Holly, the title "food stylist" does not do justice to the vast influence you've had on this book—I'm in awe of your generosity, skill, and vision. To Lucy, you're a joy and a talent. To Hannah, I'm grateful for your impeccable taste. And to Annabelle and Alice, for the extra push we needed. Those shoot days go down in my greatest memories. Fruit spirit animals and greenhouses forever.

To the great teachers: from my first (humbling) days in the kitchen at Dominique Ansel NYC—Chef Dominique, Chef Noah, Chef Karys, Chef Christian, Chef Ayako—thank you for your grace. To my time at Ottolenghi—Verena Lochmuller, a fountain of knowledge and apple of my pie. To the summers of ice cream at Happy Endings. To the life-changing experience and friendships gained at Little Bread Pedlar—Shebah (who also tested recipes and fact-checked this book—you triple threat, you!), Adam, Nichola, Stewart, Janine, to name just a few. Gabor, you are so missed. You all set me on a journey, and, in a totally non-creepy way, I hear your voices in my head when I'm stuck looking for a path forward in the kitchen. Thank you!

To my wonderful recipe testers Annabelle, Caitlin, and Steph, and all the generous KP+ subscribers who also tested recipes: Beth, Bethan, Candice, Clio, Emma H, Emma T, Georgina, Alex, Hannah, Jennie, Libbi, Melody, Natasha, Richard, Sophie, Victoria—you are superstars. A big thank you goes out to Substack and all the Kitchen Projects newsletter readers—you made this book happen!

To all my dear friends who have surfed all the waves with me, I'm OBSESSED with you. A special thank you to Claire, Kathryn, Milli, and Jordon for their endless encouragement and opining on this project. To Tim and Amelia for taking on all the shoot leftovers. To Basia, my first ever editor on Kitchen Projects, for helping me feel like a real writer. Finally, to my forever bae Giles, who also tirelessly tested recipes for this book and has always championed me—thank you, I love you.

I'm so lucky to have such a supportive, loving family: Mum and Father Richard, you gave me so much room to figure everything out; I owe it all to you. I don't know how anyone manages in life without sisters—Adrienne and Pippa, I'd be lost without you. To Carole, you generously planted so many seeds for my path, from chicken soup, to brownies, to my first ever Nigel Slater book! And finally, hugely, to Justin, you support me in extraordinary, countless ways. There's nothing I'm more excited for than spending my life with you and Pancake.

To dive even deeper into the world of baking, I've gathered together a list of reference books, research papers, and resources for you to explore. Please visit www.nicolalamb.com/furtherreading for more.

Published in the United States by Clarkson Potter/ Publishers, an imprint of the Crown Publishing Group, a division of Penguin Random House LLC, New York. ClarksonPotter.com

CLARKSON POTTER is a trademark and POTTER with colophon is a registered trademark of Penguin Random House LLC.

Originally published in the United Kingdom by Ebury Press, an imprint of Ebury Publishing, a division of Penguin Random House UK, in 2024.

Library of Congress Cataloging-in-Publication Data
Names: Lamb, Nicola, author. Title: Sift : the elements of great baking / Nicola Lamb. Description: New York : Ebury Press, 2024. | Includes index. Identifiers: LCCN 2023056094 (print) | LCCN 2023056095 (ebook) | ISBN 9780593797129 (hardcover) | ISBN 9780593797136 (ebook) Subjects: LCSH: Baking. | Baked products. | Desserts. | Cake. | Pastry. | LCGFT: Cookbooks. Classification: LCC TX763 .L268 2024 (print) | LCC TX763 (ebook) | DDC 641.7/1--dc2 3/eng/20231221 LC record: https://lccn.loc.gov/2023056094 LC ebook record: https://lccn.loc.gov/2023056095

ISBN 978-0-593-79712-9
Ebook ISBN 978-0-593-79713-6

Printed in China

Editor: Susan Roxborough
Editorial assistant: Elaine Hennig
Designer: Nueker
Production editor: Sohayla Farman
Production manager: Jessica Heim
Illustrations: Nueker
Compositor: Hannah Hunt
Food stylist: Holly Cochrane
Food stylist assistant: Lucy Turnbull
Prop stylist: Hannah Wilkinson
Photographer: Sam A Harris
Photo assistant: Matt Hague
Americanizer: Maria Ziska
Proofreader: Andrea Connolly Peabbles
Publicist: Jina Stanfill | Marketer: Andrea Portanova

10 9 8 7 6 5 4 3 2 1

First American Edition